TM

References for the Rest of Us!®

BESTSELLING BOOK SERIES

Do you find that traditional reference books are overloaded with technical details and advice you'll never use? Do you postpone important life decisions because you just don't want to deal with them? Then our *For Dummies*® business and general reference book series is for you.

For Dummies business and general reference books are written for those frustrated and hard-working souls who know they aren't dumb, but find that the myriad of personal and business issues and the accompanying horror stories make them feel helpless. *For Dummies* books use a lighthearted approach, a down-to-earth style, and even cartoons and humorous icons to dispel fears and build confidence. Lighthearted but not lightweight, these books are perfect survival guides to solve your everyday personal and business problems.

> *"More than a publishing phenomenon, 'Dummies' is a sign of the times."*
>
> — The New York Times

> *"...you won't go wrong buying them."*
>
> — Walter Mossberg, Wall Street Journal, on For Dummies books

> *"A world of detailed and authoritative information is packed into them..."*
>
> — U.S. News and World Report

Already, millions of satisfied readers agree. They have made For Dummies the #1 introductory level computer book series and a best-selling business book series. They have written asking for more. So, if you're looking for the best and easiest way to learn about business and other general reference topics, look to For Dummies to give you a helping hand.

Wiley Publishing, Inc.

U.S. Presidents

FOR

DUMMIES®

by Marcus A. Stadelmann
Associate Professor of Political Science
at the University of Texas at Tyler

WILEY

Wiley Publishing, Inc.

U.S. Presidents For Dummies®

Published by
Wiley Publishing, Inc.
111 River Street
Hoboken, NJ 07030
www.wiley.com

Copyright © 2002 by Wiley Publishing, Inc., Indianapolis, Indiana

Published by Wiley Publishing, Inc., Indianapolis, Indiana

Published simultaneously in Canada

For general information on our other products and services or to obtain technical support, please contact our Customer Care Department within the U.S. at 800-762-2974, outside the U.S. at 317-572-3993, or fax 317-572-4002.

Wiley also publishes its books in a variety of electronic formats. Some content that appears in print may not be available in electronic books.

Library of Congress Cataloging-in-Publication Data:

Library of Congress Control Number: 2002100246

ISBN: 0-7645-0885-7

Manufactured in the United States of America

10 9 8 7 6 5 4 3

3B/RV/RS/QU/IN.

About the Author

Marcus A. Stadelmann is an Associate Professor of Political Science at the University of Texas at Tyler. Dr. Stadelmann received his Ph.D. from the University of California at Riverside in 1990, and has subsequently taught at universities in California, Utah, and Texas.

He presently teaches classes on American government and comparative politics. In addition he has given many public lectures on American presidential elections and international topics such as the collapse of the Soviet Union and German unification and has presented papers at national and regional academic conferences.

Dr. Stadelmann's other publications include *The Dependent Ally-German Foreign Policy from 1949 to 1990*. In addition, Dr. Stadelmann has contributed chapters to many books and has published numerous academic articles.

Dedication

This book is dedicated to the people who had the most impact on my life, my parents Wolfgang and Heidi, my wife Betsey, and my two daughters Katarina and Holly.

Author's Acknowledgments

Special thanks go to my wife Betsey and my two daughters Katarina and Holly. They kept me on track for the last months, supported me in this endeavor, and patiently waited until my work was done. Without their support, this work would not have been possible.

I would also like to express my gratitude to my editor, Kathleen Dobie, who did an excellent job working with me on the book. Without her input, this book would not have become what it is today. Finally, I would like to thank my technical editor, James Newsom, who spent countless hours making sure that this work was as perfect as possible.

Publisher's Acknowledgments

We're proud of this book; please send us your comments through our online registration form located at www.dummies.com/register.

Some of the people who helped bring this book to market include the following:

Acquisitions, Editorial, and Media Development

Project Editor: Kathleen A. Dobie

Senior Acquisitions Editor: Greg Tubach

Copy Editor: Greg Pearson

Technical Editor: James L. Newsom, Ph.D.

Permissions Editor: Laura Moss

Editorial Manager: Christine Meloy Beck

Media Development Manager: Laura VanWinkle

Editorial Assistants: Melissa Bennett, Brian Herrmann

Cover Photos: PHX-Hagerstown

Composition

Project Coordinator: Nancee Reeves

Layout and Graphics: Beth Brooks, Joyce Haughey, Barry Offringa, Brent Savage, Jacque Schneider, Betty Schulte, Jeremey Unger, Erin Zeltner

Proofreaders: Laura Albert, TECHBOOKS Production Services

Indexer: TECHBOOKS Production Services

Publishing and Editorial for Consumer Dummies

Diane Graves Steele, Vice President and Publisher, Consumer Dummies
Joyce Pepple, Acquisitions Director, Consumer Dummies
Kristin A. Cocks, Product Development Director, Consumer Dummies
Michael Spring, Vice President and Publisher, Travel
Brice Gosnell, Associate Publisher, Travel
Suzanne Jannetta, Editorial Director, Travel

Publishing for Technology Dummies

Richard Swadley, Vice President and Executive Group Publisher
Andy Cummings, Vice President and Publisher

Composition Services

Gerry Fahey, Vice President of Production Services
Debbie Stailey, Director of Composition Services

Contents at a Glance

Cartoons at a Glance

By Rich Tennant

The 5th Wave By Rich Tennant

"Mr. President, the Confederate Army is massing in Virginia, several more of our officers have defected to the South, oh, and bad news— Mrs. Lincoln's redesigned tea setting won't be here until Friday."

page 129

The 5th Wave By Rich Tennant

Andrew Jackson, 7th president of the United States was nicknamed "Old Hickory" because "Thunderhair" "Chip" and "Slappy" were already taken.

page 77

The 5th Wave By Rich Tennant

By virtue of a single word, did Eleanor inspire FDR to create the New Deal.

Gin!

Dang!!

page 229

The 5th Wave By Rich Tennant

George Washington: Father of the Country and first US President. Originator of the White House Cabinet, established Congress's right to tax US citizens and re-wrote existing boating regulations to increase the number of people allowable in a row boat from 5 to 12.

page 29

The 5th Wave By Rich Tennant

From the very beginning, Warren G. Harding's presidency was suspect due to Harding's liberal use of the double-finger quotation mark during his swearing in ceremony.

page 349

The 5th Wave By Rich Tennant

WHY PRESIDENT JIMMY CARTER WALKED FROM THE CAPITOL TO THE WHITE HOUSE ON INAUGURATION DAY

"We're good to go, Mr. President; just waiting for your brother, Billy. He's asked to drive the limousine."

page 301

The 5th Wave By Rich Tennant

IN JAN. 1943, THE DECISION TO INVADE ITALY THROUGH SICILY WAS MADE AT THE CASABLANCA CONFERENCE.

"President Roosevelt, you know General de Gaulle, Prime Minister Churchill, Sam the piano player..."

page 7

Cartoon Information:
Fax: 978-546-7747
E-Mail: richtennant@the5thwave.com
World Wide Web: www.the5thwave.com

Table of Contents

Introduction

· ·

*O*ver the last 213 years, 42 men have dominated U.S. politics and history. Although almost every American can name the current president, less than half can tell you the name of the vice president or the Senate majority leader. No other office within the U.S. government has received as much attention as the presidency.

The successes and failures of the chief executive have become a staple of U.S. culture. Every year, the media spends thousands of hours disseminating information on their virtues and shortcomings. Their biographies become best sellers. The public marvels at their childhood plights and adult accomplishments. Stories about their personal lives and office conduct have become ingrained in American culture and literature. The public revels in the presidents' personal shortcomings and failures, and eagerly laps up scandals involving them. From Jefferson's affair with a slave, to the corruption of the Grant and Harding administrations, to Bill Clinton's sex scandals, the public is mesmerized by the presidents and their activities.

From humble beginnings, the presidency has evolved over time to become the dominant institution in the U.S. government. People look to the president for guidance in times of crisis. He (and so far, all of our presidents have been men) is held responsible for the problems the country faces and is expected to resolve these problems. In addition, the president symbolizes the United States abroad. Other countries judge the United States by what kind of president is in power. A bad president reflects poorly on all U.S. citizens.

About This Book

Most books on the U.S. presidency are either textbooks, which are usually boring and tedious, or autobiographies. Although autobiographies are interesting reading, they provide you with information on just one president — and face it, who has time to read 42 biographies?

This book is neither a textbook nor a biography — it combines the best elements of both. It won't bore you with little tedious facts or a lot of narrative. It doesn't shower you with a mass of statistics that prove to you what you already know. The information on the presidents gets to the point, highlighting only the major events of each presidency.

The book covers all 42 U.S. presidents in chronological order. Some presidents have a whole chapter to themselves, others have a section in a chapter that covers several chief executives. I detail some basic personal information for each president, and I also cover the major events that took place during each president's administration.

I designed this book to give a solid foundation on the presidents, whether you're studying political science, writing a paper, or reading for pleasure. I tried to make the book entertaining by including little-known tidbits. So, whether you're a history buff, a student, or just someone interested in America's presidents, this book is for you. My hope is that this book will prove one point: The history of our presidents is fascinating and fun.

Conventions Used in This Book

To avoid repeating certain procedures, facts, and ideas, this book uses certain conventions. For example, I use the common abbreviations *WWI* and *WWII* to refer to World War I and World War II, respectively. I also use familiar presidential initials, such as *FDR* for Franklin Delano Roosevelt and *JFK* for John Fitzgerald Kennedy.

The information in some sidebars is relevant to more than one chapter. When this is the case, the book refers to these sidebars by the title of the sidebar and chapter number. For example, Andrew Johnson was the first president to face impeachment proceedings. So I include a sidebar, "How to get impeached," explaining impeachment when I cover Johnson in Chapter 11. Most people know only too well that Andrew Johnson wasn't the last president to have impeachment charges brought against him. You'll find references to this sidebar in chapters that cover Richard Nixon and Bill Clinton.

I also provide some information in a consistent format. Early in a president's section or chapter, I include a sidebar that talks about his early years — when he was born, where he lived, what schools he attended (if he attended school at all!), and whom he married. (First ladies sometimes crop up in other places, but the facts about them are usually in these sidebars.)

How This Book is Organized

Unlike a textbook, this book is not linear in nature: You can start anywhere you want. You can go to Chapter 25 on George W. Bush and read about the historic election of 2000 and the unprecedented terrorist attack on September 11, 2001, and then go back and read Chapter 3 on our first president, George Washington. Chapters are freestanding — not dependent on each other — and they contain all the information you need to understand a president, his policies, and the time period in which he served.

To make the material more organized and easily understood, I divided the book into seven parts. Each part covers a specific part of U.S. history and its respective presidents. The following sections describe the parts of this book.

Part I: Examining the Office and the Officeholders

The first two chapters of the book describe the office of the president, and the evolution of the presidency from a weak executive with few powers, to the creation of the imperial presidency, to the current situation where the president works with Congress to get his agenda passed.

When presidents leave office, they are judged as failures or successes. Chapter 2 takes a look at how we rate and rank our presidents and the criteria we use. I give you my own subjective rankings of our ten best and ten worst presidents in Part VII: The Part of Tens.

Part II: Starting with Known Quantities: Washington to John Quincy Adams

This part covers the most prominent U.S. presidents. These presidents were founding fathers who set the foundation for the U.S. presidency. Interestingly, many of them allowed Congress to dominate and make policy for the new country.

Most U.S. citizens know about the nation's first presidents. From Washington to Jefferson and Madison, America's first presidents are well-known individuals. They legitimized America's new form of government, making it acceptable to the public.

Part III: Enduring the Best and the Worst: Jackson to Buchanan

Within a time span of 30 years, the United States saw two of its greatest presidents and many of its most abysmal failures. The period started out promisingly with Andrew Jackson, the country's first strong president. Then came the failures. With the exception of James K. Polk, who was a great president (hardworking and honest), the rest of the bunch were miserable failures. Who remembers Presidents Pierce, Fillmore, and Buchanan?

The country was in deep crisis in the 1850s, with a civil war looming. The country needed a good, strong president to settle the conflicts between the North and South. But none of the presidents of the 1850s did anything to prevent a civil war; many, in fact, contributed to the outbreak of the conflict.

Part IV: Becoming a Force in the World: Lincoln to Hoover

Who doesn't know of Abraham Lincoln and his valiant attempts to preserve the Union? Besides saving the country, Lincoln also set the foundation for the United States to become a world power. During his tenure, the country industrialized and developed economically. Most of Lincoln's successors just stood by and watched the country grow.

After the great Lincoln came some bad and ineffective presidents. Andrew Johnson was the first president to be impeached. Johnson was followed by the corrupt Grant administration and the disputed election of 1876.

The next bunch of presidents was made up of honest, capable men, who believed that Congress should run the country while they stand on the side. All of this changed in 1901.

Chapter 13 and 14 cover two of our strongest and most prominent presidents — Theodore Roosevelt and Woodrow Wilson. Roosevelt brought the United States into the arena of great world powers and Wilson saved democracy in Europe by getting the United States involved in World War I.

The 1920s then gave the country bland, ineffective presidents best known for corruption (Harding), napping (Coolidge), or slow reactions (Hoover).

Part V: Instituting the Imperial Presidency: Franklin Roosevelt to Richard Nixon

Franklin Roosevelt took the helm in 1933 with innovative ideas for the country. He started the welfare state in the United States, including social security and unemployment benefits and slowly pulled the United States out of the Great Depression. Roosevelt also turned the United States into a superpower by entering and helping to win World War II.

Harry Truman finished the job of winning the war by dropping two atomic bombs on Japan. Truman dealt with the new Cold War and staved off communism with the Truman Doctrine and the Marshall Plan. Dwight Eisenhower, the quiet president, successfully contained communism.

By the time John F. Kennedy came to power, the imperial presidency was in place. Kennedy didn't have enough time as president to enjoy its powers, but his successor Lyndon Johnson took full advantage of the power of the presidency.

If it weren't for Richard Nixon, the imperial presidency would still be around today. The Watergate scandal weakened the presidency, and Congress reasserted itself. Good-bye imperial presidency.

Part VI: Changing the Dynamics: Gerald Ford to George W. Bush

After the Nixon disaster, Congress reasserted itself, especially in foreign policy. Ever since, America's presidents have battled Congress over policy.

Part VI begins by examining the short-lived presidency of Gerald Ford and one-term president Jimmy Carter. In the 1980s, Ronald Reagan, the "Great Communicator," restored U.S. power and prestige in the world and brought communism to its knees. Reagan's successor, George Bush, oversaw the collapse of communism and waged the Gulf War.

Bill Clinton has the distinction of being the second president to be impeached by the House of Representatives. All of his scandals, however, didn't hurt his popularity with the public, proving that many U.S. citizens base their vote on their pocketbook. Part VI concludes by looking at the disputed election of 2000 and the terrorist attacks on the United States in 2001.

Part VII: The Part of Tens

The Part of Tens may annoy you or challenge you. In the first two chapters of Part VII, I rank the presidents, presenting my picks for the ten best and the ten worst. In Chapter 28, I give you possible vacation destinations in the ten best presidential libraries.

Appendix: Presidential Facts

The term *appendix* usually means "skip this section." Please don't. The appendix contains a lot of interesting and relevant information. It presents birth dates for all the presidents and death dates for deceased presidents. Wouldn't it be nice to know if you share a birthday with a president? In addition, it lists vice presidents, political party affiliation, and the outcomes of all presidential elections in U.S. history.

For the statistic buff, the results of these elections not only include the numbers and percentages for the Electoral College votes, but also for the popular vote. Enjoy!

Icons Used in This Book

As you read and enjoy this book, you will discover five different icons that alert you to specific aspects of America's 42 presidents. The five icons are

 This icon presents little-known information, or trivia, on the 42 presidents. Many of the presidents coined terms or set precedents for the presidency and the country. This icon alerts you to this type of information.

 This icon alerts you to famous statements or quotes made by the presidents. Some quotes you may be familiar with, and others you may not know. Some may shock you, and others may amuse you.

 Politics is at the heart of the U.S. presidency. This icon highlights political conflicts and positions. It covers the personal views of some presidents and the controversial issues of the day.

 This icon points out important information you should be aware of as you read the section, the chapter, or the book. This icon covers only the most important events, people, and issues.

 Historical information including treaties, important bills, strategic doctrines, and other relevant material or events have this icon beside them. This information is included for the history buff, so feel free to ignore these paragraphs if you're not interested.

Where to Go from Here

Feel free to start with any chapter and any president that interests you. Keep in mind that all the chapters are nonlinear, so you can start with any topic in any chapter.

Part I
Examining the Office and the Officeholders

The 5th Wave   By Rich Tennant

IN JAN. 1943, THE DECISION TO INVADE ITALY THROUGH SICILY WAS MADE AT THE CASABLANCA CONFERENCE.

"President Roosevelt, you know General de Gaulle, Prime Minister Churchill, Sam the piano player..."

In this part...

The story of our presidents is a fascinating one. Part of that fascination is the history and evolution of the presidency. After the war of independence was won, there was much debate over what type of government to establish. With the Articles of Confederation not working well, a new form of government had to be created. This was accomplished in 1788, when the Constitution of the United States was ratified by the states. In this part you see the reason of why a new form of government was necessary and how the Constitutional Convention established the form of government we enjoy today.

Chapter 1 discusses the constitutional powers of the president such as the veto power and also mentions some informal powers such as the power to manipulate public opinion. In addition, I trace the evolution of the presidency from a weak ceremonial post to the imperial presidency of modern times.

Chapter 2 looks at the way we evaluate and rank presidents and their administrations. I take you through both public and academic rankings of our presidents and look at upward and downward movement of some presidents.

Chapter 1

Presidents and the Presidency

● ●

In This Chapter

▶ Setting up a government for the United States

▶ Creating the presidency

▶ Changing with the times

▶ Possessing formal powers

▶ Developing informal powers

▶ Fighting Congress

● ●

This chapter looks at the U.S. presidency. It talks about how the U.S. system of government was established. It also discusses the Constitution and the evolution of the presidency from a weak ceremonial post, such as the presidency of James Madison, to the imperial presidency of FDR. Today we find a stalemate between the presidency and Congress, resulting in much bargaining and compromising and the occasional government shutdown. In addition, the chapter covers formal powers the president possesses, such as the power to cast a veto. Finally, the president has been granted or assumed some special, informal powers, especially the power to manipulate public opinion. The discussion of these informal powers rounds out the chapter.

Establishing the First U.S. Government

In 1774, 12 colonies (Georgia refused to attend) agreed to get together and set up a united legislature, or *Continental Congress,* to speak with one voice against British oppression. The Continental Congress turned into a national legislature during the Revolutionary War and stuck around after independence was declared, assuming the functions of a new national government.

In 1781, the Congress passed the *Articles of Confederation,* creating a confederation between the 13 former colonies. After the states agreed on the Articles of Confederation, the Congress renamed itself the *Congress of the Confederation* and became a weak federal legislature — it was without real powers, including the power to tax or the power to create a national army. The real power remained within the 13 states.

The Congress survived until the Constitution created a new form of government in 1789, and the Congress of the United States replaced the Congress of the Confederation.

A *confederation* is a form of government where power rests at the state level and not at the national level.

Facing problems

The confederation system caused immediate problems for the new country:

- Without the power to tax, the Congress could not support a large military, which was dangerous with the British, Russian, and Spanish empires still in North America.

- The war bonds sold to finance the war against Britain presented another problem. With the war over and the national government unable to tax, nobody redeemed the bonds. Many patriotic people who bought war bonds to support the war for independence lost their life savings when they couldn't redeem the bonds. Not surprisingly, people complained.

- Trade became a problem, with the states treating each other like they were foreign countries. How can a united country be established when its members impose trade restrictions against each other?

Writing a constitution

By 1785, many prominent politicians in the United States were worried. They felt that the new country was in serious trouble and that the new government, created by the Articles of Confederation, was not working. For this purpose, a national meeting in Philadelphia was called to change or revise the Articles of Confederation. This meeting, also referred to as the *Constitutional Convention,* began in May of 1787. Its original purpose was just to change the Articles of Confederation, not to write a new Constitution. The convention lasted until September 1787, when the delegates actually overstepped their authority and voted to approve a new constitution for the country.

Instead of revising the Articles of Confederation, the delegates created a brand new document — the Constitution of the United States. They felt that a revision of the Articles of Confederation would not accomplish the task of creating a strong, united country. So they wrote a brand new document instead, abolishing the Articles of Confederation and setting up a new form of government. The Constitution called for the following:

- The creation of a federal republic, where the states and the national-federal government shared powers

> ✔ A bicameral Congress with two chambers — the House of Representatives (selected by the people) and the Senate (equally represented by the states, with each state sending two Senators)
>
> ✔ An executive, or president, elected by an Electoral College every four years
>
> ✔ A Supreme Court nominated by the president and ratified by the Senate

Drawing up the presidency

During the Constitutional Convention in Philadelphia in 1787, the hottest topic was what kind of executive to have. Some wanted a strong executive, even a king. Others wanted a weak executive at the mercy of Congress. Some even proposed multiple executives, with more than one president serving in the various areas of government.

James Wilson, a delegate from Pennsylvania, was responsible for the presidency we have today. During the debate, he based the modern presidency on the New York and Massachusetts State constitutions.

One of the big questions at the Constitutional Convention was whether to create a parliamentary or a presidential republic. In a *parliamentary system,* the legislature, not the citizens, selects the executive. Chosen by the majority, the executive's party always controls the legislature. In a *presidential republic,* voters choose the president. This can result in a divided government, with one party controlling the legislature and the other the presidency.

A presidential system, such as the form the United States adopted, creates moderate policies, involving lots of compromise, because the executive and Congress have to bargain with each other to be successful. In a parliamentary system, the executive always gets what he or she wants, because it controls the legislature.

Being unique

The system of checks and balances is a feature unique to the United States. The delegates at the convention wanted to make sure that the president wouldn't dominate the new government. So they implemented many checks on his power. Congress and the Supreme Court can check the president in the areas the delegates considered the most important, resulting in this system of checks and balances. These areas included treaty-making, war-making and especially the power to declare war, which was given to Congress. Congress and the Supreme Court further received the power to override a president's veto and to remove him from office if necessary.

The Electoral College

The Electoral College, established by the Constitution, consists of electors who have the power to choose the president and vice president.

The first Electoral College, which met in 1789, consisted of representatives from all the states that ratified the Constitution. Depending on the state, either the people or the state legislatures chose the respective delegates for the Electoral College. In the Electoral College, each delegate cast two ballots. Whoever won the most votes became the president of the United States; the runner-up was named the vice president.

This system led to confusion. In 1800, Thomas Jefferson and Aaron Burr received the same number of votes, even though most electors favored Jefferson for president and Burr for vice president. The electors had to cast two ballots without being able to differentiate between president and vice president. The 12th Amendment fixed the system in 1804 by mandating separate ballots for the president and vice president.

In 1961, the 23rd Amendment allowed the District of Columbia to cast three votes in the Electoral College, even though it doesn't have statehood. Today, the electors in the Electoral College represent all 50 states and the District of Columbia. The electors, in turn, are chosen by their respective state legislatures. (Each party, Democrats and Republicans, draws up a list of electors. Whichever party wins the state in the presidential election gets to use its list in the Electoral College. The only exceptions to this rule are found in Maine and Nebraska, where one electoral vote goes to the winner of each Congressional district in the state and two votes go to the winner of the state itself). The number of electors representing each state equals the number of members of Congress (members of the House of Representatives plus the two senators) for each state. Today, there are 538 total votes in the Electoral College, and a candidate has to win 270 to become president. If nobody has a majority in the Electoral College, the vote goes into the House of Representatives.

Today, the president is the most powerful politician on earth, but he has to share a lot of his powers with Congress.

Over the next two centuries, the power and influence of the presidency developed and changed.

Granting formal presidential powers

The Constitution, even though a brief document, sets aside Article II to discuss the presidency. Article II outlines the Electoral College and the powers of the president. The Constitution formally mentions the following powers in Section 2 and Section 3 of Article II of the Constitution. The powers are listed in the order found in the Constitution:

 ✔ **Commander in chief of the armed forces:** This power has caused much controversy. Many presidents have interpreted it to mean that they have the power to make war. Congress, on the other hand, has the constitutional power to declare war. The War Powers Act of 1973 (discussed later in this chapter) further contributes to the controversy surrounding this power.

✔ **Granting reprieves and pardons:** The president has the power to pardon anyone for federal offenses. The only exception is impeachment. The president cannot pardon someone who has been impeached.

✔ **Making treaties:** The president has the power to negotiate treaties with foreign countries. All treaties have to be approved by the Senate with a two-thirds majority.

✔ **Appointing Supreme Court Justices and ambassadors:** The president has the power to appoint justices of the U.S. Supreme Court and ambassadors. In both instances, the Senate has to approve his choices.

✔ **Convening Congress to special sessions:** In emergency situations, the president has the power to call Congress into a special session.

✔ **Receiving ambassadors:** The president has the right to receive foreign ambassadors and other foreign dignitaries to discuss policy with them.

✔ **Ensuring that the laws are faithfully executed:** That's all the Constitution says about this power. Today, presidents interpret it as the power to make policy, as outlined in the annual budget the president submits to Congress.

Vetoing legislation

Additional powers of the president are found in Article I, Section 7. Even though Article I deals mainly with Congressional powers, it does discuss the veto power of the president. According to Section 7, the president possesses the power to veto legislation passed by Congress. He has ten days to veto a bill and has to explain to Congress why he cast the veto. Congress then has the option to override a president's veto. This requires a two-thirds majority in both houses of Congress.

If Congress passes a bill within ten days of adjourning, the president can cast a *pocket veto*. All he has to do is to let the bill sit on his desk until Congress adjourns and the bill has been vetoed. Pocket vetoes cannot be overridden, because Congress has no chance to vote on the veto. Most vetoes stand, or are not overridden by Congress. Less than 4 percent of all vetoes in U.S. history have been overridden.

Interpreting presidential powers

The Constitution is not very specific on presidential powers. Many are vague and open to broad interpretation. For example, does to "faithfully execute the laws" mean that a president just observes Congress and then makes Congressional legislation law? Or can the president make laws himself? As commander in chief, is the president just some kind of super-general reacting to Congress, which has the power to declare war, or is he the supreme war maker in the United States? It is thus left up to the president to define his role.

Different men who have held the office have interpreted their powers differently. For example, in 1861, after President Lincoln took office and before Congress reconvened, Lincoln unilaterally reacted to the attack on Fort Sumter by the Confederacy (see Chapter 10). He defined the role of commander in chief by taking over the war effort himself. In addition, he single-handedly freed the slaves in the Confederacy with the Emancipation Proclamation. He felt his actions were justified by the emergency of the Civil War. Lincoln's predecessor, James Buchanan, however, believed that his powers did not extend to preventing the Southern states from leaving the Union. So he refused to act when the first Southern states left the Union and created the Confederacy.

Examining Presidential Influence on the Presidency

Just as the president is a living, breathing person, the presidency is a living, breathing institution. The men who have so far filled the office have put their own unique stamp on the office, for better or worse. The following sections give you some examples.

During the period from 1789 to 1824, most U.S. presidents were prominent men known to most U.S. citizens. They included many of our founding fathers and others who had served their country valiantly in the Revolutionary War. With the exception of John Adams, each of the first 5 presidents served two terms, bringing a measure of stability to the young country.

They legitimized the new government, or in other words, they created public support for the new form of government. Even if one disagreed with the new form of government created by the Constitution, how could one oppose George Washington as president? These presidents set the foundation for the United States. However, during this time period, Congress dominated and made most decisions for the United States. The president was considered to be a caretaker, and his job was to implement policies passed by Congress.

Challenging Congress: Andrew Jackson

When Andrew Jackson assumed office in 1829, he believed that he had a mandate from the people and that it was his job to not only implement policies passed by Congress but to make his own. He saw himself as a guardian of the people, with a mission to protect them from the excesses of Congress.

He challenged Congress and vetoed major congressional legislation. Jackson actually vetoed more legislation than all of his predecessors combined.

Jackson's interpretation of a powerful president disappeared with him. His successors perceived their role as one of reacting to Congress.

With the exception of Abraham Lincoln, Teddy Roosevelt, and Woodrow Wilson, all presidents for the next century subordinated themselves to Congress. Congress made policy for the United States, and the presidents passively endorsed it.

Creating the imperial presidency: Franklin Roosevelt

With the Great Depression hitting the country hard in 1929, and World War II (WWII) starting in Europe in 1939, the U.S. public looked for strong leadership.

They found it in Franklin Delano Roosevelt. Starting with his election in 1932, FDR single-handedly created the imperial presidency. He was responsible for the New Deal programs, which greatly enhanced the powers of the presidency by establishing a large federal bureaucracy over which the president presides. Roosevelt put a massive welfare state in place (see Chapter 16) and had government take an active role in the economy. FDR made it the business of the president to take care of the U.S. public.

Foreign policy also came to the forefront when FDR took over in 1933. He moved the United States to support the Allies during WWII. During the war, he met with Allied leaders and hammered out major agreements. The subsequent Cold War further involved the United States in global affairs.

The trend of the president dominating foreign policy continued, and presidents today are the foreign policy leaders in the United States. By the time Lyndon Johnson assumed the presidency in 1963, Congress was reacting to the president, who now made both domestic and foreign policy for the country.

Dethroning the imperial presidency: Richard Nixon

In 1974, Richard Nixon destroyed the imperial presidency with the Watergate scandal and its aftermath. Congress saw the executive position weakened and took this chance to restore some of the power it had lost to the president.

The most visible changes Congress imposed were in the area of foreign policy and budget policies, when Congress passed the War Powers Act in 1973 over

President Nixon's veto and the Budget Reform Act in 1974. These acts brought Congress back into the realms of war-making and budgeting.

The War Powers Act of 1973 was a direct challenge to the president and the president's powers to commit U.S. troops into combat. The acts severely restricted the president by calling for the following:

- The president has to inform Congress in writing 48 hours after he commits troops into a hostile situation.

- Sixty days after committing troops into a hostile situation, Congress has to declare war or authorize continuous commitment. This gives Congress the power to recall the troops.

- Congress, at any time, can pass a *concurrent resolution* (a resolution passed by both houses of Congress) to recall the troops. The president cannot veto this resolution.

Suddenly Congress had the powers to recall troops that a president committed into a hostile situation. It didn't have to stand idly by while a president fought a war. Both institutions, Congress and the president, again shared war-making powers.

Ironically, every president affected by the act — beginning with Nixon and including George W. Bush — has claimed that the War Powers Act is unconstitutional and has refused to be bound by its terms. The Supreme Court has so far refused to rule on the constitutionality of the act.

The Budget Act of 1974 is another example of how Congress reasserted itself. Presidents had given themselves the power to refuse to spend money appropriated by Congress for certain programs. Most presidents, beginning with Jefferson, used it frequently.

This power was absolute until the Nixon era. In 1974, Congress passed the Budget Reform Act, which stated that the president can refuse to spend or delay the spending of money, but he has to tell Congress about it. Congress then has the option to pass a resolution calling for the spending of the money. After the resolution passes, the president has to spend the money. Suddenly, Congress could force a president to spend money allocated for programs the president opposed.

Perfecting the Power to Shape Public Opinion

The greatest power a U.S. president has is not found in the Constitution. It is the power to persuade and convince the U.S. public. If the president can get the public behind him, he becomes unstoppable. Congress cannot and will not oppose him if he can show Congress that the public supports him on a certain issue. For this reason, the power to shape public opinion is a great one.

Persuading the people

Theodore Roosevelt was the first U.S. president to take advantage of the power of public opinion. He used the presidency as a *bully pulpit* — a forum to use his influence to promote his causes — and preached to the U.S. public in an attempt to gather public support. When Congress began to stifle his progressive reforms (see Chapter 13), he toured the United States and attempted to convince the public of the integrity of his programs. With the public behind him, Congress had a tough time not agreeing to his agenda.

Woodrow Wilson, a political scientist, recognized this power and continued in Roosevelt's tradition. He, too, traveled around the country to rally support for his policies. In addition, Wilson established the tradition of holding regular press conferences, and addressed Congress directly by giving his State of the Union address in person to Congress. Wilson transformed the State of the Union address into the public spectacle it still is today. He set the precedent of using the media to disseminate his speeches to the U.S. public.

Making use of the media

With the invention of the radio, and later television, the power to persuade, or shape public opinion, gained new importance. Radio made it possible to reach the U.S. public easily, without ever leaving the White House.

The first president to take advantage of this was Franklin Roosevelt in the 1930s. A week after presenting his first inaugural address, FDR began addressing the U.S. public directly over the radio with his famous fireside chats, which he used to explain his policies and foster trust and confidence in the public. Roosevelt continued this practice throughout his presidency, delivering a total of 27 fireside chats.

It was John F. Kennedy who used television for similar purposes. He became our first television president. Kennedy and his advisors had figured that the best way to reach the public was through television appearances heavily laden with political messages. Nothing was more successful in gaining the support of the U.S. public than a well-timed, well-written, and well-delivered speech.

Kennedy was also the first president to allow his press conferences to be covered on live television. (Eisenhower had his press conferences taped and reserved the right to edit them before they were broadcast.) Kennedy delivered 64 live press conferences before he was assassinated.

Today, using television to reach the public is common. Inaugural addresses, State of the Union addresses, and press conference are all designed to reach out to the U.S. public and convince people that the president's policies merit their support. Clearly, a well-written and well-delivered speech can sway public opinion in a president's favor. This in turn facilitates his dealings with Congress.

Performing Many Roles: Today's President

Today the president performs many roles in society. The president has become the preeminent politician in the United States. Some of his roles include:

- **Head of state:** The president symbolizes the United States. Other countries judge the United States by what kind of president the U.S. public elects.

- **Commander in chief:** The president heads the U.S. military. The public looks to him to commit troops into combat. The public also holds him accountable for the successes or failures of military operations.

- **Chief foreign policy maker:** The president is expected to make foreign policy, meet foreign leaders, and negotiate treaties. The public holds him responsible for successes and failures in foreign policy.

- **Chief executive:** The president is in charge of the federal bureaucracy, which includes the cabinet departments, the Office of Management and Budget, and the military — more than 2 million people altogether.

- **Chief legislator:** Today, the president is responsible for most major legislation. He proposes the budget and uses his veto power to shape policy. The president acts, and Congress usually reacts to his policies.

- **Crisis manager:** Whenever crisis strikes the country, the U.S. public looks to the president to act. After the terrorist attacks on the United States in September 2001, the public expected the president, not Congress, to react. It was George W. Bush and his advisors who explained to the public and Congress what had happened, as well as what measures the government would take.

- **Leader of his party:** The public, as well as party supporters, look at the president as the leader of his party. If the president does well, the public will usually reward his party in the elections. If he performs poorly, the public will usually punish his party, especially in *off-year* (non-presidential) elections.

Today, the president is the chief politician in the United States. However, he still has to share his powers with Congress on many occasions, and Congress can keep his power in check, if necessary.

Chapter 2

Presidential Rankings and Evaluations

In This Chapter

▶ Studying presidential rankings

▶ Reviewing two presidential surveys

*T*his chapter looks at how U.S. presidents are ranked by the public and experts, such as academics. I present two surveys: One asked experts, mostly historians, to rank the presidents; the other asked the public to do the same. The differences are interesting, and I discuss the significance of those differences after the surveys themselves.

The public is aware of the founding fathers and major presidents who served during crises, such as Abraham Lincoln and Franklin Delano Roosevelt. This knowledge comes mostly from school and the emphasis that the media places on these important presidents. But when was the last time you saw a special on Rutherford Hayes or read a new biography of Millard Fillmore? On the other hand, you can choose among several movies or books about Franklin Roosevelt or Abraham Lincoln.

Polls show that most U.S. citizens know about the presidents in office during their lifetime but don't know much about the presidents of the past, especially the lesser-known executives. Therefore, the public ranks current presidents and famous presidents higher than lesser-known presidents. Academics who study presidents, on the other hand, have a better historical perspective — not too many recent presidents rank high on their scale.

Over time, the standing of a past president may change within the rankings of the U.S. public and academics, providing for renewed interest in his life and actions in office. Some presidents are highly regarded after they leave office, only to end up being considered disappointments in the long run. Andrew Johnson had this fate. Other presidents, such as Harry Truman, may be considered failures shortly after the end of their administrations and then become popular heroes later.

This chapter looks at the academic and public rankings of U.S. presidents, as well as the issues and characteristics each group uses to evaluate presidents. Chapter 26 presents my personal ranking of the ten best presidents, and Chapter 27 lists my picks for the ten worst presidents in U.S. history.

Evaluating the Presidents

U.S. presidents are evaluated in many ways. The major characteristics academic and public polls use to evaluate the 42 U.S. presidents vary from survey to survey, but the main standards remain fairly consistent.

It is important to keep in mind that times change and presidential rankings reflect this. Early in U.S. history, the United States was isolationist, so foreign policy wasn't a factor in presidential evaluations. Foreign policy became much more important in the 20th century.

Media scrutiny is a recent phenomenon. During most of the 19th and 20th centuries, the media did not delve into presidents' lives. It was considered taboo to report on private presidential scandals — the public didn't know much, if anything, about Franklin Roosevelt's or Harding's extramarital affairs. A president's private indiscretions didn't factor into how he was judged as president. This code of silence held well into the 20th century — the media didn't report on John F. Kennedy's legendary affairs in the White House, even his well-known liaison with movie star Marilyn Monroe.

The Watergate scandal in the 1970s changed things. Suddenly the media believed that it had an obligation to be a watchdog over the presidents. This new role allowed the media not only to check presidents for public mistakes and policy failures, but also to report on private wrongdoings. This role for the media won't change as long as juicy scandals continue to garner large audiences. Future presidents have to expect to have their lives scrutinized and any minor wrongdoing reported. In the 2000 election, George W. Bush figured that a 20-year-old conviction for drunk driving wouldn't be a big deal and wouldn't be reported. Boy, was he wrong. When the story came out days before the election, it almost cost him the presidency.

Policy leadership

A president has to make policy, domestic and foreign, for the country. The president outlines his policies in his inaugural address, his annual State of the Union addresses, and especially his budget. The president has a tough battle to conquer: He has to mobilize public opinion to gain the upper hand with Congress.

The president has to be careful when dealing with Congress. If he is pushy and takes a heavy-handed approach, Congress may resent him, and he is not likely to be very successful. Andrew Johnson and Richard Nixon found this out the hard way. If a president is willing to lobby Congress and bargain and deal with its members, he can be very successful. George Bush saw most of his legislation pass, even though the opposition Democrats controlled both houses of Congress.

Leadership skills are necessary for the president to succeed. The more skills a president possesses, the more likely Congress will pass his policies. This is one way that a president is judged and evaluated. The more his policies get passed, the higher his ranking.

In modern times, a president's legislation has been judged according to the impact his policies have on social equality in U.S. society. Policies that benefit minorities and the poor enhance a president's ranking in the polls.

Crisis management

The U.S. public looks to the president as its political and economic leader. He is held responsible for the political and economic climate, whether times are good or bad. A successful president has to have a program ready to stimulate the economy if necessary, and he has to be able to pass it. If he fails, he will not win reelection. Jimmy Carter and George Bush are recent presidents who lost their bids for reelection due to economic decline. At the same time, a booming economy can get a president reelected even if he is facing personal scandals, as Bill Clinton demonstrated in 1996.

Crisis management also refers to international crises. The way a president reacts to major foreign crises, such as a war or a terrorist attack, greatly impacts his standing with the public and his rankings in the polls. Abraham Lincoln and Franklin Roosevelt, two presidents who always rank in the top five, rank high mainly because of their crisis-management skills. Lincoln reacted forcefully during the Civil War and kept the Union intact. Franklin Roosevelt guided the United States through World War II and turned the country into a superpower.

Lyndon Johnson, on the other hand, couldn't deal with the conflict in Vietnam. This inability lowers his ranking, despite his major domestic accomplishments. More recently, President George W. Bush, who was not doing well in the polls as late as August 2001, turned himself into a great crisis manager after the terrorist attacks in September 2001. His handling of the situation brought new life to his presidency. He is likely to go down as one of the great crisis managers in U.S. history.

Presidential appointments

Presidents are also measured by the people they appoint to public office. This area of evaluation includes appointments to the Supreme Court and the presidential cabinet.

Presidents Harding and Grant destroyed their presidencies with inept, corrupt appointments, and their rankings reflect this. Appointing good, skilled people reflects positively on a president. George C. Marshall and Henry Kissinger, both Secretaries of State, reflected positively on the presidents that appointed them, increasing Truman's and Nixon's standings, respectively. Today, diversity has become an issue. Presidential appointments should reflect the ethnic composition of the country. The more minorities, including women, a president appoints to high-level positions, the higher his ranking. Both Bill Clinton and George W. Bush have done well in this area, with their cabinets containing a fair amount of minorities.

Foreign standing

Foreign policy is a recent addition to the criteria for ranking U.S. presidents. Most 19th century presidents can't be ranked on this issue because, during that time period, the United States was isolationist and didn't get involved in world affairs. But since Theodore Roosevelt and his active participation in international affairs (See Chapter 13), foreign policy has been a major part of the presidency. Today a president deals with many other nations: How he deals with these nations, as well as how these nations perceive him, contribute to his ranking.

Major foreign policy success can make up for domestic failure. President Nixon ranks low on many lists, but he had major accomplishments in the area of foreign policy. These accomplishments elevate him into the middle of the presidential pack. President George Bush was a great foreign policy president: During his term, the Soviet Union collapsed, the Gulf War was won, and major arms control took place. These accomplishments push him into the top 15 of U.S. presidents.

Respect from foreign nations is very important. President Nixon was widely respected by foreign nations. After his resignation, he continued to be treated as a successful president by most of the world, which led to a rise in his rankings.

Character and integrity

The attributes of character and integrity are important when judging presidents. A president who promotes corruption, lies to the public, or is involved in scandals will obviously be ranked lower than an honest president.

President Nixon single-handedly destroyed his presidency and his place in history with the Watergate scandal. President Clinton undermined a successful presidency with many personal scandals, including lying to the public. President Clinton's scandals continued even after he left office. President Harding destroyed what was left of his presidency with continuous extramarital affairs.

At the same time, a president who wasn't very successful in office, such as Jimmy Carter, can restore his reputation and rise in the rankings for being a true humanitarian and an honest person. James Polk made it into my top ten list of presidents in this book for being an honest, dedicated individual. He worked so hard that it cost him his life. There were no scandals during his presidency, and he even kept his campaign promise not to run for reelection.

Public persuasion

The ability to persuade the public to his point of view is one of the most powerful weapons a president possesses. It's also one he most needs to succeed. How a president uses this power, and how successful he is with it, impacts his standing in the ranks of presidents. Some of the masters of public persuasion are

- **Theodore Roosevelt,** who used his position and influence as president to persuade citizens to his point of view. He was able to get much of his legislation passed, despite having to deal with a hostile Congress.

- **Franklin Roosevelt,** who went straight to the public with his fireside chats and not only reassured the public after the Great Depression, but also gained support for his New Deal legislation.

- **Ronald Reagan,** who is known as the "Great Communicator" because he possessed a special ability to connect with the U.S. public.

    The public loved Reagan and the way he dealt with the average person. This adoration translated into support for his policies. Congress enacted a large part of Reagan's agenda because the public backed him — not necessarily because Congress agreed with him and his proposals.

Other presidents haven't fared as well. Jimmy Carter had a tough time connecting with the public. For this reason, much of his presidential agenda never made it through Congress, even though his own party controlled Congress. Richard Nixon failed in similar fashion. He couldn't relate to the public. By the time the Watergate scandal came around, it was too late to gather public support for his presidency.

Presidential vision

Some presidents come into office without a vision of what they want to accomplish as president: This usually results in a failed presidency. Without a master plan, a president is at the mercy of Congress, which can then take over and make policy for the country.

The more successful presidents have a vision. They want to use the office of president to change the United States. Franklin Roosevelt wanted to bring about changes to protect the average citizen from the brutal effects of the Great Depression. Reagan wanted to restore the United States to greatness and decrease the size of the federal government. With a vision to guide them, presidents tend to be active, as they try to implement their agenda. Even if they're not successful, they still get credit for having a vision.

A president without a vision accomplishes nothing, because there is nothing he wants to accomplish. Without a vision, a presidency results in failure.

The most successful presidents in U.S. history all had a vision of how they wanted the country to look and act. By the time they served out their terms, they had made a difference and changed the United States according to their plan.

Ranking U.S. Presidents

One of the best evaluations of U.S. presidents was released in 1999. C-SPAN (National Cable Satellite Corporation), a network created to show public affairs programming, conducted a survey of 58 historians and other experts on the presidency in the United States and asked them to rank the presidents. Then, the network asked its viewers to rank the presidents. The rankings of the 1,145 people who participated are similar to the rankings of the academics, but they do contain some interesting differences. I present both surveys in Table 2-1. (Our current president, George W. Bush, is not ranked.)

The 42 U.S. presidents were ranked on ten different characteristics and then put in order. The ten criteria included: public persuasion, crisis leadership, economic management, moral authority, international relations, administrative skills, relations with congress, vision/setting agenda, pursued justice for all, and performance within contexts of times.

To this day, the C-SPAN surveys are the most comprehensive surveys available to the public. You can find more information on the Web site at www.americanpresidents.org/survey.

Table 2-1	**Presidential Rankings**	
Ranking	*C-SPAN academic survey*	*C-SPAN viewer survey*
1	Abraham Lincoln	Abraham Lincoln
2	Franklin Delano Roosevelt	George Washington
3	George Washington	Theodore Roosevelt
4	Theodore Roosevelt	Franklin Delano Roosevelt
5	Harry S. Truman	Thomas Jefferson
6	Woodrow Wilson	Ronald Reagan
7	Thomas Jefferson	Harry S. Truman
8	John F. Kennedy	Dwight D. Eisenhower
9	Dwight D. Eisenhower	James Monroe
10	Lyndon Baines Johnson	James Madison
11	Ronald Reagan	John Adams
12	James K. Polk	John F. Kennedy
13	Andrew Jackson	Woodrow Wilson
14	James Monroe	Andrew Jackson
15	William McKinley	John Quincy Adams
16	John Adams	George Bush
17	Grover Cleveland	James K. Polk
18	James Madison	William McKinley
19	John Quincy Adams	Lyndon Baines Johnson
20	George Bush	Richard Nixon
21	Bill Clinton	Grover Cleveland
22	Jimmy Carter	Calvin Coolidge
23	Gerald Ford	Gerald Ford
24	William Howard Taft	William Howard Taft
25	Richard Nixon	Zachary Taylor
26	Rutherford B. Hayes	Rutherford B. Hayes
27	Calvin Coolidge	Jimmy Carter

(continued)

Table 2-1 *(continued)*

Ranking	C-SPAN academic survey	C-SPAN viewer survey
28	Zachary Taylor	James Garfield
29	James Garfield	Ulysses S. Grant
30	Martin Van Buren	Martin Van Buren
31	Benjamin Harrison	Benjamin Harrison
32	Chester Arthur	John Tyler
33	Ulysses S. Grant	Herbert Hoover
34	Herbert Hoover	Chester Arthur
35	Millard Fillmore	William Henry Harrison
36	John Tyler	Bill Clinton
37	William Henry Harrison	Millard Fillmore
38	Warren G. Harding	Andrew Johnson
39	Franklin Pierce	Franklin Pierce
40	Andrew Johnson	Warren G. Harding
41	James Buchanan	James Buchanan

Explaining the differences

Experts, such as academics, rank presidents such as John F. Kennedy and Lyndon Johnson higher than the public for their accomplishments in domestic policy. There is also a political bias among academics. Academics tend to be more liberal than the general populace, so they tend to rate liberal presidents higher than the public does.

The public doesn't have this ideological bias. The public considers Ronald Reagan one of the top ten presidents. They remember Reagan fondly, and they really don't care about the Iran-Contra scandal, which academics hold against him. The public also ranks George Bush and Richard Nixon higher than academics do.

It is interesting to observe that Richard Nixon doesn't make the five worst presidents anymore. Right after the Watergate scandal, he was considered one of the worst presidents in U.S. history. But he was able to regain some of his stature in the last two decades of his life, mostly due to his foreign policy accomplishments. (See Chapter 21 for coverage of President Nixon.)

Changing rankings over time

Presidential rankings change over time. This fluctuation especially affects recent presidents. It takes time to evaluate a presidency and to see the long-term impact of a president's accomplishments or failures. Actions that may have been considered a big mistake at the time can turn out to be a stroke of genius decades later. At the same time, a courageous move may turn into a disastrous mistake when viewed with the benefit of hindsight. So, you can expect the more recent presidents to move up and down the rankings ladder in years to come. Most of the earlier presidents, on the other hand, are unlikely to improve or worsen in the standings.

Moving up the ladder: Truman

When Harry Truman left office, many considered his presidency a failure. Contemporaneous observers believed that he was one of the worst presidents in U.S. history. He wasn't able to win the war in Korea, and his civil rights and social programs were stalled in Congress.

Decades later, the perception of Truman changed. People looked at Truman's foreign policy and recognized what he accomplished. Truman implemented the policy of containing communism, not allowing any more European countries to go communist: The Truman Doctrine, providing aid to countries fighting communist uprisings, saved Greece and Turkey from communism, and the Marshall Plan, providing economic aid to Europe, restored European economies and prevented communist parties from coming to power in Europe after World War II.

Truman also faced the toughest decision a person could make: Should he drop nuclear bombs on Japan? Truman did what he thought was best for the country. He wanted to end World War II as quickly as possible to save U.S. lives. He did this by having U.S. bombers drop atomic bombs on the cities of Hiroshima and Nagasaki.

Truman also integrated the armed forces by executive order. He could have accomplished even more if he hadn't faced a hostile Congress.

Today Truman is considered a great president, consistently ranking in the top ten. (For in-depth coverage of Truman, turn to Chapter 17.)

Reevaluating Eisenhower

When Eisenhower left office, his presidency was considered boring and bland. People thought he hadn't done much. Decades later, people looked at his presidency differently — not doing much might be a good thing.

Eisenhower ended the war in Korea and kept peace around the world. As Eisenhower proudly proclaimed, communism didn't gain an inch of territory during his tenure, and he accomplished this without shedding any U.S. blood. Not bad for a quiet, boring president.

At home, the economy was booming. Eisenhower built the U.S. interstate system and sponsored civil rights legislation. He stood up to the southern states and enforced the Supreme Court's decision to integrate U.S. public schools. Eisenhower proved that you don't have to be a flamboyant, controversial individual to be a great president. Chapter 18 gives you more reasons to like Ike.

Moving down the ladder: Andrew Johnson

Many, especially in the South, admired Andrew Johnson when he left office. He stood up to a Republican Congress that was trying to punish the former Confederate states. People thought that he was a true believer in states' rights. They also believed that he adhered to the Constitution during his short-lived presidency.

Today, Johnson is considered a horrible human being whose presidency was a massive failure. Johnson was a stubborn individual, unwilling to compromise on any issue. He tried to circumvent Congress and bring the Southern states back into the Union by himself. He was a blatant racist who didn't care at all about former slaves. He even vetoed the 13th Amendment, which made former slaves U.S. citizens. Had it been up to him, African Americans would have never had any political rights.

Johnson truly deserves to be listed among the worst presidents in U.S. history, but it took time to recognize this.

Part II
Starting with Known Quantities: Washington to John Quincy Adams

George Washington: Father of the Country and first US President. Originator of the White House Cabinet; established Congress's right to tax US citizens and re-wrote existing boating regulations to increase the number of people allowable in a row boat from 5 to 12.

In this part . . .

You see how George Washington became our first and one of our best presidents. I look at his administration and the important precedents he set for generations to come. Despite his objections to political parties, Washington could not prevent the establishment of the first political party system, and by the time he retired two parties battled for the presidency.

Next, I look at the presidency of John Adams and his attempt to curtail basic freedoms, such as freedom of speech. Fortunately, his successor proved to be a great president. Not only did Thomas Jefferson double the size of the country with the Louisiana Purchase, but he proved to be a president of the people restoring many rights taken away by Adams.

Unfortunately Jefferson's successors, James Madison and James Monroe, weren't as successful. James Madison, one of our founding fathers and author of the Bill of Rights, almost destroyed the country he helped to create in the War of 1812. James Monroe was a great foreign policy leader, adding Florida to the United States, but he allowed Congress to run the show on domestic issues.

John Quincy Adams, the only president elected by the House of Representatives, closes out the part. A great human being and superior congressman and diplomat, he suffered one of the worst presidencies to date.

Chapter 3

Starting Well with George Washington

*W*ithout question, George Washington is one of the most discussed and admired presidents in the history of the United States. The respect and admiration he holds with both academics and the U.S. public is justified. Not many people can claim to first create a new country and then successfully establish a democratic form of government. It is not just the fact that Washington defeated the British (with a little help from the French) that makes him so unique on the long list of world leaders, but that he rejected all efforts to make him a king. Throughout his life, Washington believed in the ideal of democracy and did his best to make sure that democracy survived after he left office.

George Washington truly deserves the title "founding father." Without him, there would be no United States, and there would be no democracy on the North American continent.

Washington's Early Career

George Washington grew up in the Virginia of the early 18th century, when Great Britain controlled the 13 American colonies as a part of a great British Empire that spanned most of the globe. Washington's great wish was to join the British army as an officer. Young Washington did not have any thoughts of revolution in his mind: He wanted to serve the British Empire. Nobody could have predicted that the loyal British citizen would end up as a revolutionary who created a new country.

Growing up a younger son

George Washington was born on February 22, 1732, the son of a well-to-do plantation owner in Virginia. As the youngest son in the family, Washington knew that he could not expect very much (if any) financial assistance from his father because the custom of the time dictated that the eldest son inherit any property.

George's father died when George was only 11 years old. Most of the family's plantation went to his half-brother, Lawrence. Lawrence made young George a part of his own family at their family residence in Mount Vernon and raised George like a son. With his brother's help, George, a natural when it came to mathematics, became a surveyor. His dream was to seek new lands in the American West and develop them for settlement.

By the age of 17, Washington had gained a reputation for being a top-notch surveyor, becoming the official surveyor for Culpeper County in Virginia. Washington made good use of his skills, slowly buying up some of the lands he surveyed. By the time he died, Washington owned more than 56,000 acres of land.

Set for a career in surveying, Washington's fortunes changed with the abrupt death of his beloved half-brother, Lawrence, in 1752. As his half-brother was dying of tuberculosis, Washington traveled with him to the island of Barbados, which has a good climate for people suffering from the disease, to search for a cure. In Barbados, Washington caught smallpox, which scarred him for life. On a positive note, by surviving smallpox, Washington became immune to the disease that proved to be a more deadly foe to American soldiers than the British during the Revolutionary War.

The deaths of Lawrence's wife and daughter a few years later brought Washington back to the family plantation.

Washington trained as a surveyor. The profession gave him a good living but didn't allow him to become a member of Virginia's elite, which was required to enter politics. This left Washington with only one option — a military career. So in 1752, Washington joined the Virginia militia, hoping to become an officer in the British army. His goal was to impress the governor of Virginia and the British king. He soon got his chance.

Proving his prowess in the military

In 1753, the French moved into the Ohio Valley — a move that alarmed the British. Washington left for the Ohio Valley with the order to tell the French to leave. The French refused, and Washington recommended the establishment of a British fort to counter the French settlements. The governor of Virginia agreed, and a fort was built. Before long, the French attacked, starting the French and Indian War.

Washington, who was promoted to Lieutenant Colonel, left Virginia with 159 men to defend the fort. En route, he encountered a small French unit and defeated it successfully. When Washington's exploits were published in a British magazine, his fame grew. By 1754, Washington expected to be named an officer in the British army. But because the British believed that their officers were better than Colonial officers, Washington's hopes of becoming a British officer were shattered, so he resigned his military commission.

The British decision to ignore the colonists proved costly when the French and their Indian allies defeated the British forces in 1755. The governor of Virginia decided that only Washington could save the day and appointed him commander in chief of all Colonial forces. By 1758, Colonel Washington had defeated the French. He became a national hero and accomplished his goal of joining the Virginia elite.

Turning to politics

One year after his retirement from the military, Washington became a member of the Virginia legislature. By the 1760s, Washington was an outspoken critic of policies imposed by Great Britain. Believing that the British infringed more and more on the rights of the Colonies, Washington began to oppose British policies vocally — especially the taxes imposed on the Colonies to help Britain pay for wars it fought in Europe.

Washington especially criticized the Stamp Act of 1765 and the Townshed Acts of 1767. By 1770, Washington knew that reconciliation with Britain was impossible, so he advocated the use of force to defend Colonial freedoms. The *Stamp Act of 1765* required the Colonies to pay taxes on all types of printed documents, including newspapers, marriage certificates, and all legal documents. The *Townshed Act of 1767* was even worse. It imposed taxes on all kind of goods, including paper and tea.

Martha's role

Washington met Martha Custis, a young and wealthy widow from a prominent Virginia family, and married her in 1759. Not only did the marriage enhance Washington' wealth, it also enhanced his status within the Virginia elite.

Martha Washington proved to be a loving wife. She joined her husband during the long winter encampments of the Revolutionary War. As first lady, she was a loyal supporter of her husband's policies and a graceful hostess. After Washington's death, she continued to receive visitors at Mount Vernon. Her only regret was that she was never able to have any children with Washington. As fate would have it, the founding father of the United States left no heirs.

Criticizing the empire

Chaos broke loose when the British Parliament passed the *Tea Act* in 1773. This act allowed the British East India Company to take over the American tea business. Disgusted, the colonists responded with the Boston Tea Party, where people disguised as Indians boarded three British ships and dumped 342 crates of tea into the Boston harbor. Parliament responded with the so-called *Intolerable Acts,* closing Boston harbor and repealing many basic Colonial rights, including the right to local self-government.

Becoming a disloyal citizen

The *Intolerable Acts* were the last straw for many in the Colonies. Twelve colonies decided to call for a Continental Congress in 1774 to respond to British aggression. During the second Congress in 1775, Washington was nominated as commander in chief of the continental forces. His future vice president, John Adams, nominated him in an attempt to align the southern colonies with the northern colonies. This alliance was necessary because colonists were already fighting the British in Massachusetts.

Fighting for Independence

As commander in chief of the continental forces, Washington took his troops to Massachusetts in June of 1775 to join in the rebellion. After the battle at Bunker Hill, where Massachusetts and Connecticut militia inflicted heavy losses on the British forces, Washington liberated Boston in the spring of 1776.

Washington knew that this victory was only short-lived. He immediately started organizing to defend New York City, the most likely target of the British forces.

In the summer of 1776, 30,000 British troops, commandeered by General Howe, landed on Long Island. With the American troops untrained and ill-equipped, the British forces, supported by German mercenaries, had no problem retaking New York City. By the winter of 1776, Washington had to retreat, and it looked as if the war was over. Washington faced mass desertions and had no financial support from the Continental Congress. He went so far as to pledge his own money to pay his troops and reject any kind of compensation for his services.

On December 25, 1776, Washington saved the disintegrating continental army and kept the war alive with a major victory at Trenton, New Jersey. He defeated a force of German mercenaries after surprising them by crossing the Delaware at night.

By the summer of 1777, the tide turned. After two battles with the British —
at Brandywine and Germantown — where Washington barely managed to
keep his army together, the battle of Saratoga in 1777 proved to be a major
victory for Washington. After his victory there, the French government
decided to enter into an alliance with the United States. Washington and his
troops spent the winter at Valley Forge in miserable conditions, as shown in
Figure 3-1, waiting for the French forces to arrive. Knowing that the French
fleet and ground troops were on their way, the British moved the war south
and conquered parts of Georgia and South Carolina.

Figure 3-1:
General
George
Washington
praying at
Valley
Forge.

Courtesy of the Library of Congress

Washington implemented a new strategy after realizing that victory was possible by drawing out the war until the British public and parliament were sick
of it and refused to continue. With the arrival of French troops in July 1779,
Washington was ready to move, but the French told him to wait for the arrival
of a second fleet. Finally, in the summer of 1781, Washington launched a massive counterattack that drove the British out of the United States. In his greatest military triumph, Washington was able to trap the major British force at
Yorktown. On October 19, 1781, the British forces, led by General Cornwallis,
surrendered. As Washington had hoped, the British parliament, sick and tired
of the ongoing war, voted to stop supporting the war despite the objections
of King George III.

Finalizing the peace took two more years. Finally, in September 1783, a peace
treaty between the United States and Great Britain ended the war. In December
of the same year, Washington retired from the military, expecting to spend the
rest of his life on his plantation in Mount Vernon. Boy, was he wrong!

Designing the New Country

After the United States achieved independence, it created a new government. Under the Articles of Confederation, the 13 states formed a loose federation, with power vested at the state level (see Chapter 1 for more on the country's beginnings). Problems soon arose, and by 1785, Washington was very worried. He felt that the new country was in serious trouble and that the Articles of Confederation were not working.

After meeting with his old buddies, James Madison and Alexander Hamilton, Washington supported a national meeting in Philadelphia the following year, 1787, to change or revise the Articles. The state of Virginia picked Washington to head its delegation.

Washington traveled to Philadelphia to become a member of the Constitutional Convention. There, the delegates picked him to chair the convention. Washington believed that the president of the convention should remain neutral, so he participated little in the debates, mostly listening to what the others had to say.

Within five months, the delegates were done. Instead of a revising the Articles, they created a brand new document, the Constitution of the United States.

President George Washington (1789–1797)

After a lengthy battle to ratify the Constitution, the country was ready to elect a president in 1788. It was a forgone conclusion that Washington would win. The only suspense was over who would win the vice-presidency. Washington was pleased when the Electoral College selected his friend John Adams for the position.

The Electoral College, following the guidelines outlined in the Constitution, chose the new president on February 4, 1789. (For a detailed discussion of the Electoral College, see the sidebar with that name in Chapter 1). In April 1789, Washington, shown in Figure 3-2, became the first president of the United States.

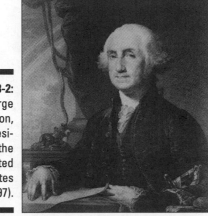

Figure 3-2:
George
Washington,
1st presi-
dent of the
United
States
(1789–1797).

Courtesy of the Library of Congress

Dealing with the Issues of the Day

One of the first decisions Washington faced as president was where to set up the new capital. He moved the seat of the new government from New York to Philadelphia.

Setting inaugural precedents

As the first president of the United States, George Washington was in the unique position of being able to establish many of the traditions we take for granted today. The only constitutional requirement for inaugural procedures is that the new president recite the following presidential oath: "I do solemnly swear that I will faithfully execute the office of president of the United States, and will to the best of my ability preserve, protect, and defend the Constitution of the United States."

As the first president of the United States, Washington established many of the traditions surrounding inaugurations today. With the Constitution silent on the issue, it was left up to

Washington to set precedent. Some of the traditions Washington started are

✔ The custom of swearing the presidential oath with the left hand on the Bible and the right hand raised to heaven

✔ Saying "So help me God" at the end of the oath

✔ An inaugural celebration (in his case, fireworks)

✔ Attending an inaugural ball given in his honor

From the presentation of an inaugural address to the festivities surrounding it, Washington set the tone for generations to come.

Adding the Bill of Rights

The first ten amendments to the Constitution are referred to as the Bill of Rights. They contain some of the most important civil liberties granted to U.S. citizens by the Constitution. Among the more important rights guaranteed by the Bill of Rights are the following:

✔ Freedom of speech, religion, press, and assembly

✔ The right to bear arms

✔ The requirement of search warrants for searches of homes and other places

✔ The prohibition of double jeopardy (being tried twice for the same crime)

✔ The right to have a lawyer present at a trial

✔ The requirement that an accused person be informed of the charges against him or her

✔ The prohibition of cruel and unusual punishment

For the complete text of the Declaration of Independence, the Constitution, and the Bill of Rights and the other amendments along with explanations and commentary, check out *Webster's New World American Words of Freedom* by Stephen Rohde, published by Hungry Minds, Inc.

But Philadelphia wasn't a popular choice: The southern states wanted the capital to be closer to the South, while Alexander Hamilton preferred for the new government to be as far away as possible from the U.S. public so politicians could make policy without public interference. A compromise was struck, and all sides agreed to build a new capital on the Potomac River at what is now Washington, D.C. Construction started soon after the location was agreed on, and it was finished by 1800. John Adams was the first U.S. president to live in the new capital, and he hated it.

Passing the Bill of Rights

When Washington assumed the presidency in 1789, his first order of business was to make sure that a Bill of Rights was added to the Constitution. During the debate over ratification, the opponents of the Constitution (also referred to as Anti-Federalists) pressed for the addition of a Bill of Rights to ensure individual freedoms, and Washington and his supporters agreed to it. So when Congress met in 1790, the first action they took was to add to the Constitution. In 1791, Congress and the states added the first ten amendments to the Constitution, also known as the *Bill of Rights*.

Article 5 of the Constitution spells out how a constitutional amendment can be added. The amendment has to be proposed, and then it has to be ratified. There are two ways to propose an amendment. First, both houses of Congress can propose an amendment with a two-thirds vote in each chamber.

Second, an amendment can be proposed if two-thirds of all state legislatures call upon Congress to hold a national convention to propose an amendment. This type of proposal has never been used. To ratify an amendment after it has been proposed, three-fourth of all state legislatures have to approve it. Up to this point, only 27 amendments have been added to the Constitution.

Splitting into two parties

By 1790, the advantages of a new stronger federal government over the system set out in the Articles of Confederation became visible. The federal government now had the power to levy duties on imports, which proved to be a major source of income.

With Alexander Hamilton heading the treasury, money started to flow in, and the federal government was able to repay the war bonds that were issued to finance the war of independence. More importantly, money was finally available to support a better military force, which proved to be vital in the wars against several Native American tribes in the western part of the United States (what was then Ohio). In 1795, the border conflicts with the Native American tribes were resolved with the Treaty of Greenville.

The first party system

Rivalry between Alexander Hamilton and Thomas Jefferson gave the United States its first party system by 1794.

Alexander Hamilton and his supporters called themselves Federalists. The Federalists supported some specific views on how the government should be run:

- They advocated a stronger national government, which would result in a weakening of states' rights.

- They advocated an active role for government in the area of economic development.

- They favored high tariffs, or duties on imports, to protect U.S. industries from foreign competition.

- When it came to foreign policy, they were closer to Great Britain than they were to France. (France and Great Britain were at war at the time.)

Thomas Jefferson and those aligned with him — labeled Democratic-Republicans — supported views that were nearly the opposite of those supported by the Federalists:

- They favored a smaller national government and powerful states.

- They believed in low tariffs to allow the average person to buy cheap foreign goods.

- They favored France in the realm of foreign policy.

By 1794, both groups had organized themselves into political parties — or factions, as Washington referred to them. The United States had its first two-party system.

Despite these early successes, quarrels broke out between the members of Washington's cabinet. Hamilton, the secretary of treasury, and Thomas Jefferson, the secretary of state, started an intense rivalry as they bid for Washington's support. This rivalry gave America its first political parties — Hamilton's Federalists and Jefferson's Democratic-Republicans — and a two party system by 1794 (check out the sidebar in this section titled "The first party system"). Although Washington was closer to the Federalists in his views, he refused to align himself with either party.

Running unopposed for a second term

Despite wanting to retire and return home to Mount Vernon, Washington decided to stand for reelection in 1792. He knew that his stature provided legitimacy for the new country and that only he could keep the fighting between Hamilton and Jefferson under control.

Not surprisingly, the founding father of the United States had no opposition in 1792 and won reelection easily. He didn't even have to campaign, because nobody opposed him in the election. The Electoral College reelected him unanimously.

Washington's second inaugural address was the shortest inaugural address in U.S. history, containing fewer than 300 words.

Establishing a policy of neutrality

In 1793, France declared war on Great Britain. Washington had to make a decision. Great Britain was still the mother country of most U.S. citizens, but France had helped the Colonies win independence, so many citizens felt an affinity for that country. With his cabinet split over which side to support, Washington made a bold decision — one that impacted U.S. foreign policy for the next century. In April 1793, Washington officially proclaimed the neutrality of the United States in the war, advocating that the United States stay out of European conflicts.

By doing so, Washington violated the 1778 Treaty of Alliance, which called for the United States to aid France in the case of war. France, bitterly disappointed, attempted to agitate Washington by sending Edmond Genet, an ambassador, to tour the United States and speak out against Washington and his policies. Genet went as far as organizing groups of pro-French U.S. citizens against Washington. This tactic backfired, leading even Jefferson, France's most ardent supporter, to endorse Washington's position. Washington prevailed and established the principle of U.S. neutrality in European affairs.

Quelling civil strife

Just when a return to normal, quiet times seemed possible, another crisis arose. In 1794, at Hamilton's urging, Congress passed a new tax on distilled liquor. This new tax threatened many distillers in western Pennsylvania. In the fall of 1794, violent resistance to the new tax broke out, ending in the murder of a federal officer in Pennsylvania.

Washington knew that he had to act quickly for a couple of reasons:

- ✔ Violence against the government could not be tolerated.
- ✔ Not responding to the violence would be considered a sign of weakness, thus threatening the new government.

Washington called on the military to stop what is now known as the *Whiskey Rebellion*. Washington even decided to head the military force himself. This military action ended the rebellion without much bloodshed. For the first time, the new government flexed its muscles and showed its critics that it was here to stay.

The final controversy of Washington's presidency was the Jay Treaty. Washington sent Chief Justice John Jay to Britain in 1794 after Britain seized U.S. ships in the West Indies. Jay returned in 1795 with a treaty that many U.S. citizens, especially Democratic-Republicans, found unacceptable.

The *Jay Treaty* contained several clauses beneficial to the United States, but it also obligated the United States to repay pre-revolutionary debts to Britain. In turn, the British agreed to pay for damages caused by the British navy's seizure of U.S. ships and to abandon some of their forts still left in the north-western part of the United States.

Despite Democratic-Republican opposition, the Federalists controlling the Senate approved the treaty. However, Republicans in the House of Representatives demanded that the House be able to vote on the treaty. They argued that because the treaty included disbursing government funds and it was the responsibility of the House to appropriate funds, representatives were entitled to vote on the treaty.

But Washington refused to submit the treaty, claiming that, based on the Constitution, only the president and the Senate should be involved in treaty negotiations. Washington prevailed, setting the precedent that still holds true today.

Stepping Down

By 1796, Washington had had enough. Disgusted with the constant partisanship in Congress, Washington wanted nothing more than to return home. He longed for Mount Vernon and was ready to retire after over 40 years of public service.

Before leaving office, however, he made one final speech to warn the U.S. public about future dangers and to set the political foundation for future presidents. He delivered his famous "Farewell Address" on September 17, 1796, saying, "The great rule of conduct for us in regard to foreign nations, is, in extending our commercial relations to have with them as little political connection as possible."

Washington's farewell address was actually a speech written for him by James Madison back in 1792, when Washington contemplated retiring after his first term. Now at odds with Madison, a Democratic-Republican, Washington turned to Hamilton to polish up the speech for him. Hamilton did so, and his influence is clearly visible in the address.

In his farewell address, Washington set out to warn the country against making any kind of alliance with foreign powers for several reasons:

- ✔ He was afraid that the United States was not yet powerful enough to face off against European countries. He was aware that any of them could easily destroy the new country in a major war.

- ✔ He stated that alliances forced the U.S. public to take sides. With the United States so ethnically divided, this could split the country and create long lasting divisions.

Finally, he warned the country against "factions" — as he called political parties — because they divided the country along partisan lines and undermined the spirit of cooperation so necessary for the new country to survive.

Although Washington's warnings on foreign alliances were listened to, his warnings against factionalism and partisan conflict fell on deaf ears, as the following presidential election showed. Thus, his address had its most lasting impact in the foreign affairs arena. True to Washington's words, the United States stayed out of world affairs (back then the equivalent of European affairs) and became isolationist until the 20th century and the presidency of Theodore Roosevelt.

Retiring Briefly

Washington left office in March 1797 to go into his well-deserved retirement. To his disappointment, his retirement didn't last long. President Adams sought his help only a year later. A conflict with France started, and Adams was afraid it would turn into a full-fledged war. So he asked Washington to take control of the U.S. armed forces. Washington reluctantly agreed. He commanded the military without ever leaving Mount Vernon, and the conflict never turned into a war.

A year later, Washington wrote his will. In it, he freed almost half of his slaves.

In December 1799, he caught pneumonia while inspecting his plantation. The founding father of the United States died on December 14, 1799, and the U.S. public mourned him for many generations.

Chapter 4

The Authoritarian and the Philosopher: John Adams and Thomas Jefferson

• •

In This Chapter

▶ Helping create a new country: Adams

▶ Contributing to the nation's intellectual and territorial expansion: Jefferson

• •

*T*his chapter deals with two presidents who were also founding fathers, John Adams and Thomas Jefferson. Without either of these prominent men, the United States would not be the same country it is today. Adams set the foundation for independence by tirelessly working in Europe as a diplomat, getting the support of France in the Revolutionary War. Jefferson wrote the Declaration of Independence, setting the foundation for our modern day form of government. As president, Adams turned authoritarian and tried to silence his opposition: This left a dark stain on his presidency. Jefferson, on the other hand, turned out to be one of our greatest presidents. One of his greatest accomplishments was the Louisiana Purchase of 1803.

Founding the Country and Almost Destroying It: John Adams

Unlike Washington, Adams didn't need the military to help him move up the social ladder. After attending the finest schools, Adams became one of the great minds of his times. Today he is considered one of the greatest political thinkers in U.S. history. He still has an impact on the field of political philosophy.

The good lawyer

Born in 1735, John Adams was the son of a prominent family in Massachusetts. He was so bright that Harvard University admitted him when he was only 16 years old. Adams studied Latin, history, and law, and decided that he wanted to be a lawyer after graduation. In 1758, he opened his own law office. Adams soon gained a reputation as one of the great legal minds in the Colonies.

After establishing a successful career, Adams married Abigail Smith in 1764 — their marriage lasted 54 years. One of their children, John Quincy Adams, later became president of the United States.

Adams's early career

Adams's legal career proved to be his way into politics. In 1765, Great Britain enacted the *Stamp Act,* a tax on all legal documents, contracts, and even newspapers, to collect more money from the Colonies. Instead of openly protesting, Adams sat down and drew up a complicated legal defense. He claimed that because the Colonies were not represented in the British parliament, they didn't have to pay the tax. Suddenly the name John Adams was a household name in the Colonies. When the British repealed the Act in 1766, a lot of credit went to Adams.

Adams was so famous that the British tried to bring him over to their side. He rejected an offer to become advocate general in the British court system in the Colonies. He chose instead to rebel against British oppression.

Defending the British

As a supporter of U.S. independence, Adams didn't mind peaceful protests to British rule. He didn't approve of violence, however. In 1770, the Boston Massacre, which started as a demonstration against the British, got out of hand. Five people were killed when British soldiers opened fire on the protestors. Rejecting violent protest, Adams not only defended the soldiers, he got them acquitted.

Adams's reputation rose. People saw him not only as a patriot, but also as a man who believed in the law and was unwilling to compromise his principles.

Entering politics

In 1773, Adams became one of the most vocal supporters of the Boston Tea Party. (See Chapter 3.) At the same time, he wrote a series of articles criticizing British policies. When the Colonies held the first Continental Congress in 1774 to discuss what to do about British oppression, Adams attended as a delegate representing Massachusetts.

The first Continental Congress accomplished nothing. By the time the Congress met again in 1775, Adams and many of his colleagues and neighbors were ready for an armed resistance. John Adams proposed establishing a continental army to oppose Britain. He further recommended that Colonel Washington from Virginia should be put in charge of the new military force.

Adams wanted Washington to be in charge of the newly created continental army for political reasons. He wanted to make sure that the Southern colonies supported a war of independence. Support was easier to garner with a Southerner in charge of the military.

Declaring independence

At the second Continental Congress in 1775, Adams called for passing a declaration of independence and chaired a special committee formed to produce such a declaration.

Thomas Jefferson, a delegate to the Congress from Virginia, wrote the declaration, and Adams presented it to the Continental Congress. The Congress signed the Declaration of Independence on July 4, 1776.

John Adams and Thomas Jefferson were the only future presidents to sign the Declaration of Independence.

Representing the new country

Adams's major contributions to the founding of the United States didn't come during his presidency — they came before he assumed the office. In his own way, Adams was as important to the revolution as George Washington. While Washington won on the battlefield, Adams succeeded in diplomacy. Without Adams's efforts, the fledgling government wouldn't have had a treaty of friendship and alliance with France and wouldn't have received financial support from the Netherlands.

Acting as chief diplomat

With the Revolutionary War in full force, Adams played the role of diplomat during his next series of missions. The Continental Congress sent him to France in 1777 to gain French support for the new country. Not only did France recognize the newly established United States, but it also signed a treaty of friendship. Not satisfied with his successes, Adams traveled to the Netherlands to set the foundation for future financial support for the United States.

After a brief stint at home in 1778, during which he wrote the constitution for the state of Massachusetts — which is still in force today — Adams went back abroad.

This time, Adams traveled to Paris to work on a peace treaty between Britain and the United States. At first, his attempts were fruitless. So he traveled to the Netherlands. This time he succeeded. Not only did he secure a $42 million loan, but he also got the Dutch to agree to recognize the newly formed United States. He then went back to Paris to negotiate with representatives of the British crown. After long negotiations, Adams, Benjamin Franklin, and John Jay worked out "The Treaty of Paris," which ended the Revolutionary War in 1783 and established U.S. independence for good.

With Adams so successful as a diplomat, the new U.S. government asked him to stay in Europe and become the U.S. representative to Great Britain. (The government at this point was run according to the provisions in the Articles of Confederation — Chapter 1 has more on the country's founding.) He accepted the position and stayed in Britain until 1788. When he returned to the United States, he found out that he was one of the candidates considered for the presidency. He thought that he had no shot at winning, so he ignored the nomination.

Becoming vice president

In February 1789, the first Electoral College (see the "The Electoral College" sidebar in Chapter 1 for information on this) in U.S. history assembled to choose the first president and vice president. Each elector was given the opportunity to cast two ballots. Whoever received the most votes became president. The person who came in second became the new vice president. To his great surprise, Adams was selected vice president of the United States.

Adams believed that the vice president's duty was to be loyal to the president — to support the president's policies publicly and raise questions only privately. For eight years, Adams publicly supported Washington on all major issues, including neutrality in the Franco-British war (even though Adams privately favored the British in the war). Clearly, Adams set a precedent for future vice presidents.

Adams didn't enjoy his role as vice president. He often complained in private of how insignificant his position was, calling the vice presidency the "most insignificant position ever invented."

Although he was loyal to Washington, Adams didn't shy away from conflict. He openly participated in the conflict between Alexander Hamilton and Thomas Jefferson (the "The first party system" sidebar in Chapter 3 explains the issues involved), in turn setting the foundation for our present political party system. Adams sided with Hamilton on the issues.

Adams was afraid of the public — especially because of the excesses of the French Revolution, where more than 20,000 members of the French political and social elite were killed — so he favored a stronger central government to maintain law and order. He felt more aligned with Great Britain than with

France, and he favored the British in foreign policy. In the realm of economics, Adams believed in limited protection for the slowly developing U.S. industries. All of these political views made him a Federalist. He soon found himself facing off with Jefferson on major issues.

Running for president

To the surprise of many, President Washington didn't run for a third term in 1796. Multiple candidates from both of the newly formed political parties ran for the office.

The Federalists favored two candidates — John Adams and Thomas Pinckney — while the Democratic-Republicans united behind Thomas Jefferson and Aaron Burr. Right away, Adams and Jefferson emerged as the front-runners. When the final tally came in, the election was close, and all four candidates received Electoral College votes. Adams came in first, winning 71 Electoral College votes. Jefferson received 68 votes, and Pinckney received 59 votes. Burr finished last with 30 votes. Adams was elected the second president of the United States.

Article 2 of the Constitution prescribes that the person with the highest number of electoral votes becomes president, while the second-highest vote-getter serves as vice president. Thus, for the only time in U.S. history, the president and vice president belonged to different political parties.

The 12th Amendment to the Constitution, ratified in 1804, altered the process, allowing members of the Electoral College to cast two ballots — one for president and one for vice president.

President John Adams (1797–1801)

As the first president from the northern colonies (Massachusetts), Adams did an admirable job of continuing to provide legitimacy for the country. Adams was often criticized as being authoritarian and unable to tolerate criticism. His presidency was characterized by the Alien and Sedition Acts, which heavily undermined personal freedom in the United States.

John Adams (shown in Figure 4-1) was inaugurated on March 4, 1797. He faced a range of problems right away.

John Adams was the first president to live in the presidential mansion in Washington D.C. Adams moved into the mansion after it was finished in the fall of 1800. But he hated Washington, D.C. so much that he was glad to leave it in March 1801.

The ABCs of the XYZ Affair

To avoid a war with France over whether the Unites States should take France's side in its war with England, Adams sent a U.S. delegation to France to negotiate. When the U.S. delegation arrived in France, the French refused to receive them. Instead, the XYZ Affair started when three agents of French foreign minister Talleyrand asked for a bribe of $250,000 from the U.S. diplomats in addition to a $12 million loan for the French government. France wanted all of this before they would meet with the U.S. delegation.

The U.S. delegation refused to comply and went back home. Adams tried to keep this insult secret, but he released it to the public after Jefferson and the Democratic-Republicans blasted him for trying to start a war. However, the names of three French diplomats were not released. Instead, Adams used the pseudonym XYZ to describe the diplomats.

Figure 4-1:
John Adams, 2nd president of the United States (1797–1801).

Courtesy of the Library of Congress

Having problems with France

The French believed that the United States owed its independence to France's efforts, and they expected the new country to support them in their current fight against the British. Washington's decision to remain neutral annoyed the French. In an effort to punish the United States, France started attacking and seizing U.S. ships in early 1797. Within months, France had seized 300 U.S. ships.

Hamilton and the Federalists called for war against France. Adams knew that war was unacceptable to Vice President Jefferson and many U.S. citizens, so he tried to negotiate instead. He sent a mission of peace to France. But at the same time, he mobilized U.S. forces just in case the mission failed.

The French refused to even meet with the U.S. delegation. (Check out the "The ABCs of the XYZ Affair" sidebar for details of the scandal.)

This diplomatic insult prompted the United States Congress and the public to prepare for war with France. Congress voted to end all treaties with France and established the Department of the Navy. Adams asked Washington to take command of the U.S. military one more time; Alexander Hamilton became Washington's second in command.

In the winter of 1799, the conflict turned violent. A U.S. frigate, the *Constellation,* successfully captured a French warship. War now seemed imminent.

Facing a crisis at home

As the nation got ready for war, partisan conflict broke out in Congress. The Democratic-Republicans under Jefferson attacked the Federalists, accusing them of trying to force the country into a war. They felt that France was their true ally and that the Federalists were overreacting. For the Democratic-Republicans, the Federalists were a bunch of closet monarchists who wanted to restore British control. The Federalists, on the other hand, thought that the Democratic-Republicans were violent radicals who wanted to initiate a French-style revolution that would end in massive bloodshed. Compromise between the two parties wasn't possible anymore. In 1798, Vice President Jefferson left the capital for a full year out of disgust for Adams and the Federalists. The political war was on.

The Alien and Sedition Acts

The Alien and Sedition Acts consisted of four separate acts designed to silence any opposition to Federalist rule:

✔ The Naturalization Act made it more difficult to become a U.S. citizen. It mandated living in the country 14 years instead of 7 to acquire citizenship. Adams and the Federalists knew that most of the country's recent immigrants were Democratic-Republicans. By making it tougher to become a citizen, the Federalists made sure that immigrants could not vote for an additional 7 years.

✔ The Alien Act allowed the government to deport foreigners that were considered a threat to the United States.

✔ The Alien Enemies Act allowed the government to imprison foreigners that were considered a threat to the United States.

✔ The Sedition Act made it a crime to criticize the federal government. Criticizing the president or the Congress was punishable by imprisonment and fines up to $5,000.

President Adams never enthusiastically enforced the first three acts, but he and his party used the Sedition Act to send reporters, newspaper publishers, and even a congressman to jail.

When Jefferson became president, his Democratic-Republican Party repealed the Naturalization Act — the other acts expired in the early years of Jefferson's presidency.

After Jefferson's departure, the Democratic-Republicans refused to collaborate with the Federalists. They even accused them publicly of trying to reestablish the monarchy. The Federalists, in turn, claimed that the Democratic-Republicans were ready to initiate a revolution in the United States and destroy democracy. President Adams became so alarmed that he started preparations to defend the presidential mansion (located in Philadelphia until 1800) against an attack.

Limiting civil liberties

Adams and the Federalists felt that the country couldn't prepare for war with constant dissent and criticism by the Democratic-Republicans. To deal with the problem, the Federalist majority in Congress passed the Alien and Sedition Acts, which severely limited the ability of U.S. citizens to criticize the government. (See "The Alien and Sedition Acts" sidebar for details of these acts.)

The Federalists thought that they were now in a secure position to dominate the country and start a war. However, the acts backfired. The average citizen didn't see the need for the acts and even feared that they undermined democracy in the United States. Furthermore, major leaders, including Jefferson and Madison, criticized the acts publicly. Two states, Kentucky and Virginia, issued statements — written by Jefferson and Madison, respectively — refusing to enforce the acts and threatening to nullify them. Virginia, fearing a federal attack, mobilized its state militia for a possible showdown with Adams. Federalist Hamilton, now in charge of the federal military, was ready to send in the troops.

Avoiding civil war

With the outbreak of a civil war looming, Adams looked for a political solution. This time, he sought to make peace with France himself. He ignored Congress and even his own cabinet, and sent one more delegation to France. He also demobilized the federal military to avoid a confrontation with Virginia. To top it off, Adams fired two of his cabinet members — Secretary of State Timothy Pickering and Secretary of War James McHenry. He distrusted them because they were loyal to Hamilton. In retaliation, Hamilton did his best to undermine Adams in the upcoming presidential elections.

The negotiations with France proved successful, and in October 1800, the two countries signed a treaty. France recognized U.S. neutrality, and the United States didn't insist that France pay reparations for the U.S. ships they seized.

Losing the presidency in 1800

The election of 1800 was a rematch between Jefferson and Adams. The outcome was very close — just as it was in 1796. The difference was Hamilton. Hamilton, who was angry with Adams, did his best to make sure that his own president lost the race. Right before the election, he published an article in which he called Adams mad and egotistical. The feud divided the Federalists, and Adams lost the race to Jefferson. The final tally gave Jefferson 73 Electoral College votes and Adams 65 votes.

Making an ungraceful escape

Adams was angry and disappointed at losing the presidency — he felt that he deserved to win reelection because he had so loyally served his country. He was so mad, that he refused to attend his successor's swearing-in ceremony. He and his wife actually snuck out of Washington, D.C. the night before Jefferson arrived to occupy the White House.

Switching parties at the end

After leaving office, Adams became a bitter enemy of Hamilton. In 1812, Adams and his son, John Quincy Adams, left the Federalist Party to become Democratic-Republicans. At the same time, Adams made peace with Jefferson. The renewal of their friendship helped restore Adams' reputation with the citizenry.

Adams lived long enough to see his son, John Quincy, win the presidency in 1824. Adams and Jefferson died on July 4, 1826, exactly 50 years after the Continental Congress passed the Declaration of Independence that both men had worked on.

John Adams is one of two presidents whose son also went on to become president of the United States. The other is George Bush (1989 to 1993), whose son, George W. Bush, became president in 2000.

Master of Multitasking: Thomas Jefferson

Many consider Thomas Jefferson, shown in Figure 4-2, to be one of the most brilliant men who ever lived. Without any doubt, Jefferson was one of the greatest thinkers in the history of the world. He was not only a politician, but also a philosopher, a diplomat, a scientist, an inventor, and an educator. Without Jefferson, there wouldn't be a Declaration of Independence or a Louisiana Purchase. Like Washington and Adams, Jefferson truly deserves the title "founding father."

How could he not succeed?

Unlike many American presidents, Thomas Jefferson was born with a silver spoon in his mouth. His father was a successful plantation owner in Virginia, and his mother belonged to the famous Randolph family, which dominated Virginia politics. With his father already active in politics, it came as no surprise that Jefferson followed in his footsteps.

Jefferson's education began when he was only five years old. With private tutors schooling him, Jefferson studied Latin, Greek, history, the natural sciences, and philosophy. In addition, he learned how to dance and play the violin. His mother wanted him to have a well-rounded education and become a true gentleman.

At age 17, Jefferson attended the College of William and Mary. He then proceeded to enter a career in law. By 1767, Jefferson was a lawyer. Jefferson decided that the law didn't provide him with sufficient income, so he moved back to his plantation to live off the land. Soon after, he entered politics and became a well-known and outspoken supporter of independence.

With all the protesting going on, Jefferson still had time to marry. He married Martha Wayles Skelton, a wealthy young widow, in 1772. The happy marriage didn't last long. Martha died in 1782. The grief-stricken Jefferson put all of his efforts into politics in an attempt to get his mind off his beloved wife.

Figure 4-2:
Thomas Jefferson, 3rd president of the United States (1801–1809).

Courtesy of the Library of Congress

Jefferson's early political career

In 1768, Jefferson was elected to the Virginia legislature. Aided by his education and writing ability, Jefferson became a powerful member of the legislature within a few years.

In 1769, Jefferson joined fellow legislator George Washington and others in condemning the Townshed Act (see Chapter 3) and embraced the cause of independence.

The British-appointed governor of Virginia shut down the legislature in response to their defiance. The legislators just moved their meeting place to a local tavern and continued their business.

After the passage of the Intolerable Acts in 1774 (see Chapter 3), Jefferson went to work. He wrote a lengthy document entitled "A Summary View of the Rights of British America," in which he provided a philosophical attack on the British right to govern the American colonies.

Jefferson was chosen as a delegate to the first Continental Congress, but he never made it to Philadelphia; he became sick on the way. He did send his documents to the first Continental Congress, which made quite an impact. Thomas Jefferson became a household name in the Colonies, and his intellectual abilities became famous. Jefferson was now a well-known radical. His path toward becoming a founding father was set.

Writing the Declaration of Independence

In 1775, Jefferson became a member of the second Continental Congress. As a delegate in Congress, Jefferson became a member of the committee charged with drawing up a declaration of independence for the American colonies. John Adams, a fellow committee member, asked Jefferson to write the declaration for the committee. After Jefferson finished the task, he sat down with Adams and Benjamin Franklin and made final corrections to his draft. In July 1776, the revised declaration was presented to the full Congress. On July 4, 1776, the Continental Congress officially adopted the declaration. A new country was born.

What did and didn't make it into the declaration

In the Declaration of Independence, Jefferson outlined his thoughts on democracy and the rights of people. In the most famous section of the piece, Jefferson proclaims that all men are created equal and have certain rights that cannot be taken away by any government. These rights include the right to life, liberty, and the pursuit of happiness. The Declaration of Independence became the foundation for the Constitution of the United States, as well as for many other democratic constitutions in Europe and around the world.

In the first draft of the Declaration of Independence, Jefferson included a critique of slavery and called for the abolition of the institution — even though he owned slaves himself. His colleagues convinced him to drop the section, because they feared that the southern colonies would object to it and refuse to ratify the declaration. Grudgingly, Jefferson consented. As president, Jefferson later outlawed the importation of new slaves into the United States.

In 1776, Jefferson went back to Virginia to continue to serve in the legislature. During this time, he developed many of his political ideas — many of which he put into effect as president. He called for *universal suffrage* — the right of everybody to vote — and he advocated land reform and public education. Most importantly, he succeeded in passing a bill that established freedom of religion in the state of Virginia. Many of his ideas became part of the Bill of Rights (see Chapter 3) when it was added to the Constitution in 1791.

Failing as governor and succeeding as diplomat

Jefferson was elected governor of Virginia and started his term in 1779. He hated the job — because the Virginia constitution gave all powers to the legislature — and he was very unsuccessful at it. When the British attacked Richmond, the capital, Jefferson fled, taking no measures to defend the city. In 1781, he retired after declaring himself sick and tired of politics. He refused to serve a second term as governor, even after he was reelected.

In 1783, the Treaty of Paris ended the Revolutionary War. Jefferson had reentered politics following the death of his wife the year before, and he was serving in the Continental Congress. He became the ambassador to France when Benjamin Franklin retired from the post.

Jefferson, who was fluent in French and enjoyed a solid reputation in Europe, proved to be a natural diplomat. He enjoyed the good life in France and served as ambassador for the next four years. He was in France during the start of the French Revolution in 1789. He initially agreed with the basic principles behind the revolution, but later condemned the violence and slowly moved away from supporting the new, revolutionary government.

Serving under Washington and Adams

Upon his return from France in 1789, Jefferson was asked by the newly elected president, George Washington, to serve as his secretary of state. Jefferson accepted the position, but he soon started clashing with the secretary of the treasury, Alexander Hamilton. (Their conflicts led to the country's first new political parties, which I explain in the "The first party system" sidebar in Chapter 3.)

The first big clash occurred over the issue of a national bank. Hamilton wanted to create a national bank, while Jefferson believed that the states should control the banking structures. Jefferson lost the battle when Washington sided with Hamilton. Continuing conflicts with Hamilton and Washington prompted Jefferson to resign in 1793. He thought that he had retired to his estate near Richmond for good. Boy, was he wrong.

In 1796, Jefferson reluctantly accepted the Democratic-Republican nomination for the presidency. It was a position he didn't want. He didn't even campaign for office, instead staying home on his plantation. To his great surprise, he came in second, losing to Adams by only three Electoral College votes. Under the Electoral College laws in effect at the time, the person who came in second became vice president. Jefferson, a Democratic-Republican, became vice president to the Federalist president Adams — not a good foundation for political success.

Jefferson was one of the few founding fathers who didn't attend the Constitutional Convention in Philadelphia in 1787. Even though Jefferson was in France at the time of the convention, James Madison kept him in the loop. When Jefferson received a copy of the proposed constitution, the lack of a bill of rights (see Chapter 3) ensuring personal freedom from government intrusion worried him. Jefferson wrote back to Madison, suggesting that a bill of rights be added. Madison agreed and used Jefferson's blueprint to propose the addition. In 1791, the new Congress of the United States added the Bill of Rights — the first ten amendments to the Constitution.

For two years, Jefferson fought a losing battle with his own president. After objecting to a war with France and, especially, to the passage of the Alien and Sedition Acts (see the sidebar, "The Alien and Sedition Acts," earlier in this chapter), Jefferson left the capital in disgust and returned home in 1798.

Jefferson started to oppose Adams and the Federalists openly from his plantation, called Monticello. He went so far as to draft the *Kentucky Resolution,* which opposed the federal government and the Alien and Sedition Acts.

President Thomas Jefferson (1801–1809)

With the 1800 election approaching, Jefferson decided to run again. This time he took the race seriously, believing that he had to save democracy from the Federalists. He defeated the incumbent Adams.

Jefferson and his running mate, Aaron Burr, received the same amount of Electoral College votes; so the selection of the president fell to the House of Representatives. It took 36 ballots in the House to decide the outcome of the election. The Federalist majority finally voted for Jefferson (after politically torturing him for a while), because they despised Aaron Burr even more.

Thomas Jefferson assumed the presidency in March 1801. One of his first tasks was to restore peace between the warring political parties. In his inaugural address, he proudly proclaimed, "we are all Republicans, we are all Federalists." This declaration satisfied many Federalists. Jefferson worked well with the Federalists during his first term.

Jefferson then freed everybody who was in jail because of the Alien and Sedition Acts. He refused to renew the acts. The acts quietly expired the same year. (See the sidebar earlier in this chapter, titled "The Alien and Sedition Acts," for more information.)

Marbury versus Madison

After Jefferson made peace with the Federalists in Congress, he attempted to reverse the packing of the federal courts. President Adams packed the courts with Federalist justices in the infamous "Midnight Appointments" before he left office. (However, not all of the appointments or commissions were sent out before Adams left office.)

Jefferson and Madison, his secretary of state, were furious at the appointments and refused to send out notifications to the rest of the appointees. William Marbury, one of the appointees whose commission was not delivered, sued, and the case went all the way to the Supreme Court.

Ironically, the new chief justice was John Marshall, who had failed to get the appointments out in the first place. Marshall faced a dilemma. If he sided with Jefferson and Madison, he would undermine the Federalist strength in the judiciary. If he sided with Marbury, Madison had already declared that he wouldn't abide by the ruling. So Marshall did what was best for himself and the Supreme Court. He declared that the Congressional Act (Judiciary Act of 1789) on which Marbury based his lawsuit was unconstitutional. So, Marshall's ruling established the principle of judicial review, allowing for the Supreme Court to declare laws of Congress unconstitutional, thus nullifying them.

Attempting to be frugal and balance the budget, Jefferson cut the size of the federal bureaucracy, including the military, and abolished several taxes, including the tax on the distilling of liquor that had prompted the Whiskey Rebellion back in 1794 (see Chapter 3).

Expanding the country: The Louisiana Purchase

Jefferson's greatest accomplishment as president is undoubtedly the purchase of the Louisiana territory from France.

France acquired the Louisiana territory in 1682 and gave it to Spain in 1762. With France's renewed power in the late eighteenth century, Jefferson expected the territory to be returned to France. Jefferson turned out to be correct: France reacquired the territory in 1802.

The weak Spanish empire constituted no threat to U.S. territorial interests, but the French empire was a different story. Jefferson sent his friend James Monroe, the former governor of Virginia and future president, to Paris to attempt to buy New Orleans from France.

The French shocked Monroe by offering to sell the whole Louisiana territory for a measly $15 million. Jefferson rejoiced and signed the treaty setting the terms for purchase. On December 20, 1803, the Senate approved the purchase, and the United States doubled in size overnight. Jefferson successfully added 828,000 square miles to the country. The territory included what would become parts of Wyoming and the following states:

Arkansas	Colorado	Iowa
Kansas	Louisiana	Minnesota
Missouri	Montana	Nebraska
North Dakota	Oklahoma	South Dakota

Jefferson's first term was a big hit with the U.S. public. It is widely considered to be one of the most successful terms of any president in U.S. history. Unfortunately, he couldn't keep it up. After easily winning reelection in 1804, Jefferson had a tough time with the problems that started during his second term.

Facing the British again

By the turn of the century, the British navy, famous for mistreating sailors, faced mass desertions and a serious manpower shortage. The solution the British Navy came up with was to not only recapture their own deserters but to *impress,* or forcefully take, U.S. sailors to serve on British ships.

By the time Jefferson started his second term, British ships were stopping U.S. ships and taking U.S. citizens to serve in the British navy. Literally thousands of U.S. sailors were kidnapped to serve on British ships.

In 1807, a U.S. frigate, the *Chesapeake,* encountered a British war ship. When the crew of the Chesapeake refused to let the British search their ship, the British opened fire on it. This was the last straw for the U.S. Congress and President Jefferson.

Not wanting to fight a war with Britain, who controlled ocean trade, Jefferson instead pushed for the passage of the *Embargo Act,* which made all exports to Europe illegal. In addition, it prohibited U.S. ships from sailing to any foreign ports. The idea behind the Embargo Act was simple. If you can't sail to foreign countries, nobody can kidnap your sailors. Of course, without trade you also cripple your economy, which is exactly what happened to the United States.

By 1809, the U.S. public had enough: National income fell by 50 percent in just two years. One of Jefferson's last acts as president was to repeal the Embargo Act. He replaced it with the Non-Intercourse Act, which banned trade only with Britain and France — the French had also seized U.S. ships.

Keeping busy in retirement

By the 1808 elections, Jefferson had enough of politics. He also wanted to abide by the two-term limit established by Washington, so he chose not to run for reelection. At the age of 65, Jefferson intended to spend the rest of his life pursuing intellectual endeavors.

While enjoying his true loves, reading and studying, Jefferson still had time to found the University of Virginia. (He even designed the campus himself.) Jefferson insisted on the acceptance of all students, rich or poor. His dream of public education, at least at the university level, came true.

Jefferson died on July 4, 1826, exactly 50 years after the adoption of the Declaration of Independence and on the same day as his presidential predecessor, John Adams.

Jefferson gave exact instructions on what to put on his gravestone, indicating what he considered to be his major accomplishments in life. His grave stone reads, "Here was buried Thomas Jefferson, Author of the Declaration of American Independence, of the Statute of Virginia for Religious Freedom and Father of the University of Virginia."

Chapter 5

Prominent but Ineffective: Madison, Monroe, and John Quincy Adams

. . . .

In This Chapter

▶ Becoming a founding father: Madison

▶ Bringing peace with foreign policy: Monroe

▶ Failing as president, but succeeding in Congress: Adams

. . . .

*T*his chapter covers three prominent U.S. presidents. James Madison is widely considered to be one of the most important founding fathers. He gave the country the Bill of Rights and was a tenacious fighter for the Constitution. As president, however, he almost destroyed the country he helped to create by going to war against Great Britain in 1812.

James Monroe fought in the Revolutionary War side by side with George Washington. He succeeded in foreign policy as president by finally making peace with Great Britain and acquiring Florida from Spain.

John Quincy Adams was a superior diplomat and congressman. However, as president, he failed. He restored his reputation by serving in Congress one more time after his defeat in 1828.

James Madison: From Founding Father to Presidential Flop

Next to Thomas Jefferson, James Madison, shown in Figure 5-1, was undoubtedly the brightest, best-educated president in the history of the United States. But, unlike his mentor Jefferson, Madison did not make a successful jump from philosophy to politics.

Madison presents a perplexing story. He was one of the least successful presidents in U.S. history, but without him, there would have been no United States. His great contributions to the country were made before he assumed office. As president, he almost destroyed the country he so loved.

Although Madison deserves the title "founding father," he does not deserve to be listed among the greatest presidents in U.S. history.

Figure 5-1:
James Madison, 4th president of the United States (1809–1817).

Courtesy of the Library of Congress

Madison's early career

After earning a degree from what is today Princeton University, Madison returned to his estate in Virginia. He was an ardent supporter of American independence from Great Britain and became a delegate to the Virginia constitutional convention in 1776. Here he met Thomas Jefferson. Madison worked closely with Jefferson on the new constitution for the state of Virginia. The two developed a close friendship, which lasted for 50 years.

As a delegate to the convention, Madison automatically became a member of the Virginia state legislature. He failed to win reelection because he refused to provide voters with free whiskey, as was commonly done back then. But in 1779, the Assembly of Virginia elected him to serve in the Continental Congress. Madison was only 29 years old — the youngest member of the Congress — but he built a reputation as a skilled legislator.

James Madison was one of the few founding fathers who didn't fight in the Revolutionary War. He thought that he was physically too weak to fight.

Working his way into politics

Like Jefferson, Madison grew up in a wealthy family. His father owned a plantation, referred to as Montpelier, in Virginia and was one of the most prominent men in the county. Madison received an excellent education, first at home by private tutors and then at a private preparatory school.

Madison also attended what today is Princeton University. He started his studies in 1769, focusing on philosophy, theology, history, and Latin and Greek. After completing his degree in 1771, Madison decided to move back to his plantation, where he battled several illnesses from 1772 until 1775. During this time, he continued his studies and developed many of the political ideas he later contributed to the Constitution and the Bill off Rights.

After the British accepted U.S. independence, Madison ran for the Virginia legislature one more time, winning easily. During the three years he served, Madison was responsible for passing Jefferson's bill to guarantee religious freedom in Virginia.

His main focus soon shifted to trade; he initiated a conference between Virginia and Maryland to discuss the issue of navigation rules on the Potomac River. It failed, because Delaware and Pennsylvania — the other states the Potomac River runs through — were not included in the talks.

Next, Madison, through a resolution passed by the Virginia legislature, called for a national conference to discuss trade regulations between the states. During that meeting, Madison and the other participants concluded that the Articles of Confederation were not working and needed to be amended. Madison proposed a constitutional convention to change the Articles of Confederation. The meeting was held in Philadelphia in 1787, and Madison himself was one of the delegates.

One of the great weaknesses of the Articles of Confederation was that the power to regulate trade and levy taxes remained with the states. States often refused to give any of their tax revenue to the federal government, as required by the Articles, leaving the national government poorly funded. In addition, some states engaged in tariff wars with each other, undermining the creation of a national economy. The country often appeared to consist of 13 independent countries rather than one United States.

Composing the Constitution

Madison was so eager to change the Articles of Confederation that he was one of the first delegates to arrive in Philadelphia for the Constitutional

Convention. He played a major role at the convention — many credit him with single-handedly making sure that the delegates wrote a new constitution. In the *Virginia Plan,* he advocated the creation of a new government with two houses, with representation in each based on population. The Virginia Plan put the larger states in control of the new government. Madison further advocated a federal judiciary and an independently elected president.

Madison wanted to make sure that the new government wasn't dependent on the states, so he called for a strong central government with independent powers. His plan was changed when the smaller states insisted on equal representation in the Senate. Madison consented to the change, knowing that it was the only way to get the Constitution ratified at the convention.

While in Philadelphia, Madison was in constant contact with Jefferson, who was in Paris at the time. Madison's notes to Jefferson represent the only information that we possess today about the proceedings in Philadelphia. Madison's notes were published in 1840 under the title "Journal of the Federal Convention" (still available, though you probably won't find it in a bookstore). Madison refused to publish the proceedings until the last member of the Constitutional Convention died — it turned out to be him.

Writing to ratify the Constitution

With the Constitution approved by the delegates, the effort to get it ratified by the states began. Madison worked tirelessly for the passage of the Constitution. He debated opponents in the Virginia legislature, and most importantly, he, along with Alexander Hamilton and John Jay, wrote *The Federalist Papers* in support of the Constitution.

The Federalist Papers

The Federalist Papers consist of 85 essays written by James Madison, Alexander Hamilton, and John Jay. (Complete text is available at the University of Oklahoma College of Law Web site at www.law.ou.edu/hist/federalist, as well as other Web sites and in print.) These essays, published beginning in October of 1787 in newspapers throughout the states, explained and supported the provisions of the Constitution and countered arguments and charges made by opponents, labeled Anti-Federalists, to its passage.

Madison wrote 29 of the essays, including the most famous ones — essays number 10 and 51. In these two essays, Madison argues that liberty is safest in a large republic, because many different interest groups compete against each other and none of them can become dominant. This assures that no group will be dominant and oppress minority viewpoints. The papers greatly contributed to the ratification of the Constitution in 1788.

Serving in Congress

With work on the Constitution finished, Madison ran for the Senate in 1788. He lost. Unwilling to give up, he ran for the House of Representatives in 1789 and defeated close friend and fellow future president James Monroe. For the next eight years, Madison served in the House of Representatives.

Madison did some of his major work as a U.S. Congressman:

- ✔ He was responsible for the legislation that attached the Bill of Rights (see Chapter 1) to the Constitution. Taking Jefferson's recommendations into account, Madison drew up the legislation and secured its passage through Congress.

- ✔ He became actively involved in the conflict between Jefferson and Hamilton over states' rights versus federal power. Madison, who started out as a Hamilton supporter, objected to the establishment of a federal bank, as well as to having the federal government pay off the states' debts. By 1792, Madison broke with Hamilton and aligned himself with Jefferson. Madison and Jefferson formed the core of the Democratic-Republican Party and worked together for the next decade. (See "The first party system," a sidebar in Chapter 3.)

By 1796, Madison had become so disillusioned with the Federalist administration and the Federalist-controlled Congress that he retired from Congress. Again his political career seemed to be over. Madison, having married Dolley Payne Todd — a young widow — in 1794, didn't mind leaving politics and looked forward to becoming a family man.

Returning to national politics

In 1796, Madison thought that he had retired from politics for good. Then the Federalist Congress passed the Alien and Sedition Acts, which made it illegal to criticize the government (see Chapter 4 for more on these acts). Madison, concerned that the acts violated the Bill of Rights, wrote the *Virginia Resolution,* which not only condemned the acts, but also encouraged states to refuse to abide by them. This brought the country close to civil war and created massive support for the Democratic-Republican Party.

In 1800, Madison campaigned tirelessly for his friend Jefferson's presidential bid. When Jefferson won the office of president, Madison became his secretary of state. For the next eight years, Madison was Jefferson's closest advisor. Madison had a hand in the Louisiana Purchase of 1803 and the Embargo Act of 1807 (Chapter 4 has more on Jefferson's presidency).

Jefferson retired in 1808 and handpicked his friend James Madison to be his successor. Madison won the election easily, defeating the Federalist candidate, Charles C. Pinckney, in a landslide.

Fighting the British for the last time

Foreign policy dominated Madison's two terms as president. Britain and France both continued seizing U.S. ships (see Chapter 4) and conscripting American sailors. Madison tried a new tactic: He reopened trade with Britain and France. The congressional authority contained in *Macon's Bill No. 2,* also stated that as soon as either Britain or France respected U.S. neutrality in their conflict and stopped seizing U.S. ships, the United States would impose an embargo against the other country. After France agreed to halt the practice, Madison punished Britain by stopping all trade.

A group of Democratic-Republicans led by Henry Clay and John Calhoun, called "War Hawks," wanted to expand U.S. influence into the British-held lands in the northern and western part of the continent, even if it meant using force.

A major uprising surfaced in 1811 when the Shawnee nation rebelled against U.S. domination. The Democratic-Republican War Hawks blamed the British for inciting the Shawnee to rebel. Combined with maritime insults and a longing for British-held lands in North America, this proved enough for Congress to declare war on Britain in June 1812. Ironically, that same month, Britain stopped seizing and raiding U.S. ships. By the time this news, which could have prevented the war, reached the United States, it was too late.

The war was a disaster for Madison. Public opinion was split — the Federalists opposed it, and some New England states refused to participate in it. "Mr. Madison's War," as the opposition labeled it, almost destroyed the United States. Despite the disastrous war, Madison managed to win reelection in 1812 by squeaking out a narrow victory.

In August of 1814, British troops attacked and destroyed Washington, D.C. When U.S. militiamen ran instead of defending the capital, Madison fled the capital and spent the next four days on horseback trying to rally his troops.

This disaster of a war officially ended in December 1814, with neither side gaining anything.

Changing policies and retiring

The last two years of Madison's presidency were much less stressful than the first six. Madison reversed his earlier position and supported Federalist policies, including the establishment of a national bank. The economy was doing well, and Jackson's victory over the British in the last, useless battle of the War of 1812 restored national pride.

After handpicking his successor, James Monroe, Madison happily retired in 1817. He spent his last years helping Jefferson establish the University of Virginia. After years of illness and the inability to recover from the loss of his friend, Jefferson, James Madison died in 1836 at the age of 85.

Succeeding Abroad, Failing at Home: James Monroe

James Monroe, shown in Figure 5-2, was the last president of the Virginia dynasty — his predecessors, except Adams, all came from Virginia. Monroe proved to be a skilled foreign policy maker — he finally established peace with Great Britain. Had he had equal success with his domestic policy, he might have been rated as one of the great presidents in U.S. history.

Figure 5-2:
James Monroe, 5th president of the United States (1817–1825).

Courtesy of the Library of Congress

Monroe's early career

In 1775, Monroe quit his studies at the College of William and Mary to enlist in the army when the fight for independence began; Monroe became a lieutenant in the Continental Army. He was with Washington during the famous crossing of the Delaware and at the battle of Trenton, where he was severely wounded by a bullet. He recovered rapidly and was made a major before participating in the battle of Monmouth, his last military engagement.

A true hero

Unlike his fellow Virginians, James Monroe didn't grow up in a wealthy family and enjoy a prosperous upbringing. He was a hard worker. And like Washington, whom he served with during the Revolutionary War, he used the military to advance in life.

James Monroe was born on a small farm in rural Virginia. He walked several miles each day to attend school. Monroe worked hard, and at the age of 16, he entered the College of William and Mary. He did not complete his studies. Monroe left the college in 1775, a year and a half into his studies, to fight in the Revolutionary War.

In 1779, Washington sent Monroe back to Virginia to raise a new military unit that never materialized. Monroe stayed in Virginia and became one of Governor Jefferson's aides. The two developed a close friendship. Monroe credited Jefferson with developing his interest in politics.

Representing Virginia and the country

In 1782, Monroe became the youngest member in the Virginia legislature. He joined the Congress of the Confederation only a year later, and his career path was set. Despite all this politicking, Monroe found time to buy an estate close to those of Jefferson and Madison, and to marry Elizabeth Kortright.

Monroe served in the Virginia legislature for three years. He dropped out of political life after his marriage in 1786, but he was elected to the Virginia legislature again the same year. He attended the Annapolis Convention on trade issues that was organized by Madison (I talk about this conference in the section, "Madison's early career," earlier in this chapter), and he supported Madison's call for a national convention to change the Articles of Confederation. To his great disappointment, he wasn't one of the delegates that attended the Philadelphia convention.

When Monroe saw the constitution that came out of the Constitutional Convention, he opposed it. He believed that the proposed government was too strong, and he demanded that a Bill of Rights be in the document. James Monroe was the only founding father to vote against the Constitution. To make matters worse, when Monroe ran for the newly established House of Representatives in 1789, he lost the race to his friend Madison.

However, in 1790, the Virginia legislature elected Monroe to serve in the U.S. Senate. Monroe, along with most of his colleagues, got involved in the struggle over establishing a federal bank (see the sidebar, "The first party system," in Chapter 3 for a discussion of these issues). Monroe became one of the leaders of the Democratic-Republican cause.

Monroe was such a supporter and admirer of France that Washington appointed him *minister plenipotentiary,* the equivalent of today's ambassador, to France in 1794. Unfortunately, Washington recalled him in 1796 for being too pro-French and anti-British. Monroe, upset at being recalled, left the administration and retired to his home in Virginia.

Serving as governor

To Monroe's surprise, the people of Virginia elected him governor in 1799. He served a quiet term until 1803, when his friend Jefferson, now president, called on him to travel to France to negotiate the Louisiana Purchase. In Paris, Monroe was one of the main architects of the treaty that sold the Louisiana Territory to the United States. Jefferson was so impressed that he named Monroe the ambassador to Great Britain, a post he held until 1807.

When Jefferson stepped down from the presidency, the Democratic-Republicans were split over who should succeed him. A small faction of the party pushed for Monroe, who did nothing to discourage them. Annoyed, Jefferson and Madison turned away from their old friend. After Madison's election as president, Monroe found himself without a job.

Serving well: Monroe's foreign policy

In 1811, Monroe was elected governor of the state of Virginia once again. By this time, Monroe and Jefferson had made up their differences. President Madison extended an olive branch to Monroe, naming him secretary of state. Monroe resigned as governor and began serving as secretary of state.

Back then, the position of secretary of state was the springboard to the presidency. By appointing Monroe to the position, Madison had ensured that Monroe would be the Democratic-Republicans' next nominee for president.

Even though Monroe personally opposed the war with Britain in 1812, he served his president loyally. When the situation became desperate in 1814, Monroe joined the war effort, leading the Maryland militia. This leadership position enhanced his reputation — he became a hero to the U.S. public. When Madison announced his retirement in 1816, there was no question who would succeed him. Monroe received the nomination of the Democratic-Republican Party and easily defeated the Federalist candidate, Rufus King.

James Monroe was responsible for saving a large number of State Department records, including the Declaration of Independence, before the British burned Washington, D.C.

Showing a flair for foreign policy

James Monroe's main love was foreign policy. Living abroad for over a decade stimulated his interest in Europe, especially Britain and France. He wanted to make sure that the United States and Britain never went to war again. At the same time, if another war was necessary, Monroe wanted to make certain that the United States was ready for it — he wanted to avoid a disaster similar to the War of 1812. So he established a permanent military force that was large enough and powerful enough to defend the country.

When he assumed office, Monroe went to work to sign a new peace treaty with Britain. In 1818, he successfully negotiated the *Rush-Bagot agreement,* which limited the size of the naval forces that both countries could use on the Great Lakes. That same year, Monroe agreed to set the U.S.-Canadian border at the 49th parallel (up to the Rocky mountains) and settle the Oregon territory jointly with Britain. With these agreements, Monroe settled all the differences between the two countries and provided the basis for the cordial relationship the United States and Great Britain enjoy to this day.

Monroe's second great foreign policy success involved the purchase of Florida. Florida, a Spanish colony, presented constant problems for the United States. It became a base from which Native Americans raided settlements in Georgia. In 1817, Monroe took action. He sent General Jackson to Florida to take care of business. Jackson did so by almost wiping out the Seminole Indians. Next, the United States told the Spanish that if they couldn't control the Native Americans in Florida they should sell Florida to the United States. Spain agreed, and Monroe purchased Florida for $5 million, though no money actually changed hands. Monroe used claims U.S. citizens had against Spain for property losses due to Indian raids in Spanish-controlled Florida and shipping losses caused by Spanish warships over the previous three decades.

Establishing the Monroe Doctrine

Monroe's most famous accomplishment in foreign policy was the Monroe Doctrine. During Monroe's two terms, Latin America rebelled against Spanish rule, and many of the former Spanish colonies became independent nations. Monroe was afraid that other European powers, especially the Holy Alliance of Russia, Austria, and Prussia, would try to interfere in, or even recolonize, the new countries. He consulted with Jefferson and his secretary of state, John Quincy Adams, to find ways to make sure that this didn't happen. The result was the Monroe Doctrine. Monroe outlined it to Congress in 1823. It became the cornerstone of U.S. foreign policy up to this day.

The Monroe Doctrine, which was actually written by John Quincy Adams, warned the European powers to stay out of the western hemisphere (the Americas). It stated that the United States wouldn't tolerate any European interference in the newly created countries. In turn, Monroe pledged to stay out of European affairs. The Monroe Doctrine drew little attention and was relatively forgotten until 1852.

Serving not so well: Monroe's domestic policy

Despite Monroe's great foreign policy accomplishments, domestic crises overshadowed his terms in office. Two issues in particular — the economy and slavery — plagued his presidency.

Dealing with slavery

The questions brought up in response to the admission of new states lead to a major crisis in 1819 when Missouri and Maine applied for statehood. The problem was Missouri's insistence on being admitted as a slave state. Before Missouri and Maine applied for statehood, the Senate was evenly split between slave and free states. The Southern states insisted that this equal division continue. The North feared that if Missouri came in as a slave state, the rest of the Louisiana Territory could follow. Monroe, who owned slaves himself, sat on the side while Congress hammered out a compromise. In 1820, the Missouri Compromise passed Congress and Monroe signed it into law.

The *Missouri Compromise* admitted Missouri as a slave state and Maine as a free state. More importantly, it outlawed slavery in new areas above the southern part of the new state of Missouri.

Monroe, a slave owner, believed that free slaves needed to be resettled in Africa. The place for resettlement was a piece of land, called Liberia, that was bought by the American Colonization Society. Monroe's support led to the naming of the capital of Liberia — Monrovia — after him.

Losing the fight with recession

In 1819, a recession hit the United States. Monroe, who believed in a weak federal government and states' rights, didn't do much about it. He got lucky: The economy recovered in time for the 1820 election, and the recession didn't undermine his popularity.

Running unopposed

Because Monroe was so successful in foreign policy, the election of 1820 wasn't much of a contest — in fact, Monroe had no opposition at all. He won every state and received all but one Electoral College vote.

One member of the Electoral College cast his vote for John Quincy Adams to assure that George Washington would remain the only president in U.S. history to be elected unanimously.

Calling it quits after two terms

James Monroe decided not to run for reelection in 1824, upholding the two-term principle established by Washington. He was also tired of the job. Unlike Madison and Jefferson, Monroe refused to name a successor, which tore the Democratic-Republican Party apart in the 1824 election.

Monroe left office in 1825 and retired to Virginia. Financial troubles forced him to sell one of his estates. After the death of his wife, Monroe's grief and poor health forced him to move in with his daughter in New York City. In a twist of fate, James Monroe became the third president to die on July 4. He passed away on July 4, 1831.

Like Father, Like Son: John Quincy Adams

John Quincy Adams, shown in Figure 5-3, is one of the most respected politicians in U.S. history. With his father having been president and vice president (check out John Adams in Chapter 4), the pressure was on for John Quincy Adams to succeed in life and in the political arena. To complement his privileged upbringing, Adams was extraordinarily bright. At the same time, he was a serious man who didn't make friends easily, and he had a tough time relating to people. This personality trait contributed to him having a tough time dealing with Congress as president.

Adams, considered a genius by many, is regarded today as one of the best secretaries of state the United States ever had. A master diplomat and superior congressman, Adams contributed greatly to the success of the United States and enjoyed a worldwide reputation. He had a friendship with Tsar Nicholas I of Russia. Despite his intelligence and accomplishments, Adams experienced one of the worst presidencies in history. It's a shame his presidency was such a failure. He deserved better.

John Quincy Adams enjoyed swimming in the nude in the Potomac River until he was 79 years old. One day, a female journalist, Anne Royall, surprised him. She sat on his clothes until he agreed to an interview and became the first woman to interview a president.

Getting elected at home

After traveling extensively in Europe, gaining experience from assisting his father and from his own endeavors, Adams returned to the United States, where being the son of a former president had its advantages. In 1802, the Federalist Party elected John Quincy Adams to the Massachusetts state senate. In 1803, he was appointed to the U.S. Senate.

Figure 5-3:
John Quincy
Adams, 6th
president of
the United
States.

Courtesy of the Library of Congress

As a senator, Adams disappointed his supporters. For Adams, it was the good of the country that mattered — not the good of his home state or his party — and his independent voting record reflected this. He crossed party lines to vote for the Louisiana Purchase in 1803 — the only Federalist senator to do so. He crossed party lines again in 1807 when he voted for Jefferson's Embargo Act. In 1808, his party was fed up with his independence and voted to replace him as senator.

Going Back to Europe

Having spent much of his childhood on the European continent, Adams continued to take an active interest in European affairs and their effects on American interests.

As a foreign ambassador

After leaving the Senate in 1808, Adams served the United States abroad for the next eight years. His independence had caught the eye of the opposition party, the Democratic-Republicans, and especially James Madison, who sent Adams back abroad.

When the War of 1812 wasn't going well for the Americans, Madison asked Adams to head the peace delegation and negotiate with the British. Adams negotiated the Treaty of Ghent, signed in 1814, which ended the War of 1812. Madison was so impressed with the way Adams handled the British that he appointed him ambassador to Britain in 1815 where he served until President James Monroe named him secretary of state.

Making his father proud

John Quincy Adams was born in 1767 on the Adams family farm in Massachusetts. As the oldest son, he received special treatment from his father, John Adams, who took him along on his travels. At the age of 10, Adams went to France when his father became the U.S. special envoy there during the Revolutionary War. Adams spent the next eight years in Europe, studying languages and diplomacy.

In 1785, Adams returned to the United States to study at Harvard. Practicing law bored him, however, and he was ready to get involved in politics. He got his chance in 1793 when President Washington appointed him the U.S. representative to the Netherlands. The next president — his father — appointed John Q. ambassador to Prussia.

John Adams met his wife, Louisa, in France. They married in 1797. Because she was born in Britain, the daughter of a U.S. diplomat, Louisa became the only foreign-born first lady in U.S. history.

As secretary of state

As secretary of state, Adams was in his milieu. First, he handled the purchase of Florida for Monroe. When General Andrew Jackson defeated the Seminoles and invaded Florida, Adams was the only member of Monroe's cabinet to defend Jackson. Adams blamed Spain for not keeping a tighter reign on the territory and told the Spanish to either control their colony or sell it to the United States. Spain, already fighting independence movements in Latin America, decided to sell Florida.

While negotiating, Adams further pressured Spain into agreeing that the Louisiana Territory purchased from France reached all the way to the Pacific Ocean. (The western borders of the Louisiana Territory had not been agreed upon in 1803.) The United States now spanned coast to coast.

The most important contribution Adams made to U.S. foreign policy occurred in 1823, when he established the Monroe Doctrine. Adams argued for years that the Americas were no longer open to colonization by Europe and that the European powers needed to stay out of the western hemisphere. President Monroe relied on Adams when he established the Monroe Doctrine: Adams actually wrote the doctrine and presented it the European powers.

Picked by the House

President Monroe was the first president in 16 years to retire without naming a successor. This complicated matters in the 1824 election. Four men, all from the Democratic-Republican Party, ran for the presidency. They were John Quincy Adams; General Andrew Jackson; the Speaker of the House, Henry Clay; and the secretary of the treasury, William Crawford.

All four of the men received Electoral College votes, but no one received a majority. Jackson won the popular vote but received only 99 Electoral College votes out of a possible 261. Adams came in second with 84 Electoral College votes. Crawford finished third, and Clay came in fourth.

With nobody receiving a majority in the Electoral College, the House of Representatives had to pick the new president. Clay, who despised Jackson, threw his support behind Adams, helping him win the presidency. Adams, in turn, appointed Clay secretary of state. Jackson and his followers cried foul. For the first time in U.S. history, the candidate that won the popular vote lost the election. This put a shadow on Adams's presidency from the beginning.

After the 1824 election, the Democratic-Republican Party fell apart. Jackson and his supporters formed the Democratic Party, still around today. Adams and his followers renamed the Democratic-Republican Party the National Republicans, but it collapsed after the 1832 election. Remnants of the National Republicans later became the Whigs.

President John Quincy Adams (1825–1829)

The Adams presidency was a disaster. Building up the U.S. infrastructure by pushing Congress to spend money on roads and canals was one of only a few bright spots. Then, in 1828, he made the political mistake of his life, which cost him reelection.

In 1828, Congress passed the "Tariff of Abominations," as opponents of the tariff called it. It established high tariffs on foreign goods and raw materials. Northern congressmen wanted it to protect their industries. The southern and western states opposed it because they depended on cheap foreign goods. When Adams didn't veto the bill, his opposition had the issue they were waiting for to help defeat him in the upcoming presidential race.

The election of 1828 turned into one of the ugliest presidential elections in U.S. history, pitting the incumbent Adams against an angry Andrew Jackson and his supporters who believed that Jackson had won the election of 1824. Jackson's supporters accused Adams of having premarital sex with his foreign-born wife, while Adams' supporters called Jackson's mother a whore. Amidst all the mudslinging, Adams lost badly.

Adams was so upset over the loss that he didn't attend Jackson's inauguration. Like his father, he snuck out of the capital and returned home.

Going back to Congress

The people of Massachusetts elected Adams to the House of Representatives two years after he retired as president. Here he accomplished more than in his four years as president. Both admirers and opponents called him "Old Man Eloquent" because of his oratory skills. Serving from 1831 until his death in 1848, Adams accomplished the following:

- He opposed the annexation of Texas, believing it would become a slave state.

- He revoked the gag rule, which made it illegal to introduce legislation that called for the abolition of slavery into Congress.

- He opposed the war with Mexico, believing that Polk tried to spread slavery (see Chapter 8).

- He helped establish the Smithsonian Institute, a museum and center for research that is dedicated to public education and national service and scholarship.

- He defended escaped slaves in the Amistad Case.

John Quincy Adams opposed slavery throughout his life. As early as 1820, he publicly condemned slavery, calling it a "foul stain upon the North American Union." In 1841, he defended a group of slaves who took over the ship carrying them to Cuba. When the ship landed in the United States and the government wanted to return the slaves to Cuba, Adams defended them in the Supreme Court and won the case.

In 1846, Adams suffered a stroke. Despite his condition, he went back to Congress. On February 21, 1848, while protesting the Mexican-American War, Adams suffered a second stroke. His colleagues took him to the speaker's chambers, where he died two days later — the only U.S. president to die in the Capitol building. His famous last words were: "This is the last of earth! I am content."

Part III
Enduring the Best and the Worst: Jackson to Buchanan

The 5th Wave   By Rich Tennant

Andrew Jackson, 7th president of the United States was nicknamed "Old Hickory" because "Thunderhair" "Chip" and "Slappy" were already taken.

In this part . . .

1 talk about two strong, successful presidents and a whole bunch of forgettable ones. Some were outright lousy.

On the positive side is Andrew Jackson, our first strong president, who challenged Congress and vetoed more legislation than all of his predecessors combined. Jackson stood up for the common person and did what he thought was right. James Polk is the other successful executive. He was an honest, dedicated president, who managed to add much of what is today the American Southwest.

Other presidents of this era, such as Martin van Buren, were unsuccessful or died early in office, like William Henry Harrison and Zachary Taylor. To make matters worse, in the 1850s — a time when the country needed its best leaders to guide the country through the issues dividing the North and South — some of the worst presidents this country ever saw ran the country. They include presidents like Millard Fillmore, a dedicated racist, Franklin Pierce, an alcoholic, and James Buchanan, who let the union fall apart, thereby almost insuring the outbreak of the Civil War.

Chapter 6

Standing Firm: Andrew Jackson

· ·

In This Chapter

▶ Entering politics

▶ Losing the presidential election in 1824

▶ Winning the presidency

▶ Paving the Trail of Tears

▶ Retiring gracefully

· ·

Compared to his predecessors, Andrew Jackson was an unlikely candidate to win the presidency. He grew up in poverty, was almost illiterate, had no political connections, and refused to identify with the ruling elite.

Jackson remains one of America's most controversial presidents. Some consider him a hero, a champion of the people, and the first strong president in U.S. history. Others see him as a gambler, wife stealer, "Indian killer," and the founding father of political corruption in the United States. The truth is that he was all of these things.

Jackson's Early Career

In 1796, the federal government formed a new state out of the western part of North Carolina, calling it Tennessee. Andrew Jackson successfully ran for the House of Representatives and became a U.S. senator one year later. In Congress, he supported the Democratic-Republicans, headed by Jefferson and Madison, and criticized President Washington for being too lenient with Native Americans.

Jackson retired from the Senate in 1798 and became a justice on the Tennessee Superior Court for the next six years. He gave up his judicial position to enjoy his marriage and dedicate himself to becoming a successful plantation owner. Within a few years, Jackson had over 100 slaves working on his Tennessee plantation, The Hermitage. To supplement his income, he got involved in horseracing and acquired a reputation as a top-notch horse breeder. Jackson seemed to have it all.

As tough as hickory

Andrew Jackson's nickname, "Old Hickory," is an apt nickname. He received the nickname during the War of 1812, when he headed the Tennessee militia. He received orders to move his troops to Mississippi, but was told to disband his troops when he arrived. Instead of doing so, he marched his unit back to Tennessee. He gave his horse to a wounded soldier and walked the whole way. His troops referred to him as "Old Hickory" because he was as tough as hardwood.

It is unclear exactly where Jackson was born, though Jackson referred to himself as a South Carolinian. Lancaster County, South Carolina and Union County, North Carolina dispute whether Jackson was born in their respective counties. In 1979, local officials in the two counties decided to settle the matter with an annual football game. They play the "Old Hickory Classic," and whoever wins gets the rights to claim Jackson's nativity for that year. It is true that his mother gave birth to him in 1767 in a log cabin a few days after Jackson's father died. Young Andrew received a fairly poor education in a frontier school, and he barely knew how to read and write.

When the Revolutionary War broke out, Jackson was ready to fight. He joined the South Carolina militia when he was just 13. He was captured by the British, and during his captivity, he refused to clean the boots of a British officer. The officer struck him across the face with a saber, scarring Jackson for life. Life got even worse for the young Jackson: Both his mother and brother caught small pox and died by the time Jackson was 14.

Jackson moved to Charleston in 1781, where he studied law. In 1787, the North Carolina bar admitted Jackson, and he began his legal career. Bored by his job, he moved west to open a law practice in Nashville. Jackson made a name for himself and became the solicitor-general for the region.

Going to war

In 1812, the United States and Britain went to war. Britain aligned itself with several Native American tribes that were also hostile to the United States. One of these tribes, the Creek, massacred 250 settlers in the Mississippi territory. Jackson organized a militia and went after the Native Americans. He found them in 1814. As a gesture of goodwill, he let all the women and children go free. Then he attacked the men, killing more than 800 Creek warriors. Later, he forced the Creek to sign a treaty with the U.S. government, ceding over half of present-day Alabama to the United States.

Impressed, President Madison appointed Jackson major-general in 1814 and sent him south to defend New Orleans. Jackson organized one of the most unique militias in U.S. history. He recruited frontiersmen, pirates, slaves, Frenchmen, and whomever else he could find. When the British launched a frontal assault on January 8, 1815, Jackson was ready. In the battle of New Orleans, Jackson's militia killed over 2,000 British soldiers, while losing only 8 men. Jackson was a national hero. (He found out later that he didn't need to fight that battle — by the time it had taken place, the war was over.)

Saved by a political enemy

President Madison named Jackson commander of the army of the southern district where the Seminole tribe, residing in Spanish-controlled Florida, made constant raids into U.S. territory. In 1817, President Monroe instructed Jackson to do whatever was necessary to stop the raids. Jackson pursued the Seminoles into Florida and wiped them out. He also executed two British citizens accused of inciting the Seminoles to make raids against U.S. settlers.

Both Spain and Britain complained bitterly about Jackson's behavior. Even some members of Monroe's cabinet wanted to send Jackson to jail. However, one — just one — member of the cabinet defended Jackson. Secretary of State John Quincy Adams, negotiating with Spain for the sale of Florida to the United States, blamed the Spanish for the debacle, arguing that it was Spain's responsibility to keep the Seminoles in order. He suggested that Spain make amendment by selling Florida to the United States. Adams prevailed, Jackson's reputation rose, and the United States bought Florida from Spain.

Even though John Quincy Adams saved Jackson's job in 1818, the two became bitter enemies. Adams beat Jackson in a bitterly contested election for the presidency in 1824, and Jackson beat Adams four years later. Jackson blamed Adams and his supporters for the death of his wife, while Adams considered Jackson unfit for the presidency. To quote Adams, Jackson was ". . . a barbarian who could not write a sentence of grammar and hardly could spell his name."

Suffering through the Stolen Election of 1824

After acquiring Florida from Spain, President Monroe appointed Jackson governor of Florida. Jackson wasn't happy in the job — he left office after serving for just four months. He returned home to Tennessee and was appointed to the U.S. Senate for the second time in 1823. A group of Jackson's supporters were planning to have him run for president, and a national-level office was the first step.

Many members of Congress disliked Jackson, and he had no real political base. However, the average citizen identified with his impoverished background, the rough times he experienced, and the hard work he put in. Jackson didn't care about the wealthy elite in the North and South. His dream was to serve the common man.

PRESIDENTIAL LORE

Dueling for his lady's honor

Andrew Jackson, while living in Nashville, met and married the love of his life, Rachel Donelson Robards. Their marriage was a happy but tragic one.

Rachel was married but separated from her husband when she met Jackson. Jackson and Rachel married in 1791, believing that her husband had signed divorce papers. When Jackson found out that Rachel was still legally married to her former husband when she and Jackson got married, he married her again in 1793.

Unfortunately, the scandal followed Jackson throughout his political career. Jackson was very sensitive about the issue, and he often challenged men he believed had insulted his wife to duel.

During his 1828 campaign for the presidency, Jackson's marriage became a campaign issue. Pamphlets attacking Rachel were distributed. Rachel's distress over the pamphlets contributed to the heart attack that killed her. Jackson blamed his opponent and never got over Rachel's death.

TECHNICAL STUFF

By the time Jackson ran for the presidency in 1824, the electoral process had changed. Previously, state legislatures decided who won the state, and many states had given this power to the people. Further, the property requirements necessary to vote had disappeared, giving every white male the vote in most states. Jackson won the states where the people selected the president but lost most of the states where the state legislatures picked the president.

In the 1824 election, Jackson came in first, winning the popular vote and 99 Electoral College votes. But it wasn't enough. With no candidate winning a majority (131) of the Electoral College votes, the election went to the House of Representatives, where each state had one vote. The Speaker of the House, Henry Clay, who came in fourth in the presidential race, threw his support behind John Quincy Adams who had come in second. With Clay's support, Adams won the presidency.

POLITICAL STUFF

So, despite coming in first and winning the popular vote, Jackson lost the presidency. When the new president appointed former opponent Henry Clay as his secretary of state, Jackson and his supporters cried foul, accusing Adams of a corrupt bargain. Bitter over their candidate's loss, Jackson's supporters left the Republican Party and formed the Jacksonian Democrats. The party platform represented the common man and called for

- Liberalizing electoral laws
- Opposing tariffs (because the average person wanted to buy cheap foreign goods)
- Favoring states' rights over the federal government

President Andrew Jackson (1829–1837)

After the bitter experience of losing the presidency in 1824, Jackson, shown in Figure 6-1, challenged the incumbent President Adams — this time with a new political party behind him. He ran as a candidate of the people, painting Adams as a candidate of the wealthy. He especially focused on the *Tariff of Abominations,* which hurt the average citizen by increasing duties on imports. Adams never had a chance. When the vote was in, Jackson received 178 electoral votes to Adams's 83.

Figure 6-1: Andrew Jackson, 7th president of the United States.

Courtesy of the Library of Congress

Andrew Jackson was truly a president of the people. He believed that government needed to look after the people who needed the most help — poor, hard-working U.S. citizens. He wanted to be a president for the poor rather than the rich. At the same time, if you were a friend or a supporter of Jackson, you could expect handsome rewards.

Andrew Jackson took the rewarding of political friends to new heights. He believed in the *spoils system,* which refers to the system of rewarding political friends and supporters with public jobs. (See the "The spoils system" sidebar in Chapter 11 for more on this.)

Jackson's inauguration almost resulted in the destruction of the White House. He opened the White House for a reception for the "common man," who, after consuming too much alcohol, roamed through the presidential mansion destroying everything in sight. Jackson snuck out of a window to avoid the chaos and spent inauguration night in a hotel.

Dealing with states' rights and tariffs

Andrew Jackson's first great political challenge occurred in the early 1830s. He urged Congress to eliminate the Tariff of Abominations, which levied high duties on foreign goods. In 1832, Congress lowered the tariff but didn't abolish it, giving Southern states reason to complain.

South Carolina pushed specifically for nullification of the tariff and passed an ordinance of nullification in 1833, declaring the federal tariff void in that state. In addition, South Carolina proclaimed that if the federal government wouldn't allow it to nullify the tariffs, it would secede.

Although Jackson supported states rights, he saw this as an act of treason. He told the state's leaders that he would do whatever was necessary to preserve the Union — including using force. Ironically, his old enemy Henry Clay came to the rescue. Clay proposed a new tariff that was acceptable to everyone, including the Southern states. South Carolina repealed its ordinance of nullification, and a civil war was narrowly avoided.

Hating banks

Throughout his life, Jackson hated banks. He considered them unnecessary and felt that they only cheated average citizens. In particular, he despised the National Bank of the United States. If it was necessary to have banks, Jackson believed that states, not the federal government, should control them.

The charter of the National Bank was not up for renewal until 1836. But the banks supporters, mostly National Republicans, introduced legislation to renew it early — a horrible political move, as it turned out. Congress passed the bill renewing the charter in 1832, but it faced a president openly opposed to it. To no one's surprise, Jackson vetoed the bill. (Jackson was not afraid to use his veto powers. In fact, he cast more vetoes than all of his predecessors combined.) Jackson decided to go after the bank itself, believing that the bank was a center of corruption and that the man in charge, Nicholas Biddle, used the bank to give rich friends low- or no-interest loans. Jackson curtailed the bank's functions, refusing to put more money into it. He withdrew money from the bank and put it into state banks.

In 1834, the Senate censured Jackson for his actions, but because the House voted to support him, the Senate's censure didn't faze him at all. The National Bank reacted by calling in loans it had given to state banks. The attempt to punish Jackson by limiting the supply of money in the United States forced the country into a recession. Jackson blamed the National Bank and its supporters, and the public backed him. With Jackson opposed to the National Bank, Congress did not renew the Bank's charter, and it went under in 1836.

Jackson's hatred for the National Bank resulted in economic chaos. He put most of the federal money into state banks, and they in turn loaned out the money. These smaller banks didn't have gold and silver reserves to back up their loans. Inflation set in, and paper money became worthless. In 1836, Jackson proclaimed that public lands could only be paid for with gold and silver. This resulted in the panic of 1837, which I discuss in the next chapter.

The sale of public land in the western parts of the United States led to a big budget surplus. Jackson used this surplus to pay off the national debt, making him the only president in U.S. history to do so.

Forcing Native Americans west

The most controversial policies of the Jackson administration were ones directed toward Native Americans. Jackson developed an intense dislike for Native American tribes after he experienced the brutality of several tribes early in his military career. As president, he supported the forced resettlement of many tribes.

When the state of Georgia insisted that the Cherokee nation abide by the laws of Georgia, as well as hand over its lands to the state, Jackson didn't interfere. He believed that the United States needed to expand. He also believed that if Native Americans stood in the way of the expansion, they needed to be removed. He officially claimed that the federal government had no jurisdiction over state matters in this case and refused to aid the Cherokee.

The Cherokee appealed to the Supreme Court. In the case of *Worcester vs. Georgia* in 1832, Chief Justice Marshall ruled that only the federal government, not the states, had jurisdiction over Native American tribes. So the Cherokee were bound only by federal law — not state law.

Jackson was so upset that he said, "John Marshall made his decision. Now let him enforce it." Without the power to enforce the decision, the Supreme Court's ruling was ignored, and the Cherokee were removed from their homeland. The U.S. government forced the Cherokee to march 800 miles from Georgia to the tribe's new homeland — a reservation in present day Oklahoma. Literally thousands died on the way.

Native Americans gave Andrew Jackson the nickname "Long Knife" for his brutality towards them.

In 1830, Congress and President Jackson passed the Indian Removal Act, and the U.S. government established the Bureau of Indian Affairs to handle all Native American issues. The Removal Act demanded the removal of many Native American tribes east of the Mississippi. When tribes refused to leave their homelands, Jackson and the military responded brutally. This brutality resulted in the Black Hawk War of 1832, when the Sac and Fox nations refused to voluntarily leave their homelands in present-day Wisconsin.

The Trail of Tears

The divisive Indian Removal Act of 1830 provided that Native Americans move or be moved to western lands, notably the Indian Territory established in what is today Oklahoma. (Davy Crockett, a representative from Tennessee, resigned in protest when the act passed.)

The Cherokee Nation, long established in Georgia, fought the act, taking their case all the way to the Supreme Court. The Court decided in Worcester versus Georgia that the Cherokee Nation was sovereign and not subject to the provisions of the Indian Removal Act — they would have to agree to move.

Though the majority of Cherokee were opposed to moving, in 1835, leaders of a faction of the Cherokee Nation signed a treaty with the U.S. government agreeing to removal from Georgia to the new Indian Territory in Oklahoma. The treaty was ratified by one vote in the Senate and General John Wool was ordered to begin the move. He resigned his commission rather than do so, but in 1838 General Winfield Scott and 7,000 troops began rounding up Cherokee citizens in makeshift forts before forcing them to travel, mostly on foot, 1,000 miles to Oklahoma.

Lack of food and the indifference of Scott and his troops contributed to the deaths of more than 4,000 of the approximately 15,000 Cherokee who were compelled to move from their homeland, and the march from Georgia to Oklahoma became known as the Trail of Tears.

In 1834, Congress and President Jackson decided to create a land for Native Americans to inhabit. They established the Indian Territory in what is now Oklahoma. Not surprisingly, most tribes weren't eager to leave their homelands. The conflict resulted in a forced resettlement of Native Americans and in the famous Trail of Tears. Not many U.S. citizens opposed Jackson's policies toward Native Americans. The country was ready to move westward. Some notable critics included Henry Clay and John Quincy Adams. Clay even thought Jackson's policies represented a stain on U.S. history.

Getting tough with France

The Jackson era didn't bring much to the realm of foreign policy, with one major exception. In 1831, France, acting in accordance with international law, agreed to pay for the damages it caused to U.S. ships during the Napoleonic Wars. (The French plundered American ships during the Napoleonic Wars.) France didn't make good on this promise until 1834, when Jackson cut off diplomatic relations with France and threatened to seize all French property in the United States. France finally caved in and paid the damages.

Cruising towards reelection

The election of 1832 is a landmark election in U.S. history for one major reason — party conventions, not members of Congress, chose the candidates for the presidency. The convention system replaced "King Caucus," which allowed the parties in Congress to nominate candidates.

The election itself was no cliffhanger. Andrew Jackson was the nominee for the Democratic Party. Henry Clay got the nod from the opposing party, the National Republicans (which would become the Whigs by 1834). Jackson slaughtered Clay in the voting booth. Jackson ended up winning 219 Electoral College votes to Clay's 49.

Deciding what to do with Texas

The question of what to do with Texas rattled several presidents. John Quincy Adams tried to buy it from Mexico, but the Mexicans refused his $1 million offer. Andrew Jackson upped the ante to $5 million, but Mexico still wouldn't bite. Texas turned into a major headache for Jackson.

When Mexico won independence from Spain in 1821, the new Mexican government allowed U.S. settlers into Texas. In the early 1830s, the U.S. settlers, headed by the Austin family, outnumbered the native Mexicans by almost 4 to 1. Mexico started to impose new laws on the settlers, and they began to rebel. Mexico's insistence that slavery be abolished and that U.S. settlers convert to Catholicism proved to be the major cause for rebellion. By 1832, many of the U.S. settlers demanded a repealing of the laws. After Mexico refused, a rebellion broke out in 1835.

In 1836, the U.S. settlers, or Texians, declared their independence from Mexico. The Mexican president, General Santa Anna, was not amused — he fought to keep his country intact. A small group of Texians, helped by U.S. citizens, set up a fort in an old Spanish mission in San Antonio called the Alamo. Shortly thereafter, the Mexican army (5,000 men strong) attacked and killed all 187 defenders. This action incensed many U.S. citizens and the remaining Texians in Texas. Six weeks later, a larger force, led by Sam Houston, defeated the Mexicans, and Texas won its independence.

After declaring independence, the new country of Texas ratified the U.S. Constitution and wanted to join the United States. Jackson faced some problems. First, Mexico made it clear that it objected to Texas joining the United States. Jackson didn't want to go to war over the matter. Second, many Northern Whigs and Democrats opposed the admission of Texas as a slave state. So Jackson did what every good politician does — he delayed the decision until his last days in office. Before he stepped down, Jackson recognized the Republic of Texas as an independent country. This move proved to be the first step toward the annexation of Texas.

Andrew Jackson was the first president to face an assassination attempt. In 1835, he was attending a funeral when a guest pulled out a pistol and tried to shoot him. The assassin had two pistols. He fired the first, which broke its cap and failed to ignite its powder, and then he drew the second, which did the same thing. The pistols were later examined and found to be in perfect working order. The odds of two such weapons malfunctioning in succession were figured as 1 in 125,000.

Reaching retirement

By 1836, Jackson was ill with tuberculosis and wanted to abide by Washington's two-term limit. Unlike Monroe, Jackson sought to make sure that his ideas and policies survived his retirement, so he handpicked his successor. His choice was Vice President Martin Van Buren, one of his most loyal allies and advisors. Van Buren won easily in 1836.

Jackson returned home to his plantation. Like his predecessors, he ran into financial troubles and borrowed heavily in his last years. In 1844, Jackson came out of retirement for the upcoming election. Disappointed with Van Buren, who lost in 1840, and now opposed to annexing Texas, Jackson turned away from his old friend and backed James Polk, another good friend, for the presidency in 1844. Jackson's selection was good enough for the Democrats. Polk received the nomination and won the presidency in 1844. A few months later, in June 1845, Andrew Jackson passed away in his sleep.

Chapter 7

Forgettable: Van Buren, William Henry Harrison, and Tyler

- -

In This Chapter

▶ Succeeding as a politician, failing as president: Van Buren

▶ Dying just one month into his term: Harrison

▶ Becoming president by default: Tyler

- -

*I*t was tough to follow in the footsteps of one of the greatest presidents in U.S. history, Andrew Jackson. Sadly, Jackson's three successors failed to duplicate his successful presidency.

Martin Van Buren was a master politician. He knew how to play the political game, manipulating issues and people, but he failed as a president.

William Henry Harrison was a great American hero. On the battlefield, he vanquished his foes. But he only lived to serve one month of his term in office.

John Tyler was an old-style southern politician and slave owner. He was almost impeached by Congress. Tyler got expelled from his party and found himself all alone when he left office.

While these three presidents served their country well before they became president, they didn't accomplish much after they entered the White House. Their terms are utterly forgettable.

Martin Van Buren, Master of Politics

Despite a well-developed understanding of politics, Martin Van Buren's presidency was unsuccessful. Like John Quincy Adams (see Chapter 5), Van Buren made his major contributions before he became president.

Van Buren, shown in Figure 7-1, was a mediocre president, but a master politician. He asked, "Is it possible to be anything in this country without being a politician?" He was instrumental in establishing the modern Democratic Party. He may also be regarded as the father of the political-machine style of politics (see "Establishing a political machine," later in this chapter) that dominated U.S. politics in the late 19th century. In his home state of New York, Van Buren single-handedly created one of the most powerful political machines in U.S. history — the Albany Regency. For more on Van Buren's influence on American politics, read *Martin Van Buren: The Romantic Age of American Politics,* by John Niven (Oxford University Press).

Figure 7-1:
Martin Van Buren, 8th president of the United States.

Courtesy of the Library of Congress

According to some sources, Martin Van Buren gave us one of the most commonly used terms in the English language — "okay." One of Van Buren's nicknames was "Old Kinderhook," from his childhood village of Kinderhook, New York. People showed approval of Van Buren and his policies by using the term "O.K."

Going from law to politics

Van Buren's legal career got him involved in politics. He was the only Democratic-Republican lawyer in Columbia County, New York, which was heavily dominated by the Federalist Party. His legal successes gave him the reputation of being one of the best lawyers in the county. The Democratic-Republican Party took notice, backing Van Buren in his successful run for the state senate in 1812.

Not an aristocrat

Martin Van Buren was born in 1782 in the small village of Kinderhook, New York. (He was the first U.S. president born a U.S. citizen. All previous presidents were British citizens.)

Van Buren truly had politics in his blood. His father was active in the Democratic-Republican Party and owned a small tavern that was a polling station, as well as a favorite stop for New York legislators on their way to the capital. Van Buren was surrounded by politicians and political talk surrounded Van Buren at an early age. This exposure sparked his interest in the legislative world.

Van Buren attended a small village school. At the age of 14, he started working for a local

lawyer. Van Buren absorbed ideas and concepts from the legal field, and at age 15, he presented his first legal argument to a local court. He liked law so much that, after turning 20, he moved to New York City to finish his legal studies. In 1803, he was admitted to the bar. He then moved back to Kinderhook to practice law.

Van Buren married in 1807. He and his wife Hannah had four sons before Hannah passed away in 1819. Van Buren never remarried. One of their sons, John Van Buren, later became the leader of the Free Soil Party.

When Van Buren entered New York politics in 1812, the Democratic-Republican Party was split into two factions. The Clinton family headed the dominant faction; "the Bucktails" referred to whoever opposed the Clintons. (The Bucktails wore tails cut from deer on their hats at political meetings, hence the name "Bucktail.")

Van Buren knew that he didn't have a shot at rising to the top of New York politics in the Clinton faction, so he took over the Bucktails to oppose the Clinton family. In 1816, he won reelection to the state senate and was also appointed the attorney general for the state of New York. To Van Buren's great dismay, DeWitt Clinton, his major political opponent, won the governorship in 1818, and Van Buren lost his job as attorney general.

After Clinton fired him, Van Buren decided that Clinton had to go. Van Buren slowly started to manipulate political meetings and conventions, packing them with his followers and using legal rules to further his political goals. For example, in 1821, his faction controlled a convention to revise the state constitution. The new constitution removed many Clintonians from office by abolishing the offices they held. Van Buren essentially had control of the state.

Establishing a political machine

In 1821, Van Buren successfully ran for a seat in the U.S. Senate. Afraid that the Clintonians might try to stage a comeback during his absence, Van Buren

established the first political machine in New York history — the Albany
Regency. For the next two decades, Van Buren ran New York politics through
his political machine while serving in Washington.

A *political machine* is a centralized organization that controls the political
structure of a city or region by rallying its membership to vote for a particular
candidate and appointing supporters to positions of power. A *party boss* heads
the organization and controls all political offices within the machine. The
machine possesses the power of *patronage,* or the power to appoint people to
political offices. The boss doesn't appoint opposition candidates to office, so
the dominant party is truly in charge.

The concept of a political machine is Irish in origin. Irish immigrants brought
the idea with them during the wave of Irish immigration that began in 1775
and lasted until 1850. By the late 19th century, political machines had control
of most large industrial cities, including Chicago, Boston, and New York.
Some political machines are still around today.

Politicking at the national level

When Martin Van Buren arrived on the national scene as a senator in 1821,
James Monroe had just won reelection without facing any opposition, and
U.S. politics were the equivalent of Democratic-Republican politics.

However, the dominant Democratic-Republican Party eventually started to fall
apart. Factions developed, and Van Buren was in his element. He aligned
himself with the faction that supported a weak federal government and states'
rights. In the presidential race of 1824, Van Buren became the campaign
manager for Secretary of Treasury William Crawford. Van Buren won
41 Electoral College votes for his candidate, even though Crawford suffered
a stroke and became paralyzed months before the election.

When Andrew Jackson lost the presidency to John Quincy Adams (see
Chapter 6), Van Buren went over to the Jackson faction. Van Buren, who
disagreed with Adams on many issues, saw that Jackson was the rising star
in the Democratic-Republican Party.

Creating a new Democratic Party

After Van Buren won reelection to the U.S. Senate in 1827, he started gearing
up for the 1828 presidential election. He decided that Jackson needed his
own political party to defeat Adams this time around. Van Buren united
several Democratic-Republican factions into the Democratic Party.

The Democratic Party adhered to truly Jeffersonian principles, supporting a
weak national government and strong states' rights, and opposing tariffs. In
1828, the new Democratic Party nominated Andrew Jackson for president and
John Calhoun for vice president.

Van Buren knew that Jackson had to win New York to win the election. So Van Buren left the U.S. Senate to run for governor of New York in 1828. He figured that he could easily win the governorship and that his coattails would be large enough to carry the state for Jackson in the presidential race. Van Buren was right. Van Buren became governor of New York, and Jackson won the state and the presidency in a landslide.

As Van Buren had expected, Jackson never forgot who helped create the Democratic Party for him or who gave up his national political career to carry New York for him.

Playing politics

For the next few years, Van Buren held a slew of political offices, including

- ✔ **Governor of New York (1829):** After only two months in office, Van Buren resigned as governor of New York when Jackson appointed him secretary of state.

- ✔ **Secretary of state (1829–1831):** Van Buren happily accepted the office of secretary of state because he knew that the position was the first step to the presidency. He proved to be a very capable secretary of state, opening trade with Turkey and the British West Indies.

- ✔ **Ambassador to Great Britain (1832):** Van Buren resigned as secretary of state during a political ploy so that Jackson could fire more members of his cabinet. Van Buren left for Great Britain but returned home when the Senate refused to ratify Jackson's choice for ambassador to Great Britain.

- ✔ **Vice president of the United States (1833–1837):** Van Buren became Jackson's choice for vice president in 1832 when Jackson sacked his old vice president, John Calhoun.

The politics of reputation

Peggy Eaton, the wife of Secretary of War John Eaton, became a hot topic in Washington D.C. in 1830. Scandalmongers disapproved of her because she had an affair with John Eaton while she was married to another man.

Van Buren defended Mrs. Eaton — probably more for political reasons than any other. Van Buren knew that Jackson's beloved and now deceased wife Rachel had been subjected to similar criticism (see Chapter 6), and he knew how much the talk angered Jackson. Jackson appreciated the fact that Van Buren stood up for Peggy Eaton. Vice President Calhoun's wife, on the other hand, ostracized the Eatons, which annoyed Jackson.

Feuding with the vice president to become the vice president

The period of 1828 until 1832 proved interesting for Van Buren. He became involved in a bitter struggle with Vice President Calhoun, who was jealous of him and his close relationship with Jackson. Calhoun didn't realize that Van Buren was an expert at playing political games. Van Buren slowly subverted his political opponent.

Van Buren defended Mrs. Eaton ("The politics of reputation" sidebar has info on the Eaton situation) and also backed Jackson when Calhoun supported *nullification,* or the right of a state to refuse to abide by federal law. To top it off, someone close to the president, possibly Van Buren, told Jackson that Calhoun had supported censuring Jackson back in 1818 when Jackson pursued the Seminoles in Florida and executed two British officers. (See Chapter 6 for more of Jackson's story.)

Calhoun struck back by publicizing the struggles within Jackson's cabinet. With Jackson angry with Calhoun, Van Buren offered to resign as the secretary of state so that Jackson could get rid of all the Calhoun supporters in his cabinet at the same time. If Van Buren were fired, it wouldn't look like Jackson was playing politics, but was just replacing a few members of his cabinet.

Jackson went along with Van Buren's plan and named him ambassador to Great Britain. The Senate refused to ratify Van Buren, with Calhoun casting the tie-breaking vote against him. Jackson trumped Calhoun's defection by naming Van Buren his choice for vice president in 1832. Van Buren had spun his magic and become the next vice president of the United States.

As vice president, Van Buren became Jackson's closest advisor and friend. He backed Jackson on all issues, including his efforts to resettle Native Americans and destroy the federal bank.

When Jackson decided not to seek a third term, he insisted that Van Buren become the presidential nominee for the Democrats. Van Buren received the nomination without any opposition within the party and won the presidency easily in 1836.

President Martin Van Buren (1837–1841)

As Andrew Jackson's successor, Martin Van Buren had very large shoes to fill. Unlike Jackson, Van Buren wasn't a man of the people. He did not feel comfortable around people, and he had a very unappealing personality — he was constantly flip-flopping on issues and scheming against other people.

On the other hand, Van Buren was a born politician. While Jackson despised politicking, Van Buren loved it. He enjoyed political intrigues and was a master at the political game. His whole political career was a political game — this was reflected in how he ran the country as president. His opponents respected his political talents by calling him "The Little Magician." Somehow Van Buren always managed to get what he wanted in politics. He truly was the first political animal in the United States.

Prolonging economic chaos

Van Buren's presidency started out disastrously, and he never recovered politically. In 1837, just after he assumed office, the Panic of 1837 started. The U.S. economy suddenly collapsed, and a worldwide recession took place.

In the United States, the financial crisis was caused by *speculation,* or the buying and selling of land at higher than normal risk with the hope of making a quick profit. From 1825 until 1836, the economy boomed, the country expanded westward, and production increased dramatically. But the demise of the National Bank, coupled with some of President Jackson's other financial blunders (check out Chapter 6 for details), led to the collapse of the state banking system, as well.

Van Buren didn't react to the banking disaster because he believed that the government shouldn't intervene in the economy. The crisis lasted for three years. Finally, in 1840, at Van Buren's urging, Congress put an independent treasury system into place, with the federal government depositing money in vaults that were located in larger cities throughout the United States.

In the midst of all his inactivity, President Van Buren did issue an executive order stating that nobody employed by the federal government should work more than 10 hours a day.

Continuing the Trail of Tears

Van Buren continued Jackson's policies of resettling Native Americans. The infamous Trail of Tears took place during his tenure. (See Chapter 6.) He sent the military to destroy the Seminoles, who rose up for the last time to fight resettlement.

Even though he opposed the institution of slavery, Van Buren did not act on his beliefs beyond refusing to admit Texas and Florida as slave states.

Battling with British Canada

During his presidency, Van Buren had a major foreign policy crisis with Canada. In 1837, Canadian citizens revolted against British rule. Many U.S. citizens were sympathetic to the uprising, so they supplied the Canadians with weapons and ammunition.

The British intercepted and destroyed a U.S. steamer carrying weapons for the Canadians, killing a U.S. citizen in the process. Enraged, some U.S. citizens raided Canada, capturing a British steamer and setting it on fire. War seemed close.

Van Buren, not wanting a war with Britain, sent the army to seal the border with Canada. The move reduced tensions, but many in the United States regarded it as a sign of weakness by their president.

In 1839, another conflict broke out with Canada. The state of Maine and the Canadian province of New Brunswick were ready to go to war over a border dispute. Both sides called out their militias. Van Buren sent the U.S. military to create a buffer between the two sides. The conflict was resolved peacefully in 1842.

Losing badly in 1840

In 1840, President Van Buren ran for reelection. He easily received the support of his own party, even though many in the United States were not very happy with him. The campaign against the Whig candidate, William Henry Harrison, proved to be a classic. Van Buren hit the campaign trail talking about issues, while the Whigs couldn't even agree on a platform. So the Whigs ran a campaign on images instead of issues and won the election.

Staging a minor comeback and retiring

In 1844, Martin Van Buren was the front-runner for the Democratic nomination. He lost the nomination to James Polk when former president Jackson refused to endorse Van Buren because he didn't support the admission of Texas into the Union.

In 1848, Van Buren, now active in the anti-slavery movement, received the nomination from the *Free Soil Party* — a political party opposed to the extension of slavery. He received almost 300,000 votes, or 10 percent of the popular vote. Van Buren siphoned off enough Democratic votes to take the election away from the Democratic nominee, Lewis Cass.

 In 1853, Van Buren toured the continent of Europe, making him the first ex-U.S. president to travel abroad. He spent two years in Europe and then returned home to finally retire. In 1860, he endorsed Stephen Douglas for the presidency. When Lincoln won the election, he supported President Lincoln and the Union in the Civil War. Van Buren died at the age of 79 in his home in Kinderhook, New York in 1862.

The Founder of the Image Campaign: William Henry Harrison

William Henry Harrison, shown in Figure 7-2, was a capable soldier and an average politician. His exploits fighting Native Americans made him a hero to the average person. He relied upon this image to win the presidency. As president, Harrison wasn't able to accomplish much because he died right after delivering his inaugural address.

Harrison's lasting legacy is the way he won in 1840. For the first time in U.S. history, a presidential candidate didn't talk much about issues — he ran a race based solely on his image. Harrison gave the United States its first *image campaign*. The image campaign has been with us ever since.

Using politics and militia against Native Americans

Like George Washington and Andrew Jackson, William Henry Harrison entered U.S. politics through the military. By 1814, he had become one of the best-known military leaders in the United States. He used his military reputation as a springboard into politics.

In 1798, Harrison, with the help of some well-connected friends, became the secretary of the Northwest Territory. Only one year later, he became the territorial delegate to the U.S. Congress for the Northwest Territory.

The educated "Indian fighter"

William Henry Harrison was born in 1773 on a large plantation in Virginia. His father was one of the signers of the Declaration of Independence and governor of Virginia. Harrison received a top-notch private schooling and then attended Hampden-Sydney College. His father wanted him to study medicine, so he sent him to the University of Pennsylvania.

Harrison really didn't want to study medicine. When his father died in 1791, he dropped out of school and joined the military. For the next seven years, Harrison served on the northwestern frontier (what is now Ohio) and participated in several battles fighting local Native American tribes, including the battle of Fallen Timbers.

While serving on the northwestern frontier, he married the love of his life, Anna Symmes. They had ten children together. William Henry Harrison's grandson, Benjamin Harrison, became the 23rd president of the United States in 1889.

As a delegate to Congress, Harrison became a champion of settlers at the expense of Native Americans. He was responsible for the *Land Act of 1800,* which parceled up and gave Native American–held lands to white settlers at low interest rates.

As soon as Congress established the Indiana territory, Harrison became its first governor — a job he held for 12 years. As governor, he continued his onslaught on Native Americans. He got some help from President Jefferson, who told him to take all Native American lands. Jefferson also told Harrison to maintain the Native American's friendship. Obviously, that didn't happen.

Harrison took almost all Native American lands in the territory. When the Shawnee opposed him, he organized a militia against them. This conflict resulted in the famous Battle of Tippecanoe, where Harrison, despite losing 20 percent of his men, defeated the Shawnee and sent them fleeing to Canada. Harrison was a national hero.

Harrison's nickname, "Old Tippecanoe," came from the Battle of Tippecanoe. The nickname became part of Harrison's presidential campaign slogan in 1840.

In 1812, war broke out with Great Britain. Harrison, as governor of the Indiana territory, always blamed the British for inciting the Shawnee and was ready to go after them. Harrison, who was now a brigadier general in the U.S. army, won major battles in the War of 1812. He liberated Detroit, Michigan, from British occupation and defeated the British army and the rest of the Shawnee in Canada. Harrison made sure that the British didn't invade from Canada, and this further enhanced his reputation. By 1814, everybody in the United States knew about the great "Indian fighter."

Focusing on politics

From 1816 until 1836, Harrison held a whole slew of political offices. These offices included

- Member of the House of Representatives
- Member of the Ohio state senate
- U.S. senator
- Ambassador to Columbia

In 1836, the Whigs were desperate for a candidate to take on the ruling Democrats. They wanted someone of similar stature to Democratic President Jackson, who was about to retire. The Whigs ran three regional candidates for office. The idea behind this odd strategy was to win enough Electoral College votes to deny the Democrat, Van Buren, a majority in the Electoral College. This would throw the election to the House of Representatives, where the Whigs believed that they could win. The Whigs nominated Harrison to run in the western part of the United States. Two other regional candidates, Hugh White and Daniel Webster, ran in the South and East, respectively.

The idea backfired. Van Buren won easily in 1836. However, Harrison did so well in the West, winning 73 Electoral College votes, that he became the front-runner for the 1840 Whig presidential nomination.

President William Henry Harrison (1841–1841)

In 1839, the Whigs, desperate to win, nominated Harrison for the presidency. At the convention, the party was so split that they couldn't agree on a party platform. So Harrison decided to run an image campaign. The party portrayed him as a common man who was born in a log cabin, like most U.S. citizens. His image became one of a hardworking, heavy-drinking commoner running against the aristocrat Van Buren. The Whigs labeled Van Buren — the son of a small tavern owner — a New York aristocrat out of touch with the common man. His nickname became "Martin Van Ruin."

A Democratic newspaper, the *Baltimore American,* was the first to try to belittle Harrison by portraying him as a frontier bumpkin. "Give him a barrel of hard cider and settle a pension of $2,000 a year on him and, my word for it, he will sit the remainder of his days in a log cabin by the side of a sea coal fire and study moral philosophy." The Whigs simply took this imagery to the frontier.

To attract southern support, former U.S. Senator John Tyler from Virginia became Harrison's vice-presidential candidate. Harrison's campaign slogan, "Tippecanoe and Tyler, too," became an instant classic. Harrison's campaign involved dragging log cabins around and providing the audience with free alcohol — a moveable party. Harrison won in a landslide, receiving 234 Electoral College votes to Van Buren's 60.

The campaign of 1840 employed massive lies. Harrison, in reality, was a wealthy aristocrat who grew up on a plantation and owned slaves. His manor in Ohio had twenty-two rooms and employed many servants. Van Buren was the commoner, not Harrison. At the end, it didn't matter. The public bought the fabricated image of Harrison, and he won big.

William Henry Harrison presented his inaugural address in March 1841. It was a cold and rainy day, and Harrison refused to wear a hat and a warm winter coat. Not surprisingly, he caught a cold, which turned into pneumonia. He never recovered and died one month later.

William Henry Harrison gave the longest inaugural address in U.S. history. He talked for almost two hours in freezing rain. He was the second oldest president to ever win office (Ronald Reagan was the oldest), and he holds the distinction of serving the shortest term of any president in U.S. history.

Stepping Into the Presidency: John Tyler

John Tyler, depicted in Figure 7-3, was the first vice president to succeed a president who died in office. Thus, he set a precedent for vice presidents to come.

A Southerner to the core

John Tyler was born in 1790, the son of a wealthy plantation owner. He attended a local school and then graduated from the College of William and Mary. In 1809, he became a lawyer in Virginia after being admitted to the bar. That same year, the people of Virginia elected his father governor of the state. It was then that Tyler's political career took off.

He became a member of the Virginia legislature in 1811 and began to serve in the House of Representatives in 1816. In between, he married Letitia Christian and fathered eight children. The marriage was a happy one until his wife died in 1842, shortly after he became president.

Tyler was a stubborn man who didn't believe in compromise. He alienated not just his opposition, but also his own supporters. He was eventually kicked out of his party. After his presidency was over, he supported the Confederacy and served it as a congressman. John Tyler was the last U.S. president to favor and defend slavery.

Throughout his congressional career, Tyler favored state rights. He didn't believe in a strong national government. He supported the institution of slavery — he owned many slaves himself — and opposed any bill that would inhibit the practice. He was a member of the southern slavocracy, as his voting record proved.

Figure 7-3:
John Tyler,
10th
president of
the United
States.

Courtesy of the Library of Congress

Supporting states' rights and slavery

As a U.S. Congressman, Tyler became a staunch supporter of states' rights and the institution of slavery. He even opposed the Missouri Compromise of 1820 because it restricted slavery. Discouraged because he was always on the losing side of such issues as slavery, he resigned his seat in 1821.

Only four years later, Tyler became governor of Virginia. The legislature subsequently elected him to the U.S. Senate in 1827. For the next nine years, Tyler served in the Senate, basing his votes on his own beliefs and ignoring his political constituency.

At first, Tyler supported President Adams. He eventually switched over to the Jacksonian Democrats, giving his support to Jackson in 1828. He felt that Adams was creating a national government that was too strong. Tyler especially hated the National Bank — Jackson's opposition to it won him over.

But by 1833, Tyler was disenchanted with Jackson. He disagreed with Jackson's threat to use force against South Carolina when it threatened to secede from the United States.

Tyler joined the newly created Whig party. When the Virginia legislature told him to vote to erase a previous vote to censure Jackson, he flat out refused and resigned his Senate seat. After serving two more years in the Virginia legislature, he was ready for the big time.

Balancing the ticket; becoming president

In 1840, the Whigs nominated William Henry Harrison for the presidency. To balance the ticket, they decided they needed to add a southerner. John Tyler was a perfect fit.

Because Tyler supported slavery, the Whig leadership told him to keep his mouth shut during Harrison's image-based campaign. The objective of the campaign was to keep Harrison vague and Tyler quiet. It worked.

Tyler was getting ready to move to Washington, D.C. when he heard that President Harrison had died. A constitutional crisis loomed. Many believed that Tyler should be the acting president until a new election could be held. Tyler objected and had himself sworn in as president in April 1841. Both foes and friends went crazy, coming up with nicknames such as "His Ascendancy," "Acting President Tyler," "Executive Ass," and "His Accidency." Soon things got worse.

President John Tyler (1841–1845)

As president, Tyler didn't change — he was still stubborn, and he refused to bargain or cooperate. His attitude made it very difficult for him to get anything accomplished, not to mention that it almost got him impeached.

Angering Congress

In 1841, Congress tried to reestablish the Bank of the United States abolished by Jackson. Tyler vetoed the bill, even though his own party proposed and passed it. Congress passed a second bill, and Tyler vetoed it again. This time, almost everyone in his cabinet resigned, his own party kicked him out, and the House of Representatives called for his impeachment.

After Tyler narrowly avoided being kicked out of office in 1843, he turned to the Democrats for help. They didn't want anything to do with him. So Tyler formed his own party, which failed miserably. Now he was all alone, and his presidency was over. In 1844, Tyler decided to back the Democrat, James Polk, who, like him, supported the annexation of Texas.

John Tyler remarried in 1844. His new wife, Julia Gardiner, was 30 years younger than him, which caused quite a stir in Washington, D.C. He fathered another 7 children with her, bringing his total to 15 children. This is the most children any U.S. president has ever had.

Faring better with foreign policy

Despite the problems Tyler was having with Congress, he did succeed in foreign policy. His most notable successes include

- Settling a border dispute between Maine and Canada
- Opening trade with China
- Annexing Texas

  Tyler truly deserved praise for the way he handled the annexation of Texas. The U.S. Senate rejected the annexation treaty in 1844. The Constitution required a two-thirds majority to ratify treaties, which Tyler wasn't able to get. Undeterred, Tyler tried again. He changed the rules of the game and proposed a joint resolution passed by both Houses of Congress to annex Texas — this required only a simple majority vote. It passed, and three days before Tyler left office, Texas joined the Union.

Dying a Confederate

Before 1861, Tyler tried his best to help preserve the Union. However, after listening to Abraham Lincoln's inaugural address, he decided that the Union was over. Tyler now backed the Confederacy and openly urged secession. Later that year, the people of Virginia elected him to the Confederate House of Representatives. He died of a stroke in early 1862, shortly before he could assume the office.

Chapter 8

Dreaming of California: James K. Polk

In This Chapter

▶ Understanding Polk's rise to power

▶ Keeping campaign promises after winning the presidency

▶ Expanding into new territories

▶ Knowing when *not* to run

*J*ames Knox Polk is one of the most underrated presidents in U.S. history. Polk had one of the most successful presidencies in U.S. history, yet presidential observers usually ignore him. In his fours years as president, Polk was not only one of the hardest working presidents, but he was also able to keep his administration free of corruption and scandals — no small feat, as recent history has shown.

Polk's legacy isn't just his able leadership but also the doubling of the size of the United States. To top it off, Polk also kept his campaign promises, making him even more unique in America's long list of presidents.

President Polk, when asked about his work habits, said, "In truth, though I occupy a very high position, I am the hardest working man in this country."

Young Hickory

Growing up in Tennessee, Polk was a fan of local hero and favorite son Andrew Jackson, who deeply affected Polk's political ideas — Polk tied his political career to Jackson's. Jackson, nicknamed "Old Hickory," was a good friend of the family. Polk was *so* dedicated to Jackson and his ideas that he was referred to as "Young Hickory."

Overcoming childhood illness

James Polk was born in 1795, the son of a small farmer in North Carolina. He later enjoyed a prosperous upbringing in Tennessee. A childhood illness kept him close to the family farm until the age of 17.

Polk, who was never able to fully use his body, was not the kind of guy you would want to hang out with! His quiet, cold, humorless, and mean personality was the result of his constantly being sick. Diagnosed with gallstones in 1812, Polk had an operation without anesthetics. Although the operation probably hurt, it allowed him to live a normal life afterwards.

Polk was exceptionally bright. He graduated first in his class from the University of North Carolina in 1818 and then studied law under the most famous lawyer in Tennessee, Felix Grundy. In 1819, Polk moved with Grundy into politics. Polk became a champion of the poor after seeing the sufferings of the poor white working class during the Panic of 1819.

Polk's wife, Sarah, who asked him to enter politics as a condition for marriage, encouraged him throughout his political career.

Polk's Early Political Career

In 1820, Polk was admitted to the bar. In 1823, he won a seat in the Tennessee state legislature. Polk, who was a fairly small man, was such a tenacious campaigner that supporters gave him the nickname "Napoleon on the Stump."

After the 1824 presidential election — when the House of Representatives selected John Quincy Adams for president over Polk's political mentor, Andrew Jackson — Polk made it his mission to get Jackson elected president in 1828. To that end, Polk ran for Jackson's old seat in the House of Representatives in 1824 and was thrilled when he won.

James Polk got involved in politics at a time when the dominant party, the Democratic-Republicans, was falling apart. The faction that was organizing the Democratic Party supported farmers and workers. Polk aligned himself with the future Democrats, calling for free public education and lower tariffs. The faction that was organizing the National Republicans championed the interests of the growing business class and merchants.

After working day and night to elect Jackson to the presidency during the 1828 presidential campaign, Polk set out to make sure that Jackson's presidential agenda made it through Congress. He soon became Jackson's right arm in Congress. In 1835, the House selected Polk to be the Speaker of the House. Because Polk was so loyal to Jackson, his opponents made fun of him, accusing him of not having a mind of his own. They insulted Polk by using terms like "slave" and "servant" to describe him.

Manifest Destiny: God's take on geography

The term *Manifest Destiny* was coined in the summer of 1845 by journalist and diplomat John Louis O' Sullivan, who supported annexing Texas. It referred to the belief that it was natural for the United States to extend its geographical borders to the Pacific.

It incorporates the view that the United States had not only the God-given right, but also the moral obligation to control the North American continent. Expansionists in all political parties used the concept to justify the acquisition of California, the Oregon Territory, and later Alaska. By the 1890s, the doctrine had gained new force and support. Many expansionists were pushing for the acquisition of islands in the Pacific and the Caribbean.

James Polk is the only Speaker of the House of Representatives to become President.

In 1836, the Whigs carried Tennessee in the presidential and gubernatorial races. Polk, who couldn't bear to see his home state governed by the opposition, ran for governor in 1839 and won back the office for the Democrats. Polk didn't hold the office of governor long, losing reelection bids in 1841 and 1843. His political career seemed to be over.

Texas to the Rescue

With the 1844 presidential election approaching, Polk let it be known that he was interested in the vice presidency. He began to support former president Martin Van Buren, who, after losing in 1840, wanted to make one more run for office. Van Buren enjoyed broad support within the Democratic Party and looked like a sure bet to win the nomination.

Then the issue of territorial expansion became a campaign issue. Polk and former president Jackson endorsed President Tyler's annexation of Texas as a slave state into the Union. But Van Buren opposed the idea — as did many Northern Democrats. Van Buren not only alienated the Southern wing of the Democratic Party but also expansionists within the party who believed that the United States should expand its borders (for info on this policy, see the "Manifest Destiny: God's take on geography" sidebar).

Congress rejected the annexation of Texas in 1844 because the Whigs and Northern Democrats feared that it would be admitted as a slave state. They were right. When Texas was admitted in 1845, it became a slave state and later joined the Confederacy.

Southern and Western Democrats decided that Van Buren had to go. So they changed the nominating rules at the Democratic convention to require that a nominee receive a two-thirds majority vote instead of a simple majority. Van Buren failed to meet the new standard.

Former president Jackson endorsed his loyal friend Polk rather than Van Buren for the presidency. After several unsuccessful ballots, the delegates realized that Van Buren wouldn't receive the necessary votes to win the Democratic nomination, so they turned to Polk as the only alternative. For the first time in its history, the United States had a *dark horse candidate* — an unexpected or unknown contestant who is not expected to win — nominated for the presidency by a major party. Suddenly the man whose career seemed to be over only a few months earlier was the presidential nominee for the Democratic Party.

Keeping His Campaign Simple

As the presidential nominee for the Democratic Party in 1844, Polk faced a formidable challenger in Henry Clay, the Whig nominee. This political battle allowed for some payback on Polk's part: Clay was the man who took away the presidency from Polk's buddy Jackson in 1824 (see Chapter 6). At first, the Whigs had fun with Polk's candidacy. They thought that he was a nobody who had no chance of beating their well-known candidate. Clay was even quoted as asking, "Who is James Polk?" His tune soon changed.

Polk ran on a limited platform, making only a few campaign promises instead of outlining a major agenda as is common today. His major theme in the campaign was the territorial expansion of the United States, promising to reoccupy the Oregon Territory and re-annex Texas, as well as acquire California.

Polk squeezed out a narrow victory with the help of Southern Democrats, who wanted the acquisition of new slave states, and the western parts of the United States, where many people believed in the concept of Manifest Destiny. The final result was close: Polk beat Clay by about 38,000 votes nationwide.

President James Polk (1845–1849)

Polk, shown in Figure 8-1, was a workaholic who set out to fulfill his campaign promises right away. He turned first to the question of tariffs. In 1846, Polk and the Democratic Congress successfully passed a new tariff, the "Walker Tariff," which lowered duties on non-luxury items, such as textiles and agricultural goods. Polk knew that low duties allowed the average person to buy goods for less. He also believed that free trade with Great Britain, especially in the area of agricultural goods, would stimulate the export of more U.S. goods to the British Empire.

Figure 8-1: James Polk, 11th president of the United States.

Courtesy of the Library of Congress

Establishing a treasury system

President Polk, being a true Jacksonian, didn't believe in a national bank or paper money — for him, only gold currency had value. After President Jackson destroyed the national bank, his successor, President Van Buren, put an independent treasury system into place.

When the Whigs were elected to office in 1840, they destroyed the independent treasury system. Polk's goal was to restore it. Because his party controlled Congress, Polk had a fairly easy time restoring the system. By 1846, the independent treasury was back in place. The independent treasury remained intact until it was replaced with the Federal Reserve System in 1913.

Expanding north and south

One of Polk's biggest tasks as president was tackling the issue of territorial expansion. Polk turned first to the Northwest — namely the Oregon Territory, which included the western parts of what today is Canada. After lengthy negotiations with Great Britain, Polk successfully added the Oregon Territory to the United States in 1846.

Without firing a shot, Polk gained access to the Pacific coast. But such achievement was not enough for a man driven by ambition. Polk decided it was time to turn south. After successfully dealing with the British Empire, what resistance could a small country — politically unstable and divided — provide against the mighty United States? Mexico became Polk's next target.

Polk's victory in November 1844, gave the Democratic party a majority in both houses of Congress. For this reason, President Tyler decided to give the annexation of Texas one more shot. Tyler asked Congress to offer annexation to Texas through a joint resolution of Congress, which required a simple majority instead of a two-thirds Senate vote. After Congressional approval, Tyler signed the bill on March 1, 1845, offering to admit Texas to statehood. Texas accepted on Dec. 29, 1845.

Polk was halfway to fulfilling his campaign promise of territorial expansion. Polk believed in Manifest Destiny. He knew that the United States could become a great power in the world only if it expanded to the Pacific Ocean. He first attempted to buy California from Mexico. In late 1845, he offered Mexico $25 million and promised to drop U.S. claims for $3 million in damages in exchange for California. Mexico, still upset over the loss of Texas (see Chapter 6), refused to discuss the offer.

To make matters worse, the Mexicans refused even to meet with the U.S. representative, John Slidell. An angry and determined Polk incited U.S. citizens living in California to rebel against Mexico. Polk also attempted to restore former Mexican dictator General Santa Anna, of Alamo fame, to power. (Later, Polk did restore Santa Anna to power — he promptly began fighting against the United States.) By early 1846, all of Polk's attempts had failed. He concluded that only war could accomplish his goals.

54-40 or fight

Both the United States and Great Britain had settled the Oregon Territory since 1818. By mutual agreement, both parties jointly claimed the territory but were able to end the arrangement at any time. Polk did just that in 1845, when he called for U.S. occupation and control of all territory up to the 54-40 parallel, which included the western part of Canada. He pretended to be especially interested in the all-important port city of Vancouver in British Columbia.

Only Polk and a few of his advisors knew that he was actually bluffing. Polk really only wanted the territory up to the 49′ parallel, which *excluded* Vancouver. His Democratic supporters in Congress, unaware of the bluffing, started to call for action against Great Britain. "54-40 or fight" became their battle cry.

Great Britain, not interested in another war, agreed to make the 49′ parallel the boundary line. Polk's supporters felt betrayed. They started to move away from their President.

Fighting a war with Mexico

Polk, not wanting to appear as the bad guy, looked for a pretense to declare war on Mexico. The Texas-Mexico border gave him the issue he was looking for. Knowing that the border was disputed, Polk sent 4,000 troops under General (and later president) Zachary Taylor to the Rio Grande area.

Mexico, who claimed the territory, wasn't amused; Mexican troops attacked a U.S. patrol, killing 11 soldiers. The attack was enough for Polk. Addressing Congress, Polk loudly proclaimed that Mexico had invaded U.S. territory and shed American blood. The war was on.

When Texas was part of Mexico, the state's borders extended only to the Nueces River, excluding what today is south Texas. But the Republic of Texas claimed that its borders extended all the way down to the Rio Grande River. When Texas was admitted to the Union, Polk aggressively supported this claim. Mexico, however, didn't recognize the Rio Grande border.

Support for the war was high in the Southern states and the American West. Whigs and Northern Democrats rejected the war because they saw it as another attempt by Polk to expand slavery. They also felt that the president deceived them by inciting a war and that the war itself was not only unjust but also illegal.

Among the most famous opponents of the war was a young congressman from Illinois named Abraham Lincoln, who condemned Polk on the floor of the House. Even a young army lieutenant involved in the war, Ulysses S. Grant, was quoted as saying that Polk started an "unjust war by a stronger nation against a weaker nation."

Commanding his troops

James Polk was the first U.S. president to truly function as commander in chief of the armed forces. Unlike modern-day presidents, who call on generals to mastermind wars for them, Polk ran the war himself, working 18-hour days and clashing with his generals. After arguing with Whig generals, Polk became so paranoid that he trusted only himself to do the job.

With the Mexican army ill-equipped and poorly led, it wasn't much of a war. Even though the United States lost 13,000 troops, only 2,000 of them actually died in battle. Most were killed by disease. In 1847, when U.S. troops captured Mexico City, the war was over.

In early 1848, Polk forced Mexico to sign the Treaty of Guadeloupe Hidalgo. This harsh and insulting treaty added New Mexico, Arizona, California, Nevada, and Utah to the United States, as well as parts of Colorado and Wyoming. The border between Texas and Mexico was fixed at the Rio Grande River. In addition, Polk agreed to pay Mexico the measly sum of $15 million — $10 million *less* than he had originally offered.

To the surprise of everybody who knew him, Polk showed some restraint after the war: He opposed those who wanted the United States to annex all of Mexico.

Even more insulting to Mexico was Polk's announcement in early 1848 that gold had been discovered in California. Polk told the American people that California's gold could not only be used to pay for the war against Mexico, but also to develop the newly acquired western part of the United States. The discovery of gold started the famous California gold rush, where thousands of U.S. citizens rushed to California to try their luck at mining gold.

Winning the War but Losing the Battle

Ironically, Polk's great successes in the war with Mexico and the compromise with Great Britain didn't add up to political success back home in Washington, D.C. The victory over Mexico and the enlargement of the country *should have* provided the president with lots of political support — but that's not how it worked out. Instead, the more successful Polk was in his quest for expansion, the more enemies he made at home. Northern Democrats and Whigs opposed him. They believed that he wanted to spread slavery by conquering more areas and making the new territories into states that supported slavery.

By the summer of 1846, the Northern Democrats and Whigs actively opposed Polk's policies. Polk never understood what all the fuss was about; he was just interested in expanding the country's borders to fulfill the Manifest Destiny that he believed in.

Unable to find a solution to the question of whether to admit new states as free or slave states, Polk and Congress avoided the issue. Polk never imagined that his actions would contribute to a civil war.

In 1846, a Northern Democratic congressman by the name of David Wilmot offered what would be called the Wilmot Proviso. It declared that any territory conquered from Mexico could not have the institution of slavery. Even though the proviso never passed Congress, it contributed greatly to the outbreak of the Civil War. Some Southern states threatened to secede if the proviso passed Congress. The Southern states in turn pushed for what they called "popular sovereignty," allowing the conquered areas themselves to decide whether to have slavery or not. Of course, they knew that most states would opt for slavery. The controversy itself wasn't resolved until after Polk's death.

Choosing Not to Run Again

Keeping his word, Polk didn't run for reelection in1848. He instead opted to retire. His decision sparked a struggle for the nomination within the Democratic Party. The Southern wing of the party eventually prevailed, nominating Lewis Cass for the presidency. Cass was a supporter of popular sovereignty.

The Northern Democrats violently opposed popular sovereignty. They rallied around former president Van Buren, who had started his own party, the Free Soil Party, and was opposed to the expansion of slavery. A divided Democratic party allowed the Whigs to win the presidency in 1848. Ironically, it was Polk's old nemesis, Zachary Taylor, the famous general from the Mexican-American War, who won the presidency for the Whigs.

President Polk literally worked himself into the grave. By the time he left office in March 1849, his work habits had taken a toll on his frail body. Polk's sickly disposition, along with his habit of working 12 to 18 hours a day, caused his immune system to weaken. Three months after leaving office, Polk caught cholera and died. His wife, Sarah, lived another 42 years and turned their home into a shrine to Polk's presidency. During the U.S. Civil War, Sarah stayed neutral publicly — though she privately supported the Confederacy.

Chapter 9

Working Up to the Civil War: Taylor, Fillmore, Pierce, and Buchanan

This chapter covers the four presidents who served in the decade before the Civil War. Zachary Taylor could have been a great president, but he died one year into his term. The other three presidents turned out to be miserable failures. With the Civil War looming, they did nothing to prevent the conflict; in fact, many of their actions contributed to the start of the war. President Fillmore destroyed his party over the issue of slavery, President Pierce openly sympathized with the South, and President Buchanan sat idly by while the Southern states seceded. None of these presidents had the backbone or the willingness to act at a time when action was desperately needed.

Trying to Preserve the Union: Zachary Taylor

When it comes to American heroes, Zachary Taylor, shown in Figure 9-1, ranks near the top of the list. During his long military career, he fought Native Americans, the British, and the Mexicans. As a military leader, he has the distinction of never being defeated in battle. Even though his enemies usually outnumbered him, he always managed to win battles somehow.

Figure 9-1:
Zachary
Taylor, 12th
president of
the United
States.

Courtesy of the Library of Congress

By the end of the Mexican-American war in 1848, Taylor had become a national hero. His status as a hero propelled him into the presidency. If he had lived to serve his full term, a bloody civil war could have been avoided. His death, a year into his presidency, allowed for weaker presidents to follow.

Fighting Native Americans and Mexicans

Like Andrew Jackson and William Henry Harrison, Zachary Taylor was a military man. He spent over 40 years serving his country.

Early campaigns

Zachary Taylor became a household name in the United States during the War of 1812. While defending the Indiana territory, he faced off against a collection of Indian tribes — including the Delaware and Kickapoos — who were followers of the Shawnee chief Tecumseh. Taylor commanded only 50 soldiers, but he was able to defend Fort Harrison, a frontier outpost, against an army of 450 Native Americans.

Taylor spent the next 19 years moving from post to post. When he got a chance to fight again, his military exploits became legendary. He was in a charge of a detachment of soldiers fighting in the Black Hawk War. After pursuing the Native Americans for three months, Taylor caught up with them and defeated them soundly. His reputation grew. President Van Buren sent him to Florida to go after the Seminoles who rose against U.S. rule. Commanding over 1,100 soldiers, he pursued the Seminoles into the Everglades and finally defeated them. President Van Buren rewarded him for his victory by naming him a brigadier general in charge of the Florida district.

"Old Rough and Ready"

Zachary Taylor was born in 1784, the son of a military officer. His father served in the Revolutionary War and received a nice chunk of land from the state of Kentucky for his services. With his father serving in the military and, later, the Kentucky state legislature, Taylor's path was set.

Taylor grew up in rural Kentucky and received a rudimentary education. In 1806, he joined the Kentucky militia. Taylor — using his father's political connections — became a lieutenant in the Seventh U.S. Infantry in 1808 and served his country for the next 40 years.

In 1810, Taylor married Margaret Smith, the daughter of a Maryland plantation owner, substantially increasing his wealth. One of their daughters, Sarah Knox Taylor, married Jefferson Davis, who became the President of the Confederate States of America. Taylor's son Richard served the Confederacy as a general.

The Mexican-American War

By 1840, Taylor was ready for a change. So he asked for a transfer. He was sent to Louisiana, where he bought a plantation and soon owned over 100 slaves. He was ready to retire when the Mexican-American War broke out in 1845. President Polk called upon him to lead the charge one more time.

In March 1845, Congress passed a resolution annexing Texas (see Chapter 7). President Polk was interested in gaining more territory from Mexico (see Chapter 8). Taylor received orders to march his troops to Corpus Christi, Texas. In early 1846, President Polk ordered Taylor to advance into disputed territory near the Rio Grande River.

During the battle of Palo Alto, a Mexican division of around 6,000 soldiers attacked Taylor. Taylor commanded only 4,000 soldiers, but he defeated the enemy soundly. Polk and Congress promoted Taylor to major general. Next, Taylor invaded Mexico. In September 1846, he attacked and conquered Monterrey, despite being outnumbered.

Taylor became the best-known and most popular man in the United States. Taylor fan clubs sprung up throughout the country, and the Whigs started to look at him as a possible presidential candidate. President Polk got jealous: He tried to undermine Taylor by moving most of the men under Taylor's command to a different division and stranding him in Mexico.

In February 1847, Mexican General Santa Anna took advantage of Taylor's situation and attacked his small army of about 5,000 men with an army of over 15,000. Taylor, who stayed right in the thick of the battle, fought the Mexican army to a standstill, and Santa Anna retreated. Taylor had not only won the battle but also the presidency. Polk's plan misfired badly.

President Zachary Taylor (1849–1850)

When Taylor returned home in late 1847, he was the leading candidate for the Whig nomination for president, despite the fact that he didn't want to be president or even a politician. Taylor's candidacy was controversial among some Whigs because he owned slaves and the Whigs opposed slavery. In the end, the Whig's desire to win overcame their politics, and they nominated Taylor for the presidency.

Taylor's platform was simple; he wanted to be a president of all the people. His reputation was such that he easily won the office. He carried the Electoral College with 163 votes to 127 for the Democratic nominee Lewis Cass.

Zachary Taylor never voted in an election before he became the nominee of the Whig party. He cast the first ballot of his life for himself in 1848.

Serving for just one year

President Taylor served a little over one year in office. During this time, he proved to be a capable leader, doing his best to preserve the Union.

In 1849, California and New Mexico, acquired in the Mexican-American War, applied for statehood. Both wanted to ban slavery in their territories. Taylor was okay with the decision to ban slavery in both territories because he felt slavery was a state matter.

Zachary Taylor supported slavery in the existing slave states — he believed that the Southern economy would collapse without slave labor. At the same time, he opposed expanding slavery into new states.

The Southern states didn't agree with Taylor's views on the issue of slavery, and some Southern congressmen, including John C. Calhoun of South Carolina, threatened to secede to put pressure on the new president. Boy, did they miscalculate. Enraged, Taylor told the Southern leadership that if they seceded, he himself would lead the U.S. army against them. For Taylor, there was no compromising on this issue — had he lived long enough to finish his term in office, the Civil War might have been avoided.

On July 4, 1850, Taylor consumed cherries and frozen milk during the Fourth of July festivities in the capital. He got sick the same night and died five days later. (Poor sanitation made it risky to eat any raw fruit or dairy products during the summer. Taylor did both. He suffered severe cramps, diarrhea, and vomiting, which led to his death.) His successor, Vice President Fillmore, put the country on the path to a civil war.

Making Things Worse: Millard Fillmore

When ranking the presidents, Millard Fillmore usually falls somewhere in the bottom ten — deservedly. As president, he didn't do much except contribute to the outbreak of the Civil War. He also did his part in destroying the Whig party, of which he was a member. He later ran for the presidency one more time as the standard bearer for the blatantly racist American Party.

Millard Fillmore, shown in Figure 9-2, was the second vice president to succeed a president who died in office. Like John Tyler, he disagreed with his predecessor on most issues and made dramatic policy changes. Fillmore even dismissed most of Taylor's cabinet and started from scratch.

Figure 9-2:
Millard
Fillmore,
13th
president of
the United
States.

Courtesy of the Library of Congress

Fillmore's early career

In 1826, a local Mason disappeared after publishing a book on the secretive Masonic order. Citizens near Buffalo, New York, formed the Anti-Mason party. Looking for candidates, they came to Fillmore. They launched his political career when they supported his successful bid for a seat in the New York state legislature.

In 1832, Fillmore was elected to the U.S. House of Representatives. He became a Whig when the Anti-Mason party fused with the Whigs in the mid-1830s. He soon became a good friend and follower of Henry Clay. He and Clay agreed on the major issues of the day, such as compromising on the issue of slavery and the need for high tariffs to protect U.S. industries.

Growing up poor and undereducated

Millard Fillmore was born in 1800, the son of a small farmer in New York State. At the age of 14, he became an apprentice to a local clothier. Fillmore educated himself slowly with the help of a local schoolteacher, Abigail Powers, whom he later married.

At the age of 19, Fillmore began studying law under a local attorney and teaching school to support himself. Finally, in 1823, he opened his own law firm near Buffalo, New York.

Fillmore expected to become the vice-presidential candidate for the Whigs in 1844, but that didn't happen. He also lost a bid for governor of New York. Fillmore reappeared on the political scene in 1847, winning the office of state comptroller in New York.

At the Whig convention in 1848, General Zachary Taylor won the presidential nomination. As a Southern slaveholder, Taylor annoyed the anti-slavery wing of the Whig party, so it looked for a Northern candidate who opposed slavery and could win in a big state — Fillmore fit the bill. He received the vice-presidential nomination and eventually became vice president.

As vice president, Fillmore took part in discussing the major issue of the day — the slave-or-free status of new states. He tried to compromise on the issue, but President Taylor refused. War loomed on the horizon.

President Millard Fillmore (1850–1853)

President Fillmore's first order of business was to settle the conflict over the admission of new states into the Union. Together with Henry Clay, Fillmore worked out a compromise known as the *Compromise of 1850*. It contained the following provisions:

- California was admitted as a free state, prohibiting slavery.

- The Utah and New Mexico territories were organized without mentioning slavery, allowing for the institution.

- A new "Fugitive Slave Law" was put into place, calling for the return of runaway slaves to their owners.

- Slavery continued to exist in Washington, D.C., although slave trading was outlawed.

- The borders of the state of Texas were defined. The state also received $10 million to pay off its state debt.

Fillmore signed the Compromise of 1850 into law. Many Northerners considered the bill pro-slavery and turned away from the Whigs. A large portion of the Whig party itself opposed the law and withdrew support from Fillmore. On the other hand, the compromise pleased the Southern states and prevented a civil war for the time being.

When Fillmore's term was up in 1854, he knew he wouldn't get the support of his own party. He attended the Whig convention, but the Whigs nominated General Winfield Scott. Scott lost the election, and the issue of slavery tore the party apart. Many of the Whigs later joined the newly established Republican Party, which advocated an anti-slavery platform.

Turning racist

In 1856, Fillmore ran for the presidency one more time. He became the candidate for the American Party, a party that opposed immigration and was anti-Catholic, anti-Black, and anti-Jewish. Fillmore won one state, Maryland, and received almost 900,000 votes in the election. After losing the election, he retired to Buffalo, New York and served as the first chancellor for the University of Buffalo. He later opposed President Lincoln for reelection and backed President Johnson during his battles with Congress. Fillmore died in 1874. He spent his last years engaged in many civic activities.

Sympathizing with the South: Franklin Pierce

Franklin Pierce, shown in Figure 9-3, is another president considered to be a major failure. He may be thought of as a failure because he was such a contradiction: He was a Northern Democrat who supported slavery and the South throughout his political career.

He not only failed to resolve the slavery issue, but couldn't achieve his political objective of territorial expansion. Added to this, no other president suffered as much in his personal life as Pierce did (see the sidebar "Facing adversity" later in this chapter), which had a great impact on his presidency. Pierce died a lonely man driven into alcoholism by a life of personal tragedy.

Figure 9-3:
Franklin
Pierce, 14th
president of
the United
States.

Courtesy of the Library of Congress

A Northern Democrat with a Southern soul

Throughout his political career, Franklin Pierce believed in the Constitution.
He tried to follow it as closely as possible. He refused to compromise on any
issues he considered unconstitutional. For this reason, he supported slavery.
He considered slavery to be immoral but constitutional. He blocked any
attempts to undermine the institution of slavery in the South.

Pierce's early political career

In Congress, Pierce became a loyal supporter of Andrew Jackson. In addition,
he aligned himself early on with the Southern wing of the Democratic Party,
favoring slavery. In 1835, he fought a petition to end slavery in the capital,
Washington, D.C. In 1836, he struck up a life-long friendship with Jefferson
Davis, the senator from Mississippi. One year later, Pierce won election to the
U.S. Senate. In the Senate, Pierce continued to support Southern causes. His
opponents blasted him, calling him a *doughface* — a term used to describe
Northern congressmen who supported the South. In 1842, he resigned his
Senate seat to spend more time with his family and opened a successful law
practice in Concord, New Hampshire.

When the Mexican-American War broke out in 1846, Pierce became a
brigadier general in the volunteer army and went to Mexico to fight.

After returning home, Pierce acted as an elder statesman, freely handing out
advice. He supported the Compromise of 1850 and territorial expansion. In
1852, Pierce received an unexpected chance at the presidency.

Facing adversity

Franklin Pierce was born in 1804 on his father's farm in New Hampshire. His father was a general during the Revolutionary War and a follower of Jefferson. His father's love of politics became a cornerstone in Pierce's childhood and prepared him for political life.

Pierce went to Bowdoin College in Maine, where he befriended Nathaniel Hawthorne, a writer whose books include *The Scarlet Letter.* The two became best friends. After graduating, Pierce studied law and began practicing in 1827. Pierce also entered politics in 1827 — the same year his father won the governorship in New Hampshire. Pierce became a member of the New Hampshire legislature in 1829, and four years later he won a seat in the U.S. House of Representatives.

In 1834, Pierce married Jane Means Appleton. Their marriage proved to be tragic. She was deeply religious, not very outgoing, and refused to move to Washington, D.C. with Pierce. So he spent most of his congressional career by himself. He gained a reputation as a heavy drinker and a frequent partier.

The Pierces had three children together. One of their children died in infancy and another died of typhus in 1843. Shortly after he won the presidency, Franklin Pierce watched his third son die in a train accident. The accident changed Pierce.

Throughout his administration, Pierce was a loner. He was frequently depressed, and he drank heavily.

President Franklin Pierce (1853–1857)

By 1852, the Democratic Party was split. On one side were the Southern Democrats favoring slavery; on the other side were the Northern Democrats, who opposed the extension of slavery. To no one's surprise, the various factions couldn't agree on a candidate. So Pierce approached some of his political friends and let it be known that he was interested in the nomination. He proved to be the ideal compromise candidate — a Northern Democrat who didn't oppose slavery. On the 49th ballot, Pierce received the nomination. He then went on to easily defeat the Whig candidate.

As president, Pierce set out to placate all factions within the Democratic Party. His cabinet included people who opposed slavery and people who favored slavery. Despite the diversity of opinion in his cabinet, Franklin Pierce has the distinction of being the only U.S. president to keep his cabinet intact. Not one of his cabinet members resigned during his administration.

Trying to expand

President Pierce believed in the concept of Manifest Destiny (see Chapter 8). He tried his best to expand the United States, but he was fairly unsuccessful. His attempts included

✔ **The Gadsden Purchase:** Pierce wanted to buy a chunk of Mexico so that he could build a railroad from New Orleans to San Diego. Pierce offered $20 million to buy all of northern Mexico (most of the existing country). The Mexican government only sold him what today is southern Arizona and southern New Mexico for $15 million.

✔ **The Ostend Manifesto:** Pierce offered Spain $130 million for Cuba. The Southern states wanted Cuba because Spain was considering freeing all slaves on the island. This would have set a dangerous precedent for the U.S. South. If Spain refused to sell, Pierce was going to threaten war. The manifesto upset Northern Democrats, who feared that the South was attempting to spread slavery, and many European powers. Pierce later disclaimed the manifesto.

Addressing slavery with the Kansas-Nebraska Act

In 1854, Senator Douglas, a Northern Democrat, introduced a bill proposing the creation of the Kansas and Nebraska territories to facilitate building a railroad from his home state of Illinois.

The question of whether the new territories should be free or slave states arose right away. President Pierce and most Democrats favored the concept of *popular sovereignty,* which allowed the people in the new states to decide for themselves. But to do this, the Missouri Compromise, which prohibited slavery in the territories, had to be repealed. In 1854, Pierce signed the repeal of the Missouri Compromise into law, and the fat was in the fire.

Nebraska opted to be a free state, but Kansas was split on the issue. When Kansas voted on the issue of slavery, thousands of people from Missouri, a slave state, crossed the border to vote. Slavery won big at the ballot box.

Northerners moved to Kansas to organize an opposition to slavery and establish their own anti-slavery government. Kansas suddenly found itself with two governments. Pierce recognized the pro-slavery government. A small civil war broke out — it was referred to as *Bleeding Kansas* (see the section of the same name later in this chapter).

With the repeal of the Missouri Compromise, Pierce committed political suicide. His own party turned away from him, and he didn't even attempt to run for reelection in 1856, saying, "There's nothing left but to get drunk."

Controversial to the end

Pierce continued to be controversial even after he retired. In 1860, he endorsed Jefferson Davis for the presidency. After Lincoln's win that same year, Pierce became an outspoken critic of Lincoln — especially of the Emancipation Proclamation.

After his wife, Jane, and his best friend, Nathaniel Hawthorne, died in 1863 and 1864, respectively, Pierce found himself all alone. He found solace in the bottle and died a bitter man in 1869.

Failing to Save the Union: James Buchanan

James Buchanan, shown in Figure 9-4, is one of the two lowest-rated presidents in U.S. history. (See Chapter 2 for more information on presidential ratings.) His notable accomplishments before becoming president in 1857 are ignored by many.

Figure 9-4:
James
Buchanan,
15th
president
of the
United
States.

Courtesy of the Library of Congress

James Buchanan loved and lived by the Constitution. He believed that, as president, he could do only what the Constitution explicitly stated. So he tolerated slavery, even though he personally opposed it. When the Southern states started to secede, Buchanan did nothing, waiting for Congress to act. Congress, split over the issue, didn't help Buchanan with the decision — so he didn't act. In turn, he, not Congress, received the blame for not saving the Union.

James Buchanan disliked the institution of slavery so much that he bought slaves in Washington, D.C. and took them back to Pennsylvania to set them free.

A self-made man

James Buchanan was born in 1791 in Pennsylvania. His father was a small town businessman. James went to average schools and proved to be a mediocre student. The college he attended, Dickinson College in Carlisle, Pennsylvania, expelled him for partying too much. He did manage to graduate after promising to change his lifestyle. Buchanan began to study law in 1809. He found his true calling and became a successful, wealthy lawyer in Lancaster, Pennsylvania.

While practicing law, Buchanan fell in love and became engaged to be married. But his fiancée broke their engagement over what Buchanan called a minor disagreement. She committed suicide shortly thereafter. Buchanan never recovered from her suicide. He remained single for the rest of his life. James Buchanan is the only unmarried president in U.S. history.

Buchanan's early career

Buchanan volunteered to fight in the War of 1812, but he didn't see any action. So he returned home and started his long political career. In 1814, he was elected to the Pennsylvania state legislature. From there, he slowly worked his way up the political ladder.

For the next half century, Buchanan served his country in many roles. Buchanan's political jobs included

- ✔ **U.S. congressman:** Buchanan started his national career in 1821 when he entered the House of Representatives as a Federalist. When the party fell apart, he became a supporter of Andrew Jackson and joined the Democrats.

- ✔ **Ambassador to Russia:** Buchanan became ambassador to Russia in 1832 and established commercial ties with the country.

- ✔ **U.S. senator:** Buchanan entered the U.S. Senate in 1834 and served 12 years.

- ✔ **Secretary of state:** In 1845, President Polk appointed Buchanan secretary of state. Buchanan proved to be a capable leader in this role, settling the Oregon Territory dispute with Great Britain (see Chapter 8). On the other hand, he failed to buy Cuba from Spain.

- ✔ **Ambassador to Great Britain:** Buchanan retired after he failed to receive the 1852 presidential nomination from the Democratic Party. But President Pierce called him out of retirement and sent him to Europe in 1853. In Europe, Buchanan participated in the disastrous Ostend Manifesto (see "Sympathizing with the South: Franklin Pierce" earlier in this chapter).

President James Buchanan (1857–1861)

In 1856, the Democratic Party was split again over the issue of slavery. The Democrats couldn't agree on a candidate for the presidency, so they started to look for a compromise candidate. They needed someone acceptable to the pro-slavery Southern wing of the party, as well as the anti-slavery Northern wing. Buchanan was a perfect fit. He was a Northerner who personally opposed slavery but believed that the institution of slavery was constitutional.

In the 1856 election, Buchanan faced a new political party. The Republican Party, which was opposed to slavery, ran a candidate for the first time in its short history. In addition, former president Fillmore ran as a third party candidate on the extreme right. Buchanan won the election easily, with the backing of all the Southern states.

Starting out with a bang

James Buchanan became president in March 1857. The infamous Dred Scott decision undermined his presidency right away.

Two days after Buchanan's inauguration, the U.S. Supreme Court handed down the Dred Scott decision (see the sidebar in this section), wherein the Court ruled that slaves were property, not people. The ruling drove the country closer to civil war.

Bleeding Kansas

Under the provisions of the Kansas-Nebraska Act, Kansas could decide for itself whether to become a slave state. (See the earlier section, "Addressing slavery with the Kansas-Nebraska Act.") By 1857, Kansas had two governments. The government in favor of slavery created the "Lecompton Constitution," allowing slavery in the state. The anti-slavery government, headquartered in Topeka, refused to recognize the new state constitution. When Kansas applied for statehood in 1857, Buchanan accepted the pro-slavery constitution, even though it failed in a statewide popular referendum. The state of Kansas held a new referendum, and slavery failed again. Congress decided not to admit Kansas, and Buchanan took blame from both sides.

President Buchanan had stated early on that he wanted to serve only one term. When the 1860 elections came around, the question of his succession split the Democratic Party. When the Northern Democrats nominated Stephen Douglas, who opposed slavery, for president, the Southern Democrats walked out. The Southern Democrats nominated their own candidate, Vice President John Breckinridge, for the presidency. Because two Democratic candidates ran for the presidency, splitting the Democratic vote, the Republican nominee, Abraham Lincoln, was elected president.

The Dred Scott decision

Dred Scott was a slave who had been taken by his owner from a slave state, Missouri, to a free state, Illinois, and then back to Missouri. Scott refused to go back to being a slave, arguing that, because he had been in a free state, he was a U.S. citizen and not a slave. The Missouri State Supreme Court agreed with Scott, so his owner took the case to the U.S. Supreme Court. In 1857, Chief Justice of the Supreme Court Roger Taney, a Southerner, wrote, "slaves are property and not people."

Taney's ruling stated that slaves were not citizens and had no political rights. The ruling also held that because slaves were property, they had to be returned to their rightful owners, even if they fled to states where slavery was illegal. Taney said that outlawing slavery was illegal, which opened the door to slavery in the new states.

The South, of course, applauded the decision, while the Northern states chose to ignore it. The decision solidified Northern support against slavery. Many Northern Democrats left their own party and joined the anti-slavery Republicans.

Sitting by through secession

After Lincoln won the presidency in 1860, Buchanan just sat out the end of his term. South Carolina and other Southern states had proclaimed that a Lincoln win would lead to secession. When the states started to secede, Buchanan stood by, believing that he didn't have the constitutional authority to prevent a state from seceding. He tried desperately to find a solution, but his compromises all failed. So he let them go.

Buchanan left the office of president on March 4, 1861, telling Lincoln, "My dear sir, if you are as happy in entering the White House as I shall feel in returning to Wheatland, you are a happy man indeed."

Throughout the Civil War, Buchanan supported the Union and defended both Presidents Lincoln and Johnson. Buchanan died at home in 1868. Shortly before his death, he published a book, *Mr. Buchanan's Administration on the Eve of the Rebellion,* in which he defended his policies.

Part IV
Becoming a Force in the World: Lincoln to Hoover

The 5th Wave   By Rich Tennant

©RICHTENNANT

"Mr. President, the Confederate Army is massing in Virginia, several more of our officers have defected to the South, oh, and bad news — Mrs. Lincoln's redesigned tea setting won't be here until Friday."

In this part . . .

1 look first at the greatest of all our presidents, Abraham Lincoln, and his valiant attempts to save the union and to end slavery in the United States.

His successors all set the foundation for the country to become an economic and military power. Some were successful, such as presidents Arthur, Cleveland, and Harrison; others failed. The failures include our first president to be impeached, Andrew Johnson, and Ulysses S. Grant, a great war hero. Both their presidencies were smeared by corruption and scandals. And, you may be surprised to discover how a candidate, Rutherford B. Hayes, lost the presidential election and still became president of the U.S.

Next, I turn to the presidents who turned the U.S. into a world power. There was William McKinley, an imperialist, who enlarged the U.S. by annexing Hawaii and winning the Spanish American War. Who can forget about Teddy Roosevelt? He not only gave us the Panama Canal and was the first American to win the Nobel Peace Prize, but he also established the tradition of protecting the average American from the excesses of big business. Woodrow Wilson is famous for saving democracy in Europe by entering World War I and reforming the country back home. He is the president who gave women the right to vote in 1920. Finally he set the foundation for the United Nations by giving us its predecessor the League of Nations.

It's a shame that I have to close this part by looking at the three presidents of the 1920s. One, Warren G. Harding, was immoral; one, Calvin Coolidge, preferred sleeping to work; and the final one, Herbert Hoover, even though a great human being and humanitarian, reacted too little too late to the Great Depression.

Chapter 10

Preserving the Union: Abraham Lincoln

Abraham Lincoln ranks first in most surveys of great U.S. presidents. It doesn't make a difference whether you ask a professor or the average U.S. citizen. Both rank Lincoln as the most successful of all U.S. presidents.

Does Lincoln deserve this honor? Certainly. Besides saving the Union, Lincoln created the modern presidency by absorbing many of the powers Congress used to possess.

Abraham Lincoln was a kind, gentle man and a true humanitarian. Had he lived to finish serving as executive officer, the process of reintegrating the Southern states into the Union might have worked better. On the other hand, one of the great misconceptions in U.S. history is that Lincoln wanted to abolish slavery. It is true that he hated the institution and considered it immoral, but at the same time, he believed that slavery was constitutional, and he pledged to maintain it in the Southern states. All he really wanted to do was to prevent the expansion of slavery into new territories.

Lincoln's Early Political Career

Lincoln ran for the Illinois state legislature in 1832. The general store he'd been working in went out of business about a month after he declared his candidacy, so he joined the military. The Black Hawk War broke out in 1832 and Lincoln became captain of a company of militiamen, though he never saw any action.

Born in a log cabin

Abraham Lincoln was born on February 12, 1809, in Kentucky. His father, Thomas, was a carpenter by trade who provided well for the family. His mother Nancy was completely illiterate. She signed her marriage certificate with an X.

Instead of going to school, Lincoln hunted and worked on his father's farm. In 1816, the family moved to Indiana. They arrived in winter and didn't have enough time to build a log cabin. So Abraham's father built an open shelter, which kept the family sheltered through the winter.

In 1818, tragedy struck when Lincoln's mother died. The following year, his father remarried a kind, gentle woman who took an interest in Lincoln and pushed him to attend the local schools. Lincoln received a crude education, but he did learn how to read and write.

After school, Lincoln became skilled at *splitting rails* — using an ax to divide logs to make fence rails — people even referred to him as the "Rail-splitter" during his presidential campaigns.

In 1830, the Lincoln family moved to Illinois where Lincoln helped his father build a livelihood and received his first introduction to politics. The manager of a local general store in New Salem, Illinois hired Lincoln for a full-time clerk position. The general store happened to be the meeting point for New Salem's citizens. The citizens discussed many issues, including politics, and Lincoln joined in on the discussions. He further added to his interest in politics by reading newspapers and books, and joining a debating society.

He returned home just two weeks before the election took place. With just a few days to campaign, Lincoln lost the election badly, which didn't surprise him. As a Whig, he figured he would have a tough time winning because the country was moving to the Democratic Party. Despite this, Lincoln had decided to run as a Whig and supported the National Republican candidate Henry Clay in 1832, who lost badly to Andrew Jackson.

After the election, Lincoln opened his own general store in New Salem. Lincoln got a break after his store went out of business. Because he was popular and well liked, he was given the job of postmaster for New Salem. The job gave him time to read. Lincoln continued his education by reading about law, politics, and the world.

Most importantly, the job of postmaster gave him the name recognition he needed to run for political office again. When he ran for the Illinois state legislature in 1834, he won — and he kept winning. He was reelected in 1836, 1838, and 1840. Soon, he was leader of the Whigs in the Illinois state legislature.

Getting ready for the national level

Abraham Lincoln used his seat in the Illinois state legislature as a springboard to national-level politics. In 1836, he spearheaded the successful effort to move the state capital of Illinois from Vandalia to Springfield.

To accomplish this feat, Lincoln employed a strategy called *logrolling,* whereby he and his colleagues who favored moving the capital voted for bills other legislators supported, and in return, those legislators voted for Lincoln's bill.

Lincoln was a Whig in the truest sense. As a legislator, he supported business interests and constructing roads and bridges in Illinois.

Lincoln improved his debating skills and his political skills while serving as a legislator. His terms as a state legislator showed his skills in compromising and illuminated his stand on slavery: While he condemned the institution of slavery, he attacked the abolitionist, anti-slavery movement as extreme and dangerous to the country.

Studying law on the side

As was common at the time, the Illinois state legislature met for just one session per year — not year-round. Lincoln used his spare time to study law. He received his license to practice in 1837. That same year, he joined the John T. Stuart law firm in Springfield, Illinois and became a successful lawyer. In 1844, he became a founding partner in the firm Logan and Lincoln. He enjoyed the law but longed for politics. By 1844, he was ready to reenter the political scene.

A Star Is Born

In 1843, Lincoln sought the nomination of the Whig party for the seventh Congressional district — one of the few safe Whig seats in Illinois. He lost. Undeterred, he tried again in 1846. This time he received the nomination and won the election. Lincoln was now a member of the U.S. House of Representatives.

Annoying everyone

In November 1846, Abraham Lincoln was elected to the U.S. House of Representatives. To his great disappointment, he didn't become one of the leaders of the body. Instead, he was one of many *freshmen* — newly elected members of Congress — and he held no important offices.

Then the war against Mexico started. Lincoln, like many Whigs, considered the war unjust and believed that Polk just wanted to spread slavery, so he opposed the war. In 1847, he blasted Polk on the floor of the House and accused him of inciting the war. He was correct in saying so, but nobody wanted to hear it at the time. Lincoln's many resolutions condemning the unjust and illegal war fell on deaf ears and annoyed his constituency.

A tragic marriage

In 1839, Lincoln met Mary Todd, a bright young socialite from Kentucky visiting New Salem. Lincoln fell in love and proposed to her in 1840. After they became engaged, Lincoln started having second thoughts, and he broke off the engagement. He regretted his decision. A year later, he started pursuing Mary again, and they married in 1842.

Tragedy struck the couple's four children — only one lived into adulthood. After losing one of his children before the age of 4, Lincoln became an overprotective father. When his second son, Willie, died in 1862 of typhoid fever,

Lincoln suffered from severe depression. His wife took the loss even worse. She went into a state of shock, claiming that she talked to the young boy at night.

Mary Todd Lincoln also became extremely jealous. She embarrassed Lincoln, who was now president, on many occasions. In addition, she spent most of the couple's money refashioning the White House and buying expensive clothing for herself. In one fit of extravagance, she bought 300 pairs of gloves. After Lincoln's death, her only surviving child, Robert, committed her to an insane asylum for a short period of time.

Lincoln actually wasn't worried much about his constituency, because according to Whig tradition, he could only serve one term. Therefore, he was able to vote his conscience.

Lincoln's resolutions condemning Polk and the Mexican-American War were called *Spot Resolutions,* because Lincoln alleged that the spot where Mexican troops attacked U.S. troops was actually on Mexican territory. This allegation would have justified the attack. His constituents gave him the nickname "Spotty Lincoln."

Voting his conscience on slavery

Lincoln continued to vote his conscience on other issues, including slavery. He supported the Wilmot Proviso, which outlawed slavery in any territory gained in the Mexican-American War (see Chapter 8.) He introduced a bill to outlaw slavery in the capital, Washington, D.C. (The bill never made it to the floor of the House, and for that reason, it wasn't voted on by Congress). He further recommended a referendum on the issue by the voters of Washington, D.C., and the full compensation of slave owners who lost their slaves if the referendum passed. Despite his anti-slavery views, Lincoln believed that neither Congress nor the president had the power to abolish slavery in the Southern states, because slavery was a state matter.

Lincoln on slavery:

> "If slavery is not wrong, nothing is wrong."

> "Whenever I hear anyone arguing for slavery, I feel a strong impulse to see it tried on him personally."

Lincoln abided by the Whig rules — he didn't run for reelection, although he wanted to serve a second term. He hoped for a nice cushy job from the new Whig President Zachary Taylor, but he only received an offer for the governorship of the Oregon Territory. Lincoln rejected the offer and returned home. Within a few years, he built his law practice into the largest and most prosperous in Illinois and became known statewide.

Debating his way to national prominence

By the early 1850s, Lincoln had lost interest in politics and resigned himself to being a lawyer. When the Kansas-Nebraska Act overturned the Missouri Compromise of 1820 (see Chapter 9), Lincoln's interest in politics was rekindled.

Lincoln opposed the Kansas-Nebraska Act vehemently, believing it would lead to extending slavery into many new states. In 1854, Lincoln participated in a debate with Stephen Douglas, the sponsor of the Kansas-Nebraska Act. Lincoln attacked Douglas for exporting slavery and criticized slavery as immoral.

By 1856, the Whigs had collapsed, so Lincoln joined the Republican Party. He soon became a leader in the new party that shared his anti-slavery views. His reputation was such that he was considered as a vice-presidential candidate for the Republican Party in 1856, but he lost out.

Lincoln ran for the U.S. Senate in 1858 against none other than Stephen Douglas, his debating opponent. The campaign became an instant classic. Lincoln challenged Douglas to seven debates, which attracted many voters (more than 15,000 people attended one debate) and national newspaper coverage. By election time, Lincoln was a household name not just in Illinois but throughout the United States. For the complete texts of the debates, please see *The Complete Lincoln-Douglas Debates of 1858,* edited by Paul M. Angle (University of Chicago Press).

In his acceptance speech as the Republican nominee for the U.S. Senate, Lincoln gave the following classic quotes: "A house divided against itself cannot stand." and "I believe this government cannot endure permanently half slave, half free. I do not expect the union to be dissolved — I do not expect the house to fall — but I do expect it will cease to be divided. It will become all one thing, or all the other."

Lincoln lost the Senate race to Douglas, even though Lincoln received more popular support. At the time, the state legislature picked the U.S. Senator — and the Democratically controlled Illinois legislature chose Douglas.

President Abraham Lincoln (1861–1865)

The election of 1860 proved to be unique in U.S. history. Four separate candidates ran for the presidency, and all won Electoral College votes. The Democratic Party split over the issue of slavery (see Chapter 9) and ran two candidates — the Northern Democrats nominated Lincoln's old nemesis Stephen Douglas, while the Southern Democrats ran Vice-President John Breckinridge. The old Whigs, renamed "Constitutional Unionists," nominated John Bell, who called for preserving the Union. Finally, the new Republican Party ran Abraham Lincoln on a moderate anti-slavery platform. The platform was enough for the South to proclaim that it wouldn't accept a Lincoln victory.

Lincoln, shown in Figure 10-1, won 180 Electoral College votes, but received only 40 percent of the popular vote. He won over 50 percent of the vote in the North and West, but received a measly 3 percent in the South. Breckinridge came in second, winning all of the Southern states, with 72 Electoral College votes. Bell and Douglas finished third and fourth, respectively.

Figure 10-1: Abraham Lincoln, 16th president of the United States.

Courtesy of the Library of Congress

Forming the Confederacy

On February 4, 1861, the seceding Southern states met in Alabama to set up a new union. The new union — the Confederate states of America — elected Jefferson Davis, the U.S. Senator from Mississippi, as its new president. The Confederacy further set up a new constitution based on the Constitution of the United States. The main difference was that the Confederate constitution emphasized the right to own slaves and stressed states' rights. The new union was closer to a *confederation,* where the states have political power, than it was to a *federation,* where the states share political power with a national government. "Dixie Land," or "Dixie" as it was called, became the unofficial anthem of the Confederacy.

When the Civil War broke out, the South faced many distinct disadvantages:

✔ The South had a population that was only a fraction of the North's — 9 million people, including 3.5 million slaves, to the North's 22 million people.

✔ The North had industries and was about to become more industrial, while the South was agricultural in nature. Because of its industrial nature, the North could supply its armies better than the South.

✔ The North, with its constant influx of immigrants, had an unlimited amount of soldiers at its disposal. At one point, new immigrants were coming off boats and going straight into the military. The South only had its native population available.

✔ The North controlled the navy and slowly strangled the South with its economic embargo.

With European powers staying neutral in the conflict, the Confederacy was all alone and vastly inferior to the Union. The only way the Confederacy could win was by immediately overpowering the North — a quick victory was the only victory possible. When an immediate victory didn't happen, it was all over for the South.

Abraham Lincoln grew a beard for the 1860 campaign at the request of a little girl by the name of Grace Bedell. She wrote him a letter telling him that all the ladies like whiskers and that they would tease their husbands to vote for Lincoln. So Lincoln became the first president to have a beard.

Dealing with secession

As threatened, Southern states started to secede as soon as Lincoln's victory became clear. On December 20, 1860, only a month after Lincoln won the election, South Carolina seceded from the Union. Other states soon followed. By the time Lincoln took office in March 1861, the following states had seceded:

Alabama	Florida
Georgia	Louisiana
Mississippi	South Carolina
Texas	

President Buchanan's inaction in the face of secession left Lincoln with a mess. By the time Lincoln assumed power, the Confederacy was in place and more Southern states were ready to secede.

Confronting the Confederacy

Lincoln assumed the presidency of the United States on March 4, 1861. His first order of business was to deal with the new Confederacy. He wanted to reassure the Southern states that there was no reason to secede, and he used his first inaugural address to do so.

In his inaugural address, Lincoln proclaimed that he believed that he had no right and no intention to interfere with slavery in the Southern states. In other words, Lincoln told the South that it could keep slavery — all he wanted was to prevent the institution of slavery from spreading to other states. At the same time, he took a strong stance on secession. He told the Confederacy that states didn't have the right to secede from the Union and that he would do everything in his power to keep the Union intact. He further warned the South that the federal government wouldn't allow the states to seize federal property — the federal government would hold it at all costs.

The Civil War

One of the headaches Lincoln inherited from his predecessor, Buchanan, was Fort Sumter, located outside of Charleston, South Carolina. Because it was a federal fort, Lincoln refused to evacuate it and hand it over to the Confederacy. Instead, he tried to reinforce it by sending additional supplies. The Confederacy, claiming the fort, subsequently attacked it and forced it to surrender. Now Lincoln had to act. He called up 75,000 militiamen from the loyal states to subdue the insurrection. While the North supported the president, the rest of the Southern states decided to join the Confederacy. Arkansas, North Carolina, Tennessee, and Virginia left the Union and joined the Confederacy.

The Civil War was about to start. Lincoln's greatest fear was that the states bordering the South would also join the Confederacy. But to his great relief, Missouri, Kentucky, and Maryland stayed in the Union.

The Civil War presented Lincoln with an unprecedented opportunity to expand the powers of the president. Lincoln felt compelled to take charge, even though he was opposed to the idea that the president, not Congress, should do so. Without a declaration of war by Congress, many felt that Lincoln couldn't do much. Because Congress was not in session, Lincoln acted on his own. So, for his first three months in office, the president ran the country by himself. Some of his unilateral actions included

✔ **Setting up blockades at all Southern ports:** Lincoln knew that the South was very dependent on imported materials and needed to export its major good — cotton — so he tried to strangle the Southern states economically.

Blockading a foreign country is considered an act of war, and only Congress has the power to do this. Lincoln chose to act unilaterally.

✔ **Increasing the size of the Union forces by more than 42,000 men:** Only Congress has the power to fund additional troops. Lincoln decided to increase the Northern army anyway.

✔ **Suspending the *habeas corpus:* *Habeas corpus* refers to the protection from illegal detainment that individuals receive from the federal government. Its suspension allowed the government to imprison people opposed to the war effort. Thousands of U.S. citizens were imprisoned because of their opposition to the war.

Lincoln justified his actions with the idea of *presidential prerogative,* meaning that, in emergencies, the executive can assume additional powers for the good of the country.

The Democrats and the Supreme Court criticized Lincoln for assuming dictatorial powers in 1861. However, by 1863, both Congress and the Supreme Court had a change of heart. They sanctioned Lincoln's actions because he had to meet the challenges caused by the Civil War.

Lincoln breathed a sigh of relief when major European powers, such as Great Britain and France, declared their neutrality in the conflict. He knew that had a European power backed the South, it would have changed everything. Ironically, Britain was closer to the South, but felt that it could not morally support a slave society.

It comes as no surprise that fighting a war can be expensive. So where did the money come from to fight the Civil War? Lincoln increased taxes to pay for most of the war. He raised income taxes and taxes on inheritances. In addition, for the first time the federal government printed money that could not be exchanged for gold.

Civil War battles

The first major battle of the Civil War occurred in July 1861. In the battle of Bull Run, the Confederate forces soundly defeated the Union troops. President Lincoln and many in the North were surprised and shocked. They had expected a quick victory. Lincoln demanded more and swifter action, and he got his wish in April 1862. In the battle of Shiloh, which was the bloodiest battle to this point, the Union suffered 13,000 casualties, while the Confederate forces lost 11,000 soldiers. By September 1862, Confederate forces, headed by General Lee, prepared for the invasion of Maryland with the ultimate goal of reaching and capturing Washington, D.C.

The Confederate armies attacked Maryland on September 17, 1862. Union forces managed to fight the South to a draw in the battle at Antietam Creek. The battle put an end to the Southern invasion of the North.

In July 1863, the turning point of the U.S. Civil War occurred with the Battle of Gettysburg. The Southern army was defeated decisively, suffering 28,000 casualties. The battle was the last major offensive the South mounted during the Civil War.

After their success at Gettysburg, the Northern armies began to move southward into Tennessee and Georgia. By the fall of 1864, Northern armies were able to occupy Atlanta. After a series of battles in Virginia (the Wilderness campaign) in late 1864, General Lee surrendered to General Grant at Appomattox, Virginia, in April 1865. The Civil War was over.

Issuing the Emancipation Proclamation

In April 1862, Lincoln signed a bill abolishing slavery in the capital of Washington, D.C., where slavery was still legal. To appease slaveholders in the capital, he offered them monetary compensation for the loss of their slaves. Because Washington D.C. was controlled by the federal government, Lincoln believed that he had the right to abolish slavery in the capital. But he decided he couldn't abolish slavery in loyal slave states, such as Missouri, because he considered slavery a state matter.

In July 1862, Lincoln presented a preliminary version of the Emancipation Proclamation to his cabinet. After receiving cabinet input, Lincoln revised the proclamation slightly and released it to Northern newspapers for publication in September 1862 — after the successful battle at Antietam, Maryland. Lincoln then issued a final version of the proclamation on January 1, 1863, and it subsequently went into effect.

In the Emancipation Proclamation, Lincoln presented an ultimatum to any state that joined the Confederacy. He referred to the Confederacy as the "rebellious states" and gave them 100 days to rejoin the Union. If they did rejoin the Union, slavery was to remain intact and protected in the eleven Southern states that made up the Confederacy. If the Confederate states failed to return to the Union, Lincoln was going to pass a declaration to end slavery in all rebellious states. He stated that he would then proclaim all slaves in the Confederacy free.

The Emancipation Proclamation did not free slaves in the slave states that remained loyal to the Union. Not until the Thirteenth Amendment to the Constitution was passed in 1865 (after Lincoln's death) were slaves freed and slavery abolished in all of the United States. In Kentucky, Maryland, Missouri, the parts of Virginia that would become West Virginia, and portions of Louisiana, slavery continued to exist. Instead of freeing the slaves in these areas outright, which would drive the states into Confederate hands, Lincoln encouraged a voluntary end to slavery by offering monetary compensation to slave owners.

Lincoln believed that he had constitutional power only to issue a military decree to free the slaves in the rebellious Southern states. The only way to end slavery in the other parts of the United States was to pass a constitutional amendment, which he urged Congress and the states to do.

Motivating the Confederacy

The Emancipation Proclamation didn't have the hoped-for effect on the Confederate states. Instead of laying their arms down, the Confederacy strengthened its resolve. Now every Confederate state knew that if they lost the war, slavery would come to an end, and their way of life would change forever. The Confederacy was ready to fight to the end.

On the bright side, the four loyal slave-owning states felt reassured that the institution of slavery would continue in their states, so they remained loyal for the rest of the Civil War. In addition, the radical wing of the Republican Party, which pushed for the abolition of slavery, applauded the proclamation and started to fall in line behind Lincoln and his policies for a short period of time.

The most important effect of the Emancipation Proclamation occurred not in the United States, but in Europe. For quite some time, the Confederacy courted Great Britain and France, hoping to gain their support for the Southern cause. With the Emancipation Proclamation, Lincoln preempted any support from the European countries, which were opposed to slavery.

After Lincoln decided that a war was necessary to preserve the Union, a group of radical Republicans known as *Jacobins* — named after a group of French revolutionaries — believed that Lincoln wasn't aggressive enough in dealing with the South.

The Jacobins wanted quicker military action. They also wanted the slaves to be freed immediately. By 1863, the Jacobins were calling for the punishment of the South and its leaders. In July 1864, the Jacobins managed to push a bill

Lincoln and his generals

The major problem the Union armies faced in the beginning was a lack of skilled leaders. Most officers, such as Robert E. Lee, sided with the South, leaving the Union troops poorly led.

When the Civil War broke out, Lincoln put General Winfield Scott in charge of the Northern armies. Scott, a veteran of the War of 1812 and the Mexican-American War, was by now not only old, but also so fat that he couldn't ride on a horse anymore. After initial defeats, Lincoln decided that he needed to change his military leaders. He sacked General Winfield Scott in November 1861 and put General George McClellan in charge. McClellan spent most of his time restoring the army's morale and creating a well-trained fighting force. McClellan's

work took time and Lincoln grew impatient. The following comment from Lincoln sheds some light on how he felt about McClellan: "My dear McClellan: if you don't want to use the army I should like to borrow it for a while." By March 1862, Lincoln was fed up with McClellan. Lincoln hated McClellan's inactivity and wanted to see more rapid action against the Confederate forces. So he replaced McClellan.

It wasn't until 1864 that Lincoln was happy with one of his choices. He finally settled on General Ulysses S. Grant to head the Northern forces. Lincoln said the following about Grant: "I wish some of you would tell the brand of whiskey that Grant drinks. I would like to send a barrel of it to my other generals."

through Congress that limited the right to vote on new state constitutions in the post-war South to those who had not supported the Confederacy, effectively disenfranchising most Southerners. The bill also permanently barred every major Confederate leader from voting. Lincoln opposed the bill and vetoed it. Incensed, the Jacobins withdrew their support for their own president.

Drafting soldiers: North and South

In 1863, the North instituted a draft as a direct response to the Confederacy's establishment of a draft. All men between the ages of 20 and 45 had to serve in the military.

However, anyone who could find a substitute or pay the government $300 didn't have to serve in the military under the terms of the Conscription Act. Many citizens saw the policy as being a way for rich people to get out of serving their country. Riots in New York City were quelled by federal troops.

It was mostly volunteers who fought the Civil War. Only 6 percent of the Union forces were draftees. The numbers for the Confederacy were a bit higher — about 20 percent of the military came from draftees.

Beginning in 1863, blacks were allowed to join the Union army — although they received only one-third of the pay of a white volunteer and had to serve under white officers. The all-black regiments fought well and bravely even though they suffered higher casualty rates than their white counterparts.

Addressing the crowds at Gettysburg

On November 19, 1863, President Lincoln delivered the most memorable speech of his career — the Gettysburg Address. Lincoln gave the address four months after the decisive battle at Gettysburg, which turned the war to the North's favor.

Lincoln spoke at a ceremony for the dedication of a cemetery to 6,000 Northern soldiers who died in the Battle of Gettysburg. (The soldiers were buried so hastily and in such shallow graves after the battle that their bodies became exposed again by the fall of 1863.) Senator Edward Everett, one of the great orators of his time, was scheduled to give the actual address, and Lincoln was invited at the last minute to say a few words. Senator Everett spoke for two hours to a crowd of 15,000 people, and then it was Lincoln's turn. Lincoln spoke for only two minutes, but his words went down in history.

In the address, Lincoln stressed the ideas of liberty and equality. He tried to provide a justification for why slavery was illegal. Because the Constitution didn't mention slavery, he relied upon the Declaration of Independence. The Declaration of Independence stated that all men were created equal. If this is true, then how could anyone justify slavery? He further proclaimed that only a Northern victory could assure the continuation of democracy and guarantee equality in the United States. The great sacrifices of the men to be buried were not in vain because their sacrifices guaranteed the future of democracy and equality in the United States.

One of the great mysteries in U.S. presidential lore is whether Lincoln really wrote the Gettysburg address on the back of an envelope on the way to Gettysburg. Although the validity of this tale is still uncertain, we do know today that there were five copies of the address. Lincoln wrote three copies for charitable purposes after the original address was delivered. One of the other two copies may be the original address, but many believe that the original has been lost.

Today the Gettysburg Address is widely considered to be one of the finest speeches ever given. This was not the case back in 1863. People forgot the speech rather quickly. It didn't even receive prominent newspaper coverage. Everett's speech, on the other hand, was widely acclaimed by the media. One of the few people who noticed the genius in Lincoln's speech was Everett himself. The day after Lincoln gave the speech, Everett told him, "I wish that I could flatter myself that I had come as near to the central idea of the occasion in two hours as you did in two minutes."

Lincoln's Short Second Term

Lincoln was not a shoo-in to win reelection in 1864. First, the radical wing of the Republican Party, the Jacobins, was unhappy with what it considered Lincoln's lenient policies toward the South. They especially opposed his ideas on Reconstruction. When Lincoln was up for renomination at the Republican convention, the Jacobins split from the Republican Party and nominated their own candidate, John C. Fremont. Now the Republican Party was split, undermining Lincoln's chances against the Democrats.

The Democratic Party, which consisted of the Northern Democrats, decided to run on a platform that called for an immediate end to the Civil War. Their choice for president was war hero and Lincoln nemesis, General George B. McClellan. Interestingly, McClellan favored the continuation of the war but disagreed with Lincoln on how the war should be conducted. The Democrats believed that McClellan was the only man capable of defeating Lincoln, so they nominated him even though he disagreed with the party on the major issues of the day.

In the early fall of 1864, it looked like Lincoln might lose the election. His party was split, and his Democratic opponent was well known and well respected.

Lincoln's luck changed when General Sherman conquered Atlanta. The victory provided a major boost for Lincoln. It was the Northern victories in the Civil War and a possible end to the conflict that got Lincoln reelected — no one wanted to vote against the possible victor.

Just to ensure that the Democrats wouldn't win, the Republican Party leaders put heavy pressure on the Jacobins and their candidate, John C. Fremont. Fremont was forced to withdraw from the race in September 1864.

With his party united again and a Northern victory looking certain, Lincoln cruised to reelection. In November 1864, Lincoln beat McClellan easily, winning 212 electoral votes to McClellan's 21. Now it was time to focus on ending the war and beginning the process of Reconstruction.

Offering terms of surrender

Abraham Lincoln started the process of Reconstruction before the Civil War was over. As early as late 1863, he outlined his ideas on reintegrating the South into the Union.

On December 8, 1863, Lincoln issued the Proclamation for Amnesty and Reconstruction, which offered full pardons and amnesty to every Southerner, with the exception of major Confederate leaders. All the Confederate states had to do was to take an oath of loyalty to the Union. They would then receive the right to vote and the right to run their own state governments. However, they were bound by the Emancipation Proclamation and had to outlaw slavery in their states. The Confederacy rejected Lincoln's terms.

Lincoln was disappointed with the South, but he continued to believe in generous terms of surrender. He knew that, in order to preserve the Union, he couldn't punish the South too strongly.

In his second inaugural address, delivered in March 1865, Lincoln outlined his ideas on Reconstruction. He advocated overcoming sectional differences, which, when dealing with the Confederacy, was only possible with generosity. He closed his address with some of the most eloquent remarks ever spoken: "With malice towards none, with charity for all, with firmness in the right as God gives us to see the right let us strive to finish the work we are in, to bind up the nation's wounds, to care for him who shall have borne the battle and for his widow and his orphan, to do all which may achieve and cherish a just and lasting peace among ourselves and with all nations." For Lincoln, it was more important to reestablish the Union than to punish the South for seceding.

Lincoln's conciliatory tone was further reflected in an address that he gave after General Lee surrendered to the Union in April 1865. Again, Lincoln reiterated his view that a national healing must come first, and that the South should be treated leniently. Lincoln, however, would not live to put his policies into place.

Serving briefly

President Lincoln had premonitions about his death. In dreams, he saw himself as a corpse and heard people say, "Lincoln is dead." On April 14, 1865, Lincoln and his wife attended a play, *Our American Cousin,* at Ford's Theatre in Washington, D.C. A pro-Southern actor, John Wilkes Booth, shot Lincoln in the head. Lincoln died the following morning. Secretary of War Stanton put it best: "Now he belongs to the ages."

Chapter 11

Reconstructing the Country: Johnson, Grant, and Hayes

• •

In This Chapter

▶ Facing the first impeachment proceedings: Johnson

▶ Gaining fame for military exploits and corruption: Grant

▶ Stealing an election and fighting corruption: Hayes

• •

*T*he first president I cover in this chapter — Andrew Johnson — was a stubborn, uncompromising president, who constantly fought with Congress. This led to his impeachment by the House of Representatives, giving him the distinction of becoming the first U.S. president to be impeached.

Next, I consider a true American hero, General Ulysses Grant. He was a great military leader, but he was a mediocre president whose administration was dominated by corruption and scandals.

Finally, Rutherford Hayes was an honest man who became president when the Republicans stole the election from the Democrats in 1876. This put a dark shadow on his presidency from the beginning. Despite this, he turned out to be a fairly capable president.

From Poverty to the Presidency: Andrew Johnson

Andrew Johnson, shown in Figure 11-1, holds the dubious distinction of being the first president impeached by the House of Representatives. He is also considered one of the least successful presidents in the history of the United States. While escaping impeachment by one vote in the Senate, Johnson, an ardent advocate of states rights and a blatant racist, managed to single-handedly prolong the plight of ex-slaves in the American South.

Courtesy of the Library of Congress

Getting into politics: Johnson's early career

Johnson entered politics in 1829. Running on a working-class platform, championing poor whites, he won the office of alderman in Greenville, Tennessee in 1829 and became the city's mayor five years later. By this point, Johnson was a committed Democrat and a great admirer of Andrew Jackson. Only one year after his successful mayoral race, Johnson was elected to the Tennessee state legislature in 1835.

In 1843, he became one of the Democratic congressmen from Tennessee, a position he would hold until 1853, when he was elected to the governorship of Tennessee. Finally, in 1857, the state legislature elected him to be one of the senators for the state. Johnson proudly proclaimed, "I have reached the summit of my ambition."

As a member of Congress, Johnson was an advocate for poor whites, having been one himself. He owned five slaves and held a staunch pro-slavery view. Despite these views, he continued to be an ardent supporter of the Union, aggressively campaigning to keep the Union intact. When the Southern states seceded from the Union in 1861, Johnson was the only Southern senator to stay in Washington, D.C.; he didn't recognize the legitimacy of the Confederacy.

Johnson's courageous act turned him into a symbol for Southerners loyal to the Union. President Lincoln rewarded him by appointing him the military governor of Tennessee.

Poorer than poor

Andrew Johnson's background foreshadowed a presidency filled with controversy. The poorest and least educated president in U.S. history was born into dire poverty on December 29, 1808. His father, who died when Johnson was only three, was a landless laborer in Raleigh, North Carolina; his mother was a seamstress. Because his family was too poor to send him to school, Johnson had to learn a trade at the tender age of 10.

While working as an apprentice to a tailor, Johnson listened to political debates and taught himself how to read and write. In 1827, he opened his own tailor shop in Greenville, Tennessee. With lots of hard work, he turned his business into a success. However, his background would always have an impact on his life, giving him a hatred for the slave-owning elites in the South and contempt for the slaves themselves. Johnson became a champion of the white lower class.

Acting on his prejudices

Johnson used his position to act upon his deep-seated hatred for white plantation owners, who dominated Tennessee politics. He replaced public officials, arrested opponents, shut down newspapers that were critical of him, and confiscated the bank of Tennessee.

In 1864, Lincoln and the Republican Party rewarded Johnson's loyalty to the Union by picking him to be Lincoln's vice-presidential candidate. Johnson appealed to Democrats in the North, and Lincoln and the Republicans believed that Johnson could establish the Republican Party in the South after the Civil War. Suddenly, Johnson, a life-long Democrat who despised the Republican Party, found himself on the Republican ticket.

President Andrew Johnson (1865–1869)

President Lincoln was assassinated six weeks after his second inauguration. Johnson found himself president of the United States on April 15, 1865; only six days after the Civil War had ended.

Reintegrating the South

The question of reintegrating the Confederate states into the Union, or *Reconstruction,* was left up to the former senator from Tennessee, a slave-owning Union advocate who hated plantation owners.

The Republican Party, which controlled Congress, pushed for punishment of the Confederate states and immediate voting rights for blacks. The Republicans mistakenly believed that the new president shared their beliefs.

The drunken clown episode

Johnson drank a considerable amount of whiskey the night before Lincoln's inauguration and even took a few shots right before entering the Senate chamber to give his vice-presidential inaugural speech, in an effort to fight a case of typhoid fever.

Johnson, heavily intoxicated and fairly incoherent, presented the most embarrassing speech in U.S. history right before Lincoln's memorable second inaugural address. The media referred to him as the "drunken clown," a label he never lost.

Johnson, however, had different ideas. Johnson believed that only plantation owners and major Confederate leaders were to blame for the Civil War. He was interested in empowering the poor whites and punishing the Southern elite he so despised. He didn't concern himself with the large slave population.

In May 1865, Johnson started implementing *his* version of Reconstruction:

✔ He offered an unconditional pardon and amnesty, and restored all property rights to any Confederate who would swear loyalty to the Union.

Excluded from the proclamation, however, were large plantation owners. They had to seek an individual presidential pardon. This requirement allowed Johnson to humiliate them. The Southern upper class now had to beg the former tailor for presidential pardons. (Most of them asked for and subsequently received the presidential pardon from Johnson.)

✔ He forced the Confederate states to abolish slavery by ratifying the Thirteenth Amendment to the Constitution.

✔ He repealed the Confederate states' ordinance of secession.

✔ He renounced all Confederate debts.

The move let the former Confederate states regulate their own business. To the great disappointment of Johnson, they did this by electing major Confederate leaders to high-level state offices.

As a slap in the face to Johnson, and especially Congress, individual Southern states ended up passing the *Black Codes,* which restricted former slaves' right to testify against whites, to serve on juries, to bear arms, to hold meetings, to vote, and to own property.

Ending a president's Reconstruction

In the summer of 1865, Johnson, undeterred by the Black Codes, started returning to their original owners plantations that had been confiscated during the war and distributed to former slaves. Johnson decided that only the former slaveholders could properly control the black population in the South. In December 1865, Johnson proudly proclaimed that Reconstruction was now over and that Congress needed to readmit representatives from the Southern states.

During Reconstruction, states in the Confederacy did not have representation in Congress from the time they seceded until after the Civil War. The last states to regain representation were Virginia, Mississippi, and Texas in 1870.

Echoing his policies, Johnson, in his 1867 message to Congress, stated that "Blacks have less capacity for government than any other race of people," and when left to themselves show a "constant tendency to relapse into barbarism."

Warring with Congress

The members of Congress were far from agreeing with Johnson's declaration that Reconstruction was over. A civil war broke out between the two branches of government.

The radical wing of the Republican Party considered Johnson a Southern sympathizer. Reports of Southern states returning Confederate leaders to public office, as well as of widespread abuse of former slaves, further undermined Johnson and pushed Congress into trying to change some of Johnson's policies.

In early 1866, Congress passed the *Civil Rights Bill,* which granted citizenship to blacks. The bill overturned the Black Codes (see the section, "Ending a president's Reconstruction," earlier in this chapter) by granting blacks the same rights as whites. After the bill was passed, blacks had access to the federal courts to prosecute discrimination.

To the shock of the Republican Party, Johnson vetoed the Civil Rights Bill. Congress overrode Johnson's veto, making the break between the president and his party complete.

Congress went on the offensive. In April 1866, Congress took the Civil Rights Bill and made it a part of the Fourteenth Amendment to the Constitution, which guaranteed "equal protection of the laws" for every U.S. citizen.

Johnson openly opposed the amendment. He stumped for Democratic candidates, who shared his views, in the 1866 Congressional elections. His campaign swing turned into a disaster when he responded to continuous heckling from Radical Republicans by entering into fierce exchanges. The last straw came when Johnson compared himself to Jesus Christ and openly suggested that Lincoln was removed by divine intervention so that Johnson could become president. The media had a field day with the president. Johnson's support for candidates from his old party backfired, and the Republican Party gained enough seats in the House to easily override any of Johnson's vetoes.

How to get impeached

The Constitution of the United States, in Article 2, Section 4, gives Congress the power to impeach the president and remove him from office for "Treason, Bribery, or other High Crimes and Misdemeanors." Political conflicts are not impeachable offenses.

An impeachment is similar to a criminal indictment. With a simple majority vote, the House of Representatives can recommend the impeachment and bring charges against the president

(or another official subject to impeachment, though, so far, impeachment proceedings have not been started against any official other than a president). The Senate then has the power to impeach and remove the president, which requires a two-thirds majority vote.

Though the House recommended impeachment for Richard Nixon, only two U.S. presidents, Andrew Johnson and Bill Clinton, faced trial in the Senate. The Senate acquitted both.

After the elections, Johnson stood by helplessly as the Republicans dismantled his efforts on Reconstruction. Congress passed the *Military Reconstruction Act,* which divided the South into five military districts and established new state governments based on the equal right to vote.

Johnson escalated the conflict with Congress in an interview with the *New York Times* when he said, "The people of the South, poor, quiet, unoffending, harmless, are to be trodden underfoot to protect n------."

Being impeached

Wanting to get rid of Johnson, the Republican leadership passed the *Tenure of Office Act* in 1867. The act prohibited the president from dismissing any federal officials without the consent of the Senate. Congress easily overrode Johnson's veto of the act. In retaliation, an angry Johnson openly encouraged Southerners to oppose the new Reconstruction plan from Congress.

Johnson then rashly suspended his secretary of war, Edwin Stanton, who was close to the Radical Republicans. When Johnson attempted to dismiss him altogether, Stanton barricaded himself in his office with several armed guards. When the Senate refused to remove Stanton under the Tenure of Office Act, Johnson declared the act unconstitutional and removed Stanton anyway. (Johnson's contention that the Tenure of Office Act was unconstitutional was upheld by the Supreme Court in 1926 — too late to help him.)

The Radical Republicans used the issue to start impeachment proceedings against the president. Johnson responded as only Johnson could — with a curse: "Let them impeach and be damned."

In the House, impeachment was a foregone conclusion. Johnson was impeached on 11 counts, with the central issue being the violation of the Tenure of Office Act. In the Senate, impeachment was less certain. Many senators believed that the Tenure of Office Act was unconstitutional in the first place, and they were less than enamored with the idea of having the Senate president pro tem, Benjamin Wade, a Radical Republican, become president. When the vote was tallied, 7 Republicans had crossed party lines and joined all 12 Democrats in the Senate by voting against impeachment. (The final tally was 35 for impeachment, 19 against.) Johnson had survived being impeached by one vote.

Serving out his term

Disgraced and disheartened, Johnson served out his term quietly, deadlocked with the Republican Congress. Even his foreign policy accomplishments were downplayed. When Johnson encouraged his secretary of state, William H. Seward, to purchase Alaska from Russia for $7,200,000, he was ridiculed. The purchase was widely referred to as "Seward's Folly."

In the summer of 1868, Johnson's hopes of becoming the presidential nominee for the Democratic Party were dashed. He returned home to Tennessee, where he received a hero's welcome. He returned to Washington, D.C. as a senator in 1875. He served just a few months of his term, though. He died of a stroke on July 31, 1875.

Enter a War Hero: Ulysses Simpson Grant

Grant's two terms as president are usually considered to be the most corrupt of any of the presidencies in U.S. history. Why did an honest man suffer such horrible terms in office? For one reason, Grant, shown in Figure 11-2, ran the presidency like a military unit and appointed his friends to high-level positions. Most of these friends turned out to be corrupt. But Grant defended and helped them, undermining his credibility and reputation.

Grant's real name was Hiram Ulysses Grant. A mistake on his West Point application had him admitted under the name Ulysses Simpson Grant. Simpson was actually his mother's maiden name. Grant liked the new name, so he stuck with it.

Grant's early career

Grant failed at many ventures early in his career. He tried his hand at farming and the selling of real estate before settling on a job as a clerk in a leather store, where he worked with his brother.

Figure 11-2:
Ulysses S.
Grant, 18th
president of
the United
States.

Courtesy of the Library of Congress

The Civil War made Grant's career. After the creation of the Confederacy and the attack on Fort Sumter (see Chapter 10), Lincoln called for local militia troops. Grant volunteered and became an officer in an Illinois regiment. He whipped the regiment into shape. Grant's commanding officer was impressed, so he made him a colonel and sent him into battle.

Just an average guy

Ulysses S. Grant was born in Ohio in 1822, the son of a middle class farmer and tanner. Young Grant attended local frontier schools, but his true interest was horses. People from all over the area brought their horses to Grant to have them broken in by the teenager.

Grant used his father's political connections to get into West Point in 1839, after his father decided that Grant needed to join the military. At West Point, Grant was a mediocre student. He graduated 21st out of a class of 39 in 1843. The topics that he enjoyed while in school were, not surprisingly, horsemanship and mathematics. He was so good at mathematics that he hoped to teach it at West Point. His dream didn't come true, so he stayed in the military.

The next two years proved to be boring, as Grant served at various locations in the Southwest. Shortly before the Mexican-American War broke out in 1846, Grant joined a new unit in Missouri, where he met the love of his life, Julia Dent. Grant's marriage was a happy one. Grant and his wife had four children. When the Mexican-American War broke out, Grant joined General Zachary Taylor's unit and fought bravely. In 1852, he received orders to go to Oregon Territory and then to California. Because Grant wasn't able to take his family when he was reassigned, he went into a severe depression and started to drink heavily. Two years later, Grant resigned from the military. The army didn't mind much, because Grant had become famous for constantly quarrelling with superiors and for drinking too much. His military career seemed to be over.

Grant's unit fought well in Missouri, and he was promoted to brigadier general in August 1861. Grant captured Forts Donelson and Henry in Tennessee, giving Lincoln the first major victories of the Civil War. In the process, he captured 14,000 Confederate soldiers and received the nickname "Unconditional Surrender" for always demanding unconditional surrender.

Becoming a war hero

The battle of Shiloh almost cost Grant his military career. He didn't fortify his positions, waiting for reinforcements instead. When Confederate forces attacked, he was unprepared. Grant took the blame for the thousands of lives lost, and congressmen and cabinet officers urged Lincoln to fire Grant.

Lincoln stood by his man, saying, "I can't spare this man, he fights." Instead of firing Grant, Lincoln appointed him commander of all the Union forces in western Tennessee and northern Mississippi. Over the next three years, Grant fought many battles and won the following major victories:

- **Battle of Vicksburg:** Grant planned to attack Vicksburg, a Confederate stronghold in Mississippi, in the fall of 1862. The city was so heavily fortified that he bypassed it and instead conquered the capital, Jackson. Then, he moved back and attacked Vicksburg. After failing to take the city, he decided to starve it. After six weeks, the Confederate forces surrendered. Grant captured 30,000 men, and the North took control of the Mississippi river.

- **Battle of Chattanooga:** In November 1863, Grant, now the commander of the western forces, attacked Confederate forces besieging Chattanooga, Tennessee. After three days, Grant won the battle and freed Tennessee of Confederate forces. Grant's victory also allowed for the invasion of the Confederacy by Northern forces.

- **The Wilderness campaign:** Grant became lieutenant general in early 1864, becoming just the third U.S. citizen to hold this position after George Washington and General Winfield Scott. In addition, Lincoln appointed Grant the commander of all Union forces, giving him command of more than half a million men and the chance to implement his own strategies. He stopped capturing cities and went after the major Confederate forces. This strategy proved bloody but successful. In May 1864, Grant attacked the Confederated forces, headed by General Lee himself. During the next month, Grant lost 60,000 men in Virginia's wilderness. The battle ended in a draw. Grant's subordinates were more successful, as General Sherman took Atlanta in the fall of 1864.

- **Appomattox:** After the fairly successful Wilderness campaign, Grant went back to his old strategy. He decided to slowly starve Lee's armies, who were cooped up outside of Richmond, the capital of Virginia. Grant remained there from June 1864 to April 1865. His other generals slowly conquered the Confederacy during the same period. On April 9, 1865, General Lee surrendered to Grant. The Civil War was over.

In 1866, Grant received the highest honor the country could bestow on him: He became a full general. Only George Washington held this position before Grant. Grant's duties were to *demobilize,* or discharge, the Northern military forces and supervise the process of Reconstruction.

Entering politics

Grant didn't want to become a politician, but because of his popularity, the Republican Party insisted that he do so. President Johnson appointed him secretary of war in 1867. Grant agreed with Johnson on treating the South leniently. He resigned his position when the Senate declared that Johnson didn't have the authority to fire his former secretary of war. (See "How to get impeached" in the Johnson section of this chapter.) Johnson accused Grant of disloyalty, and Grant subsequently joined the Radical Republicans. He even supported impeaching Johnson. Grant's path to the presidency was set.

President Ulysses Simpson Grant (1869–1877)

In 1868, there was no question who the Republican Party wanted to nominate for president — Grant was the unanimous choice. Grant won the general election in a landslide when he received 214 Electoral College votes to the Democratic nominee's (Horatio Seymour, the Governor of New York) 80.

Grant, still the number one war hero, remained popular with the U.S. public despite a horrible first term and was nominated for reelection in 1872. He won the election by a larger margin than he had won in his first term.

President Grant got off on the wrong foot right away. He handed out federal jobs on the basis of family ties and friendship. He appointed more than 40 of his relatives to federal positions. Soon, scandals broke out. Many of the people Grant appointed turned out to be corrupt. Some of the major scandals of the Grant administration included:

- ✔ The secretary of war, William Worth Belnap, resigned after defrauding Native Americans out of $100,000.

- ✔ The ambassador to Brazil, James Watson Webb, received $100,000 from the Brazilian government — the Brazilian government expected him to give a favorable report of them in Washington D.C.

> ✔ The vice president, Schuyler Colfax, resigned after he admitted to bribery during his term as Speaker of the House.
>
> ✔ The secretary of the navy, George Robeson, received $300,000 for giving out contracts to preferred businesses.
>
> ✔ The president's private secretary, Orville E. Babcock, was implicated in the Whiskey Ring for swindling the government out of millions in liquor taxes.

One of the main tasks Grant faced was reintegrating the South into the Union. By 1870, the Ku Klux Klan — an organization of white supremacists — was active in the South, and blacks were widely denied their civil rights, including the right to vote. Grant responded with the Force Acts of 1870 and 1871, which made it a federal crime to deny a person his or her civil rights. The only time that Grant used the acts was when he destroyed the Klan in South Carolina. He left the South alone after that. Slowly, segregation and legalized racism reemerged in the former Confederacy.

Passing on a third term

Grant briefly considered running for a third term. His wife loved being first lady, and Grant wanted to please her. But the Republican Party wasn't keen on the idea of renominating him after all the scandals had taken place during his administration. So he withdrew his name.

After serving out his second term, Grant took his wife on a two-year trip around the world. He briefly considered becoming the candidate for the Republican ticket in 1880, but he didn't receive enough support. So he retired from politics.

He suddenly discovered that he was broke. He had allowed his son to invest his money, and when the investments turned sour, Grant was left penniless. To make some money, he wrote his memoirs.

He finished his autobiography a week before he died from throat cancer on July 23, 1885 (at times, he smoked more than 20 cigars a day). His book became one of the finest accounts of the Civil War.

Mark Twain helped the Grants by pledging 75 percent of the royalties from his book, *Personal Memoirs,* to the Grant family. Grant's widow, Julia, received over $500,000 from Twain's pledge.

Corruption Leads to an Uncorrupt President: Rutherford Birchard Hayes

Rutherford B. Hayes was one of the most honest men ever to inhabit the White House, but he was elected under a dark cloud. He was the first president to lose the presidential race and win office through massive electoral fraud. As president, Hayes fought corruption. But his most notable achievement was ending Reconstruction.

He planned to serve just one term as president because he believed it would give him the freedom to pursue policies that he thought were right. He was willing to pursue these policies, even if it meant offending his own party and the U.S. electorate.

Hayes's early career

The controversy over slavery brought Hayes into politics. His wife was a strong Republican who opposed slavery. Hayes shared some of her views, so he joined her political party. In 1858, he became the city solicitor for Cincinnati. Shortly thereafter, the Civil War broke out.

Hayes volunteered and became a major in the Ohio Volunteer Infantry. He didn't want to do legal work for the military, so he requested to see action on the battlefield, where he was soon promoted to colonel.

Hayes's men loved him because he didn't stay behind — in a battle, Hayes would always charge first. During the next four years, Hayes was wounded four times, and he had his horse shot from under him on several occasions.

Just another lawyer

Rutherford B. Hayes was born in Ohio in 1822. His father died two months before his birth. His uncle took over, providing young Rutherford with an education. Rutherford went to private schools and then attended Kenyon College in Ohio. In 1843, he entered Harvard law school. He graduated and received his law license in 1845.

Hayes didn't like working as a lawyer, so he slacked off quite a bit to pursue his hobbies, especially the study of the natural sciences. He changed these habits when he opened a new law practice in Cincinnati in 1850 and became a famous criminal lawyer.

In 1852, he married his high school sweetheart, Lucy Ware Webb — when she became the first lady, she was the first to have a college degree. They had a wonderful marriage until her death in 1889.

One of his subordinates, future president William McKinley, said of Hayes: "His whole nature seemed to change when in battle. . . . He was, when the battle was once on . . . intense and ferocious."

Hayes's exploits became legendary. The Republican Party decided that he was a great candidate for the U.S. House of Representatives. Hayes, still fighting in the Civil War, was urged by his friends to return home to campaign. Hayes refused and won the seat in 1864 without ever campaigning. Hayes, in response to the urging from his friends, said, "An officer fit for duty who at this crisis would abandon his post to electioneer for a seat in Congress ought to be scalped."

Governing Ohio

Hayes entered Congress in 1865 and supported a tough stance on Reconstruction (for more on Reconstruction, see the section, "From Poverty to the Presidency: Andrew Johnson," earlier in this chapter). He didn't have time to accomplish much in Congress because, in 1868, the Republican Party asked him to run for governor of Ohio. Hayes accepted and won the governorship.

Hayes's administration in Ohio foreshadowed his presidency. He eliminated corruption and appointed state officials based on merit, not personal or party ties. He also founded Ohio State University. Throughout his life, Hayes was interested in education. He attempted to provide public education to as many students as possible — especially the poor.

Hayes ran for Congress again in 1871 and lost. Undeterred, he ran for a third gubernatorial term in Ohio in 1875 and defeated the popular incumbent Democratic governor. Suddenly the Republican Party looked at him as a possible presidential nominee.

President Rutherford Birchard Hayes (1877–1881)

Rutherford Hayes, shown in Figure 11-3, wasn't the frontrunner for the 1876 Republican presidential nomination. However, after all the scandals in the Grant administration, the Republican Party decided that they needed a "Mr. Clean" candidate — someone who fought corruption and was not implicated in any scandals.

Figure 11-3:
Rutherford
B. Hayes,
19th
president of
the United
States.

Courtesy of the Library of Congress

The Republican Speaker of the House of Representatives, James Blaine of Maine, was the frontrunner for the presidential nomination. However, a special committee in Congress charged him with corruption shortly before the convention. So the delegates turned to Hayes instead.

The election turned out to be the most controversial election in U.S. history (until the 2000 election). The Democratic nominee, Samuel Tilden, the governor of New York, won the popular vote by more than 200,000 votes. In the Electoral College, Tilden appeared to have won 203 electoral votes to Hayes's 166.

Although all results showed that Tilden had won, the Republican Party disputed the outcome of the election. It claimed that blacks had been denied the right to vote in many parts of the South, especially in South Carolina, Louisiana, and Florida. The election officials refused to accredit the Democratic electors in these three states. The officials instead had the three states give their electoral votes to Hayes. Now the election was tied, with each candidate receiving 184 electoral votes. Interestingly, Republican officials toured the three states and paid for *recounts,* or a second count of the votes, in many counties.

Not surprisingly, chaos ensued in the capital. The Democrats controlled the House, and the Republicans controlled the Senate. The Republican Party knew that if the election went to the House, they would lose. So they recommended a bipartisan commission to study the election and certify the results. The Republicans arranged it so that the commission would ensure a victory for Hayes.

The Democrats were furious at the machinations of the Electoral Commission and refused to attend the inauguration. The inauguration was held in secret because the Republicans feared for Hayes's life. Hayes received the title, "His Fraudulency."

Stacking an electoral commission

The Electoral Commission of 1877 consisted of 15 members — 5 from the House, 5 from the Senate, and 5 from the Supreme Court. Seven members were Democrats and seven were Republicans. The final and decisive member was Supreme Court Justice David Davis, an Independent.

Supreme Court Justice Davis became a U.S. senator for the state of Illinois shortly before the Electoral Commission was to meet. Another "Republican" justice stepped into his place. After an 8 to 7 victory from the Electoral Commission, Hayes received all of the disputed votes and became the next president of the United States.

Ending Reconstruction

To secure the promise of the Southern states not to challenge the Electoral Commission's ruling, the Republicans promised to end Reconstruction, appoint one Southerner to the new cabinet, and appropriate federal money to rebuild the South. President Hayes came through on the Republican's promise after he assumed office.

In 1877, Hayes pulled out the last Northern troops from South Carolina and Louisiana, ending Reconstruction. The Democratic Party reasserted itself and went on to control Southern politics for almost a century. The process of segregating blacks from society also started during this time. Blacks were routinely denied their civil rights, especially the right to vote.

Fighting corruption and inflation

President Hayes went after corruption as soon as he assumed the office of president. He ignored the spoils system, which handed out federal jobs based on party or family ties. He appointed the most qualified people to the positions in his administration. He further issued an executive degree, making it illegal for federal workers to work for political parties and for parties to solicit money from federal employees. The decision alienated many in both parties. In New York City, Hayes broke up a ring of federal employees working for the Republican Party. He dismissed many of the federal employees, including future president Chester A. Arthur.

Keeping his word and retiring

In 1881, Hayes kept his word and did not to run for reelection. The decision seems to have been a good one. Because he alienated Republicans and Democrats alike during his presidency, he very likely would not have received the Republican nomination anyway.

The spoils system

The spoils system is based on the concept of *patronage,* handing out government jobs based on party ties. The idea behind the spoils system was that all federal jobs belonged to the party in power and could be freely handed out to party supporters.

Andrew Jackson was the first U.S. president to widely use the spoils system extensively, and he set the tone for subsequent presidents. Following Jackson, almost all federal appointments were based on party ties. The spoils system survived until the Wilson administration (1913 to 1921), when the Civil Service Reform Act outlawed the practice.

Hayes retired to his estate in Ohio and became supportive of public education — especially for the poor in the South. He died of a heart attack in 1893, four years after his beloved wife Lucy passed away. President Hayes's last words were "I know I am going where Lucy is."

Chapter 12

Closing Out the Century: Garfield, Arthur, Cleveland, and Benjamin Harrison

. . . .

In This Chapter

▶ Being assassinated: Garfield

▶ Overcoming the odds: Arthur

▶ Serving two nonconsecutive terms: Cleveland

▶ Following in his grandfather's footsteps: Harrison

. . . .

This chapter covers the last four presidents of the 19th century. All of them concerned themselves with fighting the spoils system and protecting the U.S. public from the excesses of big business. These presidents started the practice of government interference in the U.S. economy, which is still a common practice today. All four of these presidents, three Republicans and one Democrat, were honest, hardworking men who did their best to propel the United States into the 20th century. For this accomplishment they deserve credit, even though none of them ranks among the great presidents in U.S. history.

A Promising President is Assassinated: James Abram Garfield

James Garfield, shown in Figure 12-1, has the distinction of being the second president to be assassinated (Lincoln was the first in 1865). He served only six months in office, four of them on his deathbed.

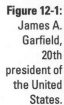

Figure 12-1:
James A.
Garfield,
20th
president of
the United
States.

Courtesy of the Library of Congress

Had he lived long enough to finish his term as president, Garfield likely would have implemented major reforms while battling the spoils system and corruption in the federal government. It would be unfair to rate him — considering that he had only two active months in office. However, judging from his long political career, Garfield would have been one of America's better presidents. Too bad he didn't have a chance to show his abilities.

Garfield's early political career

Slavery helped Garfield get involved in politics. In 1856, he campaigned for the Republican nominee for president, John Frémont, who shared his views on slavery. Both Garfield and Frémont opposed slavery. In 1859, Garfield ran for a seat in the Ohio state senate and won easily.

Garfield studied law part-time while serving in the state senate. He became a lawyer in 1861, just as the Civil War broke out. He volunteered for the military and set up the 42nd Ohio Volunteer Infantry. Garfield fought bravely in Kentucky and in the battle of Shiloh. By 1863, he was a major general.

In 1862, the people of Ohio elected James Garfield to the U.S. House of Representatives. Garfield, who was still fighting the war, refused to leave to take his seat. Only after President Lincoln personally urged him to serve in Congress did Garfield resign his military commission.

For the next 16 years, Garfield served in the House of Representatives. He joined the Radical Republicans, calling for harsh punishment of the Confederacy and the right to vote for blacks. He also backed the impeachment of

President Johnson. By 1876, Garfield was the leader of the Republican Party in the House. He achieved the position even though he was implicated in a bribery scandal. Garfield took $5,000 from a paving contractor in Washington, D.C. while he was chair of the Appropriations Committee, a group that handed out contracts for public works, such as paving streets.

James Garfield served as one of the Republican delegates on the Election Commission of 1877, which handed the election to Rutherford Hayes (see Chapter 11).

President James Abram Garfield (1881–1881)

Garfield was a Republican senator from Ohio in 1880 when the Republican Party split into two camps, the Stalwarts and the Half-Breeds. The two factions disagreed on the issue of *patronage,* the practice of handing out federal jobs to party loyalists and friends. Both groups supported patronage but disagreed over how the jobs should be handed out.

The Stalwarts backed former President Grant for the presidential nomination. The Half-Breeds favored former Speaker of the House, James Blaine. Garfield supported a third candidate, John Sherman, who was the secretary of the treasury and a fellow Ohioan. Garfield made a passionate speech for Sherman at the presidential convention. The delegates liked Garfield's speech so much that they turned to him as a compromise candidate. Even then, it was six days before he became the Republican nominee for the presidency.

In the November elections, Garfield faced off against Democrat Major General Winfield S. Hancock. Although they disagreed on the issue of tariffs, the two candidates advocated the same policies in all other areas. When the results came in, Garfield had narrowly won the popular vote (by less than 10,000 votes out of over 9 million cast), but he carried the electoral vote 214 to 155.

Being assassinated

On July 2, 1881, President Garfield was waiting for his train at the Potomac and Baltimore railroad station on his way to New England, when Charles J. Guiteau, a deranged religious fanatic, shot him twice. One bullet hit the President's arm and the other went into his back, but neither bullet killed him: Garfield's doctors did that. While looking for the bullet in Garfield's back, the doctors turned a three-inch wound into a 20-inch wound, puncturing his liver in the process. The wound became infected, and Garfield died on September 19, 1881.

The last log cabin president

James Garfield was the last U.S. president born in a log cabin. Born in 1831 in rural Ohio, Garfield lost his father when he was just two years old. Young Garfield spent his early years laboring on the family farm until he got a job on a canal boat when he was 16.

Garfield's mother persuaded him to go to school, so he enrolled in what today is Hiram College in Ohio, affiliated with the Disciples of Christ. He excelled in classical languages and became an accomplished speaker and preacher — talents that came in handy during his political career.

In 1854, Garfield, who was teaching on the side, had enough money to enroll in Williams College in Massachusetts, where he continued his study of classical languages. After he graduated, he returned to Hiram College as a professor of foreign languages and became the school's president.

In 1858, Garfield married Lucretia Rudolph, who shared his religious faith. One of Garfield's sons, James Rudolph Garfield, served in Theodore Roosevelt's administration as secretary of the interior.

Garfield's assassin had asked to be named consul to Paris but was turned down by Republican leaders. Guiteau was angry, as well as quite mad. He believed that God told him to assassinate the president to save the country and the Republican Party. The federal government hanged Guiteau in 1882.

President Garfield's deathbed quote: "He must have been crazy. None but an insane person could have done such a thing. What could he have wanted to shoot me for?"

The Unexpected President: Chester Alan Arthur

Nobody thought that Chester Arthur, shown in Figure 12-2, would ever become president, including him. Everybody expected Arthur to fail miserably and preside over a corrupt administration. He was a Republican Party loyalist who had received his political jobs based on his party loyalty.

To everybody's surprise, Arthur abandoned the *spoils system,* whereby those faithful to the party are rewarded with positions in the government, and enacted the first true civil service reform act during his administration. He became the father of the U.S. navy and was a visionary in foreign affairs. Despite expectations, Arthur turned out to be one of the better presidents of the late 19th century.

Figure 12-2:
Chester A.
Arthur, 21st
president of
the United
States.

Courtesy of the Library of Congress

Chester Arthur was a true believer in the finer things in life. He enjoyed expensive clothing, gourmet food, and a good bottle of wine. His friends loved him. He was a kind and gentle man with a great sense of humor. In other words, he was the kind of man people enjoyed hanging out with — although some considered him a snob, out of touch with the people. His parties in the White House were famous. And after the alcohol-free Hayes years, liquor flowed freely again in the White House.

Arthur's early political career

The Kansas-Nebraska Act (see Chapter 9) brought Arthur into politics, just as it had Lincoln. Because Arthur was an *abolitionist,* one who favored ending slavery, he joined the newly created Republican Party. In 1856, Arthur became a founding father of the New York Republican Party and supported Frémont, the Republican candidate for the presidency. In 1860, Arthur campaigned for Lincoln, the Republican Party nominee, and for Governor Edwin D. Morgan of New York. When both won, Arthur was ready to receive his reward under the spoils system.

When the Civil War broke out in 1861, Governor Morgan named Arthur inspector general and then quartermaster general for the New York state militia. The position paid Arthur well. He did a great job equipping over 200,000 soldiers between 1861 and 1863. Arthur resigned and returned to his law practice when the Democrats won the governorship in 1863.

Growing up religious

Chester Arthur was born in 1829, the son of a Baptist minister. Arthur attended good schools, including Union College from which he graduated in 1848. He was an average student who was more interested in living the good life than in studying. He once dumped the school bell into the Erie Canal.

After graduating from College, he taught school and became a principal. He also studied law at night. By 1853, Arthur was working for a lawyer in New York City. In 1854, he passed the bar and began to practice law in the New York area. While practicing law, Arthur became a champion of rights for blacks. He won a landmark case, which outlawed discrimination in New York's public transportation system, in 1855.

Arthur fell in love with and married Ellen Lewis Herndon in 1859. Her death, shortly before Arthur became president, affected Arthur deeply — he had fresh flowers put next to her portrait in the White House every day of his presidency.

Arthur slowly worked his way up the political ladder. By 1868, he was one of the top men in the New York State Republican Party. When Republican Ulysses S. Grant won the White House in 1868, Arthur was given the post of collector of customs in New York City — one of the most powerful positions in the federal government at the time. In his new position, Arthur oversaw more than 1,000 people and controlled almost 60 percent of all customs receipts for the country. Arthur now controlled New York City politics. All of his employees were loyal Republicans who received their jobs based on party ties. Some of them were incompetent, and many of them were corrupt.

In 1877, President Rutherford B. Hayes investigated Arthur and the customhouse. Even though Arthur was not found to be corrupt, Hayes fired him in 1878, and Arthur returned to the law.

Staging the comeback of his life

When the Republican Party split into the Stalwarts and the Half-Breeds in 1880, it couldn't agree on a presidential nominee (see the "Arthur's early political career" section earlier in this chapter). James Garfield, a Half-Breed, became the compromise presidential nominee. The party wanted to balance the ticket with a Stalwart vice-presidential candidate. Who better than Chester Arthur? In the 1880 election, Garfield and Arthur won a narrow victory. Chester Arthur was now the vice president of the United States.

President Chester Alan Arthur (1881–1885)

Chester Arthur became president on September 20, 1881, after President Garfield was assassinated. Everybody expected Arthur to be a puppet of the Stalwart branch of the Republican Party, but Arthur had other ideas. He knew that he was a one-term president — he suffered from Bright's disease, a terminal kidney disorder. So he chose to initiate reforms.

Arthur's major accomplishment as president occurred in 1883, when Congress passed the Pendleton Act, the first civil service reform bill in U.S. history. The Pendleton Act established the following provisions:

- Political tests for federal officeholders became illegal.

- Alcoholics, even if they were loyal party alcoholics, couldn't be hired anymore.

- Competitive tests for some civil service positions became mandatory. However, the act only affected 14,000 out of the 131,000 federal positions.

- Subsequent presidents were allowed to classify more civil service positions closed to the spoils/patronage system.

In the area of foreign policy, Arthur was very innovative. Some of his ideas seem visionary even today:

- The organization of an international conference to create standard time zones throughout the world

- The proposal of a single currency for North and South America to facilitate trade

- The negotiation of building a canal through Nicaragua and not Panama (The Senate, favoring Panama as the site for a canal, refused to ratify the treaty.)

Other successes during Arthur's presidency included the strengthening and modernizing of the U.S. navy.

In 1884, Arthur changed his mind about being a one-term president and wanted to run for reelection. However, his reforms had alienated many in the Republican Party. Arthur lost the Republican nomination to Senator Blaine.

Arthur went back to practicing law, but not for long. His disease caught up with him. He died on November 18, 1886 in New York City.

Making History by Serving Nonconsecutive Terms: Grover Cleveland

Grover Cleveland, shown in Figure 12-3, has the distinction of being the only president in U.S. history to serve two nonconsecutive terms. He proved to be an independent spirit, pursuing policies that he thought were right. In turn, he alienated many in his own party. His presidencies were characterized by an emphasis on fighting corruption and the spoils system.

Figure 12-3:
President Grover Cleveland, the 22nd and 24th president of the United States.

Courtesy of the Library of Congress

Cleveland was actually more conservative than his own Democratic party, which allowed him to become a Democratic president in Republican times. Because of his independence and strong character, he deserves to be ranked in the top 15 of U.S. presidents.

Independent to the end

Grover Cleveland was born in 1837 in New Jersey. His father, a Presbyterian minister, moved him to New York in 1841. Grover went to public schools and planned to attend College until his father passed away in 1853, forcing him to go to work.

For one year, he taught at a school for the blind in New York City. Then his uncle came to the rescue. He offered to have Grover live with him and work on his cattle ranch in Buffalo, New York. While working for his uncle, Cleveland studied law. In 1859, he received his license to practice law.

Cleveland's early political career

Cleveland showed his independence early: The uncle who sponsored him was one of the founders of the Republican Party in Buffalo, but Cleveland became a Democrat.

Grover Cleveland didn't fight in the Civil War. He bought a substitute, for $150, to fight in his place. This was perfectly legal under the terms of the Conscription Act (see Chapter 10).

The veto mayor

Cleveland started to work for the local Democratic Party in 1863, becoming the assistant district attorney of Erie County. He proved to be a tough crime fighter, prosecuting corruption unmercifully. The people of the county rewarded him for his work by electing him sheriff in 1871. He continued his crusade against corruption and crime and received a reputation as a hardworking, honest politician. The Democratic Party rewarded him for his loyalty by running him for mayor of Buffalo in 1881. He won easily.

Cleveland went after the corruption in the Buffalo government. He targeted politicians from both parties and consistently vetoed bills that benefited the aldermen personally. Cleveland believed that the type of corruption that was taking place shouldn't exist. His consistent vetoing of bills earned him the nickname, the "Veto Mayor."

The veto governor

To his great surprise, the Democratic Party approached him in 1882 to run for the governorship of New York. The party couldn't decide between the two frontrunners, so it decided to go with a new face instead. The public was fed up with constant corruption and wanted change. They wanted an honest person in office. The Veto Mayor fit the bill and won the governorship easily.

Not surprisingly, Cleveland continued his independence as governor of New York. He refused to hand out jobs purely on party affiliation. In addition, Cleveland continued to veto bills liberally.

In 1883, Cleveland vetoed a bill that would have lowered transit fares in New York City because he felt that it was a violation of existing laws. The so-called *Five Cent Fare Bill* was popular with many New Yorkers. After vetoing it, Cleveland said, "I shall be the most unpopular man in the state of New York." Yet, he still vetoed the bill.

A surprise nominee

In 1884, the Democratic Party went looking for a presidential candidate. The Republicans nominated Senator James Blaine of Maine, who was accused of taking money from businesses while he was the Speaker of the House. A wing of the Republican Party broke off and proclaimed that they would back any Democrat who was honest and opposed corruption. Cleveland fit the bill. He became the Democratic nominee and won the presidency in a very close election in 1884.

One of the many issues Cleveland faced while running for the presidency concerned his fathering an illegitimate child. When his campaign managers asked him how to handle the issue, Cleveland told them to admit to it. He would rather lose the election than lie to the public. His handling of the issue actually enhanced his reputation of being an honest politician.

President Stephen Grover Cleveland (1885–1889 and 1893–1897)

The election of 1884 was one of the closest elections in U.S. history. The Republican candidate, Blaine, might have won if one of his supporters had kept his mouth shut. The Reverend Samuel Burchard called the Democratic Party the "party of rum, Romanism, and rebellion." "Romanism" was a derogatory term. The slur alienated Catholic voters — they voted for Cleveland.

Cleveland continued his independent streak as president. For his cabinet, he picked the best and most capable people. He didn't care whether they were former Confederates, or even Republicans.

Cleveland's first act was to enhance the scope of the Pendleton Act to further promote civil reform. He actually doubled the number of federal jobs, which were now based on merit and not patronage. Next, he turned into the "Veto President." In his first administration, Cleveland vetoed over 200 bills; most of them were pension bills that extended money to Union war veterans. He paid a price for the vetoed bills when veterans' organizations backed his opponent, Benjamin Harrison, in 1888.

After the Civil War, Congress passed many pension bills that gave money to war veterans, including one for disabled Union veterans. The bill didn't stipulate that the disability had to be received during the war, so abuse was rampant. Cleveland vetoed the bill. Veterans' organizations started to oppose Cleveland. To make matters worse, the veteran's organizations claimed that he acted cowardly during the Civil War, because he paid someone to fight in his place.

Two years into his first term, President Cleveland married Frances Folsom, who was 28 years younger than he. The age difference caused quite a stir, with many accusing Cleveland of robbing the cradle. The accusations didn't bother him at all. The couple had five children together.

Reforming the country

Two major pieces of legislation stood out during Cleveland's first term:

- **The Dawes Act of 1887:** This act, which ended in failure, provided for the distribution of tribal American Indian lands to individual Native Americans. But, instead of becoming independent farmers, as Cleveland had hoped, many Native Americans lost their land due to fraud.

- **The Interstate Commerce Act of 1887:** This act, which proved to be the more successful of the two, fixed the price for railroad tickets at a just and reasonable level. Although the act was ignored in the beginning, it was the first major attempt by the federal government to regulate U.S. businesses. It set a precedent for many more acts to come.

Losing in 1888

Cleveland ran for reelection in 1888. He squared off against war hero Benjamin Harrison, the Republican nominee.

The Democrats were split on the issue of tariffs. Cleveland believed in lower tariffs to stimulate exports to Europe and reduce the price of foreign goods to the average U.S. citizen. Cleveland's stance annoyed many businesses, especially in the industrial North, so they turned to the Republicans, who favored higher tariffs on foreign goods. The election was close; Cleveland actually won the popular vote by 100,000 votes. However, he lost the electoral vote with 168 votes to Harrison's 233. His home state of New York was the difference in the election, as his stance on tariffs cost him the state. Undeterred, Cleveland went back to his law practice and vowed he'd be back.

In 1891, while Cleveland was practicing law in New York City, his first child, Ruth, was born. The media fell in love with her. A new candy bar, Baby Ruth, was named after her.

Serving again

In 1892, the Democratic Party was split one more time. The *Silver Democrats* supported the free, unlimited coinage of silver to increase the money supply in the United States. They believed that it would allow small farmers to repay their debts more quickly. The *Gold Democrats,* of which Cleveland was one, believed that money should be backed by gold so that currency could be exchanged into gold at any time. The amount of gold reserves determined how much money was in circulation.

Cleveland soundly defeated the incumbent Harrison, reclaiming the office of president for the Democratic Party.

During the 1892 campaign, First Lady Caroline Harrison was dying. Both candidates stopped campaigning one month before the election took place.

Cleveland's second term proved to be fairly unsuccessful. He alienated industrialists by supporting tariffs, workers by breaking a strike, and imperialists by refusing to annex the Hawaiian Islands.

In 1893, as the country was enduring a recession, doctors discovered a cancerous growth in President Cleveland's mouth. Cleveland kept his illness a secret because he didn't want to worry the public. The doctors removed Cleveland's jaw and replaced it with an artificial jaw made out of rubber. This operation wasn't made public until 1917, after Cleveland's death.

Dealing with a depression

When he came back to the White House, Cleveland faced the great depression of 1893, a worldwide depression that had spread to the United States.

The trigger industry for the economic depression in the United States was the railroads, which expanded too quickly. By 1893, the whole country faced an economic downturn. The conventional wisdom of the day dictated that Cleveland not interfere because the economy would right itself.

The depression dragged on for years, undermining the public's trust in the president. To top it all off, a group of impoverished men and their families, organized by Jacob Coxey, marched to Washington, D.C. to ask Cleveland for help. The group, called *Coxey's Army,* wanted Cleveland to spend federal money to create jobs. Cleveland just ignored them. The move was not good for his publicity. More and more Democrats turned away from their president.

Instead of trying to cure the ailing economy, Cleveland pushed for lower tariffs. He got his wish in 1894, when Congress lowered tariffs on many foreign goods. However, Republicans and Northern Democrats actually watered down the bill by increasing tariffs on certain industrial goods.

Punishing striking workers

The most damaging event to the Cleveland presidency occurred in 1894 when employees of the Pullman Company went on strike. The American Railway Union joined the strike in support of the workers at Pullman, shutting down all railroad traffic.

Because the strike handicapped the federal mail service, Cleveland believed that the federal government had the right to interfere. He sent troops to break up the strike and threw union leaders into jail. Workers began to turn away from the president.

Saying no to imperialism

Cleveland opposed *imperialism,* or the acquisition of colonies, by the United States. His predecessor, President Harrison, signed a treaty annexing Hawaii to the United States. Cleveland considered it to be imperialism, knowing that a majority of Hawaiians opposed the idea. He withdrew the treaty from the Senate, and Hawaii was not annexed. This act infuriated the many U.S. citizens who believed in imperialism.

He again passed up a chance to get involved in territorial expansion when Spain cracked down on its colony in Cuba, killing thousands, in 1895. Many U.S. citizens, including Republicans and Southern Democrats, wanted to use military action to not only help the people of Cuba, but also to annex it. Cleveland refused.

Cleveland felt so strongly about imperialism that he joined the Anti-Imperialist League, which opposed the annexation of the Philippines in 1898, after he left office.

Retiring to Princeton

By 1896, Cleveland had managed to alienate not only his own party, but also much of the public. The Democratic Party opted to nominate William Jennings Bryan for president instead of Cleveland. Cleveland didn't even campaign for Bryan.

Cleveland retired to his home in Princeton, New Jersey, and became a trustee at Princeton University. He became close friends with the university's president, a professor of government named Woodrow Wilson, who would become president of the United States in 1912.

When Cleveland died in 1908, his last words were, "I have tried so hard to do right."

The Spoiled Republican: Benjamin Harrison

Benjamin Harrison, shown in Figure 12-4, has the distinction of being the only grandson of a former president to be elected president. Harrison was a devout Republican — so much so, that many considered him a puppet of the

Republican Party. However, Harrison proved to be an honest, capable president who initiated major legislation during his term. He was actually one of the better presidents of the late 19th century.

Figure 12-4:
Benjamin
Harrison,
23rd
president of
the United
States.

Courtesy of the Library of Congress

Harrison's early political career

After moving to Indianapolis in 1854, Harrison opened a prosperous law firm and became active in the Republican Party. In 1857, he became the city attorney of Indianapolis. In 1860, he was elected Supreme Court reporter for the state of Indiana.

Growing up prominent

Benjamin Harrison came from one of the best-known families in U.S. history. His great-grandfather was one of the signers of the Declaration of Independence, and his grandfather, William Henry Harrison, was the ninth president of the United States.

Born in 1833, Benjamin Harrison grew up on his grandfather's estate in Ohio. After attending

Miami University in Oxford, Ohio, where he studied languages and religion, Benjamin studied law. In 1854, he was admitted to the Ohio bar.

Harrison married his college sweetheart, Caroline Scott, in 1853. The couple then moved to Indiana, where Harrison's grandfather had been the first governor of the territory.

At first, Harrison sat out the Civil War. But in 1862, the governor of Indiana asked him to set up the 70th Indiana Volunteer Regiment. He accepted and saw action in Kentucky and in the bloody battle of Atlanta. He proved to be an exceptional leader in the Union army, retiring with the rank of brigadier general.

Benefiting from the spoils system

After serving in the Civil War, Harrison returned to his law practice in Indiana. He stayed active in Republican politics. He tried for the Republican nomination for governor in 1872, but he was unsuccessful. He tried again four years later. This time he received the nomination. He lost the race by 5,000 votes, but he received more votes than any other Republican in Indiana history. Over the next 10 years — thanks to the spoils system (see "The spoils system" sidebar in Chapter 11) — Harrison held a slew of political offices, including:

- ✔ **Member of the Mississippi Commission:** The commission oversaw the economic development of the river.

- ✔ **Chairman of the Indiana delegation to the 1880 Republican convention:** Harrison delivered the delegation's votes for James Garfield, helping him win the nomination.

- ✔ **U.S. senator:** Harrison championed Union war veterans. The veterans became some of his staunchest supporters in the 1888 election. In addition, Harrison stood for high tariffs, which pleased business, and supported Native American rights.

Getting nominated in 1888

In 1888, the Republican field for the presidential nomination was wide open after the frontrunner, Senator Blaine, refused to stand for the nomination. He endorsed Harrison instead.

Harrison was the ideal candidate for the Republicans. He had great name recognition, thanks to his grandfather, former president William Henry Harrison. War veterans loved him and despised the Democratic incumbent, Grover Cleveland. Harrison had a good war record, while Cleveland had none. In addition, Harrison was able to deliver Ohio, where he was born, and Indiana, where he resided. After receiving the Republican presidential nomination, Harrison, despite losing the popular vote to Cleveland by 100,000 votes, defeated the incumbent president in the electoral vote, 233 to 168.

The 1888 campaign turned fairly nasty. The Republican Party not only attacked Cleveland's war record, but also engaged in open deception. A Republican from California sent a letter, pretending to be a former British citizen, Charles Murchison, who was now living in the United States, to the British ambassador to the United States. In the letter, he asked the ambassador whom Great Britain favored in the upcoming election. The ambassador naively answered the letter, stating that the British favored Cleveland. The Republican Party publicized the letter as the "Murchison Letter." Because of the letter, many Irish immigrants who despised Great Britain looked upon Cleveland as the candidate of Great Britain and voted for Harrison.

Benjamin Harrison was an excellent speaker, but he had a cold personality. His handlers made sure that he didn't have any contact with the voters after campaign appearances. His nickname became the "Human Iceberg."

President Benjamin Harrison (1889–1893)

Harrison entered office under a dark cloud. He lost the popular vote by 100,000 votes, and many looked upon him as a Republican Party stooge. To his credit, he disappointed the Republican Party by nominating people to his cabinet based on their qualifications. His cabinet included people like Theodore Roosevelt and William Howard Taft, both future presidents.

In the area of domestic policies, Harrison had several major accomplishments. These achievements included

- ✔ **The Dependent Pension Act:** This bill, passed in 1890, guaranteed pensions to all disabled Union war veterans. It further provided assistance to children and dependent parents of Union war veterans.

- ✔ **The Sherman Antitrust Act:** This act made it illegal to establish a *monopoly,* or a business that dominates a whole sector of the economy. It gave the federal government the power to break up these monopolies.

- ✔ **The McKinley Tariff Act:** This bill enacted the highest tariffs in U.S. history, about 48 percent, on foreign goods.

Harrison was also successful with his foreign policy. He increased the size of the U.S. navy and negotiated a treaty annexing Hawaii. Later, President Cleveland, opposed to imperialism, voided the treaty upon his return to the White House. Harrison set the foundation to acquire American Samoa and settled a dispute with Great Britain over fishing rights in the Bering Sea.

In 1891, electricity was installed in the White House. The Harrison's were afraid of the new technology and refused to touch the light switches.

Losing in 1892

President Harrison ran for reelection in 1892. He faced off against former President Cleveland one more time. The main campaign issue was tariffs. Harrison wanted to increase tariffs, while Cleveland advocated a reduction.

Harrison didn't have his mind on the campaign, because his wife was dying. He suspended his campaign in October, and Cleveland followed suit out of respect for the first lady. Caroline Harrison died two weeks before the 1892 election. Her husband never got over her death. Harrison lost the election in a landslide, receiving only 145 electoral votes to Cleveland's 277.

Returning to his legal career

Harrison returned to Indianapolis in 1893 and practiced law one more time. He also became an author. He wrote two books, one on the presidency and one on the state of the country.

His greatest legal accomplishment occurred between 1897 and 1899, when he represented Venezuela against Great Britain in a border dispute. Harrison filed an 800-page brief and spoke for 25 hours at the 5-day tribunal. Before he was done, the British counselor informed his government that its case was lost, though the ultimate resolution of the conflict favored Great Britain. Two years later, on March 13, 1901, Benjamin Harrison died of pneumonia.

Chapter 13

Influencing the World: McKinley, Theodore Roosevelt, and Taft

- -

In This Chapter

▶ Supporting big business and expanding the country: McKinley

▶ Fighting for the little guy and getting involved in world affairs: Roosevelt

▶ Disliking the presidency but loving the Supreme Court: Taft

- -

*T*his chapter covers three Republican presidents: One good, one great, and one failure. William McKinley was a good, capable president. He was the candidate of business, and this showed in his policies. He believed in territorial expansion, adding Hawaii, Puerto Rico, Guam, and the Samoan islands to the United States.

Theodore Roosevelt was one of the great presidents in U.S. history. He worked for the average person, protecting citizens against business excesses. He involved the country in world affairs and received the Nobel Peace Prize.

Finally, there's William Howard Taft. He loved the law and never wanted to be president. His presidency wasn't very successful. But later in life, he restored his reputation on the Supreme Court and went down in history as one of the great Supreme Court justices in U.S. history.

Discarding Isolationism: William McKinley

William McKinley, shown in Figure 13-1, was one of America's more successful presidents. During his administration, he guided the country through recovery from the depression of the early 1890s. More importantly, he brought about a major change in U.S. foreign policy: The isolationism that had been in place since George Washington's presidency finally ended. For the first time, the

United States pursued an active, expansionist foreign policy. McKinley turned the country into a world power and helped it take its place among the great powers in the world.

Figure 13-1: William McKinley, 25th president of the United States.

Courtesy of the Library of Congress

Being a loyal Republican

William McKinley's political career was characterized by party loyalty and the influence of big business. As a Republican in Congress, McKinley consistently supported high tariffs to protect U.S. businesses from foreign competition. He also relied upon the support of wealthy friends to fund his political career and pay off personal debt. As president, he showed some independence but caved in to public pressure. He started the Spanish-American War in 1898, which turned out well for him, getting him reelected.

Serving in Congress

In 1876, the year Rutherford Hayes became president, McKinley was elected a member of the House of Representatives.

He served in Congress for 12 years. He distinguished himself by supporting taxes on imports to protect U.S. industry from foreign competition. In 1890, Congress passed McKinley's greatest accomplishment, the McKinley Tariff. The tariff gave the United States the highest taxes on imports — up to 48 percent — in its history.

Governing Ohio

In 1890, McKinley lost his bid for reelection to the House of Representatives. His tariff bill alienated many farmers and middle-class workers; these groups banded together to form the coalition that defeated him.

A solid middle-class upbringing

William McKinley was born in 1843 in Niles, Ohio. His father owned a small foundry. The foundry produced enough income to allow McKinley to have a fine education. He attended a private high school.

When the Civil War broke out, McKinley volunteered and joined the 23rd Ohio Volunteer Infantry at the age of 18. He served under Major Rutherford Hayes, the future Republican president. McKinley saw action in Virginia and at Antietam. He proved to be a brave, capable soldier. He retired in 1865 with the rank of major.

McKinley studied law after retiring from the military. In 1867, he opened his own law practice in Canton, Ohio. In Canton, he became active in Republican politics and met his future wife, Ida Sexton. They married in 1871.

William McKinley's marriage was a tragic one. McKinley and his wife had two daughters. One daughter died in infancy, and the other died of typhoid fever at the age of four. Mrs. McKinley suffered a breakdown and began having epileptic seizures. Soon she became semi-invalid. McKinley proved to be a loving husband, taking care of Ida until the day he died.

Big business, however, didn't forget its friend. Mark Hanna, a Cleveland, Ohio, millionaire industrialist, became McKinley's sponsor and campaign advisor. In 1891, McKinley was elected governor of Ohio. He did a good job, building up Ohio's infrastructure — especially its roads — and providing unemployed workers with free food during the depression of 1893. The people of Ohio reelected McKinley in 1893.

President William McKinley (1897–1901)

In 1896, Hanna thought McKinley had a shot at the Republican presidential nomination. Hanna and his friends paid for a 10,000-mile trip in 1896, where McKinley delivered 370 speeches throughout the nation campaigning for Republican candidates running for Congress. McKinley became a household name.

McKinley had the Republican nomination sewn up. Hanna and his business friends raised $3.5 million for his campaign, basically buying the presidency. In contrast, the Democratic nominee, William Jennings Bryan, spent a measly $50,000. The Republicans flooded the country with pamphlets and speakers on behalf of McKinley. Major industrialists told their workers that if they voted for Bryan, a recession would follow, and they would lose their jobs.

The money and scare tactics worked — McKinley won big. He carried all the major industrial states and received 271 electoral votes to Bryan's 176.

President McKinley was the first U.S. president to use the telephone in a presidential campaign. From his home in Ohio, McKinley stayed in constant contact with his 38 campaign managers.

Restoring prosperity

By 1897, prosperity had returned to the United States, for which McKinley received full credit. He pushed for international trade, taking the United States out of economic isolation.

Within a few years, he came to the realization that high tariffs hurt trade. By 1900, he reversed his previous position and became an advocate of free trade. At the same time, he stayed on the right side of his business friends by ignoring congressional acts designed to regulate U.S. businesses.

Branching out into international affairs

McKinley, in one of the great accomplishments of his presidency, brought the United States into the international arena. For the first time, the United States flexed its muscles and showed the rest of the world that it was ready to join the ranks of the many world powers of the 1890s. Like many U.S. citizens, McKinley believed in the concept of Manifest Destiny, or the God-given right to expand (see Chapter 8 for more on this concept).

McKinley made major strides in the area of foreign policy. He started the process of U.S. *imperialism,* or the annexation and domination of weaker countries. He considered imperialism good, referring to it as "benevolent assimilation." His accomplishments in the area of imperialism included

- ✔ The Spanish-American War in 1898, which led to the annexation of Puerto Rico, Guam, and the Philippines (all parts of the Spanish colonial empire), as well as the political domination of Cuba.

- ✔ The annexation of Hawaii in 1898 after the Queen of Hawaii was overthrown in 1893 by U.S. business and U.S. troops, and the annexation of parts of the Samoan islands in 1900.

- ✔ The introduction of an open door policy in China. This policy opened up trade with China for every country. It also resulted in the *Boxer Rebellion* in 1900, where 5,000 U.S. troops were part of a multinational force that fought off Chinese nationalists, who called themselves the Boxers and objected to foreign domination of their country.

Fighting the Spanish-American War

In 1895, a revolution against Spanish rule broke out in Cuba. The Spanish government responded brutally, sending 100,000 soldiers to suppress the uprising. Thousands of Cubans were put into reconcentration camps, where many died of starvation and disease.

The Cubans were put in "reconcentrados" or *reconcentration camps.* Concentration camps hold those the government believes are dangerous or a threat, whereas reconcentration camps hold people loyal and friendly to the government. The Spanish put friendlies in camps, and therefore, anyone not in camps were rebels, an enemy who had to be destroyed.

McKinley wanted to resolve the situation peacefully, but many in the United States felt that war was the way to go. The press published horrific stories about Spanish brutality, many of them false. Nevertheless, public and Congressional reaction to these sensational reports forced McKinley to act — U.S. citizens wanted to save the Cubans from the evil Spanish empire.

McKinley sent the U.S. battleship *Maine* to Havana, Cuba, as a show of U.S. resolve. The ship blew up in the harbor, killing 260 of the U.S. soldiers aboard. The press and the public blamed Spain, and the war was on. On April 11, 1898, McKinley asked Congress for special wartime powers. Two weeks later, Congress declared war on Spain.

In 1976, the Navy published a study that determined that the Spanish weren't responsible for the explosion of the Maine. It is now believed that a spontaneous combustion on the ship was responsible for the disaster.

In May 1898, the U.S. fleet destroyed a Spanish fleet at Manila, the capital of the Philippines. Two months later, the U.S. navy destroyed a second Spanish fleet in Cuba.

The war was basically over. Spain agreed to negotiations, and the resulting Paris Treaty of 1898 gave the United States the Spanish colony of Puerto Rico, and sold the Philippines to the United States for $20 million. More than 500,000 Filipinos were killed during an uprising against new U.S. rule.

During the Spanish-American War, fewer than 400 U.S. soldiers died in battle. However, thousands died from disease and inadequate provisions.

Getting reelected and assassinated

McKinley's foreign policy proved to be popular with the U.S. public. He won reelection easily in 1900, defeating the Democrat William Jennings Bryan decisively for a second time. The only interesting fact about the 1900 presidential race was the question of who should be McKinley's vice-presidential candidate. His old vice president, Garret A. Hobart, died in 1899, and McKinley left it up to the Republican convention to pick his new vice president. The convention chose Teddy Roosevelt because he was a war hero with great name recognition.

Because Roosevelt was a progressive Republican (see the following section), a lot of Republicans considered him dangerous. They figured that if they made him vice president, an office with no powers attached to it, they could contain him and keep him out of the way. Only McKinley's major advisor saw the danger in this strategy: Mark Hanna prophetically pointed out that just one life stood between Roosevelt and the presidency.

On September 6, 1901, McKinley gave a speech at the Pan-American exposition in Buffalo, New York, and shook hands with the public afterwards. An anarchist by the name of Leon F. Czolgosz shot the president twice. McKinley clung to life, telling his closest advisors to be careful when presenting the news to his wife.

McKinley died from his wounds a week later after telling his doctors, "It is useless, gentlemen. I think we ought to have a prayer." Millions of people lined up to pay their respects to one of the country's most popular presidents, as the train carrying the president's body from New York to Ohio passed through. A month later, the federal government executed Leon Czolgosz for assassinating the president.

Vice President Roosevelt rushed back from a camping trip to be sworn in as the next president of the United States.

Building a Strong Foreign Policy: Theodore Roosevelt

Theodore Roosevelt, shown in Figure 13-2, was one of America's best presidents. He usually ranks in the top five of all presidents — a ranking he deserves. Roosevelt not only turned the United States into a true world power but he also began the long process of protecting the average U.S. citizen from the excesses of business. In the process, he increased the powers of the presidency, becoming the first strong president of the 20th century.

The use of "Teddy" in reference to the president has come into modern usage, but Roosevelt detested the abbreviation of his name.

In foreign policy, Roosevelt established the United States as a world power. He was not afraid to interfere in European affairs: He received the Nobel Peace Prize in 1906 for his work in that area. Roosevelt was the first U.S. citizen to win the award.

Teddy Roosevelt was one of the most beloved presidents in the history of the United States. To honor Roosevelt, a German toy maker named a plush bear after him. Soon it became known worldwide as the "teddy bear."

Figure 13-2:
Theodore
Roosevelt,
26th
president of
the United
States.

Courtesy of the Library of Congress

Growing up prosperous

Theodore Roosevelt was born into money in 1858. His father was a wealthy banker in New York City. Young Roosevelt received the best possible education through private tutors. Family trips around the world stimulated his interest in world affairs. By the time he became a teenager, Roosevelt had lived in Europe and traveled to Africa.

Roosevelt's true love was the natural sciences. He turned into an outdoorsman early in life. He overcame his asthma and sickly physique, and became an ardent bodybuilder. He was able to transform himself into a mountain climber, wrestler, boxer, and hunter. In 1876, he entered Harvard and became an excellent student. He graduated at the top of his class four years later and went on to study law. Roosevelt hated law and eventually dropped out of Columbia law school. He published his first book on the Naval War of 1812 while at Columbia, though and many more books followed.

Roosevelt married Alice Hathaway Lee in 1880, though on Valentine's Day in 1884, Roosevelt suffered a crushing blow. His mother died of typhoid fever, and a few hours later, his wife died after giving birth to their daughter, Alice. Roosevelt left his daughter with his sister and moved west to the Dakota Territory to become a rancher and live the life of a cowboy. While working as a rancher, he continued to publish books on hunting and the outdoor life. He is the most published president in U.S. history, with 38 books to his credit.

In 1885, Roosevelt ran into his childhood sweetheart, Edith Carow, and they fell in love again. A year later, they married and had five children together. Roosevelt returned to New York to continue his career in politics. When he finished third in a race for the governorship of New York, he was ready to retire from politics and live the life of an academic. More books followed, including his masterpiece, *The Winning of the West,* a four-volume work.

Roosevelt's early political career

Teddy Roosevelt was a progressive Republican. The term *progressive* referred to reform-minded politicians who wanted to curb the abuse of power by politicians, political parties, and especially big business. The objective was to protect the average citizen from government and business, and make the United States a better place to live.

Serving New York

In 1881, Roosevelt became a member of the New York state legislature. His independent streak was visible right away when he exposed a corrupt judge. He worked well with the Democratic governor, Grover Cleveland, and later served in Cleveland's presidential administration. His affiliation with Cleveland didn't sit well with the Republican leadership. In 1884, Roosevelt refused to run for reelection, tired of his political and personal problems (his mother and wife both died on February 14 that year), and retired from politics.

In 1888, Roosevelt returned to Republican politics, campaigning for Benjamin Harrison. When Harrison won the presidency, he appointed Roosevelt U.S. civil service commissioner. In this position, Roosevelt opposed patronage and advocated hiring people based on merit. Roosevelt's job as commissioner was to go after federal agencies that handed out jobs based on party ties or friendship. Roosevelt did such an excellent job that Democratic president Grover Cleveland, after winning the presidency in 1892, decided to keep him on the job even though he was a Republican.

In 1895, Roosevelt left the office to become the police commissioner for New York City. He went after corrupt police officers, and his reputation rose. Roosevelt disguised himself at night and went out on the streets to check that the police were doing an acceptable job. The public loved him for this tactic.

Returning to national politics

After the Republicans won the White House with McKinley in 1896, Roosevelt was ready for a return to the national scene. Roosevelt believed that the United States needed to become a great power. He thought that only a strong, powerful United States could survive against the great European powers. He also thought that the United States needed to expand and build up a powerful fleet to protect U.S. interests throughout the world.

Roosevelt served in McKinley's administration as the assistant secretary of the navy. He served well and put his effort into building up the branch. During this time, Roosevelt first envisioned building a United States–controlled canal through Central America. Then, the Spanish-American War broke out. (See the section on McKinley earlier in this chapter.)

Founding the Rough Riders

When the Spanish-American War broke out, Roosevelt longed to see action. Roosevelt, who was a captain in the New York National Guard, resigned as assistant secretary and volunteered for the first U.S. volunteer cavalry, called the "Rough Riders."

Roosevelt's unit landed in Cuba in June 1898. He and his men saw action soon after they landed. On July 1, 1898, Roosevelt led the famous charge at San Juan Hill (Roosevelt actually charged up Kettle Hill, but the battle is usually known as the battle at San Juan Hill). He took the hill despite losing a quarter of his men. The newspapers covered the charge prominently, and Roosevelt returned home a colonel and a national hero.

Becoming governor of New York and vice president

When Roosevelt returned home, the Republican Party asked him to run for governor of New York, believing that only he could win the race for the party. They were right — Roosevelt won a narrow victory.

As governor, Roosevelt managed to alienate both business and labor: He alienated business by levying a tax on public service businesses, and labor by calling out the National Guard to put down labor unrest.

The Republicans decided to get rid of Roosevelt. They figured that there was no better way to do that than to make him the vice president — a position without real power. Roosevelt knew that taking the position very likely would end his political career, but he accepted the vice-presidential nomination anyway.

President Theodore Roosevelt (1901–1909)

With the assassination of President McKinley in September 1901, Teddy Roosevelt suddenly found himself president — at the age of 42, he was the youngest president in history. Roosevelt brought a unique approach to the presidency, taking members of Congress, his cabinet, and even foreign dignitaries on walking and climbing trips.

Roosevelt also managed to alienate both Republicans and Democrats fairly quickly. For example, he invited the black educator Booker T. Washington to dinner at the White House, making Washington the first black to dine in the executive mansion. This dinner invitation alienated white Southerners, who became his staunchest foes. Soon thereafter, he annoyed the Republican Party by intervening in the Pennsylvania coal strike.

Roosevelt was aware that he acted against his party's wishes many times. He was successful because he took his case to the U.S. public. He used the presidency as a *bully pulpit* — a venue for getting his message across. When the public backed him, Congress begrudgingly followed.

President Theodore Roosevelt coined the name "White House" for the executive mansion. The term stuck and is still commonly used today.

Interfering in the coal miners' strike

In 1902, 150,000 coal miners went on strike in Pennsylvania. They wanted better pay, a nine-hour workday, and the right to organize a union — the United Mine Workers. The owners refused to even discuss the matter.

Roosevelt intervened without consulting Congress. He feared a coal shortage for the upcoming winter, so he called the mine owners to Washington, D.C. to discuss the issue. When the mine owners refused to compromise, Roosevelt threatened them. He told them that if they did not cooperate with an investigative commission, he would use federal troops to operate the mines. The owners caved in; arbitration finally took place. The next year, the mineworkers received a 10 percent pay increase, and the owners accepted the nine-hour workday. Roosevelt was successful, and the public loved it.

Going after business

For Roosevelt, the public good was what mattered. He realized that many businesses were hurting the U.S. public, so he took action. He went after the Northern Securities Company, a collection of several railroad companies that joined forces to regulate prices and reduce competition. Roosevelt used the Sherman Anti-Trust Act, passed in 1890, to dissolve the trust and protect the public. Roosevelt showed how he felt about railroad owners with these words: "A man who has never gone to school may steal from a freight car; but if he has a university education, he may steal the whole railroad."

Making his mark in foreign policy

Roosevelt's great love was foreign policy. He didn't believe in isolationism. Instead, he wanted the United States to be a great power that pursued an active foreign policy.

As president, Roosevelt had a chance to lay the foundation for his ideas. He believed in a "speak softly, and carry a big stick" foreign policy, where the United States would threaten other countries unless they pursed policies friendly and beneficial to the United States.

At the same time, he rejected taking control of weaker foreign nations. During his presidency, Roosevelt was more interested in resolving international disputes peacefully than going to war. He settled a dispute with Great Britain over the Alaskan-Canadian border peacefully and refused to annex Cuba and the Dominican Republic, which many in the United States supported. The only exception was the Philippines, where Roosevelt opposed Filipino nationalists fighting U.S. control of their country.

By 1904, Roosevelt put his foreign policy into place in the Roosevelt Corollary. The *Roosevelt Corollary* was an extension of the Monroe Doctrine. It stated that only the United States had the right to interfere in the affairs of the Americas — European powers needed to stay out. If a country in the Americas wronged a European power, the United States would take care of the problem. The United States was willing to act against any European power trying to take action in the Americas.

Building the Panama Canal

Roosevelt's greatest foreign policy accomplishment was the building of the Panama Canal. The canal was one of his pet projects, and he did everything in his power to bring it about.

Roosevelt signed a treaty with Great Britain that allowed the United States to construct and then control the canal. The canal would obviously boost world trade, and under U.S. control, it could be used as an instrument in making foreign policy.

Colombia, who at the time controlled Panama, proved to be the major obstacle. The Columbians refused to accept the $10 million Roosevelt offered for the small strip he needed to build the canal. Roosevelt then initiated a little revolution in Panama against Columbian control.

The Panamanians revolted in 1903. Roosevelt recognized the new country right away. He sent the navy to prevent Colombia from suppressing the revolt. As soon as the new Panamanian government was in power, it sold the United States a 10-mile strip of land to build the canal.

The canal was not finished until 1914. The United States retained control of the canal until President Carter signed legislation in 1977 that returned the canal to Panama by 1999 (see Chapter 22 for more on the return of the canal).

Winning reelection in 1904

In 1904, there was no question about who would win the upcoming election. Roosevelt was at the height of his popularity, and the Democratic Party nominated a virtual unknown, Alton B. Parker of New York. Roosevelt won big, carrying 336 electoral votes. He only lost the South, which was still mad at him for inviting a black to dinner at the White House (refer to the preceding section, "President Theodore Roosevelt"). Roosevelt saw the election as a mandate and pushed for even more domestic reform in his second term.

In 1904, President Roosevelt had a boxing match in the White House with heavyweight champion John L. Sullivan. The match was intense — Roosevelt lost his sight in one eye after a brutal hit by Sullivan.

Continuing a successful foreign policy

Roosevelt picked up where he left off in the area of foreign policy. In his second term, he accomplished the following:

- **The Treaty of Portsmouth:** In 1905, the Japanese and Russian empires went to war. Roosevelt decided that the United States should intervene and mediate between the two countries. Both countries agreed to U.S. mediation. The Treaty of Portsmouth settled the conflict and ended the war. Roosevelt received the Nobel Peace Prize for his successful mediation between the two empires.

- **The Algiers Conference:** In 1905, Germany and France almost went to war over Morocco. Roosevelt called for an international conference in 1906 to settle the dispute peacefully.

- **The Gentleman's Agreement:** In 1906, the city of San Francisco started to segregate its school system. The city's program singled out Asians, especially Japanese immigrants. So Roosevelt and the Japanese empire reached an agreement in 1907, voluntarily restricting Japanese immigration to the United States.

- **The Second Hague Conference:** This conference, encouraged by Roosevelt, dealt with arms control and disarmament in 1907.

- **The Great White Fleet:** To show the rest of the world how powerful the U.S. navy was, Roosevelt sent it around the world in 1907. The tour was especially intended to impress the Japanese, which it did.

Being progressive at home

Roosevelt continued his reformist policies back home. His second term brought many reform acts that still have an impact on the United States today. Roosevelt's reforms include

- **The Meat Inspection Act (1906):** This act, passed in 1906, mandated the inspection of meatpacking houses by the federal government.

Roosevelt was especially interested in the meat industry. While fighting in the Spanish-American War, he observed the poor quality of meat the soldiers consumed. Many soldiers got sick after eating the meat. When Upton Sinclair published *The Jungle,* a novel that details the unsanitary conditions in the meat industry, in 1906, the U.S. public became outraged. Roosevelt tapped into the outrage and pushed for the successful passage of the Meat Inspection Act.

✔ **The Pure Food and Drug Act (1906):** This act prohibited the production of unsafe food, liquors, medicines, and drugs.

✔ **The Hepburn Act (1906):** This act regulated the railways and allowed the federal government to supervise the railroad industry and to set prices for railroad charges. The act was later applied to telegraph and telephone companies.

During his presidency, Roosevelt set aside 235 million acres of public lands for conservation, doubling the number of national parks. He believed that he had to protect the country's public lands from private exploitation.

Salvaging the economy

In 1907, the Knickerbocker Bank in New York City, one of the largest and most powerful banks in the United States, collapsed. The collapse caused a widespread panic on Wall Street and among the public. Because the federal government didn't insure banks at the time, massive withdrawals of money could have ruined them. To prevent this, Roosevelt asked a consortium of financiers, headed by J. P. Morgan, to bail out the Knickerbocker Bank. The consortium of financiers came through, buying out other financially unstable institutions and businesses, also. Congress further stabilized the situation with the passage of the Aldrich-Vreeland Act in 1908, which provided unstable banks with federal funds. The act ended the panic and avoided a recession.

Saying no to a third term

In 1908, Roosevelt faced a difficult decision. Should he run for a third term? He knew that he could easily win reelection. However, during the 1904 campaign, he pledged not to seek a third term. He honored his pledge and handpicked a successor instead. His choice was William Howard Taft. Roosevelt believed that Taft was a progressive Republican, like himself, who would continue Roosevelt's policies. Boy, was he wrong! Roosevelt made sure that Taft won the Republican nomination. He then campaigned for him in the election. Taft won easily, and Roosevelt retired in 1909.

To allow Taft to become his own man, Roosevelt left the country and went on a safari in Africa. He went hunting and exploring. Roosevelt then went to Europe, where he was well liked and gave guest lectures at many universities. The Europeans treated him like royalty.

While vacationing in Europe, Roosevelt heard for the first time that Taft had moved away from Roosevelt's programs. More and more progressives complained about Taft, so Roosevelt returned home.

Roosevelt went on a speaking tour to promote progressive reforms. He also called for the country to move away from enriching a few individuals and instead care for all the people of the nation.

By early 1912, Roosevelt had decided that he couldn't live with Taft's policies anymore. He threw his hat into the presidential ring for the Republican nomination.

Becoming a Bull Moose

Roosevelt believed that he had a good chance of receiving the Republican nomination in 1912. However, Taft's handlers made sure that Roosevelt didn't win. At the convention, they refused to seat pro-Roosevelt delegates. This outraged supporters of Roosevelt, and they created the Progressive Party, or the so-called "Bull Moose Party." The Republican Party was split, which allowed the Democrat Woodrow Wilson to win the 1912 election.

Roosevelt campaigned throughout the country. He even survived an assassination attempt during one of his campaign appearances. After being shot in the chest on the way to a campaign appearance, he went on to deliver his campaign speech, saying at one point, "Friends, I shall ask you to be as quiet as possible. I don't know whether you fully understand that I have been shot; but it takes more than that to kill a Bull Moose." He finished his speech before collapsing and being taken to a hospital.

Roosevelt's campaigning paid off. In the 1912 election, he received 28 percent of the vote — over 4 million votes. He actually did better than the incumbent President Taft, who came in third in the election. Not surprisingly, the Democrat Wilson won in an electoral landslide, despite receiving only 42 percent of the popular vote.

The 28 percent of the vote that Roosevelt received as a third party candidate in 1912 is still the best third-party showing in U.S. history.

Retiring for good

After losing in 1912, Roosevelt retired from politics. Instead, he sought out adventure abroad. In 1913, he went to Brazil to explore the Amazon. He explored what today is the Roosevelt River in the Amazon and collected many specimens that can be seen today in the American Museum of Natural History in New York City.

Roosevelt returned home in 1914 and spoke out against President Wilson's early neutrality in World War I (WWI). For Roosevelt, neutrality was a sign of weakness. At first, Roosevelt didn't take sides in WWI because he was not sure which side to support. But after the sinking of the Lusitania in 1915 (see

Chapter 14), he moved to the Allied side. He even offered to create a new volunteer division and to fight in Europe. President Wilson turned him down, and although Roosevelt didn't fight in the war, his sons did — his son Quentin died fighting in France.

By 1918, Taft and Roosevelt had made up, and the Republican Party was united. The Republicans won big in the 1918 congressional elections and Roosevelt was expected to win the presidency easily in 1920. Fate had other plans. Roosevelt became ill and died in his sleep on January 6, 1919. Roosevelt's son Archie sent a telegram to his brothers in Europe that read: "The Lion is dead."

The President Who Hated Politics: William Howard Taft (1909–1913)

William Howard Taft, shown in Figure 13-3, was a unique figure in U.S. history. He never wanted to be president, and he hated politics. He lived his life by the frequently expressed motto, "Politics makes me sick."

President Taft didn't have the qualities of his predecessor, Theodore Roosevelt. While Roosevelt ignored Congress and went straight to the people to get backing for his programs, Taft tried to negotiate. With the Republican Party split at the time into two factions — the Conservatives and the progressives — Taft managed to alienate both wings.

Taft was a capable administrator who introduced many needed reforms but received no credit for doing so. His distaste for politics cost him reelection in 1912, and that was okay with him.

Figure 13-3:
William
Howard
Taft, 27th
president of
the United
States.

Courtesy of the Library of Congress

Born into politics

William Howard Taft was born into a prominent political and legal family. His grandfather was a judge, and his father was a Cincinnati superior court judge who served in the Grant administration as secretary of war and attorney general.

In 1874, Taft graduated second in his class at Yale. Taft wanted to be a lawyer, like his father, so he decided to attend Cincinnati Law School. In 1880, he graduated from law school, passed

the bar exam, and started to work as a court reporter. He then worked as the assistant prosecutor in Hamilton County, Ohio. By 1883, he had opened a successful law firm.

Taft married Helen Herron in 1886. She was an extremely ambitious woman, who, ever since her childhood, wanted to be first lady. She pushed Taft into an office he didn't want.

Taft loved the law, and his greatest wish was to become a member of the U.S. Supreme Court. Ironically, this wish came true only after he left the office of president. He is the only person in U.S. history to serve as both president of the United States and Chief Justice of the U.S. Supreme Court.

Taft's early career

Taft's legal career really began in 1887, when he became a judge on the Ohio superior court. In 1889, Taft's public career took off. President Harrison appointed him solicitor general for the United States. In this capacity, Taft handled all federal court cases involving the federal government. He won 18 out of the 20 cases he tried. More importantly, he met his lifelong friend and sponsor, Teddy Roosevelt, who also served in the Harrison administration.

Taft returned to Ohio after only two years in office. In Ohio, he became a member of the U.S. Sixth Circuit Court of Appeals, a position he loved. After serving eight years on the court in Ohio, he was ready for the Supreme Court. However, President McKinley had a different position in mind for Taft.

Governing in the Philippines

In 1900, President McKinley had a tough time dealing with the newly acquired Philippines. A bloody uprising against U.S. rule took place, and the military governor General Arthur MacArthur (the father of General Douglas MacArthur of World War II and Korea fame) used full force to oppress the Filipino population.

Taft had no interest in the Philippines. When McKinley first offered him the job of pacifying the Philippines, he refused. Only when McKinley offered Taft a position on the Supreme Court after he finished his job in the Philippines did Taft accept.

Taft disagreed with General MacArthur's brutal treatment of the Filipino population, and he was happy to see the general resign in 1901.

In 1901, Taft became the governor of the Philippines. He did an excellent job as governor. He reconciled the country and set the foundation for the modern-day Philippines by creating a local democratic government and building roads, medical facilities, and schools. He reorganized the civil administration. He even bought 400,000 acres from the Catholic Church and distributed the land to poor Filipinos. Taft became so involved in governing the Philippines that he actually rejected two offers to become a member of the Supreme Court. By 1904, Taft impressed the new President, Roosevelt, so much that he made him secretary of war. Taft quickly became Roosevelt's right-hand man.

Dabbling in foreign policy

As secretary of war, Taft involved himself in many diplomatic activities. Roosevelt chose him to settle disputes in Cuba and take care of the building of the canal in Panama. In addition, Taft received the task of bringing Russia and Japan, at war at the time, to the bargaining table. He succeeded, and Roosevelt won the Nobel Peace Prize. Eventually, Taft was left in charge whenever Roosevelt went on one of his many trips. According to Taft, "the president seems really to take much comfort that I am in his cabinet."

By 1908, there was no question in the Republican Party about who would be Roosevelt's successor. Roosevelt considered Taft a friend and someone who could continue his policies. The progressive wing of the Republican Party saw in Taft someone who would be another Teddy Roosevelt. The conservatives in the party saw in him someone who could help their cause and scale back some of Roosevelt's policies. Everybody liked Taft and believed that he was on their side. He easily received the nomination and went on to defeat the Democratic nominee, William Jennings Bryan, without any problems.

President Taft was a loving husband. When his wife suffered a stroke in 1909, Taft spent two hours a day for the next year teaching her how to speak again.

President William Howard Taft (1909–1913)

Problems arose as soon as Taft assumed the presidency. During the campaign, Taft promised the U.S. public that he would lower tariffs, so he called a special session of Congress to make good on his campaign promise. Instead, the Conservative Republicans, representing business interests, increased tariffs on many items. Taft believed that a president should only react to Congress and not dictate policy, so he refused to react to the bill. Taft even defended the bill, disappointing many. For Taft, it went downhill from there.

The Republican Party split into two factions during Taft's presidency. On the one hand was the Conservative wing, which was pro-business and anti-reform in nature. The Conservatives supported high tariffs, no government intervention in the economy, and no social reforms. The other wing of the Republican Party consisted of pro-Roosevelt progressives, who believed in more reformist policies, lowering tariffs, and curbing business excesses. By the end of his term, Taft had alienated both wings of the party.

Next came the Pinchot disaster. Gifford Pinchot was the head of the U.S. forestry service and one of Roosevelt's closest friends. Pinchot falsely accused the new secretary of the interior, Richard Ballinger, of allowing private companies to exploit public lands in Alaska. Taft fired Pinchot, annoying Roosevelt and many progressive Republicans.

Taft was the heaviest president in U.S. history, weighing close to 350 pounds. At one point, he got stuck in the White House bathtub and had to be pried out. Subsequently, a new and larger tub, with room for four people, was put in the White House. He was also the first U.S. president to play golf.

Beating the odds and accomplishing quite a bit

Overall, Taft's accomplishments were impressive. But he was an administrator, not a politician, and he didn't publicize his accomplishments, so he received no credit for his policies. Despite many setbacks, Taft accomplished quite a bit while in office, including

- The vigorous pursuit of monopolies and trusts. He actually pursued twice as many anti-trust lawsuits as the Roosevelt administration.
- The expansion of the powers of the Interstate Commerce Commission. He allowed the commission to regulate telephone, radio, and cable services.
- The addition of the 16th Amendment to the Constitution of the United States in 1913. This amendment, which was passed during the last days of Taft's presidency, allowed the U.S. government to collect income taxes.
- The introduction of the Publicity Act in 1910. This act forced political parties to publicize the sources of their campaign funds and their subsequent expenditures.
- The setting aside of over 72 million acres of public lands for conservation.
- The introduction of the eight-hour workday for work on federal projects.

Only Taft's foreign policy was truly a failure. He attempted to open up many regions in the world to U.S. investment. He failed in China and in the Caribbean. His greatest foreign policy triumph, the signing of a free trade agreement with Canada, failed when the Canadian population rejected the treaty in a popular vote.

Losing the presidency, gaining the Supreme Court

Taft knew that he had no chance of getting reelected in 1912. He probably would have defeated the Democrat Wilson in a two-man race, but with Roosevelt in there, he had to lose. He spent no time campaigning, so why didn't he just withdraw from the race? It has been speculated that he was mad at his former friend Roosevelt, so he wanted to make sure that Roosevelt, running on the Bull Moose ticket, didn't win either.

In the election, Taft received an abysmal 23 percent of the vote and carried only two states — the worst electoral showing by an incumbent president in U.S. history. After Taft happily retired in 1913, he taught law at Yale University. The students loved him. He also became an accomplished author of legal works. In 1921, his greatest wish came true. President Harding appointed him chief justice of the U.S. Supreme Court. Taft excelled in his new position. He reformed the judicial system and also talked Congress into giving the Supreme Court its own building. He aligned himself with the Conservative faction in the Supreme Court, but he mediated successfully with the more liberal justices. Taft was finally happy.

In February 1930, Taft became ill. He retired from the Supreme Court and died at home a few months later.

Fellow Supreme Court Justice Louis Brandeis said of Taft, "Its very difficult for me to understand how a man who is so good as chief justice could have been so bad as president."

President Taft's lasting legacy was not just his years as president or chief justice of the Supreme Court, it was his ability to serve his country. His descendants continued his legacy of serving the country. His son, Robert, became a successful United States senator, representing Ohio until his death. One of President Taft's descendents, Bob Taft, was elected governor of Ohio in 1998.

Chapter 14

Protecting Democracy: Woodrow Wilson

*W*oodrow Wilson was a visionary — ahead of his time — and one of the best presidents in U.S. history. Besides saving democracy in Europe, he implemented many reforms that propelled the United States into the 20th century. His greatest domestic accomplishment occurred shortly before he left office, when women received the right to vote.

In the area of foreign affairs, Wilson's Fourteen Points, designed to bring about an end to war in Europe and war in general, laid the foundation for the League of Nations and its successor, the United Nations.

Studying Government

Woodrow Wilson was a thinker, philosopher, and student of government. As a professor of government, Wilson was familiar with the governmental process. (His dissertation was on Congress.) Wilson used this knowledge to his advantage during his presidency. More importantly, Wilson was an idealist, believing in the goodness of people. He wanted to bring about prosperity, an egalitarian society where people enjoyed similar rights regardless of background, and world peace. He initiated major reform domestically, and worldwide, after the end of World War I (WWI).

Growing up religious

Woodrow Wilson was born in 1856 in Staunton, Virginia. His father was a Presbyterian minister and a professor at Hampton-Sydney College.

Young Woodrow received a good, private education from his parents in both religion and classical studies. (He also attended public schools during the post–Civil War era.) Wilson spent the Civil War years in the Confederacy. His father was a chaplain in the Confederate army and a Confederate supporter. This sympathy for the Confederacy stuck with Wilson. Even though he was personally opposed to slavery, he supported the right of the Confederacy to secede from the Union to protect its way of life.

After the Civil War, Wilson wanted to follow in his father's footsteps and become a minister. So he enrolled at Davidson College in North Carolina in 1873. It was not until 1875 that Wilson abandoned the idea of becoming a minister. Instead, he transferred to what today is Princeton University. At Princeton University, he studied British literature, politics, and speech. During his final year at Princeton, he published his first article. In the article, he criticized the current U.S. Congress and advocated reforms to make it more democratic in nature.

Wilson's next step was to study law. The study of law disappointed Wilson. He found it tedious and boring, but he managed to graduate in 1882 from the Virginia School of Law. He didn't enjoy practicing law, so he instead went to Johns Hopkins University to study government. He revised his article on Congress and published it as a book entitled *Congressional Government.* The book sold well. It impressed many people and earned Wilson a PhD.

Next came a career in teaching. Wilson started out at Bryn Mawr — a traditional all-female college. He hated it there, so he left for Wesleyan University in 1888. He continued to publish, achieving a nationwide reputation for being one of the best scholars on government. Finally, in 1890, his dream of receiving a professorship at Princeton University came true. Wilson settled in for a career in education. He continued to be active in his field; his books sold well. In 1902, Wilson published his masterpiece, *A History of the American People.* Wilson achieved the status of a famed writer; he became a household name in the United States.

By 1902, Wilson became so famous that Princeton University appointed him its president. He implemented tougher admission standards, turning Princeton into the well-known institution it is today.

Wilson was hardworking, but he did find time to marry. He married Ellen Louise Axson in 1885 after a long engagement. She proved to be the ideal wife for Wilson — she was always supportive of her husband. Their marriage was a happy one until her death in 1914.

Wilson is the best-educated president in U.S. history. He held a PhD in government, taught government at Princeton, and published several well-received books. He was even president of Princeton University before he became president of the United States.

Breaking into Politics in New Jersey

When Woodrow Wilson became active in New Jersey politics in 1906, it didn't look good for him. New Jersey had been a Republican state for decades. Theodore Roosevelt, a Republican, was president and at the height of his popularity.

In 1910, a political opportunity arose. More and more people in New Jersey were fed up with Republican politics. Corruption was high, and the patronage system was widespread (see "The spoils system" sidebar in Chapter 11 for info on this practice). The Democrats wanted a fresh new face, a reformer, to run for governor. Who better to fill the role than Wilson, a man well known for championing social causes at Princeton.

Wilson received the Democratic nomination. He resigned from Princeton and won big in the November election. He soon abandoned the traditional Democrats and aligned himself with progressive Democrats and Republicans who, like himself, wanted to reform New Jersey politics.

Governing New Jersey

Wilson and his allies transformed New Jersey from a conservative state, dominated by political machines and patronage, into one of the most progressive states in the Union. Among his accomplishments as governor were the following:

- ✔ **Instituting direct primaries:** Instead of having party leaders pick the nominees for the two political parties, Wilson implemented a direct primary. This system allowed for the people, not politicians, to pick whom they wanted to run for state office.

- ✔ **Setting up the Public Utilities Commission:** This commission had the power to regulate the water and power companies in New Jersey. Because the state could set rates, price gouging by these companies was prevented.

- ✔ **Establishing workmen's compensation:** With the federal government not yet providing a welfare system for the U.S. public, Wilson started to provide injured workers with workmen's compensation.

By 1911, Wilson had become one of the most famous and well-respected governors in the United States. With the incumbent President Taft having problems (see Chapter 13), Wilson was ready for the White House.

Running for president in 1912

Wilson went to the Democratic nominating convention in 1912 as an underdog. The two front-runners, Champ Clark of Missouri and Oscar Underwood of Alabama, split the vote on the first 45 ballots. Neither of them could receive the required two-thirds majority, so the delegates started to look for someone else. On the 46th ballot, Wilson received the nomination.

If the Republican Party had not split into the Taft faction, which supported the president, and the Bull Moose faction, headed by former President Theodore Roosevelt, Wilson would have lost badly to any Republican nominee.

Wilson ran on a liberal platform, reaching out to union workers and blacks. He won big in the electoral vote but garnered just under 42 percent of the popular vote. The Republican Party received over 50 percent of the popular vote. But because of its split, it lost badly in the Electoral College.

President Woodrow Wilson (1913–1921)

As president, Woodrow Wilson (shown in Figure 14-1) moved quickly to implement his progressive reform programs. He referred to his policies as the "New Freedom" programs, because they gave the average U.S. citizen more democratic freedoms in relation to the government and business. Wilson's two terms contained some of the most important legislation introduced in U.S. history. Some of his great accomplishments include:

Figure 14-1: Woodrow Wilson, 28th president of the United States.

Courtesy of the Library of Congress

✔ **The Underwood Tariff (1913):** This bill reduced tariffs for many imported goods by 25 percent. For some goods, like wool and sugar, the bill even eliminated import charges. It was the first tariff reduction since before the Civil War. The average U.S. citizen benefited from this tariff reduction by being able to buy cheap foreign goods.

✔ **The 16th Amendment to the Constitution (1913):** With the passing of the 16th Amendment, the federal government could legally tax incomes in the United States. Wilson implemented the first income tax in U.S. history. It was progressive, meaning that the more a person made, the more he paid in income taxes.

The first income tax in the United States seems ridiculously low when compared to the income taxes of today. The income tax rate on people making more than $3,000 was 1 percent. If a person made more than $20,000, the rate went up to 7 percent — the highest tax rate.

✔ **The 17th Amendment to the Constitution (1913):** This amendment allowed the people, instead of the state legislatures, to vote for their U.S. senators.

✔ **The Federal Reserve Act (1914):** Wilson implemented a new system to control the economy because he wanted to avoid continuous problems with the banks that went belly up during times of economic crisis. The new Federal Reserve System was in place by 1914. It regulated the money supply in the United States by establishing 12 regional banks that would respond to changing economic conditions, such as inflation or a recession. The Federal Reserve Act stabilized the overall economic system in the United States.

✔ **The Federal Trade Commission (1914):** Wilson believed that *monopolies,* or companies that controlled a whole sector of the economy, were bad for a democracy. So he put the Federal Trade Commission in place. The commission had the power to study suspected monopolies and recommend the destruction of them.

✔ **The Clayton Antitrust Act (1914):** This act helped unions by declaring it acceptable to strike and picket factories.

✔ **The Unemployment Compensation Act (1916):** This act provided unemployment benefits to federal employees but not to the masses of U.S. workers. It provided the foundation for the New Deal agenda of President Franklin Delano Roosevelt (see Chapter 16 for more on Roosevelt's New Deal programs).

✔ **The Child Labor Acts (1916):** These acts, later declared unconstitutional by the Supreme Court, declared child labor illegal in the United States.

✔ **The 18th Amendment to the Constitution (1919):** This amendment outlawed the production and sale of alcoholic beverages in the United States. Wilson himself drank liquor, and he made it available to guests in the White House, but he was a consummate politician, believing that the public should get what it wants.

> ✔ **The 19th Amendment to the Constitution (1920):** This amendment gave women the right to vote in 1920. Wilson supported the amendment even though he personally didn't think that women should be involved in politics.

The one area where Wilson was not progressive was civil rights. Many southerners served in high positions under Wilson, and their influence soon became visible. Within a few years, some federal agencies had become segregated.

Managing the media

Wilson liked Theodore Roosevelt: He copied much from Roosevelt in his own political career. The idea of using the presidency as a *bully pulpit,* or using his position to go directly to the people and ignoring Congress, appealed to Wilson. He adopted this idea as soon as he became president. For Wilson, the presidency was an active institution. Wilson believed that the president should lead Congress instead of just react to it.

As president, Wilson set many precedents. One of his major changes was a reverting back to the tradition of delivering the annual State of the Union address to Congress in person — something that no president had done since John Adams, more than a century earlier.

Prior presidents had sent a written copy of their address to Congress, where it was read aloud. Wilson felt that he could be more influential if he addressed Congress personally. In addition, he had his speeches published and publicized by the media to reach as many U.S. citizens as possible. He knew that if he controlled public opinion, he also controlled Congress. For example, when Wilson pushed for lower tariffs, the Senate objected. So Wilson went straight to the U.S. voters and asked them to contact their senators and push for lower tariffs. Thousands of letters poured in, and the Senate passed Wilson's lower tariff bill.

When his wife Ellen died in 1914, President Wilson was devastated. He sat next to her corpse for two days and told his aides that he hoped that someone would assassinate him.

One of the most embarrassing newspaper typographical errors regarding the presidency occurred during the Wilson administration. A year after his wife died, Wilson took a young widow, and his eventual wife, Edith Galt, to the theater. *The Washington Post* reported on this and meant to print the following: "the president spent most of his time entertaining Mrs. Galt." Instead, the printed story read: "the president spent most of his time entering Mrs. Galt."

Woodrow Wilson married Edith Galt in December 1915. She helped to run the White House after he was disabled by a stroke in 1919.

Most of Wilson's domestic accomplishments took place between 1913 and 1914. The outbreak of WWI in Europe turned Wilson's focus toward foreign policy.

Establishing a moral foreign policy

In the area of foreign policy, Wilson made important changes to the policies of Roosevelt and Taft. Unlike Roosevelt, Wilson refused to carry a big stick and bully other countries into pursuing policies that favored the United States. In contrast to Taft, Wilson believed that handing out money to foreign countries wasn't good enough. He wanted to pursue a moral foreign policy.

Wilson's foreign policy was just in nature. He respected other countries, even if they were weaker than the United States. For Wilson, it was important that all partners — not just the United States — benefit from foreign policy. For example, he considered it unjust that Roosevelt turned Panama into an independent nation for his own political purpose, namely the building of a canal. Roosevelt ignored the claims of Columbia, which controlled Panama. Wilson gave Columbia $20 million as compensation for the loss of Panama.

Mishandling Mexico

Wilson considered it illegal to intervene in the policies of other countries. Believing in the right of sovereignty, Wilson refused to intervene in the Mexican revolutions that began in 1910. Wilson declined to get involved even though many U.S. businesses that had invested in Mexico and owned property there called for military intervention to protect their investments. Roosevelt, Taft, and the Republicans agreed with this view, but Wilson refused to use the military, choosing to take a diplomatic approach instead.

Wilson refused to recognize the new Mexican government headed by General Victoriano Huerta, who seized power in 1913. Wilson backed the democratic opposition leader Venustiano Carranza instead. In 1914, Huerta's men arrested several U.S. sailors, and Wilson acted. He sent soldiers to Vera Cruz, Mexico. Over 100 people were killed in a skirmish between U.S. and Mexican soldiers in the city.

Other Latin American countries tried to mediate the Mexican civil war. However, Carranza, who was in power after Huerta's resignation, refused to recognize mediation. Carranza's refusal drove Wilson to back another reformist leader, the bandit Francisco (Pancho) Villa.

Villa believed that only the United States could overthrow the Carranza government. His idea was to raid border towns, blame the raids on Carranza, and have the United States go to war with Mexico.

Wilson didn't fall for the ruse. He recognized the Carranza government and sent troops after Pancho Villa. The troops failed to capture Villa. Many U.S.

citizens wanted a full-fledged war against Mexico and the new Mexican government. On the other side of the issue, many Mexican citizens turned against the United States because they were upset by Wilson's actions. Wilson's foreign policy towards Mexico ended in disaster.

Looking at war in Europe

In 1914, World War I broke out in Europe. Wilson announced U.S. neutrality immediately because he believed that the United States had no interest in the war in Europe. Public opinion didn't support going to war, and the minority that supported getting involved was split over which side to support. Wilson knew that taking sides in WWI could split the United States politically and ethnically, so he remained neutral, issuing ten neutrality proclamations in the fall of 1914 alone.

The two largest ethnic groups in the United States were citizens of German and English descent. This division made it tough for Wilson to take sides. He knew that he would alienate one of the two groups if the United States entered WWI.

Personally, Wilson favored the Allies — especially Great Britain, the cradle of democracy in Europe. Wilson's cabinet was also pro-British. His ambassador to Great Britain, Walter Page, consistently defended British policies.

Determining the causes of World War I

World War I (WWI) broke out in Europe in August 1914 and lasted until November 1918. The war proved to be the bloodiest and most vicious war to date. In a little over four years, 37 million people died in World War I.

The causes of the war were many. The spark that led to the outbreak of the war was the assassination of Archduke Ferdinand, the heir to the throne of the Austrian-Hungarian empire. Serbian nationalists assassinated the archduke while he was visiting Sarajevo, now the capital of Bosnia. Austria wanted revenge and demanded that Serbia accept several demands. The demands would have turned Serbia into a province of the Austrian empire. With Russian backing, the Serbs rejected the offer. Austria turned to Germany for help and received Germany's complete support. The war was on.

There are many theories on the outbreak of WWI. It is clear today that many nations wanted a war. Both Germany and Russia faced domestic problems, which the war temporarily cured. France wanted to regain territory lost to Germany during the Franco-Prussian War (1870–1871), and Italy wanted to expand. In other words, most nations in Europe, with the exception of Great Britain, welcomed the war.

However, when Germany attacked Belgium, Britain, which guaranteed Belgian security by treaty, had to act. Every major European power participated in the war. Within two years, the war had become a global war, involving 32 countries.

Being Drawn into the War

Wilson attempted to settle WWI peacefully, sending diplomatic missions to Great Britain and Germany. He was eager to ensure that the seas remain open and that U.S. trade with Europe wouldn't be affected.

The British rejected the U.S. offer. Germany, trying to disrupt British control of the seas, declared the area surrounding Great Britain a war zone and said it would attack any ships bound for Britain.

Wilson retaliated by declaring that an attack on any U.S. ship would not go unpunished. On May 7, 1915, a German submarine sank the British passenger ship *Lusitania,* killing more than 1,100 people, including 128 U.S. citizens. The U.S. public reacted angrily and demanded action. For the first time, public opinion shifted toward the Allied side. Former president Theodore Roosevelt publicly advocated a massive rearmament to get the United States ready for war.

Great Britain employed a strategy of carrying war materials, such as ammunition, on passenger ships during WWI. The strategy made it legal, under international law, for countries at war with Great Britain to sink these passenger ships. William Jennings Bryan, Wilson's secretary of state, pressured Wilson to demand that Great Britain stop this practice. Wilson refused, and Bryan resigned.

Winning reelection and preparing for war

It wasn't until 1916 that President Wilson saw a need to strengthen the U.S. military forces. For the first time, Wilson publicly stated that the U.S. military would not only be used for the defense of the country but also to protect other nations.

As he was getting the country ready for war, Wilson also faced reelection. The Republican Party united again. Roosevelt brought his Bull Moose supporters back into the party, but he refused to stand as a candidate. The Republican Party nominated Charles Evan Hughes, the former governor of New York and a member of the U.S. Supreme Court, to face Wilson.

The election was truly a cliffhanger. On election night, Wilson went to bed believing that he had lost the race. When he woke up, he found out that he'd been reelected. The voters in California, one of the most progressive states in the nation, made the difference, though Wilson carried the state by just 4,000 votes. When the final tally was in, Wilson, shown in Figure 14-2, won 277 electoral votes to Hughes's 254. Wilson's campaign slogan, "He kept us out of war," made the difference, but he couldn't continue to keep the United States neutral.

Figure 14-2:
The President and Edith Wilson on their way to the presidential inauguration in March 1917.

Courtesy of the Library of Congress

Entering World War 1

Inept German foreign policy pushed the United States into WWI. In January 1917, Germany announced a policy of unrestricted submarine warfare: Germany threatened to torpedo and sink any ship, including U.S. ships, that traded with the Allied powers.

Wilson responded by breaking off diplomatic relations with Germany and mobilizing U.S. military forces. In the next three months, German submarines sank three U.S. ships, killing 36 sailors.

On April 2, 1917, Wilson asked Congress to declare war on Germany in one of the most memorable speeches in U.S. history. The following is an excerpt from Wilson's speech:

> The world must be made safe for democracy. Its peace must be planted upon the tested foundations of political liberty. We have no selfish ends to serve. We desire no conquest, no dominion. We seek no indemnities for ourselves, no material compensation for the sacrifices we shall freely make.

Within four days, both houses passed the declaration, and the United States entered WWI on the side of the Allied powers.

The last straw for Wilson was the Zimmermann telegram. This telegram, sent to the German ambassador in Mexico and intercepted by the British in 1917, asked Mexico to join in a war against the United States. If the Mexican government agreed, Germany promised a return of the territory lost to the United States in the Mexican-American War.

Getting the public involved

Wilson moved quickly to get the country ready for war. By the end of the year, he had the following elements in place:

- ✔ The Selective Service Act was implemented. This act allowed the U.S. government to draft men between the ages of 21 and 30 to serve in the military.

- ✔ The U.S. economy turned into a wartime economy. Under the able leadership of Republican, and future president, Herbert Hoover, industries started to produce weapons, ammunition, military equipment, and food.

By the summer of 1917, the first U.S. troops were in Europe. Within a year, two million U.S. soldiers fought in Europe, making the difference in an Allied victory. Germany launched one final offensive against France in 1918 in an attempt to conquer the country before U.S. soldiers could get there to defend it. The offensive fell short. In November 1918, the German empire surrendered.

Making the Peace

The time came to make peace in Europe. Wilson speculated that the Allies would win with U.S. help. For this reason, Wilson was ready to make peace in Europe and strengthen democracy in the process.

Advocating Fourteen Points

In January 1918, Wilson outlined his famous Fourteen Points, as a condition for peace in Europe, in a speech to Congress. With the surrender of Germany in November 1918, he was ready to put these points in place. The most important provisions of the Fourteen Points were

- ✔ **Abolition of secret diplomacy:** Wilson believed that all diplomatic activity should be open to public scrutiny.

- ✔ **Protection of the seas:** Wilson wanted the seas to be open in both peace and wartime.

- ✔ **Removal of international trade barriers:** Wilson advocated lower tariffs against imports to stimulate worldwide trade.

- ✔ **Reduction of armaments and the introduction of arms control:** Wilson believed in *arms control,* or the limitation of armaments, as well as *disarmament,* or the reduction of armaments. He wanted talks to start immediately.

- ✔ **Resolution of colonial disputes:** Wilson believed that the colonial power and the people living within the colony itself should be able to resolve their differences peacefully.

- ✔ **Evacuation of Russian territory:** After the collapse of the Russian empire and the emergence of a new communist government in Russia, many foreign powers sent troops to Russia — including the United States, which tried to protect its own national interests.

- ✔ **Restoration of Belgium:** Belgium was conquered by Germany during WWI and needed to be reestablished.

- ✔ **Return of the province of Alsace-Lorraine from Germany to France:** The province of Alsace-Lorraine was conquered by Germany in 1871.

- ✔ **Creation of an independent Polish state:** The country of Poland disappeared after the Seven Year War (1756–1763). It had been divided between Austria-Hungary, Germany, and Russia. Wilson wanted it restored.

- ✔ **Creation of the League of Nations, an international peacekeeping organization:** The League of Nations operated on the concept of collective security, which stated that an attack on a member state equaled an attack on all members. In theory, this concept outlawed war in the world.

With the surrender of Germany, it was time to turn the Fourteen Points into reality.

Traveling to Europe

To Wilson's great disappointment, the U.S. public didn't reward him with majorities in Congress in the November 1918 elections. Wilson openly attacked the Republicans during the 1918 elections and urged people to vote for Democrats. Many voters felt that it was inappropriate to engage in partisan politicking while the country was still at war. They punished Wilson by voting Republican. The Republicans won both houses of Congress and began opposing Wilson's policies.

Wilson traveled to Europe in December 1918, becoming the first sitting U.S. president to do so. He received a hero's welcome. In January 1919, he opened the peace conference in Paris.

The conference in Paris proved to be disappointing to Wilson. British and French leaders disliked Wilson personally — Prime Minster Lloyd George described him as a cross between Jesus Christ and Napoleon — and they had no interest in adopting many of the Fourteen Points.

By June, Wilson had sacrificed most of the Fourteen Points in order to keep the idea of an international organization alive. By the time Germany signed the

Treaty of Versailles in 1919, ending the war, only the return of Alsace-Lorraine to France, the establishment of a League of Nations, and the establishment of independent Belgian and Polish states remained from the original 14 points.

Wilson left for home to convince the Senate to ratify the Treaty of Versailles.

Losing the peace at home

Wilson returned home in July 1919, expecting that the Senate would quickly ratify the Treaty of Versailles. But Wilson made a grave political blunder by not taking any prominent Republicans to the Paris peace conference. The Republicans felt slighted and started undermining Wilson at home while he was overseas negotiating peace.

So, when it came to ratifying the peace treaty, the Republican majority in the Senate had a few reservations. The main sticking point was the fact that the Charter of the League of Nations required the United States to make troops available to defend other member countries.

The president toured the country in an effort to drum up public support. He traveled close to 10,000 miles, exhausting himself in the process. On October 2, 1919, Wilson suffered a stroke. He ended his tour and returned home, partially paralyzed.

The Senate voted down the Treaty of Versailles in November 1919, and then voted it down again the following year. The next president, Republican Warren G. Harding, signed a separate peace treaty with Germany when he assumed office in 1921.

Woodrow Wilson received the Nobel Peace Prize in 1920 for creating the League of Nations — an organization that his own country never joined.

The *League of Nations* came into existence in 1920, with 42 nations joining the organization. It lasted until 1946, when it was replaced by the United Nations. During the League's years of existence, 63 nations were members at one time or another. The League was administered by a League Council, representing permanent members. The League Council included Great Britain, France, Italy, and later Germany, the Soviet Union, and Japan. All decisions in the council had to be unanimous, giving each member an absolute veto over the League's polices.

Serving out his term

Even though Wilson was paralyzed on the left side of his body, he decided not to resign but to remain in office until his term expired in March 1921. The public didn't receive information concerning his health problems. Wilson's wife helped him with day-to-day activities, such as writing his signature, during the last 18 months of his term.

Wilson retired from public office in 1921 and lived in seclusion until his death in 1924. To the end, he believed in the League of Nations and never forgave the Republicans for not allowing the United States to join his beloved organization.

Chapter 15

Roaring through the '20s with Harding, Coolidge, and Hoover

- -

In This Chapter

▶ Being unfit for the presidency: Harding

▶ Staying silent and accomplishing nothing: Coolidge

▶ Reacting too slowly to the Great Depression: Hoover

- -

*T*his chapter covers the three Republican presidents of the golden 1920s. Times were good: The economy was booming until 1929, and the country wasn't involved in any foreign conflicts. So the presidents didn't do much.

Harding was too busy playing poker and cheating on his wife to run the country. Coolidge didn't want to do anything but sleep. And Hoover reacted to the Great Depression a little too late. Today, all three presidents are considered failures. None of them even cracks the top-20 list of presidents.

Living the High Life: Warren G. Harding

Warren G. Harding, shown in Figure 15-1, has the distinction of being one of the worst presidents in U.S. history. He wasn't interested in the presidency. He himself thought that he was unfit for office. He only enjoyed the office because it allowed him to pursue his true loves in life: gambling, drinking, and willing women. As he said of himself, "I am a man of limited talents from a small town. I don't seem to grasp that I am president."

Harding's administration is famous for its corruption. Harding himself wasn't crooked, but he appointed many friends who used their positions to enrich themselves, which reflected badly on Harding.

Figure 15-1:
Warren G.
Harding,
29th
president of
the United
States, and
his dog
Laddie.

Harding was one of the most immoral and hypocritical individuals to ever occupy the White House. He married for money and had many adulterous affairs (fathering a child with one mistress). The Republicans paid one of his long-time girlfriends to go to Europe so that she'd be out of the way during the presidential campaign. Even though he supported prohibition, he had his own distributor provide him and his poker buddies with liquor in the White House. By 1923, these actions came back to haunt him. However, his premature death at the age of 57 saved him from many embarrassments.

Harding's early political career

The Ohio Republican Party recruited Harding to run for the Ohio state senate in 1898. He won his initial race and was reelected in 1900. In 1903, he became the lieutenant governor of Ohio, a post he held for two terms.

While working in the Ohio state government, Harding befriended Harry M. Daugherty, a major leader in the Ohio Republican Party. Daugherty became his trusted advisor and campaign manager.

When Harding lost the race for governor in 1910, he wanted to retire from politics. His wife and friends had other ideas. They talked him into staying active in politics. In 1914, he won a seat in the U.S. Senate.

Harding's years as a senator were undistinguished. He supported the conservative wing of the Republican Party, pushing for higher tariffs and the abolition of the manufacturing and sale of liquor. In 1919, he opposed the Treaty of Versailles, which established the League of Nations. In other words, Harding was a loyal Republican who pleased the party leadership.

Loving the good life

Warren G. Harding was born in Corsica, Ohio in 1865. His father was a homeopathic doctor and part-time veterinarian. After graduating from Ohio Central College in 1882, Harding tried his hand at many jobs — he taught school, sold insurance, organized a musical band, and even studied law.

Harding finally settled on a job at the local newspaper in Marion, Ohio, where he worked as a printer and reporter. He quickly lost his job because he was a Republican and the paper supported Democratic viewpoints. After losing his job, he opened his own newspaper. He bought the bankrupt *Marion Star* for $300 and turned it into a success by pledging to mention anybody living in Marion in the paper at least once a year.

Harding also joined every social club available. His personality helped him make many friends.

Harding was a fun guy who told dirty jokes and was willing to play poker and drink whiskey with just about anyone.

Harding married Florence Kling DeWolfe, a woman five years older than he, in 1891. The marriage wasn't a happy one. Harding married DeWolfe for her money. He referred to her as a shrew and gave her the nickname "The Duchess."

Harding cheated on her constantly. He had two long-lasting affairs. The first one was with Carrie Phillips, the wife of one of his closest friends. The second was with Nan Britton, whom he met while she was still in high school. The affair with Britton lasted into his presidency and produced a daughter. Britton would secretly enter the White House at night, and the two would make love in the small closet next to the president's office.

Becoming president by default

By 1919, Harding's political handler, Daugherty, believed that Harding was ready for the presidency. He sent Harding to speak all over the country.

Harding created his campaign slogan, "A Return to Normalcy," by mistake. He meant to say "normality," but he misspoke. The term stuck, and the Republican Party used it to convey that they wanted to take the country back to the good old days of pre-World War I America. The slogan sat well with a nation ready to forget about World War I.

At the Republican convention, Harding, a second-rate candidate, seemed a long shot. However, when the party couldn't agree on a candidate, Harding started looking better. After a long night in one of the famous smoke-filled rooms, the Republican Party agreed on Harding. Calvin Coolidge, the governor of Massachusetts, became his vice-presidential candidate.

After winning the nomination, Harding stayed in Ohio and campaigned from his front porch. His handlers didn't want him to mingle with the voters: They were afraid that he would offend and alienate them.

Harding won 61 percent of the popular vote and 404 electoral votes — one of the largest landslide victories in U.S. history.

President Warren Gamaliel Harding (1921–1923)

Harding's inaugural speech set the tone for what was to come. His address was the worst in U.S. history. A British reporter called it "the most illiterate statement ever made by the head of a civilized government." Harding's treasury secretary, after listening to many of Harding's speeches, said, "His speeches left the impression of pompous phrases moving over the landscape in search of an idea. Sometimes these meandering words would actually capture a straggling thought and bear it triumphantly, a prisoner in the midst, until it died of servitude and overwork."

Defrauding and scandalizing the nation

Harding's first priority as president was to organize a weekly poker game that his whole cabinet was required to attend. Many political decisions took place while the president and his cabinet played cards.

Harding's cabinet contained some of the best and worst people to ever serve the United States. Harding appointed his friends, referred to as the "Ohio Gang," to high-level cabinet positions. The Ohio Gang started defrauding the government soon after they entered office. Following are some of the more famous scandals under Harding:

- Charles Forbes, the head of the Veteran's Bureau, defrauded the government of $200 million. Harding allowed him to flee the country. When he returned, years later, Forbes went to jail. Forbes was the first U.S. cabinet member to be sentenced to jail.

- Harry M. Daugherty, the attorney general, sold alcohol during Prohibition. During Prohibition, it was illegal to make or distribute alcohol.

- Albert B. Fall, the secretary of the interior, was involved in the *Teapot Dome Scandal.*

  Teapot Dome was a federal facility where the U.S. navy drilled for and stored oil. In 1922, Fall leased the facility to two oil companies that paid him $400,000. Fall went to jail for his actions in 1929.

Reacting to all the scandals in his administration, Harding said, "My god, this is a hell of a job! I can take care of my enemies all right. But my damn friends, my g------friends . . . they're the ones that keep me walking the floor nights!"

Succeeding despite himself

Harding had his moments. His administration was successful in a few areas, where his accomplishments included

- Reducing income taxes

- Protecting U.S. industries from foreign competition with the Fordney McCumber Act — an act that increased tariffs

- Restricting immigration from Europe with the Immigration Act of 1921

- Allowing blacks in federal government positions

- Signing a separate peace treaty with Germany, officially ending the war in Europe

- Calling the Washington Conference

In 1921, Harding called for a conference in Washington between the great powers. The Washington Conference resulted in the Five Power Treaty, which limited the number of ships and aircraft carriers that the five great powers in the world could have. (The five great powers at the time were the United States, Great Britain, France, Japan, and Italy.) The conference further established the Four Power Treaty, signed by the United States, Japan, Great Britain, and France. In it, the four countries pledged to recognize each other's possessions in the Pacific. The conference proved to be the most notable achievement of the Harding administration.

Dying suddenly

By 1923, Harding had fallen into despair. All the scandals, involving some of his best friends, got to him. He decided to tour Alaska. He suddenly became ill on his trip home, so he stopped in San Francisco to rest. He died there on August 2, 1923, of a possible stroke.

Mrs. Harding didn't allow an autopsy. So nobody really knows what Harding died of. At the time, there were rumors that Mrs. Harding had poisoned him after finding out about all the affairs her husband had. So far, these rumors haven't been substantiated.

Quietly Doing Nothing: John Calvin Coolidge

Calvin Coolidge's nickname was "Silent Cal." How appropriate! As president, Coolidge didn't do much. The United States was at peace and doing well during his term. So Coolidge, shown in Figure 15-2, enjoyed the presidency — he slept a lot and was fairly anti-social. Instead of trying to prevent the approaching Great Depression, Coolidge sat back, believing that the government had no role in the economy.

Figure 15-2: Calvin Coolidge, 30th president of the United States.

Courtesy of the Library of Congress

Coolidge's early career

Coolidge won his first public office, a seat on the city council in Northampton, Massachusetts, by going door to door. He wooed the electorate with the catchy phrase, "I want your vote. I need it. I shall appreciate it." He followed up his first public office with the positions of city solicitor, clerk of courts, mayor of Northampton, and member of the Massachusetts legislature.

A true Puritan

Calvin Coolidge was born on July 4, 1872. His father owned a small shop in Vermont and was deeply religious. Young Coolidge adopted his father's values and followed them throughout his life. Coolidge believed in conservatism, honesty, thrift, and religion. He became a quiet, shy young man, who didn't like to interact with people.

While studying at Amherst College, Coolidge enjoyed the social sciences and the arts. Like many presidents, Coolidge studied law. He opened his own practice in Northampton, Massachusetts.

In 1905, he met the love of his life, Grace Anna Goodhue. She was outgoing and friendly, and she loved people. Who says opposites don't attract?

In 1912, the people elected Coolidge to the state senate, where he served four years. Coolidge became the lieutenant governor of Massachusetts in 1916 and governor in 1918.

Governing Massachusetts

As governor, Coolidge didn't do much. But one event defined his term and turned him into a household name. In 1919, police officers in Boston formed a union and asked for more money. When the city refused, they went on strike. The mayor of the city suspended the union leaders and relied on state troopers to police the city. The mayor's plan wasn't sufficient. The crime rate went up. Criminals had a field day without the normal police force in place.

On the third day of the strike, Governor Coolidge called out the National Guard. He sent cavalry to Boston and beefed up the state troopers. He even went as far as to threaten the strikers with the use of federal troops. The officers returned to work the next day, and Coolidge refused to rehire the suspended strike leaders, saying, "There is no right to strike against the public safety by anybody, anywhere, anytime."

President Wilson applauded Coolidge's actions, as did businesses nation-wide. The resulting publicity helped him win reelection easily.

Becoming vice president

At the Republican convention in 1920, the Massachusetts delegation pushed Coolidge for the presidential nomination. They failed to get him nominated, although he did get the vice-presidential slot as a consolation prize. Coolidge accepted the bid happily. In 1920, he was elected vice president after resigning as governor. As vice president, Coolidge regularly joined Harding's cabinet meetings — the first vice president to do so.

When President Harding got sick in 1923, his advisors told Vice President Coolidge that the president was fine. So Coolidge went to Vermont to spend some time with his father. When Harding died, Coolidge was unreachable because his father didn't own a phone. So messengers were sent to inform Coolidge of the president's death. They arrived late at night when Coolidge was asleep. Coolidge got up, had his father, a notary public, give him the presidential oath, and then went back to sleep.

President Calvin Coolidge (1923–1929)

When Coolidge became president, he dealt with the scandals of Harding's administration by firing the attorney general, Daugherty, and forcing the resignation of the secretary of the navy. He then proceeded to appoint well-qualified, incorruptible people to office. His best appointment was Frank Kellogg as secretary of state.

In keeping with his values, Coolidge went straight to the people to explain the changes. Coolidge held many press conferences and had his State of the Union addresses reported live on radio.

In 1924, the economy was booming, and Coolidge was a shoo-in for reelection. The Republican Party renominated him. He easily defeated Democrat John W. Davis. Coolidge received almost twice as many popular votes as Davis, as well as 382 electoral votes.

In 1924, Coolidge used the slogan, "Keep cool with Coolidge," as his campaign motto. The people loved it. They reelected him for a second term.

Serving a second term

In 1925, the world was good. The U.S. economy was doing well, and there were no major international conflicts. Coolidge reduced the national debt and fought government intrusion in the economy. He repeatedly vetoed farm bills that would have allowed the government to purchase agricultural surpluses and keep prices for these goods high. His motto was simple: If it's not broken, why fix it.

President Coolidge required a lot of sleep. He went to bed at 10 p.m. and slept until 7 a.m. But that wasn't enough. In addition, the president took one two- to four-hour nap every afternoon.

Showing his racism

On social policy issues, Coolidge held fairly racist views. He supported restrictions on immigration and publicly stated that Nordic races deteriorate when mixed with other races. In his view, the United States, being a Nordic country, had to restrict immigration from other non-Nordic countries.

Excelling in foreign policy

Coolidge's greatest accomplishment came in the area of foreign policy. The subject bored him, but his secretary of state Frank Kellogg excelled in it. The passage of the Kellogg-Briand Act in 1928 was Coolidge's crowning achievement in foreign policy. Secretary of State Kellogg received the Nobel Peace Prize for his accomplishments.

The 63 signatories of the *Kellogg-Briand Act* of 1928 renounced the use of war as an instrument of foreign policy and instead relied upon peaceful means, such as diplomacy, to settle disputes. (Aristide Briand was the foreign minister of France.)

Choosing not to run

Coolidge was immensely popular. Had he decided to run for the presidency in 1928, he could have easily won. Instead, he issued a brief statement while on vacation in the summer of 1927, saying, "I do not choose to run for President in 1928." There were no explanations attached to his message. Coolidge had just had enough. With the death of his son in 1924, Coolidge stopped enjoying the presidency. He believed that it was time to step down.

Coolidge was upset that Herbert Hoover was the Republican selection for president in 1928. At one point, Coolidge said, "This man has offered me unsolicited advice for six years, all of it bad." But Coolidge didn't do anything to prevent Hoover's nomination.

Coolidge retired in 1929 and wrote his autobiography. He sat on the boards of several corporations and became a trustee at his alma mater, Amherst College. Coolidge died of a heart attack in January 1933.

A Great Humanitarian, but a Bad President: Herbert Hoover

Herbert Hoover, shown in Figure 15-3, is the most maligned president in U.S. history. Many blame him for the Great Depression, which is quite unfair. He actually set the foundation for Franklin Roosevelt's New Deal policies (see Chapter 16 for more on these policies). Too bad his efforts weren't better publicized. Hoover wasn't a politician — he never ran for office before becoming president — and he didn't know how to reach out to the public and explain his policies. Not hearing anything different, the average U.S. citizen didn't think that the president cared. So he was voted out of office.

On the other hand, Hoover was quite a man. He was a self-made millionaire and a great humanitarian. Hoover not only organized relief efforts to Europe during and after World War I, but he also became active after World War II when President Truman called him back into service. With these efforts, Hoover literally saved millions of Europeans from starvation.

Hoover was a mediocre president and a great human being. While serving his country, Hoover refused to take a salary and instead donated the money to charities. He deserved his title as the "Great Humanitarian."

Courtesy of the Library of Congress

Hoover's early career

Hoover was in London when WWI broke out. Right away, he wanted to help. His first task was to bring home the thousands of U.S. citizens that were stranded in Europe. (He assisted over 120,000 U.S. citizens.) Hoover then took on the more demanding job of feeding and clothing thousands of Europeans. From 1914 to 1919, Hoover headed the Commission for the Relief of Belgium. He supervised the distribution of millions of tons of aid to Belgium and northern France.

President Wilson was impressed with Hoover's activities, so in 1917, he called him back home to become the U.S. food administrator. This position required Hoover to make sure that the United States could feed its military and the Allied troops in Europe. Hoover was so successful that Wilson sent him back to Europe after WWI to help starving Europeans. As the head of the American Relief Administration, Hoover provided food to 300 million people across Europe. By 1920, his job was done. It was time to move on.

Entering politics

When the Republicans retook the White House in 1921, President Harding appointed Hoover secretary of commerce. Hoover reorganized the department and extended federal control over the public airwaves and the airline industry. He also standardized sizes for basic items such as tires, nuts, and bolts.

In addition, Hoover continued to be active in the area of disaster relief. He organized aid to Russia and later took on the Mississippi river flood relief. By 1928, the Great Humanitarian was known to every U.S. citizen.

Overcoming hardships and misery

Herbert Hoover was born in the state of Iowa in 1874. Hoover grew up in a Quaker family. He was given up for dead at the age of two. When his parents pulled a sheet over his head, thinking that he was dead, his uncle, a doctor, came to the rescue and resuscitated him.

Hoover lost both of his parents by the time he was nine. Relatives divided up Hoover and his siblings, and Hoover went to Oregon to live with an uncle. He worked on his uncle's farm and studied at night, but he never graduated from high school.

Hoover became fascinated by the field of engineering after running into an engineer. Hoover was too poor to afford tuition, so he applied to what today is Stanford University. Stanford had just opened it doors in 1891. It was a well-financed private school, so it was waiving its tuition for the freshmen class to attract students. Hoover studied geology, necessary to become a mining engineer, at the university and worked many menial jobs on the side. In 1895, he graduated and started an engineering career in San Francisco.

Hoover then moved to London to work for a British mining company. His job allowed him to travel the world. He went to Australia, China, and Burma. Hoover proved to be a genius at making old mines profitable. He received a cut of the proceeds every time he succeeded and became a very wealthy man.

In 1899, Hoover married his college sweetheart, Lou Henry, the first women to graduate from Stanford with a geology degree. She accompanied him on his many trips. The Hoovers lived through the Boxer rebellion in China (see Chapter 13) and then settled in London. Hoover and his wife spoke fluent Chinese. Whenever they didn't want people in the White House to know what they were saying, they would speak to each other in Chinese.

By 1914, Hoover was one of the most respected engineers in the world. His book, *Principles of Mining,* was required reading in every college engineering class. Hoover was worth $4 million in 1914, but instead of trying to amass more money, he decided to use his money to help people. His career as a great humanitarian had begun.

Becoming president

In 1927, President Coolidge shocked the nation when he refused to run for reelection. Hoover was ready to become president, so he sought the Republican nomination. He received the nomination on the first ballot with no opposition.

The general election was even easier for Hoover. The Democrats nominated Governor Al Smith of New York for the presidency. Smith was Catholic. This topic became a hot campaign issue. Many in the United States believed that a Catholic wouldn't be loyal to the Constitution because he owed loyalty to the pope. The solid Democratic South was heavily Protestant, and it refused to back a Catholic. When the results of the presidential election came in, Hoover had won in a landslide. He won 444 electoral votes, including five Southern states not carried by a Republican since the end of Reconstruction.

President Herbert Clark Hoover (1929–1933)

In his acceptance speech at the Republican national convention, Hoover proclaimed that poverty had come to an end in the United States, saying, "The poorhouse is vanishing among us. We in America today are nearer to the final triumph over poverty than ever before in the history of the land." For the first six months, things went well. Then the Great Depression started. At first, Hoover believed that the depression was temporary, and he didn't act. As late as spring 1930, he assured the public that the recession would be over soon. Things went differently.

Dealing with the Great Depression

By spring 1930, the Great Depression was in full swing. Hoover dealt with the economic situation by implementing the following programs:

- **The Agricultural Marketing Act (1929):** This act, passed before the Great Depression started, allowed the federal government to make loans to farmers in need. The act also allowed the government to buy their surplus goods, keeping prices for these goods high.

- **The Hawley-Smoot Tariff (1930):** This tariff increased charges on foreign goods. It led to an international trade war and hurt the world economy.

- **The Reconstruction Finance Corporation (1932):** This agency provided federal money to banks, railroads, insurance companies, and, later, local and state governments in need.

- **The Glass-Steagall Act (1932):** This act released government gold reserves to stimulate the economy.

- **The Federal Home Loan Bank Act (1932):** This act provided for low interest loans to homeowners who needed money to make their mortgage payments.

Despite all of Hoover's efforts, the Great Depression got worse. Hoover refused to implement unemployment benefits because he believed that local governments could take care of unemployed citizens. Local governments were, however, broke. Now, 12 million U.S. citizens were unemployed, 5,000 banks had gone bankrupt, and 32,000 businesses had gone under. Hoover's political career was over.

Burning down Hooverville

The last straw in Hoover's presidency occurred in 1932. About 15,000 WWI veterans marched to Washington, D.C. to redeem monetary certificates they received in 1924 as payment for their military service. The certificates were not cashable until 1945.

Beginnings of the Great Depression

The Great Depression was caused by more than one event, including

✔ An abundance of agricultural goods, which drove farmers' prices down

✔ Worldwide high tariffs that stifled international trade and reduced U.S. exports

✔ Big profits were not passed from corporations to workers, causing the buying power of the average person to decrease

✔ The stock market crash of October 1929

The 1920s were a prosperous decade for most U.S. citizens. The stock market had increased dramatically in value, and many citizens speculated widely with stocks. U.S. citizens mortgaged their homes to buy stock and even bought stock on margin, which allowed them to put up only 3 percent of the stock value in cash, while borrowing the rest from stockbrokers. As a result, many U.S. citizens were in debt over their heads, owing brokerage firms billions.

In September 1929, stock prices began to fall as a response to a slowing economy. People panicked and started selling off their stocks, further decreasing stock prices. By October 1929, panic broke out, and more and more people started to sell their stocks. Stock prices collapsed. Many people lost their life savings; people who mortgaged their homes to buy stocks ended up losing them; and people who bought stocks on margin couldn't repay the brokerage firms. The brokerage firms collapsed, and then banks went under. The Great Depression had begun.

The Senate refused the veterans' request to redeem the certificates. Many veterans went home, but approximately 2,000 stayed in Washington, D.C., setting up a tent city called "Hooverville."

President Hoover ordered General MacArthur and the military to disperse the veterans. General MacArthur did more than that. He went in with tanks and burned down Hooverville. The assault lead to the death of a baby.

The public was incensed. Hoover's career was finished. With elections only months away, Hoover was likely to lose, and lose he did. In the 1932 elections, Hoover won only 59 electoral votes. His Democratic opponent, Franklin Delano Roosevelt, received 472 electoral votes. Roosevelt also won seven million more votes in the popular election than Hoover.

Staying active in retirement

Hoover retired in 1933. He went back to California and became active in charitable organizations. He started the Hoover Library on War and then donated the 200,000 books he acquired to Stanford University.

Later, Hoover toured Europe. He met Hitler and warned the United States of German aggression. In 1939, Hoover went back to the United States to organize relief funds. He provided relief to Finland after it came under attack by the Soviet Union.

After World War II, President Truman asked Hoover to analyze the need for relief in Europe and then provide whatever relief was necessary. Hoover traveled to 38 countries in Europe and again did a superb job.

Truman was impressed with Hoover's performance, so he asked him to streamline government operations. The Hoover commission completed the job successfully. In 1953, President Eisenhower asked Hoover to start a second commission for the same purpose. Again, Hoover succeeded.

In 1955, Hoover retired at age 81. He died at the age of 90 in 1964.

One of Hoover's last statements concerned the people who blamed him for the Great Depression. Hoover said of them: "I outlived the b-------."

Part V

Instituting the Imperial Presidency: Franklin Roosevelt to Richard Nixon

The 5th Wave   By Rich Tennant

By virtue of a single word, did Eleanor inspire FDR to create the New Deal.

Gin!

Dang!!

In this part . . .

1 start out by looking at a great president — Franklin
Delano Roosevelt. He pulled the country out of the
Great Depression, started long-lasting programs such as
Social Security, and preserved democracy in Europe by
entering World War II. His successor, Harry Truman, then
saved Western Europe from the expanding Soviet empire,
with programs such as the Truman Doctrine, the Marshall
Plan, and later NATO. Back home, Truman desegregates
the U.S. military.

With Truman unable to end the war in Korea, the war hero
General Dwight D. Eisenhower comes to power. Often
overlooked, he was a great president who contained the
Soviet Union without sacrificing one American life.
Eisenhower also ended the war in Korea, desegregated
U.S. public schools, and initiated the present interstate
highway system.

Who doesn't know about John F. Kennedy and his attempts
to establish better relations with the Soviet Union and to
bring civil rights to the forefront? Kennedy didn't live to
see his efforts completed, but his successor Lyndon
Johnson finished the job. His legacy includes the Civil
Rights and the Voting Rights Acts, as well as Medicare and
Medicaid. Johnson would have been a great one, but there
was Vietnam, which undermined his presidency.

Richard Nixon concludes the part. You may be amazed
at how such a successful foreign policy president was
brought down by the worst presidential scandal in U.S.
history, Watergate.

Chapter 16

Boosting the Country and Bringing Back Beer: Franklin D. Roosevelt

Franklin Delano Roosevelt, or FDR as he is referred to, is one of the best-known and most successful presidents in U.S. history. He became president at a time when the country faced a massive economic crisis — the Great Depression started in 1929, three years before he was elected. By then, the average citizen had lost faith in the ability of the capitalist system to overcome the economic crisis.

His programs restored hope, helped the economy out of a recession, and, later on, helped win a world war. Roosevelt set the foundation for modern day government interference in the economy. He is the father of the U.S. welfare state and the large federal bureaucracy that administers it.

He guided the country through World War II (WWII) and turned the United States into a superpower by 1945. For these accomplishments, he deserves to be listed among the top five presidents of the United States.

Roosevelt's Early Political Career

In 1910, the Democratic Party approached Roosevelt and asked him to run for the New York state senate. He had great name recognition, sharing a last name with the recent two-term president, plus he had the money to pay for his own campaign. Roosevelt narrowly won the seat.

Born wealthy and well connected

Franklin Delano Roosevelt was born in Hyde Park, New York in 1882, into one of the most prominent families in the United States. He was related to 11 former presidents: Theodore Roosevelt, George Washington, John and John Quincy Adams, James Madison, Martin Van Buren, Benjamin and William Henry Harrison, Zachary Taylor, Ulysses Grant, and William Howard Taft. In addition, British Prime Minister Winston Churchill was a distant cousin.

Roosevelt's father was a businessman and a conservative Democrat. Young Franklin grew up living the good life. His family took him on trips to Europe, and whatever Franklin wanted, Franklin got, including a pony when he was 4 and a sailboat when he was 16.

Private tutors gave Roosevelt a superior education. He learned to speak both German and French. His parents sent him to an elite private school when he was 14, to prepare him for Harvard, which he entered in 1899 and graduated from in 1903. His favorite subjects were political economy and history. His knowledge of economics proved especially helpful later in life.

In 1904, Roosevelt embarked on his law school career. He finished his class work at Columbia Law School, but the law bored him, so he turned to politics instead. That same year, Roosevelt, a life-long Democrat, voted for the Republican candidate for the presidency. The Republican nominee was his cousin Theodore Roosevelt.

In 1905, Roosevelt married Eleanor Roosevelt, a distant cousin. At the wedding, she was given away by her uncle, President Theodore Roosevelt.

In the New York state senate, Roosevelt turned out to be a crusader, pushing for social and economic reforms. He refused to submit to party pressure, acting more like an independent than a Democrat. Before he won reelection in 1912, Roosevelt started to support Woodrow Wilson — another Democratic reformer — which turned out to be a good political move when Wilson gave him a job.

Serving in the executive branch

After Wilson became president in 1913, he rewarded Roosevelt for his loyalty by naming him assistant secretary of the navy. Roosevelt held this position for the next seven years.

When the United States entered World War I (WWI) in 1917, Roosevelt's job acquired more importance. As assistant secretary, he recruited people into the navy and planned military strategy. This experience came in handy 24 years later, during World War II.

In 1918, the Democratic Party approached Roosevelt and asked him to run for governor of New York. He turned them down and instead sought active duty in France. President Wilson refused to let him join the military, because he considered Roosevelt too valuable as assistant secretary, but he did allow him to tour Europe to gain firsthand knowledge of the war.

In 1920, the Democrats needed a young, energetic vice-presidential candidate to balance their fairly bland candidate for the presidency, James Cox. They picked Roosevelt. Roosevelt campaigned his heart out, but the Democratic ticket lost badly to the Republican candidate, Warren G. Harding. However, Roosevelt's energetic style of campaigning paid off. The Democratic Party took notice of the young vice-presidential candidate.

Overcoming polio

In 1921, when he was 29 years old, Roosevelt went on vacation at his family's retreat at Campobello in New Brunswick, Canada. He suddenly started to feel weak, with a fever and chills. Doctors diagnosed polio. The disease crippled him for life. For the next six years, Roosevelt underwent extensive rehabilitation in an effort to walk again. But it was all to no avail.

Roosevelt retired from politics and didn't expect to return. Being in a wheelchair and unable to walk without crutches seemed to make a political career impossible. But with the encouragement of his wife Eleanor, Roosevelt returned to politics in 1924 when he gave the nominating speech for governor Al Smith of New York at the Democratic presidential convention. Smith lost in 1924, but he received the nomination in 1928.

Governing New York

When Al Smith received the Democratic presidential nomination in 1928, he gave up the governorship of New York state. Smith asked his friend Roosevelt to run for the position. Roosevelt was reluctant, but his wife and friends finally convinced him to become a candidate. He barely won the governorship, and he was back in public life.

FDR ordered a custom-made car, which allowed him to drive without having to use his feet, so that he could campaign throughout the state.

As governor, Roosevelt dealt with a Republican-controlled legislature that slowed him down when he tried to implement reforms. Despite this limitation, Roosevelt provided tax cuts to farmers.

When the Great Depression hit, Roosevelt put policies in place that previewed the New Deal policies he would champion as president. For example, he established the Temporary Emergency Relief Administration, which provided help to the unemployed in New York.

It was during his term as governor that Roosevelt developed his radio skills, addressing the citizens of New York frequently. He shied away from public appearances because of his handicap, but the radio allowed him to speak directly to the people and persuade them of the merits of his policies. During his presidency, the radio addresses evolved into his famous fireside chats.

Preparing for the presidency

By 1930, the Great Depression was in full swing. The people blamed President Hoover and the Republicans for the dismal economy. As a Democrat, Roosevelt had an easy time getting reelected as governor of New York.

After being reelected, Roosevelt became a viable candidate for the 1932 Democratic presidential nomination. Not only was he a great speaker who was well known to the electorate, but, as governor of New York, he also could deliver the largest state in the United States at the time.

In 1931, Roosevelt started campaigning by sending supporters out to travel the country and make a case for him. By 1932, he was the clear frontrunner. At the Democratic convention, Roosevelt was nominated on the fourth ballot. He chose John Nance Garner of Texas for his vice-presidential nominee to help shore up southern support.

Traditionally, the presidential nominees didn't speak at their party's convention. Instead, they sent out an acceptance letter weeks after the convention finished. Roosevelt broke with tradition: He flew to Chicago, while the convention was still going on, to make his acceptance speech to the delegates in person.

He gave an unforgettable speech in which he described a new deal for the U.S. public, saying, "I pledge you, I pledge myself, to a new deal for the American people." He promised to repeal the 18th Amendment, which prohibited the sale or distribution of alcoholic beverages, and to initiate federal public works to hire the unemployed.

Winning in 1932

After receiving his party's nod in 1932, Roosevelt knew that he would win the presidency, because the public blamed Hoover and the Republican Party for the Great Depression. Despite the favorable situation, Roosevelt campaigned hard for a couple of reasons:

- He wanted majorities in both houses of Congress to support his policies.

- He wanted to prove to the public and himself that, despite his handicap, he could campaign effectively.

Using the campaign songs "Happy Days Are Here Again" and "Kick Out The Depression with a Democratic Vote," Roosevelt traveled the country — mostly by train. Thousands listened to his speeches. By the time the election came around, Roosevelt won big. He won 42 of the 48 states and took the electoral vote, 472 to 59.

Roosevelt almost didn't become president. He won the presidency in November 1932. The swearing-in ceremony wasn't scheduled until March 1933, so Roosevelt took a vacation. He traveled to the Bahamas and Florida in February 1933. He was giving a speech in Florida on February 15, when suddenly a man took a shot at him. The man missed Roosevelt but killed the mayor of Chicago, Anton Cermak, who was standing next to Roosevelt.

President Franklin Delano Roosevelt (1933–1945)

As president, Roosevelt (shown in Figure 16-1) hit the ground running. In his inaugural address, covered live on radio, he reassured the public and told people what he was about to do. He promised help for farmers and the unemployed, and, most importantly, proposed to regulate banks, brokerage firms, and the stock exchange. He declared a four-day bank holiday, when all banks nationwide were shut down, to allow the federal government to study which banks were still sound enough to reopen.

Figure 16-1:
Franklin Delano Roosevelt, 32nd president of the United States.

Courtesy of the Library of Congress

To reassure the public and help banks, Roosevelt instituted the Federal Deposit Insurance Corporation (FDIC) in 1933. Today, the FDIC insures bank deposits by guaranteeing individual depositor's funds up to $100,000. Even if a bank collapses, the federal government guarantees individual depositor's funds.

President Roosevelt appointed the first woman in U.S. history to serve in a presidential cabinet. Frances Perkins served as secretary of labor throughout Roosevelt's administration.

Rescuing the economy

Roosevelt came to power at the worst possible time. In March 1933, millions of U.S. citizens were unemployed, thousands of businesses had collapsed, and the U.S. banking industry was in shambles. Not surprisingly, Roosevelt's first order of business was to restore the public's trust in the economic structure.

In his first inaugural address, Roosevelt uttered these unforgettable words: "Let me assert my firm belief that the only thing we have to fear is fear itself — nameless, unreasoning, unjustified terror which paralyzes needed efforts to convert retreat into advance."

Roosevelt right away called for a special session of Congress to propose programs designed to provide rapid help to the unemployed and restore faith in the U.S. economy. His most famous New Deal programs include

- **The Emergency Banking Act (1933):** This act allowed for the federal government to regulate banks and restore public faith in the banking structure.

- **The Beer and Wine Revenue Act (1933):** This act allowed for the sale and taxation of low-alcohol beer and wine (3.2 percent or less), counter to the 18th Amendment, which banned the sale of all alcoholic beverages.

- **The Economy Act (1933):** This act cut the salaries of federal employees to help save the federal government money.

- **The Federal Emergency Relief Administration (FERA) (1933):** This administration provided federal money for states and localities to fund programs to help the poor.

- **The Civilian Conservation Corps (1933):** Through this program, more than 3 million young unemployed and unmarried men constructed public works projects, such as national parks and dams. These young men had to give more than 80 percent of their salary, $30 a month, to their families.

- **The National Industrial Recovery Act (1933):** This act created the National Recovery Administration (NRA). The NRA suspended anti-trust laws temporarily and allowed *price-fixing,* where companies get together to set the same price for the same goods they produce, to help industry. More importantly, the act set a minimum wage, standardized working hours, and allowed workers to engage in collective bargaining.

The U.S. Supreme Court declared the NRA unconstitutional in 1935. Congress passed the Fair Labor Standards Act to restore parts (the minimum wage, standardized working hours, and collective bargaining) of the NRA in 1938.

✓ **The Tennessee Valley Authority (TVA) (1933):** This corporation brought the federal government into the public utilities. The federal government constructed dams to generate hydroelectric power. The government then provided the power cheaply to people in Tennessee and seven surrounding states.

✓ **The Agricultural Adjustment Administration (1933):** This administration had the tough order of saving U.S. farmers from financial ruin. It bought surplus agricultural goods and even paid farmers to produce less. With fewer goods available on the market, agricultural prices shot up, providing farmers with much-needed cash.

The Supreme Court declared the Agricultural Adjustment Administration unconstitutional in 1936. But it worked so well that Congress brought it back in 1938. Although terms have changed significantly, this act is the basis for the farms subsidies in place today.

✓ **The National Housing Act (1934):** This act created the Federal Housing Authority, which guaranteed home loans for up to 80 percent of their value. With the federal government backing mortgages, banks wouldn't lose money if homeowners defaulted on their loans, so they were willing to lend more money to more home buyers. This, in turn, stimulated the housing industry. After 1937, the U.S. Housing Authority helped build low-income housing in economically depressed areas.

✓ **The Securities Exchange Act (1934):** This act established the Securities and Exchange Commission. The commission, headed by FDR's friend Joseph Kennedy (father of future president John F. Kennedy), regulated stock and bond sales. The idea behind the Securities and Exchange Commission was to make sure that the risky speculation that led to the Great Depression wouldn't reoccur.

The Works Progress Administration (WPA) (1935): Roosevelt created this agency through an executive order. It provided jobs for the unemployed. Over four million people worked for the WPA. By 1943, the WPA had constructed 125,000 public buildings, 75,000 bridges, and 650,000 miles of roads.

✓ **The Social Security Act (1935):** This act created the country's present social security, the retirement system for people 65 and older. Employers and employees pay equally into it. Unemployment benefits and disability insurance were also included in the act. Finally, the federal government provided funds to the blind and qualifying dependent children.

- ✔ **The Wagner Act (1935):** This act guaranteed workers the right to unionize, bargain collectively, and strike.

- ✔ **The Reciprocal Trade Agreements Act (1937):** This act, often overlooked, continues to affect U.S. presidents today. It allows U.S. presidents to negotiate their own trade agreements with foreign countries without Congressional approval. If the president and the foreign country agree, tariffs can be lowered by up to 50 percent.

- ✔ **The Fair Labor Standards Act (1938):** This act set a minimum wage and limited the working hours for U.S. citizens. The minimum wage was 25¢ an hour, and the workweek was 44 hours.

Roosevelt started his famous fireside chats in March 1933 to assure the public over the radio that changes for the better were taking place. The president's warm and reassuring voice played a great role in calming the nation after the upset of the Great Depression and garnering support for the president and his policies. As president, Roosevelt gave over 20 fireside chats.

Fighting the Supreme Court in term two

By late 1935, the economy was on the slow road to recovery. (The best year the stock market ever had was 1931, just two years after its worst year, 1929.) Roosevelt received credit for the economic recovery. He was easily renominated at the 1936 Democratic convention. The Republicans nominated the governor of Kansas, Alf Landon, who supported most of the New Deal programs. Landon proceeded to lose to Roosevelt in a landslide.

After the election, the New Deal sparked controversy. Conservative Republicans and southern Democrats opposed the government intrusion into the economy, while many on the left of the Democratic Party hoped for even more government intervention.

In 1937, the economy began to decline again. The Supreme Court proved to be a major handicap to Roosevelt's plans for economic recovery. The Court, filled with conservative Democrats and Republicans, declared piece after piece of the New Deal unconstitutional.

Roosevelt decided to show the Supreme Court who was boss. He came up with a plan to pack the Supreme Court. Under the Constitution, the number of Supreme Court justices is not fixed: It is determined by Congress. When the justices started opposing his policies, Roosevelt proposed increasing the number of justices — nine — so that he could get enough like-minded justices on the Supreme Court to give him a majority.

With Roosevelt's plan, the president could appoint one additional justice for each justice over the age of 70. This revision would allow Roosevelt to appoint six more justices to the court.

Even Democrats started to desert Roosevelt, refusing to go along with his court-packing plan. He suffered a bitter defeat when Congress rejected his proposal. Ironically, the threat of packing the Court was enough to convince one of the conservative justices to switch sides. In subsequent cases, the Supreme Court let New Deal programs stand.

Winning a Third Term, Facing a World War

The public punished Roosevelt and the Democratic Party for FDR's court-packing attempt and a declining economy in the 1938 Congressional elections. Republicans increased their number of seats in Congress dramatically. It looked as if Roosevelt's presidency was coming to an end.

Events in Europe and Asia saved Roosevelt and the Democratic Party. In Asia, Japan had invaded China, while fascism was on the rise in Europe. Foreign policy suddenly came to the forefront. The public demanded an experienced foreign policy leader for president. So Roosevelt received the nomination from the Democratic Party one more time.

The general election showed Roosevelt's vulnerability. He won reelection, but by a much smaller margin than in 1936.

Fighting isolationism

When FDR assumed the presidency, he made major changes to U.S. foreign policy.

In Latin America, Franklin Roosevelt changed Theodore Roosevelt's policies of open intervention (see Chapter 13) and proclaimed a *Good Neighbor policy,* restricting U.S. intervention in Latin American domestic affairs. Franklin Roosevelt pulled U.S. troops out of Cuba and Haiti, and signed mutually beneficial trade agreements with Latin American countries.

In 1933, Roosevelt's secretary of state, Cordell Hull, proclaimed that the United States would stop interfering in the domestic and external affairs of other countries. Mexico soon put this new policy to the test when it nationalized all foreign oil companies. The U.S. government didn't react, leaving U.S. oil companies to fend for themselves.

The mood of the country became isolationist, as many people wanted the United States to stay out of world affairs. Many citizens believed that U.S. intervention in World War I was wrong and that rich companies were the only beneficiaries of the war.

The origins of World War II

In 1937, the Japanese empire invaded China. Roosevelt had opposed Japanese expansion in Asia since coming to power, and the attempted conquest of China was the last straw for him. He imposed an economic embargo on Japan, preventing even oil from reaching the country. Roosevelt also provided China with much-needed economic and military aid.

In another part of the world, fascism was expanding rapidly. Germany had started to rearm — a violation of the Versailles Treaty that ended World War I. In 1935, Germany occupied the demilitarized Rhineland and began to pursue a policy of territorial expansion. In 1936, the Spanish civil war broke out. By 1939, General Francisco Franco and his fascist allies, with the help of fascist Italy and Nazi Germany, had prevailed. Much of Eastern Europe also

went fascist, and in 1938, Hitler annexed Austria. The two great democratic powers in Europe, Great Britain and France, decided to make a deal with Hitler. So a conference was called for in 1938 to discuss Hitler's demands.

At the Munich conference in 1938, Great Britain and France appeased Hitler by giving him the parts of Czechoslovakia that were taken from Germany in 1919. Britain and France believed that Hitler was now satisfied and would stop trying to expand. Boy, were they wrong! By 1939, it had become clear that appeasement wasn't working. Hitler had seized the rest of Czechoslovakia and invaded Poland on September 1, 1939. Great Britain and France, who had pledged to defend Polish security, declared war on Germany, starting World War II. Democracy was fighting for its life in Europe.

Congress, reacting to the will of the public, passed numerous neutrality acts to make sure that the United States wouldn't become involved in another war in Europe. Congress prohibited the government from loaning money to a foreign government that hadn't paid its debts to the United States. France, which owed the U.S. money going back to WWI, was included in the ban imposed by Congress. In addition, the president couldn't send weapons to countries at war, and U.S. ships couldn't carry weapons to countries at war.

The acts tied Roosevelt's hands. He wanted to help countries in Europe and Asia, but he couldn't. Things soon changed.

Dealing with neutrality

Roosevelt's biggest problem in 1939 was Congress, which was still isolationist in nature. Roosevelt's hands were temporally tied. Events in Europe changed this. By 1940, France, Belgium, Luxemburg, the Netherlands, Denmark, and Norway fell to Germany — Great Britain was suddenly on its own in Europe.

Consensus emerged in Congress that Britain needed help. Roosevelt took advantage of this, declaring, "We are fighting to save a great and precious form of government for ourselves and for the world."

In November 1939, shortly after WWII broke out in Europe, Roosevelt signed the Neutrality Act of 1939. This act changed previous neutrality acts by allowing the United States to export weapons to countries at war. The British Empire was the main beneficiary of this policy — a fact Roosevelt was well aware of. In turn, this change in U.S. foreign policy stimulated German submarine warfare in the Atlantic.

Helping democracy survive

By 1940, Roosevelt's policies favoring the democracies in Europe became clearer. When France fell to the Germans in June 1940, Roosevelt changed official U.S. foreign policy to protect democracy in Europe. Instead of being neutral, the U.S. became non-belligerent in European affairs. This change in foreign policy allowed the United States to openly support the Allies without going to war against the Axis powers. The United States was now officially able to intervene in World War II.

Roosevelt immediately delivered 50 destroyers to Great Britain to replace the heavy losses the British suffered from German submarines. The Lend-Lease Act of 1941 allowed the president to lend arms to any country that he determined to be of vital interest to U.S. national security. He promptly lent weapons to Great Britain.

In September 1940, Roosevelt announced that all men between the ages of 21 and 35 were to register for military training. The legislation started the draft in the United States.

The term *axis* was coined in 1936 when Italy and Germany signed a treaty of alliance called the *Rome-Berlin Axis.* Later, Japan, Romania, Hungary, and Bulgaria joined the Axis.

Creeping closer to war

By the summer of 1941, German and Italian consulates were closed in the United States. U.S. marines had landed in Iceland to protect that country from Germany. Finally, in September 1941, Roosevelt initiated a massive tax increase (the Revenue Act of 1941) to pay for possible increased military expenditures. U.S. involvement in World War II appeared imminent.

Fighting World War II

On November 3, 1941, the U.S. ambassador to Japan, Joseph Grew, sent a warning that the Japanese were planning a surprise attack on U.S. military installations throughout the world. The warning alerted Roosevelt of a possible attack.

The imperial Japanese government issued a final proposal on November 20, 1941, to settle the differences between the United States and Japan peacefully. The proposal called for an end to the U.S. economic embargo and demanded that the United States stop interfering with Japanese activities in China and the Pacific. On November 26, 1941, the United States rejected the offer and, in turn, demanded the withdrawal of Japanese troops from China and Indochina.

The Japanese empire launched an attack on U.S. military installations at Pearl Harbor, Hawaii on December 7, 1941. In the evening of the same day, Japan declared war on the United States. The following day, December 8, 1941, President Roosevelt appeared in front of a joint session of Congress and asked for a declaration of war on Japan. His immortal words were: "Yesterday, December 7, 1941 — a date which will live in infamy — the United States of America was suddenly and deliberately attacked by the naval and air forces of the Empire of Japan."

Three days later, Germany and Italy declared war on the United States, and the United States found itself involved in a world war.

Roosevelt turned the U.S. economy from a peace economy into a wartime economy. The president froze wages and prices for goods for the war period. He also set production goals for armaments and other goods. In one year alone, the United States produced almost 50,000 aircraft. By 1944, the United States produced more weapons and military supplies than Germany, Italy, and Japan combined. Close to 10 million men were serving in the armed forces. Women went to work in the factories to keep the war effort going.

Roosevelt even went as far as imposing strict censorship for the wartime period and placing hundreds of thousands of Japanese Americans in internment camps.

Winning the War

By 1942, the war had turned in favor of the Allies. The U.S. navy won major victories against the Japanese in the Pacific. The Allies invaded North Africa, and more importantly, the Russians defeated the Germans in the battle of Stalingrad. The victory signaled a possible end to the German victories on the eastern front. This allowed FDR to discuss strategies to win the war and to focus in on the postwar era.

For this purpose, Roosevelt attended several conferences in the next three years. The first one, the Casablanca Conference held in January 1943 with British Prime Minister Winston Churchill, stipulated that only unconditional surrender by the Axis powers was acceptable to the United States. At the Teheran Conference, held in November 1943 in Iran, Roosevelt met with Churchill and Soviet Premier Joseph Stalin. The three leaders were referred to as the "Big Three." They agreed to invade France by the summer of 1944. After the successful invasion of France at Normandy, Roosevelt decided to run for an unprecedented fourth term. The Yalta Conference, held in February 1945, was the last conference attended by Roosevelt. The Yalta Conference laid out the structure of the postwar world. It called for the creation of the *United Nations* — an organization whose member countries pledge to defend each other and work to ensure international peace — the division and occupation of Germany, and the entry of the Soviet Union into the war with Japan.

Running and Winning One More Time

In 1944, Roosevelt faced a tough decision. Should he run for another term in office? He felt physically weak, and many believed that an unprecedented fourth term was not acceptable. On the other hand, the country was still involved in a world war, and it needed an experienced leader. So Roosevelt decided to run one more time.

During the election, Roosevelt faced Republican Thomas Dewey, the governor of New York. Roosevelt won the presidency: However, his margin of victory was even smaller than it was in 1940.

Pondering post-war problems

Roosevelt expected to achieve victory in World War II by 1944. He faced the problem of figuring out what to do with all the returning soldiers. Roosevelt knew that in a peacetime economy many of the soldiers wouldn't get jobs as soon as they returned home. This, in turn, could push the country back into a recession.

To avoid a possible recession, Roosevelt and Congress passed the Servicemen's Readjustment Act in 1944. The act stipulated that veterans would receive free medical treatment, low-interest loans to buy homes and businesses, and a free education. The bill today is known as the GI Bill of Rights. When the war ended in 1945, over 20 million soldiers went to college, greatly enhancing the educational level of the U.S. public.

Dying suddenly

Roosevelt was exhausted when he returned home from the Yalta Conference, which ironed out the details of the end of the war, in 1945. He went to Warm Springs, Georgia for a brief vacation. While sitting for an official presidential portrait, he suddenly complained of headaches. Two hours later, on April 12, 1945, Roosevelt died of a cerebral hemorrhage, and the country went into mourning. Figure 16-2 shows FDR's funeral procession. Vice President Harry Truman became the new president.

President Roosevelt had a lifelong affair with Lucy Page Mercer, one of Eleanor Roosevelt's assistants. When Eleanor found out about the affair, Roosevelt promised to end it for her. He lied. Throughout his presidency, FDR and Mercer saw each other in the White House whenever Eleanor traveled. The affair continued for the rest of Roosevelt's life. Lucy was with him when he died and was quickly escorted away by Secret Service agents when Eleanor arrived.

On hearing the news of FDR's death, Winston Churchill said to U.S. journalist Edward R. Murrow, "One day the world, and history, will know what it owes to your president."

Figure 16-2:
President Roosevelt's funeral procession.

Courtesy of the Library of Congress

Chapter 17

Stopping the Buck at Harry Truman

In This Chapter
▶ Working hard
▶ Assuming the presidency
▶ Struggling to be successful in his second term

Harry Truman is one of the most underrated presidents in U.S. history. When Truman left office in 1953, many observers considered his presidency a failure. But this view has changed over time. Today, Harry Truman is ranked among the great presidents in U.S. history. People credit him with saving western and southern Europe from Soviet domination. He also receives credit for establishing NATO (the North Atlantic Treaty Organization), which provides for the common defense of member countries.

Truman is the president who decided that the Soviet Union needed to be stopped from expanding, and his policies achieved this objective. For this accomplishment alone, he deserves to be named one of the great presidents. Domestically, Truman was ahead of his time in the area of civil rights and welfare reform, but many of his proposals didn't become law until the 1960s.

Truman's Early Political Career

In 1924, Truman approached the Pendergast family, the dominant Democratic family in Missouri, about running for public office. They liked Truman, so they ran him for judge of the eastern part of Jackson County, Missouri, even though he had no background in law. Because the Pendergasts controlled state politics at the time, Truman won the position.

Truman excelled as a judge. He actually reduced the county's debt by 60 percent while he was in charge of the infrastructure budget.

Truman lost his reelection bid, despite his solid record, when the powerful *Ku Klux Klan,* an organization that promotes supremacy of the white race and holds anti-Catholic and anti-Semitic views, opposed him.

The local Democrats asked Truman to join the Ku Klux Klan, an organization that was popular and powerful in Missouri politics at the time. Truman refused because he didn't want to be associated with the Klan's anti-black and anti-Catholic views.

The Pendergast family came to the rescue, getting Truman elected as the presiding judge for all of Jackson County in 1926. The position put Truman in control of all the county's employees and infrastructure. Truman found the county administration in shambles, with corruption running rampant, so he set to work to reform it. He fired many of the employees who held their positions based on patronage or party ties. He even toured counties throughout the country, looking for the most effective methods of governing a county.

Truman did such a great job that he easily won reelection. By 1934, he was a well-known reformer in Missouri, famous for his honesty. He was ready to enter national politics.

The last farmer president

Harry Truman was born in Missouri in 1884. When he was 6 years old, his family settled in Independence, Missouri. Truman made the city his lifelong residence. Even though he received a poor education — he didn't even go to school until he was 8 years old — Truman was a bright child. He learned many subjects by teaching himself. Truman didn't play sports. Instead, he stayed home and read. He enjoyed military history and playing the piano.

Truman graduated from high school in 1901, but his family was too poor to send him to college. He's the last U.S. president not to have a college degree.

Truman worked many menial jobs to support himself, eventually becoming a farmer. He took over his grandmother's farm near Kansas City and worked the land for the next 10 years. While working as a farmer, he became active in local

Democratic politics. Truman proved to be a good farmer but a bad investor. He invested in lead mines and oil fields and lost most of his money.

Truman joined the military when World War I broke out. Because he was as blind as a bat and wore very thick glasses, he memorized the eye chart so that he could pass the army's exam. He saw action in France and returned home a major.

When Truman returned to the United States in 1919, he married his long-time girlfriend, Bess Wallace. They met in Sunday school when he was 6 and she was 5, and started dating as teenagers. Together they opened a men's clothing store in Kansas City. The store went under in 1922. Instead of declaring bankruptcy, Truman paid all his debts over the next two decades. Having nothing else to do, Truman turned to politics.

Entering the Senate

In 1934, the Pendergast family approached Truman and asked him to run for the U.S. Senate. Truman accepted and ran a spirited campaign, pledging to support President Roosevelt's New Deal programs. His campaign — and his reputation for being an honest man — helped him win a position in the Senate.

Truman almost lost his new position as soon as he arrived in Washington, because of his connection to the Pendergast family's political machine. The Pendergast family was under investigation by the federal government after criminal elements started to dominate the political machine they ran in Missouri. The head of the family, Tom Pendergast, actually went to prison.

The federal government investigated Truman but found no evidence of wrongdoing on his part. When asked about his relationship with the Pendergast family, Truman said, "Three things ruin a man. Power, money, and women. I never wanted power. I never had any money, and the only woman in my life is up at the house right now." Truman kept his job, and the people of Missouri reelected him in 1940.

Making his mark in the Senate

After overcoming a poor start, Truman excelled in his new position. As senator, Truman was a quiet, hard-working man who soon earned his peers' respect. During his term, he successfully passed major legislation, including the following:

- ✔ **The Civil Aeronautics Act (1938):** This act regulated the aviation industry by establishing the Civil Aeronautics Board and placing it in charge of U.S. airlines.

- ✔ **The Transportation Act (1940):** Truman chaired a subcommittee proposing major regulatory changes to the railroad industry. His recommendations resulted in the Transportation Act.

- ✔ **The Truman Committee (1941):** This was Truman's major accomplishment as a senator. After Truman was encouraged by his constituents to check into suspected fraud in the defense industry, the Senate assigned him the task of chairing a congressional committee to investigate.

  Truman toured the country and found out that the military had handed out defense contracts for paybacks. Truman also discovered cheaply produced armaments, which didn't work well. To top it off, Truman revealed $25 million earmarked for a nonexistent program in Canada. By the time he completed his task in 1943, he had saved the country over $15 billion, as the investigation led to many policy changes. Truman's work was portrayed prominently by the media of the times, and he became nationally known.

Receiving the vice-presidential nomination

In 1944, everybody expected Franklin Roosevelt to run for a fourth term. The country was at war, and a change in leadership might have undermined the war effort. The big question was who would be Roosevelt's running mate. The current vice president, Henry Wallace, was a liberal who supported union rights and civil rights, which made him unacceptable to southern Democrats. So Roosevelt went searching for someone else. He found Truman, who had supported Roosevelt's foreign and domestic policies from the beginning.

Truman really didn't want the job, but he didn't dare turn down his president. So he became the vice-presidential nominee for the Democratic Party. He campaigned vigorously for the ticket and became the vice president of the United States in January 1945.

President Harry S. Truman (1945–1953)

With Franklin Roosevelt's sudden death on April 12, 1945, Harry Truman, shown in Figure 17-1, became president. Upon hearing of Roosevelt's death, Truman said, "I felt like the moon, the stars, and all the planets had fallen on me."

Figure 17-1:
Harry Truman, 33rd president of the United States.

Courtesy of the Library of Congress

Getting up to speed on the war effort

Truman and Franklin Roosevelt were never close. Truman wasn't privy to many of Roosevelt's secrets and strategies. For example, Truman wasn't aware that the United States had two atomic bombs ready. To make matters worse, Truman wasn't informed about Allied strategy in Europe — he had never met with Russian leader Joseph Stalin or British Prime Minister Winston Churchill, and he had no experience in foreign affairs.

Truman spent his first month in office being briefed by Franklin Roosevelt's aides. His first official foreign policy decision was to hold a conference in San Francisco to establish the United Nations (see Chapter 16). He then got the Senate to approve U.S. membership.

Waging peace in Europe

Truman became president on April 12, 1945 and World War II ended in Europe on May 8, 1945. In July, Truman traveled to Europe to attend the Potsdam Conference to discuss postwar European affairs with the major Allied leaders, Stalin and Churchill, and later Clement Atlee, who followed Churchill as prime minister of Great Britain. Figure 17-2 shows Truman, Stalin, and Atlee meeting in Potsdam, Germany.

Figure 17-2:
Atlee, Truman, and Stalin at the Potsdam Conference.

Courtesy of the Library of Congress

Truman was especially interested in getting the Soviet Union involved in the war with Japan. Even though the war in Europe was over, the United States was still losing close to 1,000 soldiers a day in the Pacific. Truman believed that with the help of the Soviets, the war would be over sooner rather than later.

An aggressive ideology

Since the Russian Revolution of 1917, the term *communism* has referred to a form of government in which the state nationalizes private property and controls the economy and the lives of its people. In theory, the state does what is best for the public and meets all public needs.

At first, the Soviets hoped that communism would spread rapidly throughout the world, with little help from them. When this didn't happen, Stalin started spreading communism by force, with the ultimate objective of destroying every other form of government. Only world communism was acceptable to Stalin.

Soviet President Gorbachev abandoned the concept of world communism in the late 1980s.

Dropping the A-bomb

On July 26, Truman issued the *Potsdam Declaration,* calling for Japan's unconditional surrender. If the Japanese didn't accept the terms, Truman was ready to use the atomic bomb. His military advisors told him that sending U.S. troops to invade Japan could result in the deaths of up to half a million U.S. soldiers.

On August 6, 1945, Truman, trying to avoid the potential deaths of so many soldiers, authorized U.S. bombers to drop a nuclear bomb on the city of Hiroshima, killing about 70,000 men, women, and children. Three days later, he sent planes to drop a second atomic bomb on the city of Nagasaki, killing 40,000 more civilians. At the same time, the Soviet Union invaded Japanese-controlled Manchuria and Korea.

The Japanese government surrendered on August 14, 1945. World War II was finally over.

Stopping the spread of communism and recognizing Israel

When World War II came to an end in 1945, a power vacuum existed in Europe. The former great powers on the continent — Germany, France, and Great Britain — were in shambles. The Soviet Union, under the leadership of Joseph Stalin, tried to take advantage of the confusion.

The Soviet Union expanded aggressively. By 1946, it had control of most of eastern Europe. Stalin decided to break the Yalta and Potsdam agreements, which called for holding free elections and establishing democracy in eastern Europe; instead, he imposed communist dictatorships on eastern European countries.

But control of the eastern European countries wasn't enough for Stalin. He then sought to expand into southern Europe. The Soviet Union began to actively support communist uprisings in Turkey and Greece. In 1947, Great Britain informed the United States that it could no longer afford to support the anti-communist government of Greece. Truman knew that he had to act.

To save Greece and Turkey from Soviet control, he proposed the Truman Doctrine (see the next section). The Soviet Union, in turn, perceived Truman's actions as aggression, and the Cold War — the ideological and political conflict between the Soviet Union and the United States — began. The wartime friendship between the United States and the Soviet Union came to an end.

President Truman supported the *Balfour Declaration* of 1917, which called for the establishment of a Jewish home state in Palestine. The United Nations separated Palestine into two parts to create the state of Israel in 1948. Truman supported the reorganization and recognized the new Israeli state right away.

Implementing the Truman Doctrine

In March 1947, President Truman addressed Congress. In his speech, he outlined what was to become known as the *Truman Doctrine,* saying, "I believe that it must be the policy of the United States to support free peoples who are resisting attempted subjugation by armed minorities or by outside pressures." The doctrine called for military and economic aid for Greece and Turkey — to save the countries from communist rebels. Congress agreed with the provisions of the doctrine and approved $400 million to help the two countries.

Official U.S. foreign policy became one of containment of communism, though there was no intention to try to overthrow already-existing communist regimes. Any government threatened by communism could call upon the United States for aid.

The Truman Doctrine saved Greece and Turkey from communism. Both countries joined NATO and became close U.S. allies.

Instituting the anti-communist Marshall Plan

Truman was also worried about western Europe in 1947. The Communist party became the largest political party in France. Many people flocked to it because the economic conditions in France were so bad. The Communist party promised to end unemployment and provide for the basic needs of all.

The same happened in Italy. Suddenly it looked like the communists might come to power democratically in these two major European countries. Something needed to be done.

Together with his secretary of state, George C. Marshall, Truman came up with the European Recovery Plan. This plan, also referred to as the *Marshall Plan,* called for rebuilding the war-torn European continent.

The *Marshall Plan* was both economic and political in nature. The United States offered billions of dollars in loans to any European country that applied for it. As a condition for the aid, the European country had to buy U.S. goods with the money, thereby stimulating the U.S. economy.

Marshall announced the plan in June 1947, and every western European country accepted the offer of aid. Some eastern European countries wanted to accept aid, but the Soviet Union prevented them from doing so. The last democratic government in eastern Europe, Czechoslovakia, asked for aid under the Marshall plan, but the Soviet Union intervened, destroying democracy and killing the country's democratically elected prime minister.

Under the Marshall Plan, the United States provided Europe with over $13 billion in economic aid between 1947 and 1951.

Truman knew that he could help undermine communist efforts in Europe by restoring economic prosperity to the continent. He was right. He single-handedly saved western European democracies. This accomplishment was one of the greatest successes in the history of U.S. foreign policy.

Airlifting food to Berlin

The four victorious Allies from World War II — the United States, France, Great Britain, and the Soviet Union — divided Germany and its capital, Berlin, into four zones after their victory. Each ally received one zone to control. Great Britain was on the verge of financial collapse in 1947. The country couldn't afford to run its zone, so the United States took it over in 1948. Later that year, the French zone fused with the U.S. zone, creating *Trizonia.*

With control of three zones, the United States established a new independent West German state. Currency reform took place, and Truman asked for a new, democratic constitution. Alarmed, the Soviet Union shut off all access to the western part of Berlin, which was located within the Soviet zone of occupation. The idea was simple — prevent food from getting into West Berlin and starve the Germans into submission.

Truman implemented the *Berlin airlift* in June 1948. For the next 11 months, the United States flew supplies and food to the city, feeding close to two million people. At one point, a U.S. plane landed in Berlin every minute of the day. By May 1949, the Soviet Union caved in. Truman won again.

Reforming the country

With the end of World War II, Truman turned his attention to reforming his own country, with a special focus on civil rights and social reform. He called his program the *Fair Deal* — a continuation of Roosevelt's New Deal programs.

Truman proposed the creation of a Fair Employment Practices Commission to stop discrimination against blacks. He also requested an increase in un-employment benefits, national healthcare insurance to cover every U.S. citizen, wage and price controls to slow inflation, public housing, and a higher minimum wage.

Furious, the Republicans and southern Democrats formed a coalition to block Truman's programs. Truman decided to act unilaterally in the areas he could. As president, he was in control of the U.S. armed forces. He issued an executive order, number 9981, which desegregated the U.S. military. Discrimination against blacks serving in the U.S. military finally came to an end.

In the 1946 election, backlash from Truman's policies gave the Republicans a majority in both houses of Congress — the first time since 1928. This majority proceeded to stifle Truman's reforms for the next two years.

Fighting labor

In 1946, labor unrest broke out in the United States. From locomotive engineers to telephone mechanics, everybody seemed to be on strike. By the summer of 1946, national transportation and phone service came to a halt.

Truman didn't respond to the labor strikes. The Republican Congress decided to show him up by passing the *Taft-Hartley Act,* which was designed to dramatically weaken unions in the country. Truman, a union supporter, was outraged and vetoed the bill. Undeterred, the Republican Congress, with the support of southern Democrats, overrode Truman's veto. The act stood.

The Taft-Hartley Act stipulated the following:

- The closed shop, which demanded that you had to be a union member to work in certain industries, was outlawed.
- Secondary strikes, where a union went on strike on behalf of another union, became illegal.
- Unions could no longer contribute money to political campaigns.
- Courts could now block strikes that jeopardized national safety.

Overall, the act greatly weakened unions in the United States. It also led to the start of their decline.

In 1947, Harry Truman became the first president to give a State of the Union address on television. He was also the first president to address the NAACP (National Association For the Advancement of Colored People) since its inception in 1910.

Facing opposition in 1948

Despite his great successes in foreign policy, Truman was not a shoo-in for reelection in 1948. His domestic programs alienated the southern wing of the Democratic Party, which organized its own party, the Dixiecrats. The *Dixiecrats* opposed civil rights and ran their own candidate for the presidency, South Carolina governor Strom Thurmond. Truman's anti-communist policies and perceived enmity to unions (Truman had called out the army to operate the nation's railroads in May 1948, after unions had shut it down) encouraged Roosevelt's former vice president, Henry Wallace, to form the pro-union Progressive party and run against Truman.

In the summer of 1948, the Democratic Party was split into three factions: the Progressives on the left, the Dixiecrats on the right, and Truman somewhere in the middle. The Republican Party was unified, nominating Thomas Dewey, the governor of New York, for president. Dewey had done well against Franklin Roosevelt in 1944, and he was now the frontrunner.

The Dixiecrat candidate in 1948 was Strom Thurmond, who is now a Republican senator from South Carolina. He turned 99 years old in December, 2001, but expects to finish his term, which goes until January 2003. When he turns 100, he will be the first senator in U.S. history to serve in the Senate at that age.

Defeating Dewey in 1948

Truman received the Democratic presidential nomination, but everybody expected him to lose the election in 1948. Boy, did he prove the pundits wrong.

Truman called a special session of the Republican-controlled Congress as a political ploy. When the Republican Congress didn't accomplish anything, Truman had his campaign issue, and he attacked the Republicans as a do-nothing party. He toured the United States by train, beginning his famous whistle stop tour. He stopped everywhere, giving up to 16 speeches a day.

Truman gained extra support when the Soviet Union endorsed Progressive Party candidate Henry Wallace. The endorsement killed Wallace's candidacy and sent his supporters to Truman.

When the election results came in, Truman had unexpectedly, but decisively, won by more than two million votes. He received 303 electoral votes to Dewey's 189. The Dixiecrats carried most of the southern states.

During the 1948 campaign, Truman enjoyed telling the following story: "In the middle of the speech, some big voice up in the corner hollered out, 'Give 'em hell, Harry!' Well, I never gave anybody hell — I just told the truth on these fellows and they thought it was hell."

Hating His Second Term

Truman's second term was not nearly as successful as his first one. It was dominated by foreign policy issues and a war in Korea. The year 1949 brought one of Truman's major successes and a dismal failure.

First, at Truman's urging, the North Atlantic Treaty Organization (NATO) was established in Europe. Truman designed the organization to help contain the Soviet Union in Europe. With NATO, Soviet expansionism could successfully be curtailed within the continent. The idea behind NATO was similar to the idea behind the United Nations. Both organizations used the concept of *collective security.* This concept stated that an attack on any member equaled an attack on all members. Thus, if the Soviet Union attacked Italy, a NATO member, it would have to fight all the other NATO members, including the United States. The concept, in turn, ruled out an attack on any NATO member by the Soviet Union.

Losing China to communism

In 1945, a communist uprising started in China. The pro-western government of China found itself all alone. None of the major western powers supported it. Great Britain was broke, France was fighting in Indochina, and Truman didn't consider China to be that important — his first priority was Europe. The Soviets helped their communist brethren, and by 1949, the communists were in power.

The remaining members of the pro-western government fled to Formosa and established what today is known as Taiwan. The Truman administration received the blame for not helping the anti-communist forces and thus losing China. Communist China then came to hound Truman later on in his presidency, when the United States got involved with China in Korea.

The loss of China to communism also encouraged right-wing Republicans to charge that Truman's administration was full of communists. Senator Joseph McCarthy from Wisconsin spent his whole political career trying to track down communists in the State Department. His accusations weren't substantiated, but they led to Congress passing the *Internal Security Act* in 1947, which made it illegal "to combine, conspire, or agree with any other person to perform any act which would substantially contribute to . . . the establishment of a totalitarian dictatorship." The government could jail communists in the United States and refuse entrance to any member of a totalitarian — namely communist — organization.

Fighting in Korea

In 1950, the Korean War broke out. Truman, haunted by the disaster in China, sent U.S. troops to defend South Korea and ignored warnings from the Chinese, who asked the United States not to invade North Korea.

However, General Douglas MacArthur did just that, which prompted China to enter the war on the North Korean side. The Chinese helped stop the advance of the United States. By 1951, the pre-war borders were restored, and the war dragged on for two more years with neither side being able to advance much.

General MacArthur, who was in charge of the U.S. and United Nations forces in Korea, wanted to extend the war into China, but Truman refused. When MacArthur publicly criticized the president, Truman promptly fired him, ending MacArthur's long military career. Truman had the following to say: "I fired MacArthur because he wouldn't respect the authority of the president. I didn't fire him because he was a dumb son of a bitch, although he was, but that's not against the law for generals. If it was, half to three-quarters of them would be in jail."

Succeeding at home

The 1948 elections gave Truman a Democratically controlled Congress. So he again pursued his Fair Deal legislation (see "Reforming the Country," earlier in this chapter). He was more successful in passing the legislation during his second term. Major proposals that passed Congress included

- The minimum wage was increased.
- Social Security coverage was increased.
- The Public Housing Bill, providing federal money to construct public housing all over the country, was passed.

TECHNICAL STUFF

The Korean conflict

At the end of World War II, Japan was forced out of Korea, a country it had occupied since 1910. Korea was divided into a communist North Korea and a pro-western South Korea. An unpopular military dictator ran South Korea. The North Korean communist dictator, with Soviet encouragement, launched an attack on South Korea in 1950.

The United Nations condemned the North Korean attack and voted to punish North Korea.

Fifteen United Nations members sent troops to support South Korea. General Douglas MacArthur was put in charge of all U.S. and United Nations forces. Western troops fought back the communist forces and pushed them back into North Korea.

The conflict ultimately resulted in a stalemate — the situation in Korea returned to what it had been after the Japanese left after WWII.

At the same time, southern Democrats and Republicans rejected Truman's civil rights agenda. Congress refused to repeal the Taft-Hartley Act, which Truman so despised, and which had weakened unions severely.

Truman's major domestic crisis in his second term occurred in 1952. Steel workers were ready to strike, and Truman had to make a tough decision. He was pro-union, but the country was fighting in Korea and needed steel for the war effort. So he announced that the federal government would seize the steel mills to ensure continued production. This strategy alienated unions and management alike. The Supreme Court later declared his actions unconstitutional.

Ceding to Stevenson

By the spring of 1952, Truman knew that his presidency was over. He was fairly unpopular with the U.S. public. In addition, the Republicans had found an unbeatable candidate in General Dwight D. Eisenhower. So instead of going out in defeat, Truman decided that he was done. He announced his retirement and supported the candidacy of Adlai Stevenson.

When Truman left office, his presidency seemed to be a failure. Comments such as "To err is Truman" were popular. It took time for his reputation to recover.

Truman stayed active in politics. He supported and campaigned for the Democratic presidential nominees in 1956, 1960, and 1964.

Truman didn't think much of his Republican successors, as the following quotes demonstrate:

> The trouble with Eisenhower is he's just a coward. He hasn't got any backbone at all.

> Nixon is a shifty-eyed g------ liar, and people know it. He's one of the few in the history of this country to run for high office talking out of both sides of his mouth at the same time and lying out of both sides.

Truman's greatest political triumph came in the 1960s when President Johnson put much of his Fair Deal policies, rejected by Congress in the 1940s, into place.

After retiring from politics, Truman wrote his memoirs and toured the country, giving speeches at many colleges. Truman died in 1972 at the age of 88.

Chapter 18

Liking Ike: Dwight David Eisenhower

Dwight David Eisenhower is one of the most beloved presidents in U.S. history. He presided over the booming economy of the golden 1950s when times were good. He ended the war in Korea, prevented the Soviet Union from expanding, and stood up for U.S. rights in regard to U.S. allies. Later in his presidency, he became the godfather of U.S. nuclear military might. At home, Eisenhower built the U.S. interstate highway system and started the long process of desegregation. He was a moderate who appealed to a broad range of U.S. citizens. His political legacy is one of comprise and bargaining.

Eisenhower's Early Military Career

Eisenhower graduated from West Point military academy in 1915. After World War I (WWI) broke out, Eisenhower went to Gettysburg, Pennsylvania, to train a tank corps. After World War I ended, Eisenhower became a career soldier. He was transferred to Camp Meade, Maryland, where he met his lifelong friend, George Patton. Next, in 1922, Eisenhower went to Panama to serve under General Conner, an expert on U.S. military history. Conner renewed Eisenhower's interest in the topic of U.S. military history and encouraged him to attend the Command and Generals Staff School in Kansas. Eisenhower attended the school and graduated first in his class in 1926. He continued his studies at the Army War College, from which he graduated in 1929.

A true hero

David Dwight Eisenhower was born in Denison, Texas in 1890. He was named for his father, David Jacob Eisenhower. To avoid confusion, Eisenhower was called by his middle name. The name stuck, and he eventually became Dwight David Eisenhower.

Eisenhower's family moved to Kansas when he was 1 year old. His parents ran a small farm. His father worked in a local creamery to help supplement the family income. The family was so poor that young Eisenhower had to wear his mother's shoes for a time, because his parents couldn't afford shoes for him.

Eisenhower went to local schools, where he excelled in athletics. He had a hot temper, and he was constantly involved in fights. He loved military history: He was constantly reading about battles. His interest in reading about military battles upset his mother, a pacifist, so much that she took his books away from him. His family was too poor to pay for college. Eisenhower entered West Point in 1911, after finding out that he could attend for free if he passed the entrance exams. Ironically, one of the greatest soldiers in U.S. history started his military career merely to get a free education.

At West Point, Eisenhower was an average student who graduated 61st out of a class of 164. After graduation, Eisenhower went to San Antonio to start his career in the military. In San Antonio, he met Marie "Mamie" Geneva Doud, whom he married in 1916.

In 1932, Eisenhower became an aide to General Douglas MacArthur. He went with MacArthur to the Philippines to prepare the island for a possible Japanese attack. In the Philippines, Eisenhower organized his first military unit. He trained native Filipinos and prepared them for independence. (The Philippines, at this point, was still controlled by the United States.). His unit fought with distinction when the Japanese attacked. In 1939, Eisenhower returned to the United States.

Getting ready for World War II

In 1939, WWII broke out in Europe when Germany attacked Poland. The United States slowly became involved in the conflict (see Chapter 16). Eisenhower continued to train troops. After the Japanese attack on Pearl Harbor, he was chosen to head the War Plans Division, which put him in charge of planning all U.S. military operations. Eisenhower supported the successful "Europe First" strategy. He believed that it was essential to defeat Germany first, before the United States turned against Japan. Franklin Roosevelt agreed, placing Eisenhower in charge of European operations.

Eisenhower went to Great Britain to organize the Allied offensive against Germany. Eisenhower was ready to invade and liberate France from German control, but British Prime Minister Winston Churchill objected and instead argued for an invasion of North Africa. Eisenhower disagreed with Churchill, but he followed his orders. The invasion of North Africa turned into a disaster at first, when German forces defeated Eisenhower's troops. It took months for the Allies to recover and finally drive German forces out of North Africa.

Next came the invasion of Italy. Again, Eisenhower disagreed with his superiors and argued against the attack. Eisenhower was right to disagree with his superiors — they should have listened to him. The Allied forces didn't gain control of Italy until Germany surrendered in 1945.

Liberating France

In December 1943, Eisenhower finally received the command he wanted. He was put in charge of "Operation Overlord," the invasion of France. As supreme commander of all Allied forces, Eisenhower controlled over 150,000 troops and thousands of aircraft and tanks.

To succeed, Eisenhower had to take a gamble. The Germans expected him to attack in northeastern France. German fortifications were heavy there, and the Allies would have had a tough fight on their hands. But Eisenhower changed plans at the last minute and attacked at Normandy. To fool the Germans, Eisenhower had the Allied Air Force attack the northeastern part of France: He wanted the Germans to believe that he was about to attack there. His gamble paid off. On June 6, 1944, the invasion of France, or D-Day, started at Normandy. By September 1944, Allied forces had liberated France. Eisenhower was an international hero.

Finishing off Germany

After the successful invasion of France, Eisenhower became a five-star general — the highest rank in the army. He didn't have time to celebrate. Germany launched its final offensive of World War II (WWII) in December 1944. It took Eisenhower three months to stop the attack and go back on the offensive. He entered southern Germany in March 1945. The German military surrendered to Eisenhower on May 7, 1945, ending the war in Europe.

Britain wanted Eisenhower to attack the German capital of Berlin before Soviet troops could reach it. Eisenhower refused. He knew that an attack on Berlin would kill thousands of U.S. soldiers. More importantly, the Yalta agreement had already divided the German capital into four zones of occupation. So he would have had to sacrifice thousands of U.S. lives and then give the Soviets their zone. Instead of acting, he sat back and let the Soviets attack and conquer Berlin. The Soviet Union lost over 100,000 men in the attack.

Retiring from the Military

When the war was over, Eisenhower had the unpleasant duty of *demobilizing,* or releasing soldiers from their military service. In the next two years, the size of the U.S. army shrunk from over 8 million troops down to 1 million troops. Eisenhower was appalled by the massive cutbacks, so he retired from the military in 1948.

Both the Republicans and the Democrats approached Eisenhower to ask him to run for the presidency. He refused. Instead, he wrote a bestseller on his exploits in WWII entitled *Crusade in Europe,* and he became the president of Columbia University in New York. He served as president of the university for two years, but he didn't like academia very much.

Defending NATO

In 1950, Eisenhower eagerly accepted President Truman's offer to head the new North Atlantic Treaty Organization (NATO). Eisenhower, a firm believer in NATO, went back to Europe.

Republican Party politics brought Eisenhower into the presidential race in 1952. The frontrunner for the Republican nomination was Senator Taft of Ohio, who opposed NATO. Eisenhower considered NATO necessary for the survival of a free Europe. Eisenhower feared that without it, the Soviet Union would dominate the whole continent. Eisenhower announced his candidacy for the Republican nomination in an effort to prevent Taft from becoming the nominee.

Squeaking by

In 1952, Eisenhower was the most popular politician in the United States. Unfortunately, presidential nominees weren't chosen by the people: They were chosen by a small number of party activists. The party activists supported Taft.

At the Republican presidential convention, a junior senator from California saved the day for Eisenhower. He put pressure on the California delegation, leading them to cast all of their 70 votes for Eisenhower. The junior senator from California was none other than Richard Nixon, who received the vice-presidential nod for his deeds.

Eisenhower was 62 years old, and he wanted a young, energetic vice president. Nixon was only 39 years old and had made a name for himself by fighting communism throughout his career. Nixon worked on the committees that established the Truman doctrine and the Marshall plan (see Chapter 17).

Nixon also balanced the ticket nicely: He was a conservative Republican, while Eisenhower was a moderate. Nixon became one of the best and most active vice presidents in U.S. history.

Campaigning in 1952

President Truman knew that nobody could beat Eisenhower. Truman actually decided in 1948 that he wouldn't seek reelection. When Eisenhower became the Republican nominee, Truman almost changed his mind. He figured that he was the only Democrat who might be able to beat Eisenhower. However, in March 1952, he announced that he wouldn't seek reelection. Eisenhower easily defeated the Democratic candidate, Adlai Stevenson.

Eisenhower's campaign told the public that only he could end the war in Korea, which had started in 1950. His slogan was simple: "I shall go to Korea." Both the left and the right loved him for his approach to the war. The right believed that he would invade China to end the war, and the left thought that he would sit down and work out a peace agreement. In addition, Eisenhower proclaimed that he would roll back communism, or liberate countries under communist control. When the votes were in, Eisenhower had won big. He received 55 percent of the vote and won 39 of the 48 states.

In 1952, Eisenhower's campaign used the catchy slogan "I like Ike." (Ike is a nickname for Dwight.) The Eisenhower campaign also commissioned Walt Disney to make campaign commercials for Eisenhower.

President Dwight David Eisenhower (1953–1961)

When Eisenhower, shown in Figure 18-1, entered the White House, many conservatives hoped that he would roll back or even destroy the welfare state Roosevelt had created with his New Deal policies. Eisenhower disappointed them. He actually increased the welfare state by including the self-employed in the Social Security program — this added seven million people to social security roles. In addition, Eisenhower increased the minimum wage to $1 an hour and spent heavily on public works projects. It was Eisenhower who provided the money to build our present day interstate highway system.

Eisenhower was moderate in the area of civil rights, believing that the states should deal with the issue that was a thorn in his side throughout his presidency. But, when forced into it, Eisenhower acted strongly and provided the foundation for desegregating the country in the 1960s.

Figure 18-1:
Dwight D.
Eisenhower,
34th
president of
the United
States.

Dealing with the Brown vs. the Board of Education case

Early in his term, Eisenhower ignored civil rights. It was an explosive issue that polarized the country, and he didn't want to upset his numerous supporters in the South. Eisenhower also believed in states' rights. He claimed that the issue of civil rights was one for the states, and not the federal government, to deal with.

But, in 1954, the Supreme Court forced Eisenhower to deal with the civil rights issue with its landmark ruling in the case of *Brown vs. the Board of Education of Topeka, Kansas.* The Supreme Court declared segregation in public schools illegal in the United States, sparking a storm of protest in the South.

Some southern states blatantly refused to accept the decision to start integrating public schools. It was up to Eisenhower to enforce the ruling, which he did in 1957 when the governor of Arkansas, Orval Faubus, called out the National Guard to prevent black children from attending white schools. Eisenhower sent federal troops to Arkansas to enforce the Supreme Court decision and protect the black children from white mobs. As Eisenhower said, "Mob rule cannot be allowed to override the decisions of our courts."

President Eisenhower sponsored the first civil rights bill since the post-Civil War era. The bill guaranteed blacks the right to vote. It also called for the punishment of officials who refused blacks this right. Senate Majority Leader Lyndon Johnson watered down the bill and made it ineffective.

Background on Brown vs. Board of Education

In 1896, the U.S. Supreme Court ruled in the case of *Plessy vs. Ferguson* that segregation was legal as long as it was based on the concept of separate but equal facilities. In other words, schools and other public institutions could legally segregate blacks and whites as long as each race had comparable amenities. This, of course, wasn't the case.

Oliver Brown, an African-American who lived in Topeka, Kansas, tried to enroll his daughter in an all-white school. She was refused admission, so Mr. Brown sued the Topeka Board of Education.

The Supreme Court took up the case and set down a new ruling in *Brown vs. the Board of Education of Topeka, Kansas.* The Supreme Court declared segregation unconstitutional because it created a feeling of inferiority in black children.

Managing military matters

Eisenhower changed U.S. military strategy, mostly as a means to balance the budget, as soon as he entered office. Under Truman, the United States ran a large budget deficit, which Eisenhower considered unacceptable. So he looked for a way to save money. He found it in the military.

Changing nuclear strategy

In 1953, the United States relied upon a large standing army, with nuclear weapons to back up the armed forces. Eisenhower changed this strategy. He knew that nuclear weapons were cheaper than troops, so he cut back the size of conventional forces and increased the number of nuclear weapons in the U.S. arsenal. The change allowed him to balance the budget. However, a new military strategy had to be put into place to justify his cutbacks. The Doctrine of Massive Retaliation was the answer.

The *Doctrine of Massive Retaliation* was simple. The United States threatened any country that committed an act of aggression against it or any of its allies with a massive nuclear attack. This stance, in turn, ruled out such an attack, because the aggressor faced total destruction.

At the time, the doctrine seemed a credible way to make the United States safe from a nuclear attack. Although the Soviet Union possessed nuclear weapons, it didn't have the means to deliver them. Missiles were not yet available, and the Soviets didn't have any air bases close enough to the United States to launch a strike.

Eisenhower was deeply concerned about nuclear weapons. He realized their destructiveness, and he knew that the weapons should never be used. Eisenhower addressed the United Nations in 1953, because he wanted to curtail the danger of nuclear war. He called for a new international organization, controlled by the United Nations, to oversee the peaceful use of nuclear weapons and prevent the spread of the weapons to non-nuclear powers. His speech led to the creation of the International Atomic Energy Agency in 1957.

Ending the war in Korea

To the great disappointment of many, Eisenhower did not escalate the war in Korea, which began in 1950 when North Korea invaded South Korea. (See Chapter 17.) Many conservatives hoped that Eisenhower would invade China to end the war. Eisenhower refused, seeking instead a peaceful solution.

Eisenhower told the Chinese leadership that unless they agreed to an armistice, he would use whatever weapons it took to finish the war, including nuclear weapons. Within months, the war was over.

Getting involved in Vietnam

In 1954, France's efforts to squash a grassroots movement for independence in Indochina weren't going well, so they asked Eisenhower for help. (See the "Conflict in Vietnam" sidebar in Chapter 20 for background on Indochina.) Eisenhower refused, stating that ". . . the jungles of Vietnam would swallow up division after division of U.S. troops."

Instead, Eisenhower supported peace talks, which resulted in the division of Vietnam in 1954: North Vietnam became a communist state, while South Vietnam turned itself into an anti-communist right-wing dictatorship.

Eisenhower feared that the North might threaten the South. Eisenhower worked to protect the South by helping the South Vietnamese both militarily and economically. He feared that if South Vietnam went communist, the rest of Asia might follow suit. Eisenhower justified U.S. involvement by saying, "You might have the broader consideration that might follow what you would call the falling domino principle. You have a row of dominos set up, you knock over the first one, and what will happen to the last one is the certainty that it will go over very quickly." Before Eisenhower left office, the United States had military advisors in South Vietnam to train soldiers.

Changing foreign policy

A major change in U.S. foreign policy took place in 1954. Previously, the country had operated under the Truman Doctrine and the idea of *containment* — the policy of not allowing the Soviet Union to expand any further.

During Eisenhower's campaign for the presidency in 1954, he announced a new *Rollback Doctrine* that was designed to roll back communism. So, instead of working to limit the spread of communism, the United States now pledged to liberate countries under communist control. As Eisenhower said, "We face a hostile ideology — global in scope, atheistic in nature, ruthless in purpose, and insidious in method."

Leading Hungary astray

Hungary put the Rollback Doctrine to a test in 1956 and discovered that it was all talk. Hungary was a part of the Soviet empire that dominated Eastern Europe. In 1956, a new reformist government came to power in Hungary. The leader, Imre Nagy, tried to remove Hungary from the Soviet bloc.

Believing that they could rely upon U.S. help, as the Rollback Doctrine claimed, the Hungarians seceded from the Warsaw Pact. The Soviets weren't amused: They invaded Hungary. Hungary, hoping for and expecting U.S. aid, fought back.

Help never came — Eisenhower did not want to risk nuclear war — and almost 50,000 Hungarians died in two weeks of fighting before it was all over. Hungary remained communist until 1989.

Disappointing allies over the Suez Canal

The Suez Canal crisis took up Eisenhower's time in 1956 (see the sidebar in this section titled "The story of the Suez Canal").

Eisenhower faced a dilemma when Britain and France asked the United States to help defend their rights to control the Suez Canal in Egypt. He didn't want the United States to appear to be restoring colonialism in the area. Eisenhower didn't want to help the British and French maintain control in the Middle East, either, so he denied U.S. aid.

The story of the Suez Canal

Great Britain and France had owned the Suez Canal jointly since 1875. Both still jointly controlled the Egyptian canal in 1956 when a revolutionary government, with ties to the Soviet Union, was in power in Egypt. When Britain and France rejected Egypt's call for more economic aid, Egyptian President Nasser *nationalized* (took over) the canal. Britain and France reacted harshly by invading Egypt. Israel invaded the country at the same time to conquer the Sinai Peninsula.

Egypt had no hope of fending off all three challengers, so it turned to the Soviet Union for help. When the Soviets threatened Britain and France, both nations turned to the United States for help.

Britain and France withdrew from Egypt, and the conflict was resolved peacefully. But France was furious. The new French President Charles de Gaulle pulled France out of NATO and started to build nuclear weapons.

To protect the Middle East from Soviet aggression, Eisenhower created the *Eisenhower Doctrine,* which stated that any Middle Eastern country could rely upon help from the United States, including the use of U.S. military personnel, in the fight against communism. The United States was now involved in the Middle East.

Running for reelection

In 1955, Eisenhower suffered a heart attack and was ready to retire. But the Republican Party pleaded with him to run for reelection. The party knew that he was the only candidate who could beat the Democrats, who had regained control of Congress in the 1954 elections.

Eisenhower begrudgingly agreed to run again. He faced off against Democrat Adlai Stevenson one more time. This time he won big, garnering 57 percent of the vote and 457 electoral votes, compared to Stevenson's 42 percent of the vote and 73 electoral votes.

Losing the technology race to the Soviets

In 1957, the United States was in for a major shock. The Soviet Union not only perfected missile technology but also put the first satellite (Sputnik) into orbit around the Earth. Having nuclear missiles allowed the Soviet Union to target the U.S. mainland for the first time, making the Doctrine of Massive Retaliation obsolete.

Eisenhower replaced the Doctrine of Massive Retaliation with one called *Flexible Response.* The new doctrine stated that the United States would keep its options open in case of an attack against it or an ally. Eisenhower proclaimed that the United States would reserve the right to use either conventional or nuclear forces.

With the Soviet threat suddenly real, the U.S. populace went into a state of shock and panic. People built bunkers in their backyards to protect themselves and their families in the case of a nuclear attack, and schools held drills teaching children to "duck and cover."

Eisenhower had to act — and act he did. The navy, air force, and army received money to build nuclear missiles. By 1961, all three branches had missiles, and the United States had regained its military superiority.

Changing military strategy one last time

Eisenhower developed the doctrine of the *TRIAD,* relying on three different types of nuclear weapons for the defense of the country. The three types were

- **Land-based missiles:** These were located in silos throughout the country.

- **Submarine-based missiles:** Eisenhower based these in submarines that were located throughout the world.

- **Atomic bombs carried in strategic bombers:** These bombers were located in the United States and Europe.

The idea behind TRIAD was simple: If the Soviet Union launched a first strike, it might destroy the U.S. land-based missiles and/or the U.S. bombers before the United States had a chance to launch them. But the missiles in submarines would be intact and could be used to initiate a counterstrike against the Soviet Union. This strategy made an attack against the United States irrational, because the U.S. could still destroy the Soviet Union in a second strike. This strategy is referred to as *deterrence.*

Facing communism in the backyard

In 1959, the unthinkable happened: A country in Latin America went communist. Suddenly the United States faced a communist country in its own hemisphere. The country was Cuba, where Fidel Castro initiated a communist revolution in 1959. Castro toppled the pro-U.S. dictator, Battista, and established a communist regime in Cuba.

Eisenhower responded fairly aggressively. He drew up plans for an invasion of Cuba, but he didn't have enough time left in his term to finish the job. So he left it up to his successor.

Trying to negotiate a test ban

Eisenhower wanted to go out with a bang in 1960. He was concerned about the arms race and the possible use of nuclear weapons. He called for a major arms control meeting between the United States, the Soviet Union, Great Britain, and France. Eisenhower wanted to push the Soviet leader Khrushchev into accepting a ban on nuclear testing.

Before the countries were to meet for the conference, a U.S. spy plane was shot down over the Soviet Union, and its pilot, Gary Powers, was captured by the Soviets. Khrushchev wanted Eisenhower to apologize for the incident. When Eisenhower refused to apologize, the arms control meeting was cancelled.

Staying active in retirement

Eisenhower wasn't able to run for a third term — the Republican party passed the 22nd Amendment in 1951, restricting presidents to serving only two terms. In 1961, Eisenhower retired to his farm in Gettysburg, Pennsylvania to write his memoirs.

In 1960 and 1964, Eisenhower hit the campaign trail for Republican candidates Richard Nixon and Barry Goldwater. He was disappointed when John Kennedy won the presidency in 1960. Eisenhower believed that Kennedy was too young and inexperienced to be a successful president.

When asked to comment on his presidency, Eisenhower responded, "The United States never lost a soldier or a foot of ground in my administration. We kept the peace. People asked how it happened — by God, it didn't just happen, I'll tell you that."

Between 1965 and 1969, Eisenhower suffered three more heart attacks. The third attack, in 1969, killed him. Eisenhower died at the age of 78. He is still one of the most beloved presidents in U.S. history. Eisenhower's last words were "I want to go; God take me."

Chapter 19

Fulfilling Family Expectations: John Fitzgerald Kennedy

*J*ohn F. Kennedy is one of the most admired and revered presidents in U.S. history. He brought about dramatic changes in U.S. foreign policy — changes that ultimately failed, forcing him to return to the policies of Truman and Eisenhower.

On the domestic front, Kennedy set the foundation for the Civil Rights Act and the Voting Rights Act. For this achievement he deserves much credit. He could have been a great president. But with his foreign policy being fairly unsuccessful, he barely makes it into the top 15 in many presidential ranking surveys.

Kennedy's Early Political Career

Kennedy started his political career in 1946. He went after the Democratic nomination for the 11th Congressional district in Massachusetts. The district included parts of Boston, where his grandfather had been mayor. During his campaign, Kennedy emphasized his heroic war record. He easily won the Democratic primary. The general election against the Republican candidate was even easier. John F. Kennedy entered the U.S. House of Representatives at the age of 29.

Poor little rich boy

John Fitzgerald Kennedy was born in 1917 in Brookline, Massachusetts. Politics ran in his family's blood. Kennedy's father, Joseph Kennedy, served in Franklin Roosevelt's cabinet and was the U.S. ambassador to Great Britain, and his grandfather was the mayor of Boston.

Joseph Kennedy was one of the wealthiest men in the United States. Young John Kennedy enjoyed the good life, though he was a sickly child. He survived whooping cough, tonsillitis, jaundice, measles, chicken pox, scarlet fever, and appendicitis.

Kennedy went to the best private schools and studied at Princeton and Harvard. In 1940, Kennedy graduated from Harvard. When the United States entered World War II a year later, he volunteered for the army. The army rejected him because of a back problem, but the navy accepted him.

In 1943, Kennedy was given command of his own gunboat in the Pacific. A few months later, a Japanese destroyer rammed Kennedy's gunboat. The future president swam 3 miles in shark-infested waters to the nearest island, pulling a wounded sailor behind him. On the island, he carved a message into a coconut and gave it to the friendly natives to take to U.S. soldiers. Kennedy was rescued and sent home to recover from the malaria he'd contracted.

Kennedy couldn't wait to return to active duty. However, his back problem resurfaced and he was given an honorable discharge. Then his brother Joseph, who was planning to enter politics, died fighting in Europe. So Kennedy went into politics to honor his brother.

In 1953, while serving in the Senate, Kennedy married Jacqueline Lee Bouvier, a socialite 12 years his junior. Jackie Kennedy became one of the most popular first ladies in U.S. history. John and Jackie Kennedy had three children: Caroline, a lawyer, John Kennedy Jr., who died in a plane crash in 1999, and Patrick who died at birth just weeks before his father was assassinated.

In Congress, Kennedy showed an independent streak. He criticized his own president, Truman, for losing China to communist control, but he supported most of the Fair Deal legislation (see Chapter 17 for more on China and the Fair Deal). Most of the legislation he sponsored benefited his constituents, helping him get reelected in 1948 and 1950.

Serving in the Senate

In 1952, Kennedy ran for the Senate. It was a long-shot campaign against one of the most prominent Republicans in the Senate, Henry Cabot Lodge. Kennedy traveled the state, campaigning for a full two years. In the end, his efforts paid off — he narrowly beat Lodge.

As a senator, Kennedy continued his efforts to bring as much money as possible home to Massachusetts. Then his old back problems resurfaced. Kennedy spent most of 1954 and 1955 in the hospital. While in the hospital, he wrote a book entitled *Profiles in Courage,* in which he discussed U.S. politicians who risked their political careers to support unpopular issues. The book won the Pulitzer Prize and transformed Kennedy into a national phenomenon.

Kennedy transformed himself before returning to the Senate. He became more liberal, supporting integration and the 1957 civil rights legislation. One area of controversy for Kennedy was his refusal to criticize fellow senator and family friend Joseph McCarthy, who was still going after suspected communists in the Truman and Eisenhower administrations. Many liberals believed that Kennedy should condemn him openly, but Kennedy remained quiet on the issue.

In 1957, Kennedy became a member of the Senate Foreign Relations Committee, where he developed many of his ideas on foreign policy. He supported economic aid to the Third World, and independence for Algeria from France. He supported building nuclear missiles in 1957 — a stance he used against Nixon in the 1960 presidential campaign. Kennedy easily won reelection to the Senate in 1958.

Campaigning for the presidency

As soon as Kennedy won reelection to the Senate in 1958, he started campaigning for the presidency. He knew that it would take time to convince the Democratic Party leadership that someone like him could win. He faced three major obstacles:

- ✔ **He was too young.** He was only 41 when he started campaigning for the presidency. The United States had never elected such a young president.

- ✔ **He was Catholic.** Many voters, especially in the South, were reluctant to vote for a Catholic president, because they believed that a Catholic would be loyal to the pope and not the Constitution. The United States had never had a Catholic president.

- ✔ **He was considered too conservative.** Kennedy's opposition to some of Truman's policies didn't sit too well with the Democratic Party leadership.

Kennedy's strategy to overcome the Democratic Party's objection was simple: Win in all the states that held primaries to select delegates to the Democratic nominating convention. He poured all of his resources into these primaries and focused especially on West Virginia. West Virginia was a predominantly Protestant state, bordering the South. If he could win in West Virginia, he could win anywhere. Kennedy won the state, and the party leadership recognized that he was a viable candidate who could win the presidency.

At the Democratic convention in 1960, Kennedy won the nomination on the first ballot. He named the Senate majority leader from Texas, Lyndon Johnson, as his running mate to help shore up southern support.

Debating with Nixon

Before the 2000 election, the 1960 election was the closest of the 20th century. Kennedy faced Republican Vice President Richard Nixon. Kennedy campaigned on a platform he called the *New Frontier*. It consisted of economic and social reforms, with an emphasis on civil rights, which ensured him the liberal and black votes.

The four nationally televised debates made the difference in 1960. Kennedy looked vigorous, knowledgeable, and not too young. Nixon didn't fare as well, especially in the first debate, as he had just been released from the hospital after treatment for a knee infection. The hot studio lights made him sweat noticeably, and he had a heavy beard that gave him a five o'clock shadow. People who listened on the radio gave the debates to Nixon. The people who watched the debates on television picked Kennedy as the winner. Image decided the 1960 election.

Kennedy won the election with 49.7 percent of the vote to Nixon's 49.6 percent. Kennedy assumed office in January 1961.

Benefiting from voter fraud

The election of 1960 produced allegations of massive vote fraud in Illinois and Texas — two states Kennedy narrowly won. In both states, the *graveyard vote,* or votes cast using the identities of dead people, made the difference. In Illinois, Chicago mayor Richard Daley's political machine was well known for stuffing ballot boxes. Vice-presidential candidate Lyndon Johnson put his home state network into play in Texas.

Many Republicans wanted Nixon to contest the election, but he refused. The country was involved in the *Cold War,* the ongoing ideological conflict with the Soviet Union, and Nixon didn't want to undermine public confidence in a new government by going to court.

President John Fitzgerald Kennedy (1961–1963)

John F. Kennedy, shown in Figure 19-1, was the first president born in the 20th century. He was also the youngest president, at 43 years of age, to be elected to office. (Theodore Roosevelt assumed the office at age 42, after the assassination of President William McKinley, but he wasn't elected to it until he was 46.) Kennedy was also the youngest president to die in office. He was only 46 when he was assassinated.

On January 20, 1961, President Kennedy presented one of the most unforgettable inaugural addresses in U.S. history. He outlined his "New Frontier" proposals and proclaimed that a new generation of U.S. citizens had taken over the country. In his conclusion, he called upon the U.S. citizenry to "Ask not what your country can do for you — ask what you can do for you country."

President Kennedy committed a first by appointing his brother Robert attorney general. For the first time, a president had a brother in his cabinet. Kennedy's other surviving brother, Teddy, was elected to the Senate in 1962 and still represents Massachusetts in the Senate today.

Changing Foreign Policy

John F. Kennedy was prepared to make major changes to U.S. foreign policy. He wanted to abandon the policy of containing communism and instead work with the Soviet Union to create a better, less violent world. Soviet aggression in Berlin and Cuba changed his mind.

Another major change in U.S. foreign policy came in the area of Third World relations. Kennedy believed in helping third-world countries. He backed up his beliefs by providing the Third World with monetary aid and U.S. volunteers in the form of the Peace Corps.

At the same time, he supported his predecessor's policies in Vietnam, actually increasing the number of U.S. military advisors in the country.

Dealing with arms and the U.S.S.R.

Unlike Truman and Eisenhower, Kennedy believed that it was possible to bargain and compromise with the Soviet Union, and that the two superpowers could coexist peacefully. Because Nikita Khrushchev, the Soviet premier, had been liberalizing Soviet society and had abandoned Stalinism, Kennedy thought that he could deal with him.

Kennedy wanted to stop the arms race rather than build more weapons. He proposed meeting with Khrushchev to discuss arms control and even *disarmament* — the destruction of nuclear weapons.

Kennedy was disappointed. The Soviet Union saw Kennedy's offer to negotiate as a sign of weakness. Instead of reaching out to the United States and its new leader, The Soviet Union started to behave aggressively in Europe (Berlin) and Latin America (Cuba). The Soviet Union miscalculated. Kennedy's response was: "Let every nation know, whether it wishes us well or ill, that we shall pay any price, bear any burden, meet any hardship, support any friend, oppose any foe to assure the survival and success of liberty."

By 1962, Kennedy had returned to the policies of his predecessors — working to stop Soviet aggression and contain the Soviet Union's sphere of influence.

The only tangible benefit of Kennedy's efforts was the Limited Nuclear Test Ban Treaty signed in 1963. It outlawed testing nuclear weapons in the atmosphere. After signing the treaty, Kennedy said, "Today the fear is a little less and the hope a little greater. For the first time we have been able to reach an agreement which can limit the dangers of this nuclear age."

Helping the Third World: Creating the Peace Corps

Kennedy believed that it was the obligation of the United States not only to help the Third World economically but also to spread democracy to its countries.

To further that mission, Kennedy created the *Peace Corps* in 1961 to send U.S. volunteers to the people living in third-world countries. Thousands of U.S. citizens went abroad to help build roads and hospitals, and to help educate citizens around the world.

Stepping into the Bay of Pigs

Ironically, the first major foreign policy move of the new administration ended in disaster when Kennedy decided to proceed with the Bay of Pigs invasion of Cuba planned by the Eisenhower administration.

The *Bay of Pigs* was an attempt to aid Cuban exiles after their country fell to communism in 1959. The United States provided training, equipment, and logistical support to Cubans bent on recapturing their country. The 1961 invasion failed miserably, and, as a result, Cuba turned to the Soviet Union.

The Soviets were more than happy to provide assistance to Cuba. Khrushchev had been looking for an ally in Latin America so that he could build a base for Soviet missiles. While the U.S. had missiles in Europe targeting the Soviet Union, the Soviets had none close to the U.S. mainland. What better place than Cuba?

The Cuban Missile Crisis was the defining moment for the Kennedy administration. On October 16, 1962, U.S. intelligence found out that the Soviets were building missile sites in Cuba. The U.S. air force wanted to take out the sites, and many in the military called for an invasion of Cuba. Kennedy was afraid that an invasion would lead to a world war, so he set up a blockade of Cuba instead.

Kennedy vowed that Soviet ships headed for Cuba carrying missile parts would not be allowed through the blockade. In addition, he demanded that the Soviets remove their bases and all Soviet weaponry from Cuba.

At the last moment, the Soviets backed down and recalled their ships. The Soviet Union subsequently agreed to remove the missiles and their bases from Cuba, and the United States pledged not to invade the island. World War III had been narrowly avoided. Soviet Premier Khrushchev lost his job over the debacle.

Building a wall in Berlin

The Potsdam Conference, organized after World War II (see Chapter 17 for more on WWII and the conference), divided the German capital of Berlin into four zones — one for each victorious ally. By the 1950s, the three Western allies had created West Berlin, while the Soviet Union had set up East Berlin. During most of the 1950s, hundreds of thousands of East Germans, unhappy with their communist government, fled to the West, crossing over in Berlin because it was the easiest place to leave the country.

By the early 1960s, the number of people fleeing to West Germany had created a problem for the East German government. The country's best educated and most skilled citizens were leaving. East Germany faced a brain drain and a shortage of skilled laborers.

In August 1961, the Soviet Union and the communist East German government built a wall to close off East Berlin from the West and prevent the flow of people fleeing the country. Border guards had instructions to shoot to kill anyone who attempted to leave East Germany.

Initially, the Western powers didn't react to the building of the wall — a move that shocked Germans. The Kennedy administration publicly condemned the building of the wall but did nothing more. At the time, Kennedy still believed that he could establish cordial relations with the Soviet Union and didn't want to compromise his foreign policy over Berlin.

Kennedy's outlook changed after the Cuban Missile Crisis. Thereafter, Kennedy adopted a policy of containment toward the Soviet Union. He traveled to West Berlin in June 1963 to show his support for the people there and to demonstrate that the United States would pursue a hard-line anti-communist foreign policy.

Kennedy was received enthusiastically by over two million Germans. He gave one of the most unforgettable speeches in history. He reassured the citizens of West Berlin of the commitment of the United States to the city and its defense. To demonstrate this point, Kennedy uttered the unforgettable sentence, "All free men, wherever they may live, are citizens of Berlin, and, therefore, as a free man, I take pride in the words: Ich Bin Ein Berliner." (I am a citizen of Berlin.)

Increasing U.S. involvement in Vietnam

When President Kennedy took office, the United States was already involved in Vietnam. President Eisenhower had guaranteed South Vietnam's security. Eisenhower had sent military and economic aid, as well as U.S. military advisors, to South Vietnam. Kennedy escalated U.S. involvement. (Check out the "Conflict in Vietnam" sidebar in Chapter 20 for a brief history of the Vietnam conflict.)

South Vietnam was fighting for its survival after North Vietnam supported communist rebels' attempts to overthrow the South Vietnamese government. Kennedy believed that North Vietnam needed to be stopped at all costs, so he sent more U.S. forces to Vietnam. By the time Kennedy was assassinated, he had increased the number of U.S. *military advisors,* military personal that trained and fought with South Vietnamese troops, from 700 to 15,000.

Attending to Domestic Policy

At home, Kennedy attempted to put his New Frontier agenda into place. Kennedy successfully pushed for economic reforms, such as increasing the minimum wage and aiding the poor, underdeveloped parts of the United States. A coalition of Republicans and conservative southern Democrats stifled other aspects of Kennedy's New Frontier agenda. They successfully defeated his Medicare bill, which was intended to provide subsidized medical care for the elderly. The coalition also destroyed Kennedy's idea of a new department of urban affairs, because he chose a black to head it. To top it off, Congress delayed his civil rights legislation until after his death.

Pushing for civil rights

President Kennedy set the foundation for the civil rights movement in the United States. He got the ball rolling on civil rights legislation, but he was unable to carry it through to completion. It was left to his successor, Lyndon Johnson, to finish the job.

Civil rights was included in Kennedy's New Frontier agenda, but the issue lost importance for him as soon as he entered the White House. He didn't think that the close election of 1960 provided him with a mandate to bring about sweeping changes in civil rights, and he was afraid that southern Democrats would desert his administration if he touched the topic. So he ignored the issue.

In 1962, Kennedy was forced to change his tune on civil rights. Ironically, it was southern Democrats who brought about this change. In 1962, the governor of Mississippi, Ross R. Barnett, attempted to prevent the first African American admitted to the University of Mississippi, James Meredith, from enrolling at the university. Rioting broke out among the white students, and Kennedy sent in federal troops to protect Mr. Meredith and restore order. In a similar situation in 1963, the Governor of Alabama, George Wallace, attempted to prevent two black students from attending the University of Alabama. Kennedy was again forced to react by federalizing the Alabama National Guard and using it against its own governor.

More and more blacks engaged in civil rights marches were being brutalized by southern police. Kennedy presented a bill to Congress, asking for the passage of a civil rights act. This civil rights legislation guaranteed blacks the right to vote, the right to attend public schools, the right to jobs, the right to public accommodations, and the right not to be discriminated against.

A coalition of Republicans and conservative southern Democrats delayed the civil rights legislation. Kennedy didn't live to see it become law. However, Kennedy's legislation provided the foundation for the 1964 Civil Rights Act and the 1965 Voting Rights Act (these acts are covered in Chapter 20).

Heading to the moon

One of Kennedy's greatest accomplishments was to convince Congress to approve money to explore space. Congress gave the National Aeronautics and Space Administration (NASA) more than $1 billion. In May 1961, the first U.S. astronaut traveled into space.

In 1962, John Glenn became the first U.S. citizen to orbit the earth. Kennedy didn't live to see the first American walk on the moon in 1969, but he is considered the godfather of the U.S. space program.

A Promising Life Cut Short

On November 22, 1963, President Kennedy traveled to Dallas to mediate a split in the Texas Democratic Party. The president and his wife were riding in an open convertible on the way to a luncheon, when the president was shot twice — once in the neck and once in the head. He died half an hour later.

Days later, one million people lined the route that the president's casket took to Arlington Cemetery in Washington D.C.

Dallas night club owner Jack Ruby killed President Kennedy's assassin, Lee Harvey Oswald, when Oswald was being transported from one jail to another. Oswald died at the same hospital that President Kennedy died in days earlier.

Rumors of a conspiracy to assassinate the president prompted the appointment of the Warren Commission, headed by Supreme Court Chief Justice Earl Warren. The Warren Commission found no such conspiracy, but rumors persist to this day.

Chapter 20

Fighting for Might and Right: Lyndon Johnson

● ●

In This Chapter

▶ Growing up a career politician

▶ Becoming president

▶ Dealing with Vietnam

● ●

*L*yndon Johnson is one of the most contentious presidents in U.S. history. A political genius, Johnson ran the Senate like his personal fiefdom during his tenure as majority leader. He knew how to bargain and compromise to get what he wanted from his colleagues.

As president, he was responsible for the passing of the Civil Rights Act and the Voting Rights Act. Both acts enhanced the political power of blacks in the United States and reduced discrimination greatly. Johnson built upon Franklin Roosevelt's New Deal policies by adding Medicare to Social Security, helping millions of elderly citizens.

His accomplishments should put him on top of the list of U.S. presidents. However, there was Vietnam. Johnson escalated U.S. involvement, committing thousands of troops to a cause that turned into one of the greatest disasters in the history of U.S. foreign policy. Considering Vietnam, Johnson was a good but not a great president.

Johnson's Early Political Career

After a brief career as a schoolteacher, Johnson used his father's political connections to get appointed secretary to Democratic Congressman Richard Kleberg in 1931. Johnson traveled with Kleberg to Washington, D.C. and did his best to impress the Democratic leadership on Capitol Hill. He went as far as showering in the communal bathroom four times a day just to meet people.

Just a country bumpkin

Lyndon Johnson was born in 1908 near Johnson City, Texas. His grandfather had moved the family from Georgia to Texas in 1846 to raise cattle. Unfortunately, he wasn't very successful at it. Johnson's father abandoned ranching to sell real estate. Johnson's father was deeply involved in Texas politics, serving six terms in the Texas legislature. When Lyndon Johnson was born, his father told a neighbor that a United States senator had been born. He was right.

Johnson went to local schools and held many menial jobs on the side. By the time he graduated from high school, he had worked as a shoeshine boy, a hired hand, and an animal trapper.

Growing up poor, Johnson saw a need for a government that would give a helping hand to the average citizen. He became a staunch supporter of Franklin Roosevelt's New Deal policies. Johnson fulfilled his desire to help people by becoming a teacher. In 1927, he borrowed money to attend Southwest Texas Teachers College. He graduated in 1930 and became a public school teacher in Houston, Texas, until politics interfered with his educational career.

In 1934, Lyndon Johnson met his future wife, Claudia Alta "Lady Bird" Taylor. He asked her to marry him on their first date, and she said "no." He was very persistent, and she said "yes" two months later. On the day of their wedding, he forgot her wedding ring. So he ran to a Sears store right before the ceremony to pick up a ring for $2.50. The couple had two daughters. Lady Bird Johnson is still the grand old lady of Texas politics.

Johnson impressed the Speaker of the House, Texas Democrat Sam Rayburn, and even President Franklin Roosevelt. In 1935, the president appointed Johnson the director of the Texas National Youth Administration. Johnson put thousands of young Texans to work.

Johnson also made many friends and political connections. Then fate took a turn. The Democratic incumbent of Johnson's home district in Central Texas suddenly died in 1937. Johnson ran for the open seat in the special election held to fill the position. He borrowed money from his wife and, with his many friends backing him, won the seat.

Serving in the House of Representatives

As soon as Johnson entered the House of Representatives, he became one of the staunchest supporters of President Franklin Delano Roosevelt (FDR) and the New Deal. He worked tirelessly for the president and for his constituents. Roosevelt was so impressed with Johnson that he gave him a one-time invitation to ride on the presidential train.

With FDR's help, Johnson brought public electricity to Texas and rebuilt some roads and dams in his home state. Johnson's dedication to his constituents was so great that he demanded that his staff answer every constituent letter within 24 hours of receiving it.

Trying for the Senate

In 1941, one of the Texas senators died in office. Johnson decided to run for the vacant seat. Even President Roosevelt endorsed him, saying that Johnson was a good old friend. Johnson almost pulled off a victory. In the end, he lost the race by just 1,311 votes out of over 600,000 cast.

Johnson was still serving in the House when the United States entered World War II. He became the first congressman to volunteer for the military. He served in Australia and New Guinea, where the Japanese shot down his plane in 1942. Johnson received the Silver Star for bravery and returned home a hero.

The death of Franklin Roosevelt in 1945 affected Johnson deeply. He told friends that he felt as if he had lost his second father. He vowed to continue Roosevelt's legacy in Congress. To do this, he had to become a senator. So he ran again for the Senate in 1948. The election was even closer than the 1941 election, but the result was in Johnson's favor this time — he won by 87 votes out of 900,000 cast. His political enemies made fun of the closeness of the election and called him "Landslide Lyndon."

Serving in the Senate

When Johnson arrived in the Senate in 1949, he was well-known and had great connections. He had served in the House for 12 years and made many friends. His friend and mentor Sam Rayburn was again the Speaker of the House. Johnson was a moderate southern senator, and both liberal northern Democrats and conservative southern Democrats trusted him.

Showing leadership

Johnson, despite being a freshman in the Senate, was appointed to the prestigious Senate Armed Services Committee, where he advocated strong defense and the containment of communism. In 1952, when the Republicans regained control of the Senate in the Eisenhower landslide, Johnson suddenly found himself minority leader in the Senate.

As minority leader, Johnson built a loyal following of Democratic senators. He campaigned for them and gave them good committee assignments — even when they were new to the Senate. In addition, Johnson believed that, as minority leader, he had to work with the Eisenhower administration. Instead of obstructing the Republicans, he bargained and compromised with them. Johnson's work with the Eisenhower administration earned him the respect of many Republicans.

In 1954, Johnson won reelection, and the Democrats recaptured the Senate. This made Lyndon Johnson the new majority leader. When the missile gap crisis developed and the Soviet Union put the first Sputnik satellite into space in 1957, Johnson, as Senate majority leader, took charge and personally oversaw the development of the U.S. space program.

In 1955, Lyndon Johnson suffered a massive heart attack. He was put on a special diet and had to give up his three-packs-a-day smoking habit. He recuperated quickly and went back to work.

Dealing with civil rights

Civil rights presented a problem for Johnson. He knew that most of his southern colleagues opposed any reforms, while his northern friends pushed for them. The Eisenhower administration bailed him out. Eisenhower pushed for the 1957 civil rights legislation, and Johnson went to work. He watered down the legislation, making it acceptable to southerners, while at the same time assuring passage of at least parts of it. His compromise stood, and Congress passed the first civil rights legislation since the days of Reconstruction.

The 1957 civil rights bill originally provided for non-jury trials for public officials who interfered with blacks' right to vote. Johnson changed the bill to provide for jury trials because he knew that southern juries were all white and wouldn't convict public officials. This revision made the bill acceptable to southern Democrats.

Becoming vice president and president

Johnson disliked Republican Vice President Richard Nixon and wanted to make sure that he wouldn't become president in 1960. Johnson devised a strategy to become the Democratic presidential nominee. He figured that convention delegates wouldn't be able to agree on a candidate. He stayed out of the primaries so that he could offer himself as a compromise choice.

Johnson miscalculated, and John F. Kennedy won the presidential nomination on the first ballot. To Johnson's surprise, Kennedy offered him the vice-presidential spot. Johnson accepted and campaigned his heart out. He targeted southerners to make sure that they would vote for Kennedy, who was Catholic. Johnson succeeded — Kennedy won narrowly in the Carolinas, Louisiana, and Texas.

Johnson was one of the strongest vice presidents in U.S. history. He had more experience than the new president, and he had the connections in Congress to make sure that Kennedy's programs passed. Kennedy took full advantage of Johnson's political savvy. He listened to Johnson's advice and even briefed the vice president consistently on his policies. By 1963, Johnson ranked second in importance only to Robert Kennedy in the White House power structure.

As vice president, Johnson continued to focus on the space program. He was responsible for its successful completion, which was accomplished earlier than expected. He also pushed for moving NASA's (National Aeronautics and Space Administration) headquarters to Houston.

On November 22, 1963, tragedy struck. President Kennedy was assassinated in Dallas, Texas. Lyndon Johnson was sworn in as president only 112 minutes after the president died. Johnson's first order of business as president was to reassure a grieving public. In his first address to the country, Johnson said, "An assassin's bullet has thrust upon me the awesome burden of the presidency. I am here to say that I need the help of all Americans, in all of America."

President Lyndon Baines Johnson (1963–1969)

On November 27, 1963 — five days after becoming president — Lyndon Johnson, pictured in Figure 20-1, addressed both houses of Congress. He pledged to continue Kennedy's policies and asked Congress to pass Kennedy's stalled agenda, especially his civil rights agenda, quickly. Johnson knew that the timing was perfect. Under the circumstances, very few representatives would refuse to vote against Kennedy's polices.

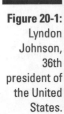

Figure 20-1:
Lyndon
Johnson,
36th
president of
the United
States.

Courtesy of the Library of Congress

Honoring Kennedy's agenda

President Johnson outlined his agenda to Congress and the nation in early 1964: "Let this session of Congress be known as the session which did more for civil rights than the last hundred sessions combined; as the session which enacted the most far-reaching tax cut of our time; as the session which declared all-out war on human poverty and unemployment in these United States; as the session which finally recognized the health needs of all our citizens . . . as the session which helped to build more homes, and more schools, and more libraries, and more hospitals than any single session of Congress in the history of our Republic."

The highlights of Kennedy's civil rights agenda, signed into law by Johnson, include the following:

✔ **The Civil Rights Act:** This act outlawed discrimination based upon gender, race, and religion. Further, it declared discrimination in public accommodations illegal. Johnson signed the act into law in 1964.

To support passage of the Civil Rights Act, Johnson stated: "The promise of America is a simple promise: Every person shall share in the blessings of this land. And they shall share on the basis of their merits as a person. They shall not be judged by their color, or by their beliefs, or by their religion, or by where they were born, or the neighborhood in which they live."

✔ **The Voting Rights Act:** This act, passed by Congress in 1965, guaranteed all U.S. citizens, including blacks, the right to vote in all states. The act outlawed all of the barriers to voting that were established by the southern states. In addition, it allowed for federal observers to be sent anywhere in the United States to supervise elections and prevent voting irregularities from taking place.

Many barriers to voting had been established in the South. These barriers included literacy tests, which discriminated against poor, uneducated blacks and whites equally. *Poll taxes,* which required individuals to pay to vote, were declared illegal, and the infamous *grandfather clause,* which stated that you could vote only if your grandfather had voted, and therefore automatically excluded most blacks, was abolished.

✔ **The long delayed tax cut that Kennedy had been pushing for:** This tax cut was finally passed in the summer of 1964.

Pushing his own agenda: The Great Society

The result of the 1964 presidential election was a foregone conclusion. The Democrats nominated Lyndon Johnson on the first ballot. The Republicans, on the other hand, went to the conservative right of their party and picked Barry Goldwater, a senator from Arizona, as their candidate. Goldwater opposed the Civil Rights Act, wanted to curtail Social Security, and advocated the use of tactical nuclear weapons in Vietnam.

Johnson won the 1964 election in one of the greatest landslides in U.S. history. He received 61 percent of the vote, won by almost 16 million votes, and carried all but 6 states. In addition, he was given large Democratic majorities in both houses of Congress. Now he could push for further reform.

Johnson quickly turned to his pet project, the Great Society. He outlined the Great Society in a commencement address at the University of Michigan. In the address, Johnson claimed that the United States had become a rich and powerful society, but that many problems still persisted. These problems included poverty, racial injustice, and poor education. Unless the problems were resolved, a Great Society couldn't exist in the United States. Johnson proposed to reduce crime, rebuild inner city areas, make college more affordable, reduce classroom crowding, and hire better and more-qualified teachers to help bring about his dream society.

The Great Society project resulted in many programs, passed by Congress between 1965 and 1967, that are still with us today:

✔ **The Higher Education Act:** This act established scholarships and low interest student loans to help poor students attend college.

✔ **The Elementary and Secondary Education Act:** This act provided billions of dollars in funding to help improve public schools.

✔ **The Medicare Act:** This act provided federal hospital and medical insurance for the elderly (those over 65). The act further created Medicaid, which provides hospital and medical benefits for the poor, regardless of age.

- ✔ **The Model Cities Act:** This act gave $1.2 billion to improve housing and education in inner city areas.

- ✔ **The National Endowment for the Arts and Humanities:** This independent agency provides grants to art programs and artists throughout the United States and its territories.

- ✔ **The Highway Beautification Act:** This act limited billboards on federal highways.

- ✔ **The Department of Transportation (DOT):** This department was created to oversee national transportation issues.

- ✔ **The Department of Housing and Urban Development (HUD):** This department provides funds and resources for homebuyers and community groups (HUD).

President Johnson appointed the first African American to the Supreme Court. Thurgood Marshall, who argued the case of *Brown vs. the Board of Education of Topeka, Kansas* before the Court in 1954 (see Chapter 18), was appointed to the Supreme Court in 1967.

Getting involved in Vietnam

Johnson supported Eisenhower and Kennedy in their decision to get the United States involved in Vietnam (see the "Conflict in Vietnam" sidebar in this section). As Johnson put it, "If we quit Vietnam, tomorrow we'll be fighting in Hawaii, and next week we'll have to fight in San Francisco."

By 1964, Johnson knew that he had to do more to help South Vietnam fight off communist aggression: "Just like the Alamo, somebody damn well needed to go to their aid. Well, by God, I'm going to Vietnam's aid." He increased the number of U.S. military advisors, who were training the South Vietnamese army, to 25,000. Many of the military advisors were now fighting in the field with their South Vietnamese allies. It wasn't enough.

Johnson issued the Gulf of Tonkin report to Congress in August 1964. The report claimed that North Vietnamese forces in the Gulf of Tonkin attacked U.S. warships. To punish North Vietnam for this outrage, Johnson asked Congress to pass the Gulf of Tonkin resolution, which allowed him to increase U.S. military presence in South Vietnam. Congress passed the resolution, and the United States escalated the war.

In 1965, the United States increased its troop presence to 200,000 and began bombing North Vietnam. In addition, the United States asked some of its Asian allies to contribute troops to the effort. Most of them did. By the end of 1965, South Korea, Australia, New Zealand, Thailand, and the Philippines had committed troops. The war in Vietnam was now an international affair.

TECHNICAL STUFF

Conflict in Vietnam

In 1945, France regained its colony of Indochina, consisting of what is today Vietnam, Cambodia, and Laos. Indochina had been conquered by Japan during World War II (WWII), but a native force, organized by communist leader Ho Chi Minh, fought the Japanese. After WWII ended, Indochina was returned to France, which refused to implement reforms demanded by the natives. After France objected to the reforms, a bitter eight-year war of independence followed.

At first, the United States stayed out of the conflict. But when China went communist in 1949, U.S. policy changed. The United States didn't want to see another communist country in Asia. President Truman sent military and economic aid to France to help the country fight communism in Indochina. But by 1954, France seemed to have lost the war.

Before giving up, France asked the United States for more help. It wanted the United States to initiate air strikes against the communists. Eisenhower agreed to help destroy the communists, but he wanted France to abandon Indochina afterwards. France refused, so peace talks took place in Geneva, Switzerland. At the 1954 Geneva conference, the following provisions were agreed to:

- ✔ French withdrawal from Indochina

- ✔ The division of Vietnam into a communist North Vietnam and an anti-communist South Vietnam

- ✔ Democratic elections in Vietnam, which were to be held in 1956, to unify the country

By 1956, it looked like the communists might win democratic elections. So the United States backed South Vietnam's refusal to hold elections. North Vietnam, in retaliation, started a communist uprising in South Vietnam. Eisenhower decided to intervene. He sent military and economic aid and committed America's first troops, namely military advisors. Now the United States was involved in Vietnam. Eisenhower's successor, John F. Kennedy, increased U.S. military presence dramatically.

By 1967, the war was taking a horrible toll on the United States. About 15,000 soldiers had died already, and the war had cost the United States $25 billion. Public opinion started to shift. At first, most U.S. citizens supported the war to stop communism. The horrible cost in human lives and the graphic pictures from the front changed public opinion. Johnson was ready to end the war. He approached North Vietnam and offered peace talks. North Vietnam rejected the offer, and the war continued.

Mounting the Tet offensive

In January 1968, North Vietnam launched a major offensive against the United States and its South Vietnamese allies. The campaign began during the Vietnamese New Year's celebrations — *Tet*. The North Vietnamese and its South Vietnamese communist allies, the Vietcong, attacked every large city and provincial capital in South Vietnam.

The U.S. response to the Tet offensive turned out to be a major victory. In the counterattacks, 85,000 communist troops were killed, eliminating the Vietcong as a viable fighting force. From then on, the United States fought regular North Vietnamese soldiers.

Despite subsequently liberating almost all the cities taken, the U.S. media declared that the war was lost after the Tet offensive. The public followed the media, and for the first time, a majority of U.S. citizens opposed the war in Vietnam.

Getting out

On March 31, 1968, President Johnson announced major changes in his policies towards Vietnam in a nationally televised address. He called for peace and offered to stop bombing North Vietnam if they agreed to negotiate. As a sign of goodwill, the United States stopped bombing about 90 percent of the country right away.

Johnson proceeded to tell the nation about a new strategy in Vietnam. It called for South Vietnam to build up its forces, which allowed the United States to cut back its troop size. At the same time, the United States would continue to equip the new and larger South Vietnamese army with the best possible weaponry. According to Johnson, the destruction of South Vietnam wasn't acceptable. He told the world that the United States would do whatever it took to protect its ally in Asia.

Johnson's address to the nation had two purposes. First, he outlined the new policies in Vietnam. Second, Johnson shocked the nation by declaring that he wouldn't run for reelection. Johnson had decided to run for reelection in early 1968, but he suddenly faced opposition from the liberal anti-war wing of his party. Senator Eugene McCarthy, a liberal Democrat from Minnesota, entered the race and won 42 percent of vote in the New Hampshire primary. His victory emboldened more challengers. Senator Robert Kennedy from New York was next to challenge Johnson. Polls showed that Johnson would lose the race to any Republican challenger. Johnson knew that he had a tough race coming up, so he decided to quit while he was ahead.

Johnson stayed out of the ensuing battle for the Democratic nomination. He personally favored his vice president, Hubert Humphrey, over Robert Kennedy, but he didn't intervene on Humphrey's behalf because he was fed up with politics and wasn't happy that people from his own party were challenging him. He didn't even campaign for Humphrey in the battle against the Republican candidate, Richard Nixon. After Nixon's victory, Johnson retired to his Texas ranch and wrote his memoirs. He died of heart failure in January 1973.

Chapter 21

Covering Up: Richard Nixon

●●●

In This Chapter

▶ Pursuing a career in politics

▶ Contending for the presidency

▶ Serving as president

▶ Losing the presidency

●●●

*T*his chapter deals with the most controversial president in U.S. history — Richard Milhous Nixon. Nixon had a distinguished career in Congress and was an active vice-president under Dwight Eisenhower. He resolved many problems for Ike before ascending to the slot of chief executive.

As president, Nixon was a foreign policy genius. If rankings were based on foreign policy alone, he would be one of the top five presidents in the history of the United States. However, there was Watergate, the scandal that ruined Nixon's presidency, smeared his reputation, and undermined public confidence in the presidency.

In retirement, Nixon became an elder statesman, advising presidents such as Ronald Reagan, George Bush, and even Democrat Bill Clinton. He managed to repair his tarnished reputation somewhat, but the Watergate controversy continues to linger. Richard Nixon may not have been one of America's better presidents, but he doesn't deserve to be listed among the worst.

Nixon's Early Political Career

In 1946, when Nixon got back from serving in the South Pacific during World War II, the Californian Republican Party approached the returning war hero and asked him to run for the 12th district's congressional seat, held by long-time Democratic Congressman Jerry Voorhis.

Nixon had no issues to attack Voorhis on, so he researched Voorhis's past and found that he had been a *socialist,* believing in powerful unions and government-owned industries. Nixon accused Voorhis of still being a socialist

Growing up modest

Richard Nixon was born on his family's lemon farm in California in 1913. The young Nixon was a quiet, obedient child who seemed gloomy and depressed. In high school, Nixon debated competitively at the national level.

Nixon's life was characterized by two tragedies early in his life. His two beloved brothers, the only two people he was ever close to, had both died of tuberculosis by the time Nixon was 20. Nixon never got over their deaths.

Nixon attended Whittier College in California, where he proved to be an exceptional student. He graduated second in his class and received a scholarship to attend Duke University to study law. A troubling incident occurred while Nixon attended Duke University: Nixon was worried about his grades, so he and a classmate broke into a professor's office to look at the grade sheets. But he did well in law school, graduating third in his class.

After graduation, Nixon returned to California to practice law at a small law firm in Whittier. He met the love of his life in 1937 and fell in love with Thelma (Pat) Catherine Ryan, a typing and shorthand teacher, who was active in amateur theater. He went as far as auditioning for a part in a play so that he could be close to her. On their first date, he asked her to marry him. She refused. But Nixon persisted, and in 1940 they were married.

Shortly after World War II broke out, Nixon joined the Navy. He spent all of the war years in the South Pacific. Nixon retired from the military with the rank of lieutenant commander in 1946.

and of being soft on communism. The *Cold War* — the period after the end of World War II when the relationship between the Unites States and the Soviet Union was characterized by suspicion and animosity — was just starting, and with Americans feeling scared and belligerent about communism, the accusation was enough to help Nixon win the seat.

Nixon learned a valuable lesson during that campaign race: Attacking an opponent for being soft on communism was a great strategy. Nixon went on to build a career on being a staunch anti-communist.

Pursuing communists in the House

As a member of the House of Representatives, Nixon accomplished much. He was a member of the Herter Committee, which studied and supported the Marshall Plan, and he served on the House Education and Labor Committee, where he helped draw up the Taft-Hartley Act in 1947 (see Chapter 17 for more information on the Marshall Plan and the Taft-Hartley Act).

Nixon's reputation as an anti-communist got him on the House Un-American Activities Committee, which was assigned to investigate and uncover communists and subversive organizations in the federal government and other areas of the United States, notably the film industry.

Nixon made a name for himself by doggedly pursuing the Alger Hiss case, when even President Truman was tired of pursuing the matter. A State Department official who was accused of treason, Hiss was ultimately convicted of perjury in 1950 due to Nixon's pursuit, and Nixon became a hero to the conservative right.

Red-baiting his way to the Senate

In 1950, Nixon ran for the Senate. His opponent was longtime liberal Democratic senator Helen Gahagan Douglas. Nixon used the same tactics he'd used in his first House, labeling Douglas as soft on communism. He called her "The Pink Lady," despite having no basis for the accusation. The tactic worked, and Nixon won the election by almost 700,000 votes.

After he won the seat, Nixon didn't spend a lot of time in the Senate. In 1951, he toured the United States, giving speeches to Republican organizations. He became a household name among Republicans across the country.

Delivering California and being chosen vice president

Nixon saved the day for Eisenhower at the Republican presidential convention in 1952, when he delivered all of California's votes to Eisenhower, making the difference for the general. The grateful Eisenhower picked Nixon as his vice-presidential candidate.

After being selected as Eisenhower's vice-presidential nominee, Nixon was accused of financial improprieties. The *New York Post* reported that Nixon had set up a fund to help out fellow Republicans and that many wealthy Californians had donated money to it. While this type of fundraising was perfectly legal, Eisenhower was running on a platform of political morality.

Many in the Republican Party called for Nixon's resignation as the vice-dential nominee. In September 1952, Nixon went live on national television and gave his famous *Checkers Speech*. He disclosed all of his financial assets and told the U.S. public that he was innocent of any wrongdoing. He further revealed that he had received a puppy, by the name of Checkers, as a gift. He told the public that his children loved the dog and that he would rather resign as Eisenhower's vice-presidential nominee than return the little puppy and hurt his children. To quote Nixon: "The kids, like all kids, loved the dog, and I just want to say this, right now, that regardless of what they say about it, we are going to keep it."

When he left the studio, Nixon thought his career was over. But letters expressing support for Nixon poured in, and Nixon's career was saved.

Serving as vice president

The Eisenhower-Nixon ticket easily won the presidential election of 1952. Richard Nixon became the youngest vice president in U.S. history — in 1953, he was only 40 years old. Unlike previous vice presidents, Nixon wasn't a quiet bystander but an active participant in forming the administration's policies. Eisenhower hated partisan politics, so he sent Nixon to defend his policies in front of Congress.

Nixon traveled the world for Eisenhower, visiting more than 50 countries and becoming the goodwill ambassador for the Eisenhower administration. In 1959, Nixon traveled to Moscow and appeared in a televised debate with Soviet Premier Khrushchev on the merits of democracy and communism. This *kitchen debate* was later broadcast in both countries. Nixon became the first U.S. politician to address the Soviet public on live television.

In 1960, Nixon was the clear frontrunner for the Republican presidential nomination. He received the nomination on the first ballot and went into the 1960 election as the clear favorite.

Losing the Presidential Race in 1960

Before the 2000 election, the 1960 presidential election was the closest presidential election since the early days of the democracy. Nixon campaigned hard and would have won had it not been for four televised debates — the first-ever nationally televised presidential debates.

Nixon looked old and tired during the first debate. He had just come of out of the hospital after recovering from a life-threatening infection, and he looked ill. Despite his weary looks, he refused to wear makeup. Even his mother called him afterwards to ask if he was all right. John F. Kennedy, the Democratic nominee, looked young and energetic in comparison.

Kennedy went on to win the election by 112,803 votes out of almost 70 million cast. Despite charges of vote fraud in Illinois and Texas — states that Nixon lost by a few thousand votes — Nixon refused to go to court, saying, "to drag out the decision would do incalculable and lasting damage throughout the country" (from *Rating the Presidents,* William J. Ridings, Jr. and Stuart B. McIver, published by Citadel Press, 2000). Nixon congratulated Kennedy and returned to his law practice in California.

Contending from Coast to Coast

After returning to California, Nixon wrote his autobiography, entitled *Six Crises,* and was content to practice law. The California Republican Party approached him about running for governor in 1962. Only Nixon had a shot at winning against the popular Democratic incumbent Edmund G. Brown.

Nixon accepted the challenge and used his practiced tactic — he accused Brown of being soft on communism. But his strategy backfired this time, because the public wasn't concerned with this issue in a state-level race.

When the votes were in, Nixon lost badly. Instead of giving a concession speech on election night, though, Nixon lashed out at the press, concluding with these famous words: "You won't have Nixon to kick around anymore, because, gentlemen, this is my last press conference." Boy, was he wrong!

After his defeat, Nixon moved to New York City to practice law. He campaigned for Republicans all over the country, including Barry Goldwater, the Republican presidential nominee, in 1964. His loyalty and effort paid off. By 1968, many in the Republican Party owed Nixon.

Nixon decided to give the presidency one more shot, announcing his candidacy in February 1968. He won the Republican nomination easily and launched his campaign on two issues: The unsuccessful war in Vietnam and the growing violent protest at home. He argued that only an experienced foreign policy leader could end the war and restore order on the home front.

Nixon faced Democratic vice president Hubert Humphrey and third-party candidate George Wallace, who ran on a platform supporting racial segregation. Wallace almost took the election away from Nixon by winning five southern states, but in the end, Nixon won with 43.4 percent of the popular vote to Humphrey's 42.7 percent.

Nixon didn't want to offend anyone, so he ran a very bland campaign in 1968. And, he refused to debate. He had learned the lesson of 1960 well.

President Richard Milhous Nixon (1969–1974)

As president, Nixon set out to make major changes in U.S. foreign policy. His priority was to end the war in Vietnam. In addition, Nixon believed that it was necessary to enter into arms control negotiations with the Soviet Union and achieve cordial relations with communist China.

In the domestic arena, Nixon attempted to control inflation and started some of the most important environmental legislation in U.S. history. Figure 21-1 depicts President Nixon.

Figure 21-1:
Richard
Nixon, 37th
president of
the United
States.

Courtesy of the Library of Congress

Ending the war in Vietnam

Vietnam was Nixon's first priority when he took office in 1968. He built on the policy changes that Johnson implemented shortly before he left office (see Chapter 20, especially the "Conflict in Vietnam" sidebar).

Nixon's strategy was called *Vietnamization*. It called upon South Vietnam to do more of the fighting so that the United States could withdraw its troops. In addition, Nixon proclaimed what became known as the *Nixon Doctrine,* which stated that Asia could expect only military and economic aid in the fight against communism — the United States would not send more troops.

When Nixon entered the White House in January 1969, more than 500,000 U.S. soldiers were stationed in Vietnam. Nixon had pledged to reduce the number of U.S. soldiers fighting in Vietnam during his campaign, and this he did. By late 1969, Nixon had withdrawn 90,000 troops. When Nixon was up for reelection in 1972, only 30,000 soldiers remained in Vietnam.

When secret peace talks collapsed in 1972, Nixon decided to bomb North Vietnam and force them to the bargaining table. The increased air strikes proved to be the most severe in history to that point, but they worked. In January 1973, a cease-fire agreement was signed between the United States, South Vietnam, and North Vietnam, ending U.S. involvement in Vietnam.

The two Vietnams broke the agreement shortly thereafter, and the war dragged on for two more years. Without U.S. aid, the South Vietnamese army collapsed, and on April 30, 1975, the South Vietnamese capital of Saigon fell to North Vietnamese forces. The war was over, and the country reunified under communist control. Vietnam and the United States finally started to reopen diplomatic relations during the Clinton administration.

Having more successes in foreign policy

President Nixon was very successful in the realm of foreign policy. Some of Nixon's important foreign policy accomplishments include the following:

- He traveled to the Soviet Union to sign the Strategic Arms Limitation Talks Treaty (SALT I) in 1972. The treaty was the first arms control treaty with the Soviet Union since World War II. It set a ceiling of how many ICBM's (Intercontinental Ballistic Missiles) each country could have. It also limited antiballistic missile systems (designed to shoot down incoming missiles) to two per country.

- He became the first U.S. president to travel to Communist China. Secret negotiations to reestablish ties between the U.S. and China started in 1969. Nixon's visit in 1972 led to a reestablishment of diplomatic relations between the United States and China.

- He intervened in the 1973 war between Israel and Egypt and restored peace between the two countries. Egypt appealed to its ally, the Soviet Union, for help when things got tough. The Soviets didn't want to see one of their allies destroyed, so they asked the United States to settle the conflict peacefully by forcing the Israelis to negotiate. When Nixon visited the Middle East in 1974, he received a hero's welcome from both Israelis and Arabs.

Dealing with domestic issues

Nixon was also very successful in the area of domestic politics. From 1969 to 1973, he accomplished the following:

- Landed the first U.S. astronauts on the moon in 1969, bringing the efforts of three administrations to fruition.

- Established the Environmental Protection Agency in 1970.

- Implemented the Water Pollution Act, which established funds for the creation of sewage treatment plants and prohibited dumping industrial waste into the nation's waterways. The National Air Quality Standards Act of 1970 restricted auto emissions and established clean air standards.

✔ Passed the 26th Amendment to the Constitution, which gave 18 to 21 year olds the right to vote.

✔ Froze prices and wages to reduce inflation.

✔ Curtailed government spending and raised interest rates to combat inflation.

✔ Ended the draft in the United States.

Serving Part of a Second Term

With the 1972 election approaching, Nixon was a shoo-in to win. He had great successes in foreign policy, brought inflation under control, and was about to end the war in Vietnam. His opponent, Senator George McGovern of South Dakota, belonged to the liberal wing of the Democratic Party and had no support in the South.

The 1972 election produced one of the greatest landslides in U.S. history, as Nixon won 49 of the 50 states. Nixon won the election by almost 20 million votes. He was ready to make history. This he did, but not in the way he imagined.

Falling prey to the Watergate scandal

In 1972, five men were caught breaking into the Democratic Party National Headquarters at the Watergate hotel in Washington, D.C. At first, nobody thought much of it. The situation didn't become a campaign issue in 1972, and it didn't gain very much attention until police discovered an address book listing names, phone numbers, and even checks tying the burglars to the Committee to Reelect the President (CREEP) — the Nixon reelection committee.

Congress began investigating the issue in February 1973 and found that hush money from the Nixon campaign had been deposited in one of the burglar's bank accounts. In addition, the burglars were tied to some of Nixon's closest aides. Mass resignations of most of Nixon's aides followed.

Then came the big question: What did the President know, and when did he know it? The Senate named a special prosecutor, Archibald Cox, in the spring of 1973 to investigate the ties between the burglars and the administration.

In July, one of Nixon's aides revealed the existence of a secret taping system in the White House. Nixon used the taping device to record conversations for use when he wrote his memoirs. The special prosecutor wanted the tapes, but Nixon refused, citing executive privilege. Nixon became involved in a bitter court battle over the secret tapes. For the first time, members of Congress were demanding Nixon's resignation.

Initiating the Saturday Night Massacre

When the special prosecutor of the investigation, Archibald Cox, continued to subpoena the tapes, Nixon told Attorney General Elliot Richardson to fire Cox on Saturday, October 20, 1973. Richardson refused and resigned instead. Deputy Attorney General William Ruckelshaus also resigned rather than fire Cox, and it was left to Robert Bork, Nixon's solicitor general, to actually accomplish the deed. This series of resignations and firings became known as the *Saturday Night Massacre.*

The House Judiciary Committee instituted impeachment procedures against Nixon. In response, Nixon handed over some of the tapes to Congress on October 23, 1973. When Congress discovered that the tapes had been edited, they were forced to appoint a new special prosecutor, Leon Jaworski.

As if Nixon didn't have enough trouble in the early 1970s, his vice president, Spiro Agnew, was involved in his own scandal, which had nothing to do with Watergate. Agnew took bribes while serving as governor of Maryland and continued to do so after he became vice president in 1969. Federal prosecutors brought charges against Agnew in 1973. Instead of going to court, he plea-bargained, paid a $10,000 fine, and resigned as vice president. Nixon promptly replaced him with the Republican leader in the House, Gerald R. Ford of Michigan.

Returning to the tapes

In March 1974, Special Prosecutor Leon Jaworski asked for more of Nixon's tapes. Nixon refused to hand them over. This time the case went before the U.S. Supreme Court, which ruled on July 24, 1974, that Nixon had to hand the tapes over to Jaworski. That same day, the Judiciary Committee in the House of Representatives started impeachment procedures against Nixon. Nixon was charged with three articles of impeachment (see the "How to get impeached" sidebar in Chapter 11 for the basics on impeachment):

✔ Article One included obstructing justice, making false or misleading statements, withholding evidence, counseling perjury, misusing the CIA, and misusing FBI information.

✔ Article Two included abuse of power, misusing the Internal Revenue Service, the FBI, and the Secret Service, interfering with the Watergate investigation, and other crimes.

✔ Article Three included failure to comply with Congressional subpoenas.

The House Judiciary Committee voted overwhelmingly to recommend that Nixon be impeached on all counts by the full House.

Resigning the presidency

The House and the Senate never got the chance to impeach Nixon. On August 5, 1974, the White House released tapes containing evidence that Nixon had instructed the CIA to stop the FBI investigation of the Watergate break-in. Even Nixon's staunchest supporters turned away from him at this revelation.

Nixon addressed the nation on August 8, 1974, to announce his resignation. In his speech, he told the country that he no longer had the support he needed to continue the fight. He never admitted any guilt or error in the Watergate affair, and he continued to claim that he was innocent.

Nixon left office on August 9, 1974, and flew to California. The new president, Gerald Ford, gave Nixon an unconditional pardon on September 8, 1974, making Nixon safe from any prosecution.

Retiring and rehabilitating

As soon as Nixon left office, he set out to restore his reputation. Over the next 20 years, he wrote seven books, including his memoirs. He became a trusted foreign policy advisor to Presidents Reagan, George H. Bush, and Clinton.

Many considered Nixon one of the best foreign policy experts in the country. His visits to China and Russia became international events. He often received a hero's welcome during his visits, especially in the Republic of China.

Nixon died suddenly of a stroke in 1994 and received a national burial. His funeral was attended not only by five U.S. presidents but by every major foreign leader in the world. Nixon rehabilitated himself to some extent, but he will always be associated with the Watergate scandal.

Part VI

Changing the Dynamics: Gerald Ford to George W. Bush

The 5th Wave   By Rich Tennant

WHY PRESIDENT JIMMY CARTER WALKED FROM THE CAPITOL TO THE WHITE HOUSE ON INAUGURATION DAY

"We're good to go, Mr. President, just waiting for your brother, Billy. He's asked to drive the limousine."

In this part . . .

I cover our most recent presidents. I begin with Gerald Ford, who served less than two years in office. Pardoning former President Nixon tarnished his presidency, and Ford never recovered form this. President Carter was a decent, honest, individual who nonetheless was brought down by economic problems and the hostage crisis in Iran.

The Great Communicator succeeded him. Ronald Reagan was able to connect to the U.S. public in a special way. The people loved his style and the way he restored national pride and worldwide power. By the time he left office, the Soviet Union was on the verge of collapse and the United States was number one, one more time.

Reagan's vice president, George Herbert Walker Bush, finished the job of overseeing the collapse of communism in the Soviet Union and Eastern Europe. He also expelled Iraq from Kuwait, but that wasn't enough to overcome a downturn in the economy.

Bill Clinton gave the country eight years of unexpected economic growth. The people loved him for this and even forgave Clinton for many of his personal shortcomings.

Our most recent president, George W. Bush closes out this part. I look at the disputed election of 2000 and the rough start Bush had as president. All this changed on September 11, 2001, when a terrorist attack brought out the best in a country and in a president.

Chapter 22

The Career Politician and the Peanut Farmer: Ford and Carter

*P*residents Ford and Carter were similar in style and character. Both were honest men who showed character and integrity in office. Both dealt with the aftermath of Vietnam and Watergate and restored credibility to the White House. The two were also similar politically: Ford was a moderate Republican, and Carter was a moderate Democrat.

Ford and Carter both had their problems in office. During Ford's presidency, Vietnam was lost to communism, and Ford issued the controversial pardon of former President Nixon. Carter tried to pursue a moral, humanitarian foreign policy, which ended in failure when the Soviet Union took advantage of perceived weaknesses in U.S. foreign policy.

Today, President Carter is recognized as a great humanitarian. Carter goes on peace missions all over the world. President Ford, meanwhile, has become the grand old man in the Republican Party. He freely hands out advice to his successors. Both men are great human beings, but their presidencies were merely average.

Stepping in for Nixon: Gerald Ford

Gerald Ford, shown in Figure 22-1, became president by default. He never wanted to be president. Ford actually turned down the vice presidency when Nixon asked him to be his running mate in 1968. Ford's great desire was to become Speaker of the House. When he didn't receive the position in 1972, he planned to retire in 1976. Fate intervened.

A model guy

Gerald Ford was born in Nebraska in 1913 as Leslie Lynch King, Jr. His mother left her abusive husband — Ford's father — the same year and remarried in 1916. Her new husband, Gerald R. Ford, legally adopted her son and gave him his name.

Ford grew up in Michigan. He was an exceptional athlete and a model — in 1939, he modeled winter sports clothing for *Look* magazine.

He attended the University of Michigan on a football scholarship. He was named the most valuable player and received offers from two professional football teams. He turned down the offers and accepted a coaching job at Yale University, which allowed him to study law at Yale. He graduated in 1941.

Ford had just started practicing law when World War II broke out. He joined the navy and served in the South Pacific. He saw heavy combat and won ten battle stars for his bravery.

Returning home, he married Elizabeth "Betty" Bloomer Warren, a model and professional dancer. Betty Ford was one of the most controversial and beloved first ladies in U.S. history. She favored abortion rights and supported the Equal Rights Amendment, which the Republican Party opposed. Her fight with breast cancer increased public awareness of the disease. After leaving the White House, she revealed her addiction to painkillers and alcohol and proceeded to establish the Betty Ford clinic in California, which has become a favorite treatment center for movie stars and politicians with dependency problems.

When Vice President Spiro Agnew resigned, Nixon needed a replacement fast. He chose Ford. Just a few months later, Ford suddenly found himself president of the United States, without ever running for the office.

Ford's presidency is characterized by two major events: His controversial pardon of former president Nixon, which cost him reelection in 1976, and the loss of South Vietnam to communist North Vietnamese forces.

Ford did what he thought was right and did his best to restore honesty and prestige to the office of the presidency. For this he deserves credit.

It isn't really fair to rank Ford's presidency, because he served just a little over two years in office. Taking his whole political career into account, he can be rated as a great politician and an average president.

Figure 22-1:
Gerald Ford,
38th
president of
the United
States.

Courtesy of the Library of Congress

Ford's early political career

Ford joined the Republican Party in 1940. He shared his stepfather's opposition to big government, and support for U.S. isolationism in foreign policy. However, Ford changed his views on foreign policy after serving in the military. He now believed that the United States needed to be involved in international affairs.

In 1948, the local Republican Party in Grand Rapids, Michigan, approached Ford and asked him to challenge incumbent Republican Congressman Bartel Jonkman, an isolationist, in the primary. Ford, running on the strength of his war record, beat Jonkman easily. He then cruised to victory in the general election and began a long, distinguished Congressional career.

Serving in Congress

Ford served in the House of Representatives for the next 25 years. As a congressman, Ford was very conservative on defense issues — he voted to increase the defense budget and became a staunch anti-communist. At the same time, he consistently supported civil rights legislation.

Ford rose quickly through the Republican ranks. In 1963, he became the chairman of the House Republican conference. In 1965, he took over as the House minority leader. Now he had his eyes set on the speakership. For Ford to get the position, however, the Republicans had to win a majority in the House, because the majority party selects the Speaker. Ford expected Nixon's landslide reelection in 1972 to help the Republicans get the majority in the House, but that didn't happen. So Ford decided to make it his last term in office.

Being approved for the vice presidency

In 1973, President Nixon's vice president, Spiro Agnew, resigned because he had been involved in a bribery scandal (see Chapter 21). Nixon needed a replacement quickly. He considered Ronald Reagan, the governor of California, but opted for Ford. Ford had good ties to Congress, was well liked and respected by his peers, and could easily win confirmation.

The Senate ratified Ford by a vote of 92 to 3. The House followed suit and approved Ford by a vote of 387 to 35. Gerald Ford became the vice president of the United States on December 6, 1973.

Under the provisions of the 25th Amendment to the U.S. Constitution, the president has to submit the name of a new vice president to Congress if the former vice president dies or resigns. Congress then has to approve the president's choice.

Stepping into the presidency

As the new vice president, Ford soon became involved in the Watergate scandal (President Nixon and the Watergate scandal are covered in Chapter 21). Ford had to publicly defend the president, even though he privately believed that Nixon was guilty.

As the Watergate affair continued, it became increasingly clear to Ford that he might become president. Early in the summer of 1974, Ford's personal advisor Phil Buchen began to set up a transition team, without Ford's direct knowledge, just in case.

On August 8, 1974, President Nixon announced his resignation to the U.S. public. One day later, Gerald Ford became the new president. He had an unenviable task ahead of him. He needed to reassure the nation and restore faith in the presidency.

President Ford is the only person in U.S. history to serve as both vice president and president without being elected to either office. He was appointed to both positions.

President Gerald Rudolph Ford, Jr. (1974–1977)

On August 9, 1974, Ford addressed the nation to reassure the U.S. public. He announced that the long nightmare was over and that it was time to go on with politics as usual.

A month later, Ford destroyed his presidency for the good of the country when he announced that he had issued a full pardon to former President Nixon. The media and many U.S. citizens were incensed. Calls poured in, condemning Ford's actions. His approval rating fell from 71 percent to 50 percent. Ford lost all the goodwill that he had accumulated in Congress. His presidency seemed doomed.

Why did he do it? A public trial of the president of the United States would have undermined the U.S. position abroad and split the U.S. public. Ford knew this and was willing to sacrifice his own career to save the country international embarrassment.

Taking on domestic problems

The 1974 Congressional election gave the Democratic Party an overwhelming majority in Congress. Now Ford faced a hostile Congress. Over the next two years, Congress overrode more than 20 percent of Ford's vetoes, the highest percentage in over a century.

To make matters worse, the economy took a nosedive. Inflation skyrocketed, driven by increased government spending and an increase in the price of oil. Ford cut government spending to help combat the rise in inflation. By the time he left office, inflation had fallen from 11.2 percent to 5.3 percent.

The unemployment rate also rose. Ford cut taxes to stimulate the economy and create jobs. Congress, however, blocked his tax cuts until 1976; by then it was too late for them to have an impact on the 1976 elections.

To placate critics on the left, Ford proclaimed a full amnesty for draft dodgers. *Draft dodgers* were young men who either avoided the draft or deserted the military during the Vietnam War. Under Ford's amnesty plan, these men would be welcomed back into the country if they completed two years of public or military service. Over 20,000 people applied for amnesty.

Ford didn't face opposition only from the Congressional Democrats. The conservative right of the Republican Party also opposed him. They rallied around Ronald Reagan, the former governor of California. Reagan publicly opposed Ford beginning in 1975 and announced his candidacy for the Republican presidential nomination the same year.

Dealing with foreign policy problems

When Gerald Ford assumed the presidency, the United States had withdrawn completely from South Vietnam. But the war between North Vietnam and South Vietnam continued.

In 1975, North Vietnam violated the peace treaty of 1973 (see the "Conflict in Vietnam" sidebar in Chapter 20) and invaded South Vietnam. Ford wanted to help South Vietnam, but Congress refused to go along. Within months, the South Vietnamese government fell, and all of Vietnam was now communist. More than 50,000 U.S. soldiers had died for nothing.

The Ford administration handled many other foreign policy events, including

- ✔ **The Helsinki Accords:** In 1975, 35 countries met in Helsinki, Finland and ratified accords that recognized all post–World War II borders in Europe as legitimate. The Soviet Union, as part of the agreement, pledged to respect human rights and ease travel restrictions for Soviet citizens and foreigners traveling to the Soviet Union.

- ✔ **The Vladivostock Agreements:** Ford and Soviet Premier Brezhnev signed these agreements in 1974. The agreements amended the SALT I arms treaty (see Chapter 21) and allowed for only one antiballistic missile site per country.

In the fall of 1975, President Ford survived two assassination attempts. In one case, the gun didn't fire. In the other case, a bystander intervened and the bullet missed.

Winning the Republican nomination and losing the presidency

In the fall of 1975, Ronald Reagan entered the race for the Republican presidential nomination. Reagan ran to the right of Ford, opposing the Helsinki accords and advocating a tough line against the Soviet Union. Reagan won several southern primaries. But in the end, Ford narrowly prevailed at the Republican convention. Ford picked Senator Robert Dole of Kansas for his vice-presidential running mate.

In the campaign against Democrat Jimmy Carter, Ford started out as the underdog. The economy was not doing well, and many people never forgave Ford for pardoning Nixon. His vice-presidential nominee, Robert Dole, came across as a bitter, mean-spirited man, labeling the Democratic Party the "party of warfare."

Ford committed a major gaffe during the presidential debates. He said that Poland wasn't under Soviet domination, when it clearly was. This error undermined his campaign.

At one point, Ford trailed Carter by over 50 points in the polls. He managed to close the gap considerably, losing by only 2 percentage points.

President Ford earned a reputation for being clumsy. Ford once fell out of presidential airplane Air Force One, and he often fell while skiing. He also had a tendency to hit people with his golf balls. Comedian Chevy Chase, who portrayed the president as accident-prone on the television show *Saturday Night Live,* cemented this image of President Ford.

Retiring publicly

After leaving office in 1977, President Ford undertook many public activities. He taught at the University of Michigan, founded the American Enterprise Institute, a think tank that studies public policy, and wrote his memoirs while staying active in politics.

Ford has campaigned for Republicans throughout the country. In 1980, he almost became Reagan's vice-presidential candidate. He has actively supported every Republican presidential candidate since then.

In 1999, President Clinton awarded Ford the Presidential Medal of Freedom for his many years of service to the country. Ford suffered a minor stroke at the Republican convention in 2000, but he has recuperated fully.

Sharing Faith and Principles: Jimmy Carter

Jimmy Carter, shown in Figure 22-2, was the Democrat least likely to win the presidency in 1976. He was the governor of a small southern state, Georgia, and had no national political experience. In earlier times, the lack of experience would have sunk any other candidacy. But, after the Watergate scandal in Richard Nixon's term (see Chapter 21), the U.S. public was sick and tired of politics as usual. They wanted someone new — an outsider — with no ties to Washington.

Carter ran on an outsider platform. He promised to return morality to the White House and to fight corruption in the capital. Carter's platform was good enough to win the presidency. However, as president, Carter paid a bitter price for being an outsider. He didn't have the connections in Congress to get his agenda passed, even though his party controlled both Houses of Congress. A declining economy and a foreign policy crisis undermined Carter. He lost his reelection bid in 1980.

Growing up in the South

Jimmy Carter was born in Georgia in 1924. He grew up in the small rural town of Plains, where his father grew and brokered peanuts, and owned a local store. His father was a conservative southern Democrat who served in the Georgia legislature and favored racial segregation. His mother was a liberal nurse who favored civil rights.

Carter attended Georgia Southwestern College and the Georgia Institute of Technology. He started his military career in 1943, when he entered the U.S. Naval Academy in Annapolis,

Maryland. He graduated in 1946, married Rosalynn Smith, his high school sweetheart, and entered the navy. He didn't participate in any fighting while serving in the military, but he did spend many months serving on submarines.

In 1953, Carter's father was diagnosed with cancer. Carter returned home to take over the family business. He proved to be an excellent businessman, as he turned the small concern into a large peanut warehouse business. By the time Jimmy Carter became president, he was a millionaire.

Figure 22-2:
Jimmy Carter, 39th president of the United States.

Courtesy of the Library of Congress

Carter's early political career

Carter's political career started in 19z60, when he won a seat on a local school board in Plains, Georgia. Two years later, he was elected to the Georgia state senate. Carter appeared to have lost the race at first, but he challenged the results, claiming vote fraud. He won the case and the seat.

By 1966, Carter thought that he was ready for the governorship. He entered the race and finished a disappointing third. Carter didn't take the loss lightly; he went into a major depression and thought that his political career was over. His sister encouraged him to find religion, and Carter became born again, turning himself into an Evangelical Christian. Encouraged, he ran for governor again in 1970.

Governing Georgia

Jimmy Carter learned from his 1966 gubernatorial run that a moderate Democrat couldn't win in Georgia. So he turned his campaign around and ran as a conservative Democrat. He also played the race card. His campaign showed his major opponent, Carl Sanders, joking with a black athlete. The strategy won him the segregationist vote and the governorship.

As governor, Carter changed his tune right away. He pushed for education reform, protection of the environment, and especially civil rights. In his inaugural address, he declared, "The time for racial discrimination is over." He hung a picture of Dr. Martin Luther King, Jr. in the governor's mansion. Carter wasn't just talk: He actually appointed many blacks to high-level state offices.

Running for the presidency

As early as 1972, Carter wanted to be president. He established a campaign committee and had a detailed strategy drawn up. In 1974, the Democratic Party appointed Carter to head the Democratic National Campaign Committee, a committee in charge of raising money for Democratic candidates throughout the country. From there, he decided to make a run for the presidency.

In early 1975, Carter announced his candidacy. He was a virtual unknown, and nobody gave him much of a chance. But Carter prevailed. He campaigned hard and kept discussion of his position vague on various issues while calling for a return to morality and an end to corruption in the federal government. Carter's platform resonated with a public that had recently dealt with Vietnam and Watergate. Carter won 17 of the 30 primaries.

At the Democratic convention, Carter received the nomination on the first ballot. To placate northern liberals and unions, Carter nominated liberal Minnesota Senator Walter Mondale as his vice president.

During the campaign, Carter blew a huge lead in the polls. But he managed to hang on to win the presidency. Much of his support came from African Americans and the southern states. Carter won the presidency with 297 electoral votes to Ford's 240. (One elector cast a vote for Ronald Reagan, who was not a candidate).

One of the most embarrassing moments in the 1976 campaign involved Carter giving an interview to *Playboy* magazine, in which he said, "I've looked on a lot of women with lust. I've committed adultery in my heart many times. This is something that God recognizes I will do — and I have done — and God forgives me."

President James Earl Carter, Jr. (1977–1981)

Carter's results as president were mixed. He had some successes, but at the same time, he experienced massive failures. One of his greatest mistakes was to make good on his campaign promise to rely on outsiders who didn't have strong ties to Congress. Even though his party controlled both Houses of Congress, he had less success in dealing with Congress than did presidents who didn't have that advantage — George Bush, for example.

Things started out well for Carter. On his first day in office, he pardoned all Vietnam draft evaders. He was able to get important environmental legislation passed, and he established the Department of Education to improve instructional standards throughout the United States.

Dealing with foreign policy issues

Carter attempted to base his foreign policy on human rights considerations. He cut off aid to friendly dictatorships if they violated human rights, which led to disastrous results. By 1978, the pro-American governments in Nicaragua and Iran had collapsed. The fall of the Shah of Iran in 1978 came back to haunt Carter. Major foreign policy events during the Carter administration include

- ✔ **The Panama Canal Treaty:** Despite objections by many U.S. citizens, Carter signed a treaty to return the canal to Panama by December 31, 1999. The United States reserved the right to defend the canal.

- ✔ **The Camp David Accords:** In September 1978, the crowning moment of the Carter administration's foreign policy took place. Carter met with Israeli Prime Minister Menachem Begin and Egyptian President Anwar Sadat in Camp David, Maryland. After long negotiations, the Camp David Accords, which ended the state of war between Israel and Egypt, were finalized. Sadat and Begin won the Nobel Peace Prize for negotiating the accord.

- ✔ **SALT II:** Carter and Soviet Premier Leonid Brezhnev signed SALT II (Strategic Arms Limitations Talks) in 1979. The treaty imposed ceilings on strategic weapons for both countries. The Senate never ratified SALT II. Carter withdrew it from consideration when the Soviets invaded Afghanistan.

- ✔ **The Soviet Invasion of Afghanistan:** In 1979, the Soviet Union invaded Afghanistan to maintain a communist government in power. Carter reacted strongly, withdrawing SALT II from the Senate, boycotting the Olympics held in Moscow, and prohibiting the sale of grain to the Soviet Union. The Soviets stayed in Afghanistan until 1988, when troops were recalled.

- ✔ **The Carter Doctrine:** The Carter Doctrine stated that the United States would use military force to prevent the Soviet Union from expanding further into the Middle East.

Facing U.S. hostages in Iran

In 1979, the Shah of Iran, the major U.S. ally in the Middle East, was toppled by a Muslim fundamentalist regime headed by the Ayatollah Khomeini. Carter refused to help the U.S. ally.

After the fall of the Shah of Iran, relations between the new Muslim fundamentalist regime and the United States deteriorated. When the Shah was diagnosed with cancer, the United States allowed him into the country for medical treatment. Iran was outraged. They wanted the Shah extradited so that he could be put on trial, but Carter refused.

On November 4, 1979, Iranian militants seized the U.S. embassy in Teheran, the capital of Iran — a clear violation of international law. After Carter protested, the Iranian government released all the women and minorities they had seized but continued to keep 53 white men hostage. Carter tried to negotiate the hostages' release, but he failed.

In April 1980, Carter authorized a military special forces unit to go in and get the hostages out. The attempt failed when a sandstorm caused two choppers to collide, killing eight servicemen.

Carter was blamed for the failure of the rescue attempt. The ongoing hostage crisis contributed greatly to his defeat in his 1980 reelection bid. Republican Ronald Reagan, while campaigning for the presidency, openly threatened Iran with a military strike unless the hostages were released. Iran released the hostages on January 20, 1981 — the day Reagan was inaugurated.

Handling problems at home

Most of Carter's domestic problems centered on the issue of energy. In 1979, OPEC (Organization of Petroleum Exporting Countries) increased oil prices dramatically. This led to inflation. By 1980, loan interest rates hit 20 percent. Most people were unable to finance homes and cars. Carter took the blame for the high interest rates.

On the bright side, Carter managed to pass legislation that encouraged the development of alternative energy in an effort to decrease dependence on foreign oil. Unfortunately, these programs were dismantled by his successors.

With the 1980 election approaching, Carter seemed vulnerable. Democratic Senator Ted Kennedy of Massachusetts launched a bid for the presidency. He and Carter battled it out for most of the spring of 1980. Kennedy refused to concede and took the fight to the convention, splitting the Democratic Party. Carter prevailed in the end, but the fight with Kennedy took a heavy toll, as Carter was forced to accept Kennedy's liberal platform.

The Republicans nominated Ronald Reagan, the former governor of California, on the first ballot. His vice-presidential nominee was George Bush, the former head of the CIA and former Texas congressman. The Republican ticket was formidable, indeed.

Losing his reelection bid

In 1980, Carter was forced to campaign on a liberal platform. He also had a lot of political baggage hanging over him, especially the hostages still held by Iran. Reagan, on the other hand, campaigned on an agenda of making the United States great again. Carter hoped that he would have an advantage in the debates. However, Reagan, who was a former actor, excelled at the debates and bested Carter.

When the election results came in, Carter had lost in a landslide, winning just 41 percent of the vote to Reagan's 51 percent. In addition, the Democrats lost control of the Senate for the first time since the 1950s.

Carter left office in January 1981, with his presidency considered a failure. He himself was considered a weak, ineffective president.

Retiring but not retreating

After leaving office, Carter proceeded to restore his reputation. He founded the Carter Center at Emory University to study democracy and human rights. Carter became an even more vocal advocate of human rights throughout the world.

Carter has traveled extensively, monitoring elections in many countries, and has served as a special peace emissary on more than one occasion. As a peace emissary, he traveled to North Korea and Haiti in 1994.

Carter and his wife Rosalynn also participate in Habitat for Humanity, where they don't just raise money but actually help build low-income housing with their own hands.

In 1999, President Clinton awarded Jimmy and Rosalynn Carter the Presidential Medal of Freedom for their humanitarian service. Today, Jimmy Carter is one of the most respected individuals not just in the United States but in the world. What a way to restore one's reputation.

Chapter 23

A Starring Role for Ronald Reagan

● ●

In This Chapter

▶ Taking up careers in acting and politics

▶ Becoming president

▶ Establishing a stronger foreign policy

▶ Handling the Iran-Contra scandal

▶ Retiring popular

● ●

*R*onald Reagan is one of the most beloved presidents in U.S. history. While academics rank him low on the presidential scale, the public adores him and ranks him in the top ten of all presidents (see Chapter 2). He was able to communicate in a unique way with the U.S. public: He reassured the country and instilled a new patriotism. He truly deserves the title bestowed upon him by the media: "The Great Communicator."

As president, Reagan restored U.S. pride and prestige in the world. He not only contained communism but also liberated communist countries. Trying to match his increase in U.S. defense spending crippled the Soviet economy and contributed to the collapse of the Soviet Union. At the same time, he left office with the largest budget deficit in U.S. history and the cloud of the Iran-Contra scandal hanging over him.

For his foreign policy successes, Reagan deserves to be listed in my top ten of U.S. presidents. Had his economic policies worked, he could have broken into the top five.

President Reagan gave the United States many firsts: He was the oldest president at age 69 to be elected to office, and he was the first president to have been divorced.

Dreaming of Hollywood

Ronald Wilson Reagan was born in Tampico, Illinois in 1911. His father was a traveling shoe salesman who moved the family to Dixon, Illinois, when Reagan was 9 years old. Reagan considers Dixon his hometown. His father was an alcoholic — he had the "Irish disease," as Reagan put it — and the family was barely able to make ends meet.

In high school, Reagan played football and was the student council president. Reagan developed his theatrical and political interests at Eureka College, which he attended from 1928 to 1932. He starred in plays and organized a strike against the college president in response to curriculum cutbacks. Reagan forced the resignation of the college president.

After graduating with a degree in economics, Reagan wanted to act, but no acting jobs were available in the Midwest. He became a sportscaster instead, signing on with radio station WHO in Des Moines, Iowa.

In 1937, Reagan traveled to California to report on the Chicago Cubs's spring training camp. While he was there, a friend of his arranged a screen test with the Warner Brothers movie studio. Warner Brothers signed him to a seven-year contract, and over the next 25 years, Reagan made more than 50 movies.

Reagan met actress Jane Wyman in 1938. They got married in 1940. The marriage failed, and they were divorced by 1948. During World War II, Reagan enlisted in the army. He made training films for the military, but he never saw any action.

Reagan's Early Career

Reagan started his political career in 1947 when he became president of the *Screen Actors Guild,* a union representing actors and actresses. Reagan was a lifelong Democrat, but, as president of the Screen Actors Guild, he was called to Washington to testify on communist involvement in the film industry. He took a strong anti-communist stance and started moving to the right.

Actress Nancy Davis contacted Reagan because her name appeared by mistake on a list of communist sympathizers in Hollywood. Reagan, as president of the Screen Actors Guild, took care of the problem for Nancy and also fell in love with her. They were married in 1952.

In 1954, Reagan turned to television. He hosted a half-hour television show, *General Electric Theater,* and traveled around the country giving speeches on behalf of General Electric. In his speeches, Reagan tackled many political issues, such as tax cuts and the superiority of the *free enterprise system* — wherein the government does not interfere in the economy.

After campaigning and voting for Republicans Eisenhower and Nixon, Reagan officially changed his party affiliation from Democrat to Republican in 1962.

Reagan's big political break occurred in 1964. The Republican nominee for president, Barry Goldwater, was doing poorly in the polls and having problems raising money. Reagan gave an impassioned speech on Goldwater's behalf, blasting big government and praising individual initiative. The televised speech raised hundreds of thousands of dollars for Goldwater and turned Reagan into a national conservative icon.

Governing California

In 1966, a group of businesspeople asked Reagan to run for governor of California. He accepted and ran a tough campaign, appealing to Republicans and to Democrats who belonged to labor unions. (He used the same technique when he ran for the presidency in 1980.) Reagan beat the incumbent Pat Brown, who had beaten Nixon back in 1962, by almost a million votes.

Reagan's terms as governor of California foreshadowed his presidency. To combat a budget deficit, Reagan cut spending. He initiated a 10 percent budget cut in all state agencies.

Reagan became known for being tough on protesters, especially the counterculture movement that grew up at many universities in the 1960s. This stance pleased many voters. Reagan easily won reelection in 1970.

During his second term, Reagan's major accomplishment was welfare reform in California. To combat welfare fraud, Reagan cut more than 300,000 people from the welfare rolls. In 1974, everybody expected Reagan to run for and easily win a third term. But he had his sights set on the White House.

Challenging Ford in 1976

In 1975, Reagan announced his candidacy for the Republican presidential nomination. President Ford had been in office for just a year, and he was experiencing many problems (see Chapter 22). The conservative wing of the Republican Party backed Reagan.

Not doing well in the early primaries, Reagan accused Ford of not being conservative enough. This strategy worked, especially in the South and West. In the end, Ford won the nomination by a slim, 57-vote margin.

Winning the presidency in 1980

After losing by a narrow margin in 1976, Reagan ran for the Republican nomination again in 1980. He was the clear frontrunner for the nomination until George Bush entered the race and won several primaries.

At the Republican convention, Reagan won the nomination and planned to name former president Gerald Ford as his vice-president. Ford, however, wanted to have a co-presidency, where he could be involved in decision making. Reagan opted for George Bush instead. He didn't want the media or the public to think that he needed help from a former president.

Reagan faced incumbent president Jimmy Carter in the general election. Reagan focused on Carter's weaknesses and called for a restoration of U.S. power, major rearmament, and, especially, a smaller government with less regulation and a major tax cut.

The *Reagan Democrats* — white, male, working class voters — paired with support from corporations across the country, contributed to Reagan's a landslide victory. He got 489 electoral votes and 51 percent of the popular vote, and the mandate he was looking for to bring about major changes.

President Ronald Wilson Reagan (1981–1989)

Ronald Reagan, shown in Figure 23-1, entered the White House intending to bring about major changes in economic and social policy. He believed in less government regulation of the economy, and lower taxes for both businesses and individuals. Reagan opposed the welfare state and wanted to cut welfare benefits. He also intended to appoint conservative Supreme Court justices who would help promote his conservative social agenda.

Figure 23-1:
Ronald Reagan, 40th president of the United States.

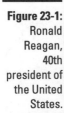

Courtesy of the Library of Congress

Surviving an assassination attempt

Before Reagan was able to get started on his agenda, an assassin's bullet almost killed him. Reagan survived the assassination attempt, although his press secretary, James Brady, was crippled for life.

On March 30, 1981, Reagan delivered a speech at a hotel in Washington. He was shot by a crazed assassin, John Hinckley, while waiting outside the hotel. Doctors found that the bullet had hit the president's left lung and lodged itself just an inch from his heart. On his way to the operating table, Reagan cracked several jokes, which turned him into a hero with most U.S. citizens. Reagan returned to work only 12 days later, having achieved almost mythical status.

After the assassination attempt, Congress felt that it had to go along with Reagan's policies because the public stood behind him. Who could oppose a president who survived being shot?

Stimulating the economy

When Reagan took office in 1981, the economy was in bad shape. By 1982, unemployment had hit 11 percent, the budget deficit had increased, and interest rates were still high. Reagan pushed many reforms through Congress in his first term (1981 to 1984) to help the economy. These reforms included

- Major tax cuts of up to 30 percent and increases in tax write-offs for U.S. citizens and U.S. businesses with the Economic Recovery Act of 1981. (See the "Supply-side economics" sidebar in this section for more on this theory.)

- Major cut backs in social spending. Reagan cut spending on programs such as job training, college loans, and medical programs.

- Reductions in regulations for the economy. For example, Reagan pushed to deregulate the savings-and-loan industry which resulted in the savings-and-loan crises of the late 1980s.

- Reductions in environmental standards. Reagan believed that stringent environmental and pollution standards imposed unnecessary costs on U.S. businesses. So the standards were lowered or eliminated.

- Massive increases in defense spending. Reagan doubled the defense budget to almost $300 billion.

Supply-side economics

Reagan believed in the economic theory of supply-side economics. The idea behind supply-side economics is simple: The government initiates major tax cuts for U.S. businesses and the public, and the businesses use the tax savings to invest in the economy, leading to new technologies and more jobs. At the same time, the government implements major spending cuts to balance the budget and curb inflation.

The formerly unemployed can now buy goods, which helps stimulate the economy. They can also pay taxes, replacing the revenues lost in the initial tax cut.

The theory is sound on paper. However, businesses didn't use the tax cuts as intended. They didn't invest their tax savings, no new high-paying jobs were created, and no new tax revenue filled the government's coffers. In addition, Congress refused to cut spending, resulting in a major budget deficit.

Reagan's economic programs, though controversial in nature, worked fairly well. By 1983, the economy had recovered, and by 1984, it was booming. Reagan left the most popular welfare programs untouched, actually increasing Social Security and Medicare spending. Reagan's policies created 20 million new jobs during his eight years in office. Unemployment had sunk to 5.5 percent by 1988, and inflation virtually disappeared. Things looked good in America. However, Reagan's policies also had negative side effects.

Increasing the national debt

With tax cuts reducing government income, Reagan had to borrow heavily to finance his increase in expenditures. By the time he left office, the national debt had reached a record $3 trillion. The government needed to set aside almost 15 percent of the annual budget just to make the interest payments.

The government was competing with private businesses for loans, so interest rates shot up. This increase encouraged foreigners to buy dollars and put them into U.S. banks to take advantage of the high interest rates. The value of the dollar appreciated, making foreign goods cheaper and U.S. exports more expensive, resulting in a massive trade deficit. The government was forced to intervene: It *devalued* the dollar, or reduced the value of the dollar in relation to foreign currencies, in 1986 to correct the trade deficit.

Breaking a strike

In August 1981, the union representing air traffic controllers, PATCO (Professional Air Traffic Controllers Organization) went on strike, effectively shutting down the country's major airports.

The union's actions were illegal under federal law. But instead of negotiating, as the union leaders expected, Reagan fired all 13,000 air traffic controllers, hired replacements, and disbanded the union. Reagan refused to rehire the controllers even after major labor leaders in the United States asked him to do so. No other union challenged Reagan during the rest of his presidency.

Implementing conservative social policies

Reagan changed U.S. social policies — a promise made during his campaign. The emphasis on civil rights stopped. Reagan attempted to curtail affirmative action and stop court-ordered *busing*, where white students were bused to inner city schools and black students to affluent suburban schools.

Federal affirmative action, which set aside government contracts for minorities, was stopped in 1981. In addition, Reagan's administration supported lawsuits challenging the legality of affirmative action.

Packing the Supreme Court

Reagan knew that to be successful he had to have the support of the Supreme Court, so he appointed conservatives to the bench. His first selection was Sandra Day O'Connor, a conservative judge from Arizona and the first woman on the Supreme Court. She was confirmed by the U.S. Senate easily.

Reagan then appointed Antonin Scalia, a conservative Catholic who became one of the most conservative members on the court. Reagan elevated William Rehnquist to Chief Justice, and conservatives controlled the Supreme Court. However, to Reagan's great disappointment, the conservative court did not roll back affirmative action or end the practice of abortion.

Reestablishing U.S. World Domination

Before Reagan took office, U.S. prestige and power had suffered greatly. The Soviet Union used the Carter years to expand and rearm. After Cuba, a second country in Latin America, Nicaragua, went communist and was destabilizing its neighbor, El Salvador. Reagan was especially concerned with growing Soviet power in Latin America. The United States was perceived as weak, while Soviet power was growing.

Influencing events around the globe

Reagan took decisive action on the foreign policy front, especially in the cause of wiping out communism. Some of the more notable events are

- **The Reagan Doctrine:** This doctrine pledged economic and military aid to any movement fighting communism. Under the doctrine, the United States gave aid to rebels fighting communism in Angola and Nicaragua.

- **Central America:** The United States cut off support from the socialist government of Nicaragua in 1981. After Nicaragua signed a pact with the Soviet Union, the United States gave support to the anticommunist forces in Nicaragua, known as the *Contras.* In addition, Reagan started to support the right wing government in El Salvador, which was fighting a communist uprising sponsored by Nicaragua.

- **Grenada:** In 1983, Reagan invaded the Caribbean island of Grenada. The island had gone communist after a pro-American government was overthrown. Cuban military advisors were present to help build up the infrastructure of the island. Because Reagan feared another Soviet ally in Latin America, he invaded and liberated the island nation.

- **Lebanon:** In 1982, Reagan sent marines to Lebanon to protect a new Christian government. A suicide bomber attacked the headquarters of the marines, killing 241 marines. Reagan withdrew the marines in 1984.

- **Afghanistan:** The United States began supporting the Afghan freedom fighters, or *mujahidin,* opposing the Soviet Union, supplying them with stinger missiles, which gave the Afghans the ability to shoot down Soviet aircraft and take away the Soviet's air superiority.

- **Libya:** In 1986, a Muslim terrorist killed a U.S. soldier in a dance hall in Berlin, Germany. Reagan blamed Libya and its leader Muammar Qaddafi. He initiated an air strike against Libya.

- **SDI:** In 1983, Reagan proposed the *Strategic Defense Initiative (SDI),* also referred to as "Star Wars," an antiballistic missile system designed to shoot down incoming nuclear missiles before they hit the United States.

In theory, the system would protect the country from nuclear attack, thus restoring U.S. superiority in the nuclear arms race. Billions of dollars were spent on it before President George Bush abandoned it.

✔ **Massive rearmament:** Reagan poured billions of dollars into defense to restore U.S. military might. The Soviet Union tried to match the strength of the U.S. military, but couldn't. By 1986, Soviet leader Mikhail Gorbachev decided that it was time to end the arms race, and arms control negotiations took place.

Dealing with the Soviets

In 1985, Mikhail Gorbachev came to power in the Soviet Union. He was young and energetic, and he wanted to reform the Soviet Union. He recognized that his country couldn't keep up with the United States in the arms race and approached Reagan to discuss ending the arms race. The two met in 1985 and 1986 and hit it off on a personal level. *Détente,* or peaceful coexistence, was reestablished. In the following years, many weapons treaties were negotiated, including:

✔ **The Intermediate Range Nuclear Forces Treaty:** Gorbachev and Reagan signed this historic treaty in 1987. Both countries agreed to engage in *disarmament* — the destruction of existing weapons. Intermediate range missiles scattered all over Europe were to be destroyed, with foreign observers acting as witnesses. Close to 2,000 intermediate range missiles were destroyed under the provisions of the treaty.

✔ **The Conventional Forces in Europe Treaty:** This treaty provided for massive cutbacks among conventional forces, such as tanks located throughout Europe.

The Soviet Union also agreed to withdraw its troops from Afghanistan and abandon the objective of world communism. The collapse of the Soviet Empire had begun.

Dealing with Scandal in his Second Term

In 1984, Reagan ran for reelection. The economy was doing well and the United States seemed more powerful than ever. At 73, Reagan was the oldest man ever to run for the presidency: His age became an issue, but one he put to rest with a stellar performance in the second debate. Reagan went on to win the largest victory in the history of the country with 49 states and 525 electoral votes. Former vice president Walter Mondale carried only his home state of Minnesota and the District of Columbia.

Reagan's policy successes came to an abrupt halt in late 1986, as he spent the remainder of his term dealing with the Iran-Contra scandal.

A story broke in Lebanon in November 1986, revealing that the Reagan administration had been selling weapons to Iran in exchange for freeing U.S. hostages in Lebanon. The exchange was illegal, and it embarrassed the Reagan administration. The profits from the illegal arms sales were then used to fund the Contras in Nicaragua, which was also illegal. Congress had repeatedly refused Reagan's requests to give aid to the *Contras* — so-called freedom fighters trying to overthrow the Nicaraguan government. Congress instead passed a bill making military aid to the Contras illegal.

In the end, Congress issued a 690-page report stating that Reagan was unaware of the illegal doings of some of his staff, though it criticized Reagan's management style. This analysis was no surprise to many political observers who knew that Reagan liked to delegate authority: He wasn't involved in day-to-day decisions.

Even though many believed that Reagan was aware of the dealings in the Iran-Contra scandal, the public never blamed him for it, and his approval ratings remained high. The media gave him the nickname the "Teflon president," because none of the accusations stuck.

Keeping the Revolution Alive during Retirement

After Reagan left office, he stayed active in Republican politics, campaigning for his vice president, George Bush, in 1988 and contributing to Bush's victory. The Reagan Democrats transferred their votes to Bush, who ran on a platform built around continuing Reagan's policies. Though he campaigned for Bush again in 1992, Bill Clinton won that election.

Reagan's memoirs, *An American Life,* became a bestseller. The opening of the Reagan library in Simi Valley, California in 1991 was one of the big highlights of the former president's career. The library is considered the best presidential library in the country (that's where I rank it in Chapter 28).

In November 1994, Reagan announced that he had Alzheimer's disease. His public appearances decreased, and his wife Nancy attended the 1996 Republican national convention on his behalf. At the time of this writing, Ronald Reagan, who turned 91 in 2002, is the oldest living president in the history of the United States.

Chapter 24

Acting Out: George Bush and Bill Clinton

....

In This Chapter

▶ Ending the Cold War, starting a war with Iraq: Bush

▶ Generating prosperity and scandal: Clinton

....

*T*his chapter covers two of the country's recent presidents — George Bush and Bill Clinton. Together, the two of them would have made a potent combination, with Bush's expertise in foreign affairs and Clinton's ability to connect with the average voter. Unfortunately, they were each undermined by their weaknesses — Bush by his domestic policy weakness and Clinton by his personal weakness.

George Bush won the presidency in 1988 on the coattails of the Reagan revolution but disappointed both conservatives and liberals. He broke a campaign pledge when he raised taxes to cover an increasing deficit, and he pursued conservative social policies.

Bush's major successes came in the area of foreign relations. He presided over the end of the Cold War and the collapse of the Soviet Union, and he punished aggression in the Middle East by forcefully expelling Iraq from Kuwait with Operation Desert Storm. For his foreign policy accomplishments, he deserves credit. Bush is arguably one of the best foreign policy presidents in U.S. history. He loved foreign policy and excelled at it. But his domestic policies destroyed his presidency — especially his tax hike in 1991.

Bill Clinton, on the other hand, excelled in domestic politics. He gave the United States 10 years of economic growth and prosperity. He disliked foreign policy, and this showed in unsuccessful endeavors in Somalia and Haiti. His second term was hamstrung by sexual scandals.

Bringing an End to the Cold War: George Bush

George H. Bush, shown in Figure 24-1, will go down in history as one of the great foreign policy presidents in U.S. history. During his administration, the Soviet Union collapsed and the Cold War came to an end. After almost 50 years of competition between the United States and the Soviet Union, the United States emerged victorious. Bush handled the liberation of Eastern Europe skillfully. Without his diplomatic skills, the reunification of Germany, divided since the end of World War II, would not have occurred so quickly. Bush added to his foreign policy success by implementing major arms control agreements with the Soviet Union, and later Russia, to reduce the threat of nuclear war in the world.

When Saddam Hussein invaded Kuwait in 1990, Bush stood up to him, punished him for his aggression by defeating the Iraqi army, and liberated Kuwait, defending American national oil interests. Bush was a great foreign policy leader, indeed, and history will look kindly upon his presidency.

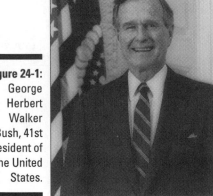

Figure 24-1: George Herbert Walker Bush, 41st president of the United States.

Courtesy of the Library of Congress

George Bush was just the second sitting vice president in more than 150 years to win the presidency — Martin Van Buren was the first in 1836. Bush was also the second sitting vice president in history to lose reelection — again, Martin Van Buren was the first in 1840.

Growing up prominent

George Bush was born into one of the most prominent families in the United States. He grew up in a wealthy family committed to civil service, and his parents instilled in him a sense of civic obligation. Bush was born in Massachusetts in 1924, but he grew up in Connecticut. His father was a prominent Wall Street lawyer who later served two terms in the U.S. Senate.

Young Bush attended the best schools and was ready to go to Yale when World War II broke out. He enlisted in the navy in 1942 and became a torpedo bomber pilot. While serving his country, Bush became one of the youngest and most distinguished pilots of World War II. He flew more than 50 bombing missions against Japan.

In 1944, his plane was shot down by the Japanese. Bush survived hours in the Pacific Ocean before a U.S. submarine rescued him.

Bush returned home in late 1944. He married Barbara Pierce, the daughter of a magazine publishing magnate — her father published *Redbook* and *McCall's* magazines — in 1945. Bush also returned to Yale, graduating in 1948 with a degree in economics.

Instead of relying on his family connections in the Northeast, Bush moved to Texas to make a life of his own. He started a business producing oil-drilling equipment. Within a few years, Bush was a millionaire.

Bush's early political career

Like his father, Bush was a moderate Republican. In 1962, he became the chairman of the Republican Party in Harris County (Houston), Texas. A couple of years later, Bush thought he was ready to run for office. His father had been a senator, so Bush figured he should be one, too. He ran against incumbent Democrat Ralph Yarborough in 1964 and lost. However, he gained the attention of the Republican Party by receiving a record number of votes for a Republican in Texas. Former vice-president Richard Nixon took Bush under his wing, and in 1966, Bush became the first Republican to represent Houston in the House of Representatives.

Bush's career in Congress was a distinguished one. He pushed to give 18-year-olds the right to vote, and he pushed to abolish the military draft. In 1970, Bush ran for the Senate one more time. This time he faced Lloyd Bentsen. Again he lost the race for the Senate. President Nixon, still seeing a lot of potential in Bush, came to the rescue by appointing Bush ambassador to the United Nations.

Gaining a wide variety of experience

From 1971 to 1977, Bush served in a lot of government positions, including

- **Ambassador to the United Nations (1971–1973):** In this position, Bush gained knowledge of foreign affairs and established many personal ties. These ties came in handy during his presidency.

> ✔ **Chairman of the Republican National Committee (1973–1974):** In this function, Bush raised money for the Republican Party and was forced to defend President Nixon to the public.
>
> Bush came to believe that Nixon was guilty in the Watergate scandal. In 1974, Bush actually sent his mentor a letter asking him to resign.
>
> ✔ **U.S. Envoy to China (1974–1975):** In this position, Bush laid the foundation for establishing diplomatic relations between the United States and China, which was accomplished in 1979.
>
> ✔ **Head of the CIA (1976–1977):** As the head of the CIA (Central Intelligence Agency), Bush had to defend the agency to Congress many times. He is widely credited for restoring trust and prestige to the CIA.

With the Democrats winning the White House in 1976, Bush's public career was over for the time being. So he turned his attention to the big prize — the presidency.

Becoming vice president

In 1980, Bush ran for the Republican presidential nomination — he was the only real challenger to Ronald Reagan. He ran as a moderate, pointing out his differences with the more conservative Reagan. In the campaign, Bush even referred to Reagan's economic agenda as "voodoo economics."

When Reagan won the nomination, he selected Bush to be his running mate. Bush had to promise to support Reagan's policies, even if he disagreed with them.

President Reagan believed strongly in delegating authority, which made Bush a very active player in the Reagan administration. Bush attended all cabinet meetings and defended Reagan's policies in speeches he gave throughout the country and around the world. His world travel gave him more foreign policy connections.

At home, Bush was put in charge of the task forces on terrorism and drugs. Bush was involved in the Iran-Contra scandal, but he denied any wrongdoing and was later cleared of all charges.

Running for the presidency one more time

In 1988, Bush was the frontrunner for the Republican nomination. He easily beat a challenge by Senator Robert Dole of Kansas. Bush benefited from the fact that Reagan had retired as one of the most popular presidents in U.S. history. Reagan actively campaigned for Bush, and Bush promised to continue Reagan's policies. Bush promised the U.S. public that, as president, he would preside over a "kinder, gentler America," where especially the poor would benefit. At the Republican convention, he further pledged not to raise taxes, saying "The Congress will push me to raise taxes, and I'll say no, and they'll push, and I'll say no, and they'll push again and I'll say to them, 'read my lips, no new taxes.'" — a promise he later had to break.

The 1988 campaign got nasty. Bush, trailing in the polls, attacked his Democratic opponent, Michael Dukakis, the governor of Massachusetts, by accusing him of being soft on crime. Bush also highlighted Dukakis's plan to make cuts in the military and attacked him for supporting the right to burn the U.S. flag. Bush's negative attacks worked. He won 54 percent of the vote and carried 426 electoral votes to Dukakis's 111.

President George Herbert Walker Bush (1989–1993)

Unlike Reagan, Bush was a hands-on president. He showed up early for work, and he deeply immersed himself in decision making. This work ethic showed especially in the area of foreign affairs, where Bush had many major accomplishments. However, Bush wasn't nearly as successful in domestic policy.

Excelling in foreign policy

Foreign policy was Bush's great love, and he excelled at it. His major foreign policy accomplishments include

- ✔ **The invasion of Panama:** In December 1989, President Bush ordered the invasion of Panama. The Panamanian dictator, Manuel Noriega, was actively involved in drug smuggling, and he nullified a democratic vote that he had lost. The murder of a U.S. marine by Noriega's forces was the last straw that prompted Bush to invade the country with 24,000 U.S. troops. The troops captured and removed Noriega from office in January 1990. He was brought back to the United States for trial. Noriega was subsequently tried in the United States in April 1992, convicted of drug trafficking, and incarcerated.

- ✔ **German unification:** President Bush played an active role in convincing Soviet president Gorbachev to allow Germany, which had been divided since 1945 (see Chapter 17), to reunify in 1990.

- ✔ **START I (Strategic Arms Reduction Treaty):** This treaty, ratified in 1991, reduced U.S. and Soviet nuclear arsenals. The number of nuclear warheads was cut to 8,500 for the United States and 6,500 for the Soviet Union.

- ✔ **The Understanding on Nuclear Arms Reduction Resolution:** This resolution, signed in 1992, further reduced the nuclear arsenals of the United States and Russia (after the collapse of the Soviet Union). The new numbers were 3,500 warheads for the United States and 3,000 for Russia.

✔ **The end of the Cold War:** With the collapse of the Soviet Union in late 1991, the United States had won the Cold War. It was the only remaining superpower. Bush proceeded slowly, trying not to antagonize Russia, and assured Russia economic aid.

Bush was also actively involved in the liberation of Eastern Europe from Soviet control. He advocated a slow, cautious transition and extended economic aid to the new democracies in Eastern Europe.

✔ **The Gulf War:** In 1990, Saddam Hussein, the leader of Iraq, invaded neighboring Kuwait. Kuwait holds some of the largest oil reserves in the world, and it neighbors U.S. ally Saudi Arabia. Bush was afraid that Saudi Arabia would be Iraq's next target. Bush created an international alliance sanctioned by the United Nations, including such unlikely allies as the Soviet Union and many Arab countries, to punish Iraq.

Having problems at home

President Bush's foreign policy successes lifted his approval rating to an astonishing 91 percent, the highest ever for a sitting president. He seemed to be a shoo-in for reelection in 1992, but domestic problems interfered. Bush wasn't nearly as successful with domestic politics as he was with foreign policy. His problems at home included:

✔ **The deficit:** By 1989, the budget deficit had risen to $350 billion annually. The overall budget deficit reached $3.2 trillion — the highest it had ever been. In 1991, the Bush administration, together with Congress, increased taxes to reduce the deficit.

✔ **The collapse of the savings and loan industry:** President Reagan and Congress deregulated the savings and loan industry in 1982. This freed institutions to engage in risky speculation, and many institutions were mismanaged. By 1989, approximately 1,000 savings and loan businesses had collapsed or were on the verge of collapsing. The government had to step in and spend an estimated $500 billion to bail these industries out so that millions of Americans didn't lose their savings.

Operation Desert Storm

Operation Desert Storm — the liberation of Kuwait — began on January 17, 1991, and lasted just a few weeks. On February 27, 1991, United States marines liberated Kuwait City, the capital of Kuwait. Iraq was defeated, and the war was over. The allied alliance lost fewer than 200 soldiers, while Iraq lost 100,000 soldiers.

Kuwait was free, but Hussein was still in power. Bush knew that removing Hussein would anger his Arab allies and destabilize the Persian Gulf region, allowing Iran to take over the region. Bush is still widely criticized for his decision not to remove Hussein from power in Iraq.

Finding some success with domestic policy

The Bush administration succeeded in some areas of domestic policy. The following are some of the most notable successes:

- ✔ **The Americans with Disabilities Act:** This act made it mandatory for government installations, businesses, and public places to eliminate any physical obstacle that handicapped citizens may be facing. For example, elevators had to be installed in all government facilities.

- ✔ **The Clean Air Act:** This act provided higher standards for air quality.

- ✔ **NAFTA (The North American Free Trade Agreement):** Bush proposed NAFTA in 1991. It eliminated most tariffs between the United States, Canada, and Mexico, and made provision for eligible Latin American countries to join at a later date. Congress stalled the agreement until President Clinton signed it in 1993.

President Bush appointed the second African American justice to the Supreme Court. (The first was Thurgood Marshall, who was appointed by President Johnson in 1967). In 1991, he appointed Clarence Thomas, who narrowly won confirmation in a bitter Senate battle.

Losing reelection in 1992

President Bush fully expected to win reelection in 1992. He had many great foreign policy successes, and he thought that would be good enough. In addition, he was opposed by a Democratic governor, with a lot of personal baggage, from a small state.

But what ultimately cost Bush the election was a third party candidate, H. Ross Perot, a billionaire from Texas. Perot siphoned off conservative votes and won almost 20 percent of the total vote. Studies show that almost two-thirds of all Perot voters would have voted for Bush had Perot withdrawn.

During the candidate debates, Bush seemed disinterested. On election night, he lost badly, receiving only 37 percent of the popular vote and 168 electoral votes. The Democrat Bill Clinton won the presidency with 43 percent of the popular vote and 370 electoral votes.

Retiring, and advising

George Bush left office in 1993 and moved back to Houston, Texas. He wrote his memoirs, and at press time, was still giving speeches around the country. When asked about his greatest success as president, Bush replied, "By the grace of God, America won the Cold War."

Bush's proudest moments involved his sons. In 1994, his son George W. Bush became governor of Texas, and in 1998, another son, Jeb, won the governorship of Florida. Then, Governor George W. Bush became president in 2001.

Today, George Bush is involved in his son's administration, advising him on foreign affairs.

Scandal Amid Domestic Policy Success: Bill Clinton

Bill Clinton, shown in Figure 24-2, is one of the most controversial U.S. presidents in history. He achieved great successes in domestic policy and was the first Democrat to be elected to two terms since Franklin Roosevelt.

Clinton single-handedly transformed the Democratic Party, moving it to the center of the political spectrum. He effectively used the media to communicate with the public. He was also a wizard at campaigning.

Clinton could have been considered a great U.S. president if it had not been for the many scandals involving him and his administration. From the Whitewater financial scandal to his affair with intern Monica Lewinsky, which got him impeached by the House of Representatives but not convicted in the Senate, to Pardongate — the money-for-pardons scandal that marred his last days in office and beyond — Clinton's terms seemed to be full of scandals. He is the only president to have been involved in a scandal as he left office. His record doesn't bode well for his future ranking among U.S. presidents.

Figure 24-2:
Bill Clinton,
42nd
president of
the United
States.

Courtesy of the Library of Congress

Overcoming the odds

Bill Clinton was born William Jefferson Blythe, IV, in Hope, Arkansas in 1946. His father, a traveling salesman, was killed a few months before his birth. His mother remarried, and Bill took his stepfather's last name, Clinton. His stepfather was an alcoholic who frequently beat his wife and the two boys (Bill and his stepbrother, Roger). At the age of 14, Clinton stood up to his stepfather and threatened him. The violence stopped.

Clinton was an excellent student and very active in school politics — he ran for so many offices that the principal finally told him that he'd held enough offices. He was also an avid saxophone player. He won first prize in a statewide contest and started a band with two friends called the "Three Blind Mice."

In 1963, the American Legion's Boys Nation Program selected Clinton to travel to Washington to meet President Kennedy. After this meeting, Clinton made up his mind to enter politics. To this end, he attended Georgetown University and graduated with a degree in international affairs in 1968.

After graduating from Georgetown, he received a Rhodes scholarship to travel and study at Oxford University in Great Britain. At Oxford, he protested the United State's involvement in the ongoing war in Vietnam. Clinton knew that he wouldn't have to serve in Vietnam because he had a very high number in the draft lottery.

In 1970, Clinton received a scholarship to study law at Yale, where he met his future wife, Hillary Rodham. They shared the same political views, and both worked for George McGovern during his 1972 presidential campaign.

Clinton graduated in 1973 and moved back to Arkansas to teach law at the University of Arkansas. Hillary Rodham joined the faculty in 1974 and married Clinton in 1975.

Clinton's early political career

In 1974, Clinton ran for a seat in the U.S. House of Representatives. He figured the timing was good, with the Republican Party discredited by Watergate. He faced incumbent Republican congressman John Paul Hammerschmidt and nearly won, receiving 48 percent of the vote.

Clinton's near-upset brought him to the attention of the Arkansas Democratic Party. The party saw him as an up-and-coming politician and nominated him for attorney general in 1976. Clinton easily won the race. In 1978, the governor of Arkansas, David Pryor, ran for the Senate, leaving the governorship open. Clinton won the election for the governorship and became the nation's youngest governor at the age of 32.

Governing Arkansas — Part 1

When Clinton took over in Arkansas, the state was in shambles. It ranked low in national rankings of income, education, and standard of living. Clinton wanted to change all that.

Clinton needed money to improve education and the Arkansas infrastructure, so he implemented a tax increase. As an environmentalist, Clinton opposed the tree-harvesting practices of Arkansas's largest employers — paper companies. His tax increase and opposition to tree harvesting made him widely disliked in the state and led to his defeat when he ran for reelection in 1980.

Clinton wasn't discouraged. He learned from his mistakes and was ready to run again in 1982. He apologized to the people of Arkansas for the mistakes he made during his first term and won the election with 55 percent of the vote. He governed Arkansas for the next 10 years, winning reelection three more times.

Governing Arkansas — Part 2

Clinton became one of the most successful governors in the United States. In 1986, *Newsweek* magazine ranked him the fifth-best governor in the country, and in 1991, he was ranked the best governor by his fellow governors.

As governor, Clinton pushed for education reform, job growth, and the inclusion of minorities in state government. He increased taxes to help pay teachers higher salaries, provided poor students with scholarships, and changed the high school curriculum in Arkansas to emphasize hard sciences, such as mathematics and physics. As a result of Clinton's programs, the graduation rate in Arkansas increased, and tests showed that Arkansan children were learning much more and much better than they had been.

Clinton also pushed for laws to make Arkansas attractive to large businesses. This strategy worked: Many businesses moved to Arkansas to take advantage of cheap, skilled labor and tax breaks.

Running for president in 1992

Clinton had announced his candidacy for the Democratic nomination in October 1991, starting his path to the presidency. He was active in the *Democratic Leadership Council,* a group of moderate Democrats trying to impact national politics through progressive policies. This group provided him with the political foundation and issues necessary to run for the presidency, though he still faced an uphill battle to win the Democratic presidential nomination. He was helped by the fact that many prominent Democrats sat out the 1992 election, believing that President Bush was unbeatable.

By the spring of 1992, Clinton had emerged as the frontrunner for the Democratic nomination, which he easily received that summer.

He ran his campaign as a New Democrat, conservative on many social issues, such as the death penalty, which he supported. He based his campaign solely on domestic issues, knowing that Bush was stronger on foreign policy. Clinton emphasized the weakening economy and promised a turnaround. He advocated a tax cut for the middle class, promised to reduce the deficit, and called for a cut in defense spending. Most importantly, he advocated health care reform and welfare reform.

During his campaign, Clinton had to overcome personal attacks involving a long-lasting relationship he had with an Arkansas state employee and night-club singer, Gennifer Flowers. Clinton and his wife appeared on the television show *60 Minutes* to defend their marriage and ask the media and the public to respect their privacy. The strategy worked. Clinton's affair didn't become an issue in the 1992 campaign.

Clinton excelled in the candidate debates and went on to beat Bush in November. An independent candidate, H. Ross Perot, helped Clinton by draining votes from Bush. At 46, Clinton became the third-youngest president in U.S. history and the first president born after WWII.

President William Jefferson Clinton (1993–2001)

Clinton assumed office in January 1993, saying in his inaugural address, "There is nothing wrong with America that can't be fixed with what is right in America."

Clinton was ready to implement reforms quickly. However, one of his first proposals almost destroyed his presidency. Clinton proposed legislation lifting the ban on homosexuals serving openly in the military. The military, the Republican Party, and many Democrats were incensed and opposed to the plan. This opposition, combined with the public's negative reaction to the change in policy, forced Clinton to back down. A compromise was struck. Today a *don't ask, don't tell* policy is in place. In other words, superiors cannot ask whether a serviceperson is homosexual, and gays and lesbians in the military cannot openly admit to their sexual orientation.

Succeeding at home

Clinton achieved major domestic successes, giving the U.S. economy eight years of unprecedented growth. Clinton's successes include the following:

✔ **Reducing the federal deficit:** When Clinton assumed office, the budget deficit had reached $290 billion. To combat the deficit, Clinton passed a major tax increase in 1993, which together with spending cuts was supposed to reduce the deficit by $500 billion over the next five years. By 1997, the federal government ran a surplus of $70 billion, the first surplus since 1969. The surplus was available to pay off the country's national debt, which topped $5 trillion.

- ✔ **The Crime Bill:** This bill put more police officers on the street to help reduce crime. It also banned assault weapons and implemented controls on handgun purchases.

- ✔ **The Family and Medical Leave Act:** This act, passed in 1993, provided new parents with an unpaid 12-week leave. It also included similar leaves for people caring for sick relatives or recovering from serious illness.

- ✔ **Americorps:** This new program allowed students to perform community service to finance college or repay student loans.

- ✔ **Welfare reform:** In 1996, Bill Clinton initiated major welfare reform. The bill limited lifetime welfare benefits to 5 years and required able adults on welfare to go back to work after being on welfare for 2 years.

- ✔ **The 1997 tax cut:** Clinton kept his 1992 campaign promise when he signed a major tax cut into law in 1997.

- ✔ **Safe Drinking Water Act:** This act, passed in 1996, improved the quality of drinking water by tightening the standards of the Clean Water Act, passed in 1977 to regulate water pollution nationwide. Under the act, the Environmental Protection Agency (EPA) can set water quality standards to assure safe drinking water for the U.S. public.

Failing with healthcare

One of Clinton's major campaign promises was to reform the healthcare system in the United States. To fulfill this promise, Clinton appointed his wife, Hillary Rodham Clinton, as the leader of a task force. This task force, entitled the Presidential Task Force on National Healthcare Reform, had the job of coming up with a way to restructure the U.S. healthcare system.

The task force's plan was more than 240,000 words long and contained provisions that would obligate businesses to provide medical insurance for their employees. Opponents — primarily insurance companies, other businesses, and Republicans — criticized the plan as too complicated and charged that it gave the federal government too much control over medical care. The opponents launched a successful public relations effort to get the public on their side. With the public opposed to it, the task force's plan was never even submitted to Congress.

Losing Congress in 1994

By 1994, Bill Clinton had become an unpopular president. His support for the rights of homosexual military personnel and his failed healthcare plan created resentment, especially among white male voters. These voters turned out heavily in 1994 and voted for Republican congressional candidates.

The Democrats lost both Houses of Congress for the first time since the Eisenhower era. Clinton faced a hostile Congress and its new Speaker of the House, Newt Gingrich. Gridlock resulted: The Democratic President and Republican Congress battled each other to a standstill on most issues.

In late 1995 and early 1996, the federal government was shut down twice because Congress and the president could not agree on a budget. The Republicans wanted to cut spending for Medicare and educational and environmental programs, while the president planned to increase spending in these areas. Republicans paid a bitter price for this conflict in the 1996 elections, receiving the blame for shutting down the government.

During the summer of 1996, Clinton and Congress did reach agreement on increasing the minimum wage and reforming the welfare system.

Winning reelection in 1996

In 1996, President Clinton ran against Republican senator Robert Dole of Kansas. Dole desperately tried to make Clinton's character a campaign issue, but he was unsuccessful. With the economy doing well, the voters were happy with Clinton's performance. He won reelection easily with 49 percent of the popular vote and 379 electoral votes. Dole, on the other hand, received 41 percent of the popular vote and 159 electoral votes. Third-party candidate H. Ross Perot ran a distant third, winning only 8 percent of the vote.

Dealing with foreign policy

During the Clinton presidency, many foreign policy crises took place. With Clinton specializing in domestic policies, it was clear that foreign policy wasn't as important to him. The major events included:

- **NAFTA (The North American Free Trade Agreement):** Clinton's predecessor, George Bush, laid the foundation for NAFTA before he left office (see "Having problems at home" earlier in this chapter for the details). Many in the United States, especially labor unions, feared that NAFTA would take jobs away from U.S. workers because people could buy cheaper foreign goods and companies could move to Mexico to take advantage of cheap labor. Clinton went against many in his own party and pushed for passage of the agreement in 1993.

- **Somalia:** Clinton inherited the mess in Somalia from his predecessor, George Bush. Bush sent troops to Somalia to protect United Nations food deliveries. President Clinton increased U.S. troops and attempted to restore order in the country, which was torn by civil war. In 1993, 18 U.S. soldiers were killed and by 1994, the troops were recalled.

✔ **Haiti:** In 1991, a military coup ousted democratically elected president Aristide. By 1993, thousands of Haitians tried to flee to the United States, and Clinton acted. He demanded that President Aristide be returned to power. The Haitian military refused and Clinton sent troops.

Before military personnel reached Haiti, a peace delegation headed by former president Jimmy Carter reached an agreement to restore Aristide to power.

✔ **The bombing of U.S. embassies in Africa:** In 1998, al Qaeda (see Chapter 25) bombed U.S. embassies in Kenya and Tanzania, killing hundreds. Clinton ordered missile attacks against Sudan and Afghanistan, the two countries harboring al Qaeda.

✔ **The Dayton Peace Accords:** These accords, reached in 1995, settled the conflict in Bosnia by dividing the country into three parts, with each faction in the conflict — Croats, Serbs, and Bosnians — controlling one part.

✔ **The attack on Yugoslavia:** By 1998, Serbian troops were committing genocide, or mass murder, in the province of Kosovo, inhabited by ethnic Albanians. The North Atlantic Treaty Organization (NATO) and President Clinton initiated strikes against Serbia in the spring of 1999. By the summer of 1999, Yugoslavia had agreed to the presence of United Nations peacekeeping forces in Kosovo.

In 2000, a democratic rebellion toppled the communist leader of Yugoslavia, settling the crisis for good.

All the president's scandals

Scandals surfaced throughout the Clinton presidency. The most famous of these include

✔ **The Whitewater affair:** In 1993, a financial dealing the Clintons had in Arkansas became an issue for the Clinton presidency. The Clintons were involved in a land-development deal in Arkansas in 1978, called the Whitewater Development Corporation. When the deal went sour, the Clintons lost a chunk of money, as did their business partners. Later, these partners, James and Susan McDougal, opened a small savings and loan. The savings and loan went under in 1989; it was later bailed out by the federal government. President Clinton was accused of using his position as governor of Arkansas to help out his former business partners. A federal investigation, headed by independent counsel Kenneth Starr, filed no charges against the Clintons. But the Clintons's former business partners, the McDougals, and the governor of Arkansas, Jim Guy Tucker, were convicted of wrongdoing.

✔ **The Paula Jones case:** In 1994, Paula Jones, a former secretary for the state of Arkansas, accused President Clinton of sexual harassment. The case was at first dismissed, but Jones appealed it. Rather than go to court, Clinton paid her $850,000 to drop the case.

✔ **The Lewinsky affair:** During the Paula Jones case, lawyers became aware of a rumor that president Clinton was having an affair with one of his interns, 24-year-old Monica Lewinsky. In early 1998, President Clinton denied the affair under oath. Evidence later contradicted his testimony.

Ms. Lewinsky admitted to the affair and stated that Clinton told her to lie in front of a grand jury — a criminal offense.

In August 1998, the President appeared in front of a grand jury and admitted the affair — contradicting his earlier testimony. A few days later, the president apologized for the affair and admitted to the U.S. public that he had lied.

In December 1998, the House voted to impeach President Clinton on two charges — obstruction of justice and perjury (lying under oath). The Senate, however, failed to muster the two-thirds majority needed to convict and remove Clinton. Clinton's presidency was saved, and he served out his term. (For an explanation of the impeachment process, turn to the "How to get impeached" sidebar in Chapter 11.)

Bill Clinton was the first elected U.S. president to be impeached in the House of Representatives. The only other president to be impeached by the House was Andrew Johnson, who succeeded Lincoln after Lincoln's assassination.

Leaving under a cloud

Throughout the impeachment hearings, much of the public stood behind Clinton. While they disapproved of his behavior and his character, they approved of his politics.

Clinton served out the last two years in office enjoying an ever-expanding economy. By 1999, the budget surplus grew to $123 billion, and it looked as if the federal deficit could be paid off by 2002 — a feat that hadn't been accomplished since Andrew Jackson's time in office.

Democratic nominee Vice President Al Gore didn't ask Clinton to campaign for him in 2000 because he didn't want to be tied to Clinton's scandals. Clinton and others later blamed this decision for Gore's eventual loss.

Clinton campaigned heavily for his wife, Hillary Rodham Clinton, who won a Senate seat in the state of New York, where Clinton was very popular. Hillary Rodham Clinton is the first "first lady" to win a seat in the U.S. Senate.

Clinton retired to New York after the 2000 elections to write his memoirs and oversee the construction of his presidential library in Arkansas.

His scandals followed him into retirement. Right before leaving office, President Clinton granted pardons for criminal convictions to 140 people, some of them major donors to the Democratic Party. "Pardongate" further tarnished Clinton's reputation.

Chapter 25

Getting the Call: George W. Bush

• •

In This Chapter
▶ Governing Texas
▶ Winning a disputed election
▶ Leading the country through the unimagined

• •

George W. Bush, shown in Figure 25-1, certainly has the background for the presidency: His grandfather served in the U.S. Senate, and his father was president. However, it wasn't until his father was defeated in his bid for reelection as president in 1992 that George W. became involved in politics. He ran for governor of Texas, defeating a popular incumbent, and after being reelected by a record margin, he decided to go for the White House.

The 1992 election, which saw his father lose the presidency, hurt George W. Bush deeply. He felt that the Democrats had smeared his father's reputation, and he vowed revenge. Many see his father's loss to Bill Clinton as the catalyst for Bush's ambitions in politics.

George W. Bush prevailed in the most disputed election in U.S. history, and he seemed destined to preside over a contentious and partisan presidency. Then terrorism struck the United States, and President Bush was called upon to answer the attack. He has done an outstanding job to this point. He has the chance to become one of the great presidents in U.S. history.

Growing up prominent

George Walker Bush was born in 1946 in New Haven, Connecticut. He came from one of the most prominent families in the United States. When George W. was 2 years old, the family moved to Texas, where his father made millions in the oil business.

Bush attended and graduated from Yale University with a degree in history in 1968. He served in the Texas Air National Guard from 1968 until 1973, but he didn't see any action in the ongoing Vietnam War. Bush was famous for his partying and drinking in these years, though he stopped drinking alcohol in 1986.

In 1973 went to Harvard University to get a Master of Business Administration (MBA). After completing the degree, Bush moved back to Texas and worked in the oil industry.

While campaigning for a seat in the House of Representatives in 1977, Bush met his future wife, Laura Welch, a schoolteacher and librarian. They married in November 1977.

Figure 25-1:
George W. Bush, 43rd president of the United States.

©AFP/CORBIS

Bush's Early Career

In 1977, Bush ran for a seat in the U.S. House of Representatives, but lost. After his defeat, Bush went back to the oil industry, which he'd worked in after getting his MBA in 1975. He started his own company, Arbusto Energy Inc. (*Arbusto* means "bush" in Spanish.) The company didn't do well, though when it merged with a larger company, George W. stayed on as CEO. Bush was paid handsomely when he sold the company in 1986.

In 1987, Bush went to Washington to help his father run for the presidency. He had worked on his father's 1980 presidential campaign and became an advisor when his father entered the White House. In 1989, he returned to Texas to buy a stake in the Texas Rangers, a professional baseball team. He became the spokesman for the team, which made him well-known in Texas.

The oil business did not make Bush a millionaire; rather, it was the sale of his share of the Texas Rangers that made him his fortune. He was in debt until he sold his oil company and used the money to buy into the Texas Rangers.

Running for governor

After exploring the possibility, Bush ran for governor of Texas in 1994. Going into the race, Bush knew it would be tough to overcome his underdog status. The incumbent governor, Ann Richards, enjoyed good ratings and was well liked. But, instead of launching bitter personal attacks as his opponent did, Bush talked about issues, emphasizing education reform and reducing crime. He even campaigned in traditional Democratic strongholds, where his fluency in Spanish helped him with Mexican-Americans.

Bush's victory in Texas was the great surprise of the 1994 elections. Bush won in some traditional Democratic areas such as East Texas. Victory was sweet for Bush. He defeated the politician who had savagely attacked his father in her keynote address to the 1988 Democratic national convention.

Governing Texas

As governor of Texas, Bush showed his ability to negotiate, compromise, and make friends. He courted the most important Democrats in the state — the Democrats still controlled the legislature and the powerful lieutenant governor's position — and quickly established close friendships with the Democratic speaker of the house and the lieutenant governor.

Bush accomplished much in his first term as the governor of Texas. He reduced the number of Texans on welfare, reformed the education system, and put a ceiling on lawsuit judgments. By the time he was up for reelection in 1998, Bush was a shoo-in. Many prominent Democrats endorsed him, including the Democratic lieutenant governor, and he beat his Democratic opponent with 69 percent of the vote. He received 49 percent of the Hispanic vote in Texas, a record for a Republican.

Bush accomplished even more in his second term as governor. He raised salaries for teachers and pledged to have every child reading by the time he or she graduated from school. Statistics showed that his education reforms were working, as educational test scores increased throughout the state.

Running for the Presidency

In early 1999, Bush formed an exploratory committee to evaluate his chances of making a successful bid for the presidency. Bush knew that he would face tough competition for the nomination, especially from Senator John McCain from Arizona and former Secretary of Labor Elizabeth Dole., but he emerged as the Republican nominee.

Bush returned to his Texas themes — education and welfare reform — believing that they would work well nationwide. He labeled himself a compassionate conservative to attract women and minority voters, on whom the election hinged. Bush emphasized education and social security reform and pledged to strengthen the military and cut taxes. The strategy worked.

Debating and Campaigning

Three debates between the major-party presidential candidates — Republican George W. Bush and Democrat Al Gore — were a decisive component of the election. On paper, the debates favored Gore, a seasoned debater, but during the first debate Bush appeared knowledgeable and experienced, while Gore appeared bored and arrogant. The media declared Bush the winner, and he regained a small lead in the polls. Both candidates performed well in the next two debates, and the polls didn't change. Bush clung to a small lead.

Five days before the election took place, it was revealed that Governor Bush had been arrested for drunken driving more than 20 years prior. Not many people were affected by the story, but a small minority moved to Al Gore, giving him a small lead in the polls. The night before the election, two polls favored Bush and two favored Gore. It would be a close race indeed.

Surviving the 2000 Election

On Election Day, both candidates won the states they were expected to. The election seemed to be over when the networks called the state of Florida for Al Gore. Bush couldn't win without its electoral votes. But, two hours later the networks put Florida back in the undecided column.

This error proved costly for Bush. Subsequent studies show that the networks' error depressed Republican voter turnout in key states that Bush ended up losing by just a few thousand votes.

At 1 o'clock in the morning Eastern Standard Time, the networks declared Bush the winner in Florida. Gore was on the phone with Bush, congratulating him, when he was informed that Bush's lead in Florida was dwindling. Gore retracted his concession, and Florida moved back to the undecided column. When the country woke up the next morning, there was no winner. Al Gore won the popular vote, but neither candidate had a majority in the Electoral College. Florida would decide the election.

Going to court

On November 9, 2000, two days after the election, Bush's lead in Florida was 1,784 votes out of 6 million votes cast. The closeness of the race triggered an automatic recount under Florida law. The recount was completed by November 10, and Bush's lead had declined to 327 votes.

The Democratic Party asked for a manual recount in four traditionally Democratic counties in Florida. The Bush campaign objected and went to court to block the recount, claiming that it would be partisan, and therefore unreliable. The Gore campaign argued that the ballot in Palm Beach County was confusing and that questionable ballots should be inspected and counted. The federal courts refused to stop the recounts, and Florida gave the four counties until November 14, 2000 to complete their recounts.

The Gore campaign objected, claiming that a thorough recount would take longer than the court-imposed deadline of November 14. A district court upheld the deadline, but ruled that all recounts could be included in the final tally. Now the Bush campaign objected. The Florida Supreme Court finally ruled on November 21, 2000 that all manual recounts had to be included in the final vote totals and set a new deadline for the recounts to be completed: November 26, 2000. On that date, the Republican secretary of state for Florida, Katherine Harris, certified George W. Bush as the winner of Florida's electoral votes. The final margin was 537 votes.

Because the final vote didn't include Miami-Dade County, which stopped the recounts because it couldn't complete them on time, the Gore campaign contested the final results. Gore appealed to the Florida Supreme Court which called for a new statewide manual recount.

Being appointed

The Bush campaign took the case to the United States Supreme Court which stopped all recounts on December 9, 2000. Three days later, the U.S. Supreme Court ruled in a split 5 to 4 decision that no further recounts could be held in Florida. It was all over for the Gore campaign. One day later, Vice President Gore conceded and congratulated George W. Bush in a nationally televised address. Bush was now the new president of the United States.

President George Walker Bush (2001–Present)

George W. Bush assumed the presidency on January 20, 2001. With the hotly contested election behind him, many observers predicted that he would have a tough time as president. He didn't receive a mandate from the public, and many in the United States considered him a court-appointed president.

Bush attempted to use his inaugural address to appeal to the people who had voted against him. He emphasized a need to reform education and social security, and highlighted his tax cut plan. Tough times lay ahead.

Domestic policies

Bush proceeded quickly after entering the White House. He proposed a new education plan and a faith-based initiative to give more funds to faith-based organizations helping the needy.

In June 2001, Congress passed Bush's tax cut proposal. Bush's plan initiated a $1.25 trillion tax cut over ten years. Under its provisions, most U.S. taxpayers received a tax refund in the summer of 2001.

In the summer of 2001, Republican Senator James Jeffords of Vermont left the Republican Party to become an Independent. The transition returned the Senate to the Democrats, and instead of having Republican majorities in both chambers of Congress, Bush had to work with a hostile Senate.

Foreign policy

Bush's foreign policy faced criticism. Bush proposed to build an antiballistic missile system and had to withdraw from the longstanding Antiballistic

Missile Treaty signed with the Soviet Union to do so. Despite the objections of most European allies and Russia, Bush announced in December 2001 that the United States would pull out of the treaty.

Bush also refused to recognize the Kyoto protocol, an international treaty that calls for lowering the emission of gases destroying the ozone layer. The rest of the world was furious. Bush looked like an isolationist out to antagonize the rest of the world.

Disaster Strikes

On September 11, 2001, the unimaginable happened. Terrorists hit the United States. Two hijacked passenger airplanes struck the twin towers of the World Trade Center, in New York City, leading to their collapse. As this book went to press, officials listed almost 3,000 U.S. and foreign citizens who died in the attack on the twin towers.

Soon after the two buildings were hit, a third hijacked plane struck the Pentagon, killing close to 200 people. A fourth hijacked plane crashed in Pennsylvania when the passengers attempted to overtake the hijackers. Its assumed target was the White House or Camp David.

The shocked and angry nation demanded action. President Bush went on national television on September 20, 2001 to reassure the U.S. public and explain what had happened. Bush laid blame for the attack on the al Qaeda terrorist network and its founder, Osama Bin Laden. Al Qaeda was headquartered in Afghanistan. Bush told the ruling Taliban regime to hand over Bin Laden or face the consequences.

Fighting terrorism

On October 7, 2001, U.S. and British planes attacked Afghanistan. The objective of the attack was to knock out al Qaeda training camps, eliminate the organization and its followers, and destroy the Taliban regime.

Negotiations began with the Northern Alliance, an opposition group, which controlled about 5 percent of Afghanistan. The U.S. supplied the Northern Alliance with weapons and military advisors. Within weeks it became a powerful force, successfully attacking the Taliban.

Very slowly, the Northern Alliance conquered city after city and, in November, Kabul, the capital of Afghanistan fell. By December 2001, the Northern Alliance with the help of U.S. ground troops had taken the rest of the country. The Taliban were surrendering en masse, but its leader Mullah Omar, as well as Osama Bin Laden, the head of al Qaeda, escaped capture. A new government was set up in Afghanistan, and an interim leader, Hamid Karzai, was put in charge to transition the country toward democracy.

Punishing terrorists

After the attack on September 11, 2001, President Bush set out to create an international alliance to fight terrorism. Most European countries pledged military aid and NATO invoked Article 5 of its charter. Invoking this article obligates all NATO countries to join the U.S. in the fight against terrorism — to treat the attack on the United States as an attack on their own soil.

Even the Islamic world condemned the attack and assured support for U.S. efforts. Pakistan offered much-needed military bases that the United States could use to strike at Afghanistan. To the surprise of many, even Russia agreed to help and provide bases if necessary.

The coalition came together by late September 2001. The U.S. was ready to strike at Afghanistan, which still harbored Osama Bin Laden.

Becoming a national hero

The U.S. public has stood behind its president. Instead of disrupting life in the United States, as the terrorists had hoped, the public rallied around the flag. A new wave of patriotism swept the country, and U.S. citizens turned out by the millions to help. President Bush rode a record wave of approval. Bush's ratings were as high as 90 percent in the winter of 2001 with the war in Afghanistan going well.

Despite starting out as a president without a mandate, George W. Bush may go down in history as one of the country's great presidents.

Part VII
The Part of Tens

The 5th Wave — By Rich Tennant

From the very beginning, Warren G. Harding's presidency was suspect due to Harding's liberal use of the double-finger quotation mark during his swearing in ceremony.

In this part . . .

I give you the traditional Dummies part of tens. First, I present a list of the ten best presidents in U.S. history. These are my choices, so feel free to disagree with me. The ten worst presidents follow. Again, these are my subjective choices and any disagreement is welcome.

Next, I look at the ten most memorable presidential libraries. Every American should visit some of these at least once. So the next time you plan a vacation or a weekend trip, keep these in mind.

Following this part is a presidential facts appendix that lists all kinds of information about the presidents, from presidential birth dates to death dates; election results, including Electoral College and popular votes, are included.

Chapter 26

The Ten Best Presidents

*I*n this chapter, I undertake a truly difficult task. Selecting the ten best presidents out of the 42 on the list isn't easy. Of course, some choices are no-brainers; some presidents, such as Washington, Lincoln, and Franklin Delano Roosevelt stand out so much that they have to be included in any list of the top ten presidents. Other picks may cause a little controversy — this is good. Feel free to disagree with me on these ten choices, because every list of presidents is subjective in nature.

I base my evaluation on the seven characteristics I discuss in Chapter 2, and they consist of policy leadership, crisis management, quality of their appointments, how they're regarded by foreign leaders, their character and integrity, how effective they are at getting the public's support, and the vision they have for the country. For a president to be listed in the top ten list, he has to have shown superior abilities in all seven categories.

Without any further ado, here are my picks for the ten best presidents in U.S. history, with the best president being listed first and the tenth best listed last.

Abraham Lincoln

Abraham Lincoln not only saved the Union, but he also issued the Emancipation Proclamation, declaring the slaves in the Confederacy free, and pushed for the 13th Amendment, outlawing slavery in the United States. He expanded the war-making powers of the president, and he was a founding father of the Republican Party.

If Lincoln had lived longer, the reintegration of the Confederate states into the union (See Chapters 10 and 11) would have proceeded differently, leading to less controversy.

Franklin Delano Roosevelt

Franklin Delano Roosevelt has the distinction of being the only president elected to four terms. He assumed the presidency during the Great Depression and provided practical help to the people affected by it. His New Deal programs provided help and hope to millions of U.S. citizens and set the foundation for the modern welfare state.

Franklin Roosevelt saved democracy in Europe by aiding Great Britain early on in its struggle with Nazi Germany, and turned the U.S. economy into a wartime economy capable of winning World War II. During the war, he became one of the founding fathers of the United Nations, committing the United States to an active interventionist foreign policy.

Theodore Roosevelt

Theodore Roosevelt broke the longstanding isolationist tradition that kept the United States deliberately uninvolved in world affairs. By getting involved in world affairs, he set the foundation for the United States to become a world power in the 20th century.

Theodore Roosevelt gave the world the Panama Canal (see Chapter 13), and he was the first U.S. citizen to receive the Nobel Peace Prize for settling the war between Japan and Russia in 1906.

Roosevelt further protected average citizens from business excesses by regulating industries.

George Washington

As the first president, George Washington kept the new country together. He legitimized the new form of government and set the foundation for democracy in the United States.

Washington also established many traditions, some of which are still around today. From the ceremony and protocols surrounding inaugural addresses to the isolationist foreign policy in place until the early 20th century, Washington's ideas stuck around.

Harry Truman

Harry Truman is one of the most underrated presidents in U.S. history. He made the difficult choice of dropping two atomic bombs on Japan, which ended World War II. In the opinion of many scholars, Truman's decision saved untold lives that would have been lost if the United States had been forced to invade Japan.

Truman single-handedly saved Western and Southern Europe from communism with the Truman Doctrine, extending military aid to countries fighting communist uprisings, and the Marshall Plan, which helped to rebuild the economies of post-war Europe. He was the first president to realize the Soviet threat. He acted to stop communism from expanding, establishing organizations such as NATO (North Atlantic Treaty Organization) to contain Soviet expansionism. (Turn to Chapter 17 for more detail on Truman.)

Ronald Reagan

Ronald Reagan was elected president in a time of crisis, as U.S. power was declining internationally. He restored U.S. power and prestige throughout the world. His military spending led to the destruction of the Soviet economy, which wasn't able to keep up with U.S. spending, and the subsequent collapse of the Soviet empire. Without Reagan, the United States may not have won the Cold War in 1991.

Reagan's economic polices, while increasing the U.S. debt, provided for years of unheard of growth for the U.S. economy. When he left office in 1989, he was one of the most idolized and admired presidents in U.S. history.

Thomas Jefferson

Thomas Jefferson was the most intellectual president in U.S. history. He enjoyed a worldwide reputation for his writings, and he was the chief author of the Declaration of Independence.

As president, Jefferson doubled the size of the country with the Louisiana Purchase, and he kept the country from going to war with major European powers.

Woodrow Wilson

Woodrow Wilson saved democracy in Europe. He made the decision to enter World War I on the side of the democratic allies in Europe. Wilson's decision provided for the difference in WWI, as democracy emerged victorious over the authoritarian German and Austrian-Hungarian empires. The League of Nations, the predecessor to the United Nations, was his brainchild. Even though the U.S. Senate refused to join the League of Nations, the foundation for the United Nations was set.

Domestically, Wilson was a reformer who gave women the right to vote in 1920. He also oversaw the newly established way to elect U.S. senators, which put the selection in the hands of voters instead of the state legislatures.

Dwight D. Eisenhower

This choice may surprise some. Dwight D. Eisenhower was a president who accomplished much in a very quiet way. He ended the war in Korea and managed to contain the Soviet Union for the eight years he held office. He gave the United States eight years of peace. During his tenure in office, not one U.S. soldier was lost in combat.

Eisenhower passed the first civil rights legislation since the end of the Civil War. He stood up to several Southern governors who refused to implement the Supreme Court's decision to integrate public schools. Finally, Eisenhower also gave us our present day Interstate Highway System. (There's more on Ike in Chapter 18.)

James Polk

This is another choice that may surprise some readers. I consider James Polk the most underrated president in U.S. history. He arranged a dramatic expansion of the country by acquiring most of what today is the southwestern United States.

Polk was a hardworking, honest man, who actually worked himself into an early grave. During Polk's administration, there were no scandals involving him or his cabinet.

This president stuck to his promise to serve only one term, and he put the good of the country before his own interests, earning the right to be listed as one of the top ten U.S. presidents. (I explain his deeds in more detail in Chapter 8.)

Chapter 27

The Ten Worst Presidents

- -

- -

*W*hile the United States had many mediocre presidents, only a few were really bad. Choosing the five worst presidents is fairly easy, because there is agreement among the public and academics as to who belongs in a list of the bottom five (see Chapter 2). But selecting the bottom ten presidents is a more difficult task. Nonetheless, I give it a shot. Please feel free to disagree with my selections.

The rankings are subjective, so I ask you to cut me some slack. I base my rankings on characteristics including, policy leadership, crisis management, presidential appointments, foreign standing, character and integrity, public persuasion, and presidential vision. (Historians and other people who rank presidents often base their decisions on many of these same qualities, as noted in Chapter 2.) The presidents in this list appear with the worst president coming first.

Andrew Johnson

Andrew Johnson is widely considered one of the worst presidents. He became president only because President Lincoln was assassinated.

His Reconstruction plan for the Southern states after the Civil War was lenient for the former Confederate states, and it didn't benefit former slaves at all. He pushed Congress to the point where he was impeached by the House of Representatives for violating the Tenure of Office Act (see Chapter 11).

In addition, Johnson was an unpleasant, bigoted fellow with a bad temper. Had it been up to him, African Americans would have never received citizenship or any civil rights.

Warren G. Harding

President Warren G. Harding's administration was a massive failure. He appointed friends to high-level government positions, and they repaid him by creating many financial scandals. His administration accomplished nothing of value, and his years as president are utterly forgettable.

Harding was a hypocrite and womanizer. He supported Prohibition and drank in secret. He married his wife for her money, and then he cheated on her in a White House closet (just off the Oval Office) while she slept in her bedroom. Harding put it best himself: "I am not fit for this office [the presidency] and never should have been here."

Franklin Pierce

Franklin Pierce was a Northern Democrat with a Southern soul. He supported slavery throughout his career because he believed that the Constitution allowed the states to decide whether to be slave states or free states. More importantly, Pierce laid the foundation for the Civil War by not opposing the Kansas-Nebraska Act in 1854. The act overturned the Missouri Compromise of 1820 and allowed new states to choose whether to allow slavery.

Pierce drank heavily as he ignored the conflict that tore Kansas apart. He didn't even run for reelection in 1856. He retired and drank himself to death instead.

James Buchanan

James Buchanan served his country loyally and faithfully until he became president. As a Northern Democrat, he personally opposed slavery, but he believed that the Constitution allowed it. So he refused to do anything about the issue. Instead, he supported the Supreme Court's Dred Scott decision in 1857, which declared that slaves were not people or citizens.

When most Southern states seceded after Lincoln's victory in 1860, Buchanan stood by and did nothing, just waiting for his term to end. When Lincoln arrived in the White House, Buchanan hurriedly left and disappeared into oblivion.

John Tyler

John Tyler became president by default when President Harrison died in office in 1841. He wasn't a Whig like Harrison, but he had been selected because he could appeal to Southern voters. He alienated his own party to the point where its members threatened to impeach him.

Tyler accomplished almost nothing while in office, with the exception of bringing Texas into the Union. Without this one accomplishment, Tyler would rank even lower on the presidential scale.

Millard Fillmore

Millard Fillmore was another vice president who became president by default. He took over after President Zachary Taylor died one year into his term.

Shortly after taking office, Fillmore destroyed his own party by backing the Compromise of 1850 (see Chapter 9 for more information), which many Whigs considered pro-slavery. To make matters worse, Fillmore ran for the presidency in 1856 as a candidate for the racist American party, which advocated against blacks, Jews, and Catholics.

In 1864, Fillmore turned against Lincoln by backing Lincoln's opponent, General George McClellan. He then later he backed Andrew Johnson in his fight with Congress (see Chapter 11). I guess it takes one bad president to try to help out another bad president.

Ulysses S. Grant

Ulysses S. Grant was one of the most capable soldiers in U.S. history — for this, he deserves much credit. As president, however, he was the opposite of capable. Grant filled cabinet positions with his friends and relatives, resulting in rampant corruption and many scandals. Grant was an honest man, but he didn't have many honest friends. To make matters worse, he defended his corrupt friends, undermining his own credibility in the eyes of the public.

Grant's trust in people was so high that he lost all of his money when his son invested it improperly. He retired a pauper and wrote his memoirs to help feed his family.

William Henry Harrison

It is not fair to judge William Henry Harrison on his term in office. He served only a little over a month, most of it on his deathbed. It is justified, however, to rank him on his campaign and his agenda. Well, there was no agenda, because Harrison stood for nothing and ran without a platform. His campaign portrayed him as a hard-drinking man of the people, who was born in a log cabin. He did drink hard cider, but he grew up wealthy on a large estate in Virginia. His campaign was based on a lie, but it got him elected.

Martin Van Buren

Martin Van Buren was one of the best politicians in U.S. history. He knew how to play the political game. He helped create the Democratic Party on Andrew Jackson's behalf. He served his country well until he reached the presidency. Suddenly, his accomplishments stopped. How could such a great politician be such a bad president?

He wasn't responsible for the depression of 1837, but he also didn't do anything about it, which undermined his chances for reelection. He refused to address slurs against him in the 1840 election and lost badly. In 1848, he took the presidency away from his own Democratic Party by running as a third-party candidate.

Herbert Hoover

It pains me to put Herbert Hoover on the list of the ten worst presidents. Hoover was a self-made man and a great humanitarian who was responsible for saving millions of Europeans from starving to death after both world wars. How could such a great human being be such a bad president? Well, although he can't be blamed for causing the Great Depression of the 1920s and early 1930s, he can be blamed for reacting to it too late — a classic example of doing too little, too late.

Hoover shows that being a great person and being a great president don't necessarily go hand in hand.

Chapter 28

Ten Presidential Libraries Worth Visiting

● ●

In This Chapter

▶ Finding information about U.S. presidents

▶ Visiting the top presidential libraries

● ●

*I*n this chapter, I look at presidential libraries. Most of America's older, historical presidents don't have libraries, so a lot of the libraries worth visiting are those of more modern presidents.

Franklin Delano Roosevelt established the first presidential library in 1939. Every U.S. president since Franklin Roosevelt has set up a presidential library after finishing his term in office. The National Archives and Records administration operate all presidential libraries. Getting the financing to build his library, through private donations, is up to the president. After it is built, the federal government takes over and operates the library.

The ten libraries listed below are the ones I recommend that you visit at some point in your life. The list begins with the best coming first. (Remember, this list is subjective in nature; it represents my own personal preferences.)

When mentioning presidential libraries, it is important to keep in mind that the libraries are found in the home state of each particular president, or the state he considered his home. For example, Truman was born in Missouri: He considered it his home, and he represented it in the Senate. Thus, he chose Missouri as the site for his presidential library. Ronald Reagan, on the other hand, was born in Illinois, but he considered California, the state he governed, his home. So, his library is in California.

Presidential libraries contain all the public papers of a president, including information concerning his public career before his presidency. The presidential libraries even include some private information on the chief executives. In addition, the libraries contain pictures and films, and tapes of presidential speeches. Finally, gifts from foreign dignitaries are on display, because the president, as a public official, is not allowed to keep them.

Many of the presidential libraries have become important research facilities for scholars studying the respective presidents. All presidential libraries are open to the public and have a wealth of information available to anybody interested in learning more about the president.

Ronald Reagan Presidential Library

The Ronald Reagan Presidential Library is the largest presidential library in the United States. The library — located in beautiful Simi Valley, California — contains all of Reagan's public and personal papers. In addition, the library contains many displays that portray Reagan's life.

Contact Info: 40 Presidential Drive, Simi Valley, CA 93065; phone 800-410-8354; Web site: www.reagan.utexas.edu.

George Bush Presidential Library and Museum

The George Bush Presidential Library and Museum is on the campus of Texas A&M University in College Station, Texas. Bush chose to build the library on the campus of the second most prestigious university in Texas, his home state, because Lyndon Johnson had already built his presidential library at the University of Texas.

The library, which contains the private and public papers of America's 41st president, opened in 1997 and is the most highly computerized of all the presidential libraries. The library's computer system allows for easy access to all kinds of information on George H. Bush.

Contact Info: 1000 George Bush Drive West, College Station, TX 77845; phone 979-260-9552; Web site: http://bushlibrary.tamu.edu.

John Fitzgerald Kennedy Presidential Library and Museum

The John Fitzgerald Kennedy Library and Museum is in Boston, Massachusetts. The library is one of the best research facilities in the United States for the social sciences. The museum contains many displays of Kennedy's life. It also has gift shops for the public.

Contact Info: Columbia Point, Boston, MA 02125; phone 877-616-4599 or 617-929-4500; Web site: www.jfklibrary.org.

Lyndon Baines Johnson Library and Museum

The Lyndon Baines Johnson Library and Museum is on the campus of the University of Texas in Austin. It is a top-notch research facility for the social sciences and the humanities, containing over 35 million documents. The museum traces the life of Lyndon Johnson.

Contact Info: 2313 Red River Street, Austin, TX 78705; phone 512-916-5137; Web site: www.lbjlib.utexas.edu.

Franklin D. Roosevelt Library and Museum

The Franklin D. Roosevelt Library is part of a larger center that contains President Roosevelt's childhood home and the burial place of the president and his wife, Eleanor. It is the first presidential library in U.S. history.

Contact Info: 4079 Albany Post Road, Hyde Park, NY 12538; phone 845-229-8114; Web site: www.fdrlibrary.marist.edu.

Dwight D. Eisenhower Library and Museum

Located in Abilene, Kansas, the Dwight D. Eisenhower Library is one of five buildings within the Eisenhower Center. The center also contains Eisenhower's boyhood home, his burial place, a visitors' center, and the Eisenhower museum.

Contact Info: 200 Southeast Fourth Street, Abilene, KS 67410; phone 1-877-746-4453 or 785-263-4751; Web site: www.eisenhower.utexas.edu.

Richard Nixon Library and Birthplace

The Richard Nixon Library is in Yorba Linda, California, the birthplace of the former president. The library contains most of Nixon's papers and tapes, including the controversial Watergate tapes. It is surrounded by a beautiful park open to the public. The burial places of Richard Nixon and his wife, Pat, are also at the site.

Contact Info: 18001 Yorba Linda Boulevard, Yorba Linda, CA 92886; phone 714-993-3393; Web site: www.nixonfoundation.org.

Jimmy Carter Library and Museum

The Jimmy Carter Library is part of the Carter Center in Atlanta, Georgia. It contains a research center, which houses Carter's presidential documents (over 27 million pages), and a museum.

Contact Info: 441 Freedom Parkway, Atlanta, GA 30307; phone 404-331-3942; Web site: www.jimmycarterlibrary.org.

Harry S. Truman Presidential Museum and Library

The Harry Truman Library is in Independence, Missouri. It contains a museum detailing Truman's life and accomplishments. Truman is also buried at this site.

Contact Info: 500 West U.S. Highway 24, Independence, MO 64050; phone 1-800-833-1225 or 816-833-1400; Web site: www.trumanlibrary.org.

Gerald R. Ford Library and Museum

The Gerald R. Ford Library is on the campus of the University of Michigan. It is attached to the central campus library, and it contains 20 million documents on the Ford presidency.

Contact Info: 1000 Beal Avenue, Ann Arbor, MI 48109; phone 734-741-2218; Web site: www.ford.utexas.edu.

Appendix

Presidential Facts

• •

*T*he table that is this appendix contains a lot of interesting and relevant information. It gives birth dates for all the presidents and death dates for deceased presidents. In addition, it lists the presidents' respective vice-presidents, including the ones who died in office. The appendix further presents the political party affiliation for every president and the names of the opponents in their respective elections. To top it off, both the Electoral College votes and the popular vote are provided for the presidential elections. The popular vote is presented in a format that gives the number and percentage of votes received.

Note: The popular vote is not available for the first five presidents, so only the number of electoral votes is provided. Beginning with the 1824 elections, both totals are available. In addition, there were no political parties in 1789 and 1792, so no party affiliation is listed for these two elections.

Personal Information	Year	Candidate	Party	Popular Vote	Electoral Vote
George Washington Term: 1789–1797 Birth date: February 22, 1732 Death date: December 14, 1799 Vice President: John Adams	1789	George Washington			69
		John Adams			34
		Others			35
	1792	George Washington			132
		John Adams			77
		George Clinton			50
		Others			5
John Adams Term: 1797–1801 Birth date: October 30, 1735 Death date: July 4, 1826 Vice President: Thomas Jefferson	1796	John Adams	Federalist		71
		Thomas Jefferson	Democratic-Republican		68
		Thomas Pinckney	Federalist		59
		Aaron Burr	Democratic-Republican		30
		Others			48
Thomas Jefferson Term: 1801–1809 Birth date: April 13, 1743 Death date: July 4, 1826 Vice Presidents: Aaron Burr (1801–1805); George Clinton (1805–1809)	1800	Thomas Jefferson	Democratic-Republican		73
		Aaron Burr	Democratic-Republican		73
		John Adams	Federalist		65
		Charles C. Pinckney	Federalist		64
	1804	Thomas Jefferson	Democratic-Republican		162
		Charles C. Pinckney	Federalist		14
James Madison Term: 1809–1817 Birth date: March 16, 1751 Death date: June 28, 1836 Vice Presidents: George Clinton (1809–1812) died in office; Elbridge Gerry (1813–1814) died in office	1808	James Madison	Democratic-Republican		122
		Charles C. Pinckney	Federalist		47
		George Clinton	Independent-Republican		6
	1812	James Madison	Democratic-Republican		128
		DeWitt Clinton	Federalist		89

Personal Information	Year	Candidate	Party	Popular Vote	Electoral Vote
James Monroe Term: 1817–1825 Birth date: April 28, 1758 Death date: July 4, 1831 Vice President: Daniel D. Tompkins	1816	James Monroe Rufus King	Democratic-Republican Federalist		183 34
	1820	James Monroe John Quincy Adams	Democratic-Republican Independent-Republican		231 1
John Quincy Adams Term: 1825–1829 Birth date: July 11, 1767 Death date: February 23, 1848 Vice President: John C. Calhoun	1824	John Quincy Adams Andrew Jackson Henry Clay William H. Crawford	Democratic-Republican Democratic-Republican Democratic-Republican Democratic-Republican	108,740 (30.5%) 153,544 (43.1%) 47,136 (13.2%) 46,618 (13.1%)	84 99 37 41
Andrew Jackson Term: 1829–1837 Birth date: March 15, 1767 Death date: June 8, 1845 Vice Presidents: John C. Calhoun (1829–1832); Martin Van Buren (1833–1837)	1828	Andrew Jackson John Quincy Adams	Democratic National Republican	647,231 (56%) 509,097 (44%)	178 83
	1832	Andrew Jackson Henry Clay John Floyd	Democratic National Republican National Republican	687,502 (55%) 530,189 (42.4%) 33,108 (2.6%)	219 49 11
Martin Van Buren Term: 1837–1841 Birth date: December 5, 1782 Death date: July 24, 1862 Vice President: Richard M. Johnson	1836	Martin Van Buren William Henry Harrison Hugh L. White Daniel Webster	Democratic Whig Whig Whig	761,549 (50.9%) 549,567 (36.7%) 145,396 (9.7%) 41,287 (2.7%)	170 73 26 14
William Henry Harrison Term: 1841–1841 Birth date: February 9, 1773 Death date: April 4, 1841 Vice President: John Tyler	1840	William Henry Harrison Martin Van Buren	Whig Democratic	1,275,017 (53.1%) 1,128,702 (46.9%)	234 60

(continued)

Personal Information	Year	Candidate	Party	Popular Vote	Electoral Vote
John Tyler Term: 1841–1845 Birth date: March 29, 1790 Death date: January 18, 1862 Vice President: Vacant					
James Knox Polk Term: 1845–1849 Birth date: November 2, 1795 Death date: June 15, 1849 Vice President: George M. Dallas	1844	James K. Polk Henry Clay James G. Birney	Democratic Whig Liberty	1,337,243 (49.6%) 1,299,068 (48.1%) 62,300 (2.3%)	170 105 0
Zachary Taylor Term: 1849–1850 Birth date: November 24, 1784 Death date: July 9, 1850 Vice President: Millard Fillmore	1848	Zachary Taylor Lewis Cass Martin Van Buren	Whig Democratic Free Soil	1,360,101 (47.4%) 1,220,544 (42.5%) 291,263 (10.1%)	163 127 0
Millard Fillmore Term: 1850–1853 Birth date: January 7, 1800 Death date: March 8, 1874 Vice President: Vacant					
Franklin Pierce Term: 1853–1857 Birth date: November 23, 1804 Death date: October 8, 1869 Vice President: William R. King (1853) died in office	1852	Franklin Pierce Winfield Scott	Democratic Whig	1,601,474 (50.9%) 1,386,578 (44.1%)	254 42

Personal Information	Year	Candidate	Party	Popular Vote	Electoral Vote
James Buchanan Term: 1857–1861 Birth date: April 23, 1791 Death date: June 1, 1868 Vice President: John C. Breckinridge	1856	James Buchanan John C. Fremont Millard Fillmore	Democratic Republican American	1,838,169 (45.4%) 1,335,264 (33.0%) 874,534 (21.6%)	174 114 114
Abraham Lincoln Term: 1861–1865 Birth date: February 12, 1809 Death date: April 15, 1865 Vice Presidents: Hannibal Hamlin (1861–1865); Andrew Johnson (1865–1865)	1860	Abraham Lincoln Stephen A. Douglas John C. Breckinridge John Bell	Republican Democratic Democratic-Constitutional Union	1,865,593 (39.8%) 1,382,713 (29.5%) 848,356 (18.1%) 592,906 (12.6%)	180 12 72 39
	1864	Abraham Lincoln George B. McClellan	Republican Democratic	2,206,938 (55.0%) 1,803,787 (45.0%)	212 21
Andrew Johnson Term: 1865–1869 Birth date: December 29, 1808 Death date: July 31, 1875 Vice President: Vacant					
Ulysses S. Grant Term: 1869–1877 Birth date: April 27, 1822 Death date: July 23, 1885 Vice Presidents: Schuyler Colfax (1869–1873); Henry Wilson (1873–1875) died in office	1868	Ulysses S. Grant Horatio Seymour	Republican Democratic	3,013,421 (52.7%) 2,706,829 (47.3)	214 80
	1872	Ulysses S. Grant Horace Greeley	Republican Democratic	3,596,745 (55.6%) 2,843,446 (43.9%)	286 66
Rutherford B. Hayes Term: 1877–1881 Birth date: October 4, 1822 Death date: January 17, 1893 Vice President: William A. Wheeler	1876	Rutherford B. Hayes Samuel Tilden	Republican Democratic	4,036,572 (48.0%) 4,284,020 (51.0%)	185 184

(continued)

Personal Information	Year	Candidate	Party	Popular Vote	Electoral Vote
James Garfield Term: 1881–1881 Birth date: November 19, 1831 Death date: September 19, 1881 Vice President: Chester Arthur	1880	James Garfield Winfield S. Hancock	Republican Democratic	4,449,053 (48.3%) 4,442,035 (48.2%)	214 155
Chester A. Arthur Term: 1881–1885 Birth date: October 5, 1829 Death date: November 18, 1886 Vice President: Vacant					
Grover Cleveland Term: 1885–1889 Birth date: March 18, 1837 Death date: June 24, 1908 Vice President: Thomas A. Hendricks (1885) died in office	1884	Grover Cleveland James Blaine	Democratic Republican	4,874,986 (48.5%) 4,851,981 (48.2%)	219 182
Benjamin Harrison Term: 1889–1893 Birth date: August 20, 1833 Death date: March 13, 1901 Vice President: Levi P. Morton	1888	Benjamin Harrison Grover Cleveland	Republican Democratic	5,444,337 (47.8%) 5,540,050 (48.6%)	233 168
Grover Cleveland Term: 1893–1897 Birth date: March 18, 1837 Death date: June 24, 1908 Vice President: Adlai E. Stevenson	1892	Grover Cleveland Benjamin Harrison James B. Weaver	Democratic Republican People's	5,554,414 (46.0%) 5,190,802 (43.0%) 1,027,329 (8.5%)	277 145 22

Personal Information	Year	Candidate	Party	Popular Vote	Electoral Vote
William McKinley Term: 1897–1901 Birth date: January 29, 1843 Death date: September 14, 1901 Vice Presidents: Garret A. Hobart (1897–1899) died in office; Theodore Roosevelt (1901–1901)	1896	William McKinley William Jennings Bryan	Republican Democratic	7,035,638 (50.8%) 6,467,946 (46.7%)	271 176
	1900	William McKinley William Jennings Bryan	Republican Democratic; Populist	7,219,530 (51.7%) 6,356,734 (45.5%)	292 155
Theodore Roosevelt Term: 1901–1909 Birth date: October 27, 1858 Death date: January 6, 1919 Vice President: Vacant (1901–1905); Charles W. Fairbanks (1905–1909)	1904	Theodore Roosevelt Alton B. Parker	Republican Democratic	7,628,834 (56.4%) 5,084,401 (37.6%)	336 140
William Howard Taft Term: 1909–1913 Birth date: September 15, 1857 Death date: March 8, 1930 Vice President: James S. Sherman (1909–1912) died in office	1908	William Howard Taft William Jennings Bryan	Republican Democratic	7,679,006 (51.6%) 6,409,106 (43.1%)	321 162
Woodrow Wilson Term: 1913–1921 Birth date: December 28, 1856 Death date: February 3, 1924 Vice President: Thomas R. Marshall	1912	Woodrow Wilson Theodore Roosevelt William Howard Taft	Democratic Bull Moose Republican	6,286,820 (41.8%) 4,126,020 (27.4%) 3,483,922 (23.2%)	435 88 8
	1916	Woodrow Wilson Charles E. Hughes	Democratic Republican	9,129,606 (49.3%) 8,538,221) (46.1%)	277 254
Warren G. Harding Term: 1921–1923 Birth date: November 2, 1865 Death date: August 2, 1923 Vice President: Calvin Coolidge	1920	Warren G. Harding James M. Cox	Republican Democratic	16,152,200 (61%) 9,147,353 (34.6%)	404 127

(continued)

Personal Information	Year	Candidate	Party	Popular Vote	Electoral Vote
Calvin Coolidge Term: 1923–1929 Birth date: July 4, 1872 Death date: January 5, 1933 Vice President: Vacant (1923–1925); Charles G. Dawes (1925–1929)	1924	Calvin Coolidge John W. Davis Robert LaFollette	Republican Democratic Progressive	15,725,016 (54.1%) 8,385,586 (28.8%) 4,822,856 (16.6%)	382 136 13
Herbert Hoover Term: 1929–1933 Birth date: August 10, 1874 Death date: October 20, 1964 Vice President: Charles Curtis	1928	Herbert Hoover Alfred E. Smith	Republican Democratic	21,392,190 (58.2%) 15,016,443 (40.8%)	444 87
Franklin Delano Roosevelt Term: 1933–1945 Birth date: January 30, 1882 Death date: April 12, 1945 Vice Presidents: John N. Garner (1933–1941); Henry A. Wallace (1941–1945); Harry Truman (1945–1945)	1932	Franklin Roosevelt Herbert Hoover	Democratic Republican	22,809,638 (57.3%) 15,758,901 (39.6%)	472 59
	1936	Franklin Roosevelt Alfred M. Landon	Democratic Republican	27,751,612 (60.7%) 16,681,913 (36.4%)	523 8
	1940	Franklin Roosevelt Wendell L. Wilkie	Democratic Republican	27,243,466 (54.7%) 22,304,755 (44.8%)	449 82
	1944	Franklin Roosevelt Thomas E. Dewey	Republican Democratic	25,602,505 (52.8%) 22,006,278 (44.5%)	432 99
Harry Truman Term: 1945–1953 Birth date: May 8, 1884 Death date: December 26, 1972 Vice President: Vacant (1945–1949); Alben W. Barkley (1949–1953)	1948	Harry Truman Thomas E. Dewey J. Strom Thurmond	Democratic Republican States' Rights Party	24,105,587 (49.5%) 21,970,017 (45.1%) 1,169,063 (2.4%)	303 189 39

Personal Information	Year	Candidate	Party	Popular Vote	Electoral Vote
Dwight D. Eisenhower Term: 1953–1961 Birth date: October 14, 1890 Death date: March 28, 1969 Vice President: Richard Nixon	1952	Dwight Eisenhower Adlai E. Stevenson	Republican Democratic	33,936,234 (55.2%) 27,314,922 (44.5%)	442 89
	1956	Dwight Eisenhower Adlai E. Stevenson	Republican Democratic	35,590,472 (57.4%) 26,022,752 (42.0%)	457 73
John F. Kennedy Term: 1961–1963 Birth date: May 29, 1917 Death date: November 22, 1963 Vice President: Lyndon Johnson	1960	John F. Kennedy Richard Nixon	Democratic Republican	34,227,096 (49.9%) 34,108,546 (49.6%)	303 219
Lyndon Baines Johnson Term: 1963–1969 Birth date: August 27, 1908 Death date: January 22, 1973 Vice President: Vacant (1963–1965); Hubert H. Humphrey (1965–1969)	1964	Lyndon Johnson Barry Goldwater	Democratic Republican	43,126,233 (61.1%) 27,174,989 (38.5%)	486 52
Richard Milhous Nixon Term: 1969–1974 Birth date: January 9, 1913 Death date: April 22, 1994 Vice Presidents: Spiro Agnew (1969–1973); Gerald Ford (1973–1974)	1968	Richard Nixon Hubert Humphrey George Wallace	Republican Democratic American-Independent	31,785,148 (43.4%) 31,274,503 (42.7%) 9,899,557 (13.5%)	301 191 46
	1972	Richard Nixon George McGovern	Republican Democratic	45,767,218 (60.6%) 28,357,668 (37.5%)	520 17
Gerald Ford Term: 1974–1977 Birth date: July 14, 1913 Death date: Vice President: Nelson A. Rockefeller					

(continued)

Personal Information	Year	Candidate	Party	Popular Vote	Electoral Vote
James Earl Carter, Jr. Term: 1977–1981 Birth date: October 1, 1924 Death date: Vice President: Walter Mondale	1976	Jimmy Carter Gerald Ford	Democratic Republican	40,274,975 (50.6%) 38,530,614 (48.4%)	297 240
Ronald Reagan Term: 1981–1989 Birth date: February 6, 1911 Death date: Vice President: George Herbert Walker Bush	1980	Ronald Reagan Jimmy Carter John Anderson	Republican Democratic Independent	43,899,248 (51.0%) 36,481,435 (42.3%) 5,719,437 (6.6%)	489 49 0
	1984	Ronald Reagan Walter Mondale	Republican Democratic	52,606,797 (59.0%) 36,450,613 (41.0%)	525 13
George Herbert Walker Bush Term: 1989–1993 Birth date: June 12, 1924 Death date: Vice President: Dan Quayle	1988	George Bush Michael Dukakis	Republican Democratic	48,881,278 (53.4%) 41,805,374 (45.6%)	426 112
Bill Clinton Term: 1993–2001 Birth date: August 19, 1946 Death date: Vice President: Albert Gore, Jr.	1992	Bill Clinton George Bush Ross Perot	Democratic Republican Independent	44,909,889 (43.2%) 39,104,545 (37.7%) 19,742,267 (19.0%)	370 168 0
	1996	Bill Clinton Robert Dole Ross Perot	Democratic Republican Reform	47,401,185 (49.0%) 39,197,469 (41.0%) 8,085,294 (8.0%)	379 159 0
George Walker Bush Term: 2001–Present Birth date: July 6, 1946 Death date: Vice President: Richard "Dick" Cheney	2000	George W. Bush Albert Gore, Jr. Ralph Nader	Republican Democratic Green	50,455,156 (47.9%) 50,992,335 (48.4%) 2,882,897 (2.8%)	271 269 0

Index

●●

• C •

• K •

• T •